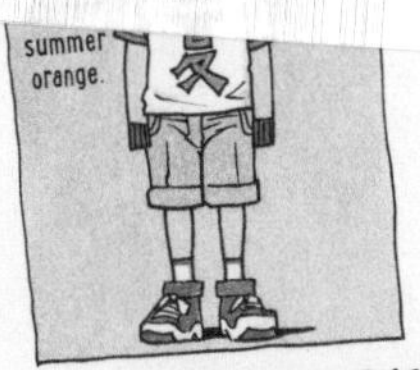
summer
orange.

NOBUAKI ENOKI

Hello! It's nice to meet you! This is my first manga to become a graphic novel...so to everyone who has picked up a copy, thank you very much! Calling this a courtroom drama makes it sound a bit complex, but it's just a mystery series, so it'd make me happy if you could casually enjoy it while solving all the whodunits!

And so...ahem...

I hereby call this Classroom Session to order!!!

Nobuaki Enoki received the Jump Treasure New Cartoonist Prize in April 2009 for his work *Rikuo*. *School Judgment: Gakkyu Hotei* was his first work to be serialized in *Weekly Shonen Jump*.

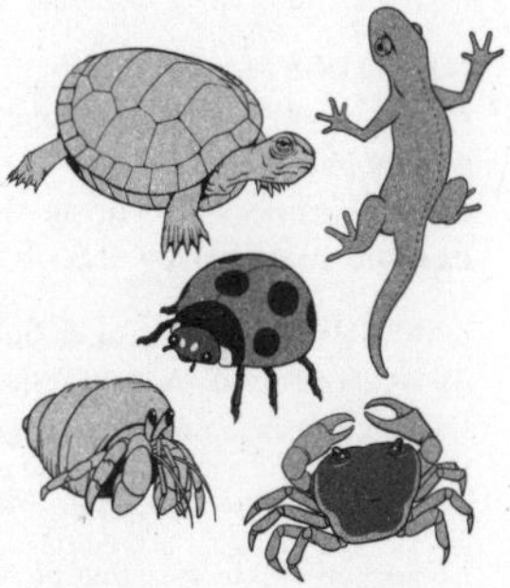

TAKESHI OBATA

Everyone wants to be the creature keeper!

I assembled some of the creatures that I like.

Takeshi Obata was born in 1969 in Niigata, Japan, and first achieved international recognition as the artist of the wildly popular *Shonen Jump* title *Hikaru no Go*, which won the 2003 Tezuka Osamu Cultural Prize: Shinsei "New Hope" Award and the 2000 Shogakukan Manga Award. He went on to illustrate the smash hit *Death Note* as well as the hugely successful manga *Bakuman。* and *All You Need Is Kill*.

School Judgment

GAKKYU HOTEI

SHONEN JUMP MANGA EDITION

1

STORY BY Nobuaki Enoki
ART BY Takeshi Obata

TRANSLATION Mari Morimoto
TOUCH-UP ART & LETTERING James Gaubatz
DESIGN Shawn Carrico
WEEKLY SHONEN JUMP EDITOR Alexis Kirsch
GRAPHIC NOVEL EDITOR Marlene First

GAKKYU HOTEI © 2014 by Nobuaki Enoki, Takeshi Obata
All rights reserved. First published in Japan in 2014 by SHUEISHA Inc., Tokyo.
English translation rights arranged by SHUEISHA Inc.

Printed in the U.S.A.

Published by VIZ Media, LLC
P.O. Box 77010
San Francisco, CA 94107

10 9 8 7 6 5 4 3 2 1
First printing, February 2016

School Judgment

GAKKYU HOTEI

1

The Suzuki Murder and Dismemberment Case

STORY BY Nobuaki Enoki
ART BY Takeshi Obata

CLASS SCHEDULE

	MON	TUE	WED	THU	FRI
1	School Judgment GAKKYU HOTEI				1
2	**Chapter 1** The Suzuki Murder and Dismemberment Case p. 5	Phys Ed	**Chapter 3** The Pretty Idol Airi Takanashi Photo Voyeurism Case p. 87	Ethics	Social Studies
3	Language	**Chapter 2** The Suzuki Murder and Dismemberment Case (2) p. 61	Science	**Chapter 6** The Shuichi Higashide Cheating Case (2) p. 151	Art
4	Science	Foreign Language	**Chapter 4** The Pretty Idol Airi Takanashi Photo Voyeurism Case (2) p. 111	Math	Art
5	Phys Ed	Music	Classroom Arbitration	**Chapter 7** Beware of the Magical Powder p. 171	General Studies
6	Math	Social Studies	**Chapter 5** The Shuichi Higashide Cheating Case p. 131	Phys Ed	**Glossary** p. 191

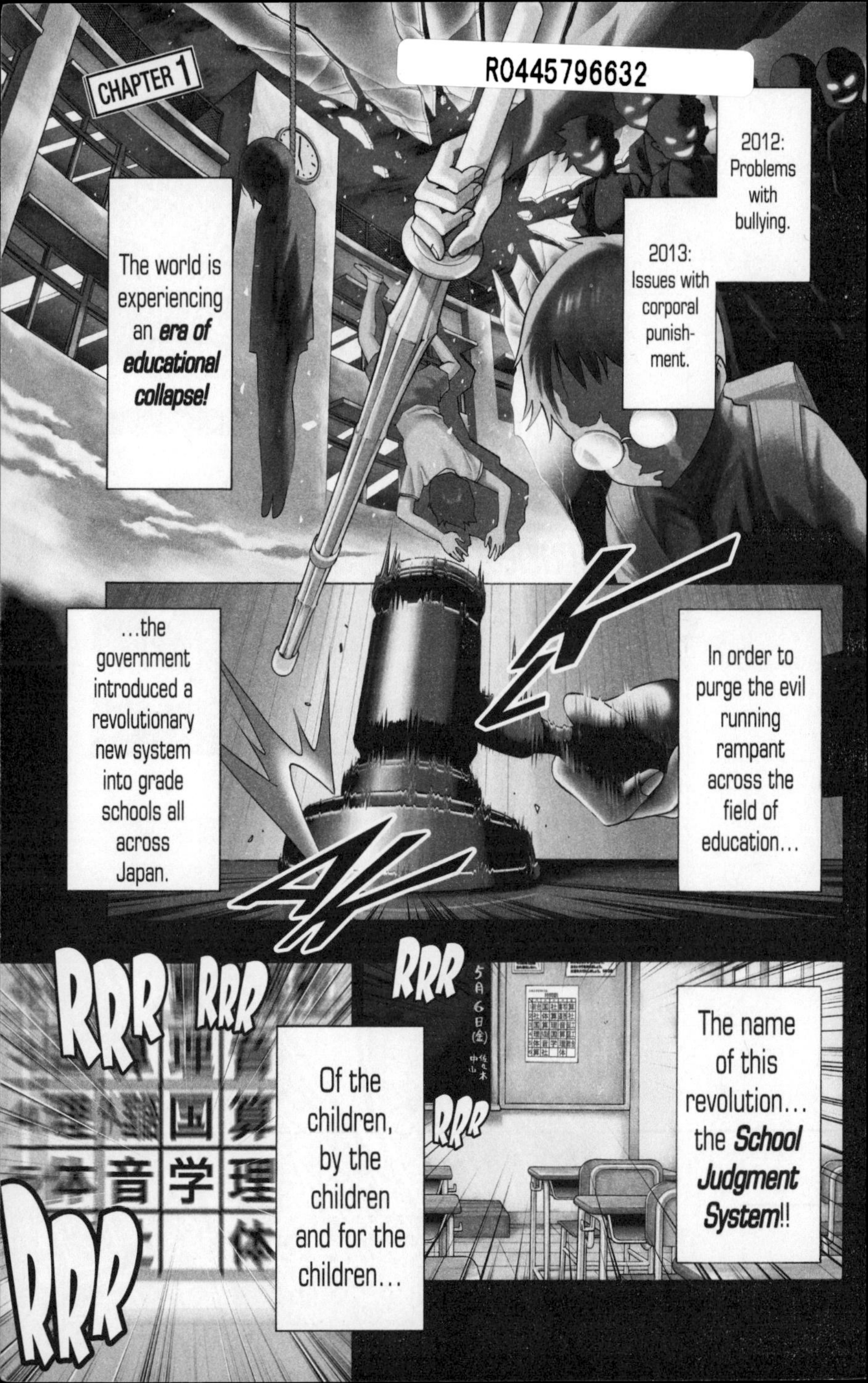
CHAPTER 1
2012: Problems with bullying.
2013: Issues with corporal punish-ment.
The world is experiencing an ***era of educational collapse!***
In order to purge the evil running rampant across the field of education…
…the government introduced a revolutionary new system into grade schools all across Japan.
RRR
5月6日(金)
The name of this revolution… the ***School Judgment System***!!
RRR
RRR
RRR
Of the children, by the children and for the children…
RRR

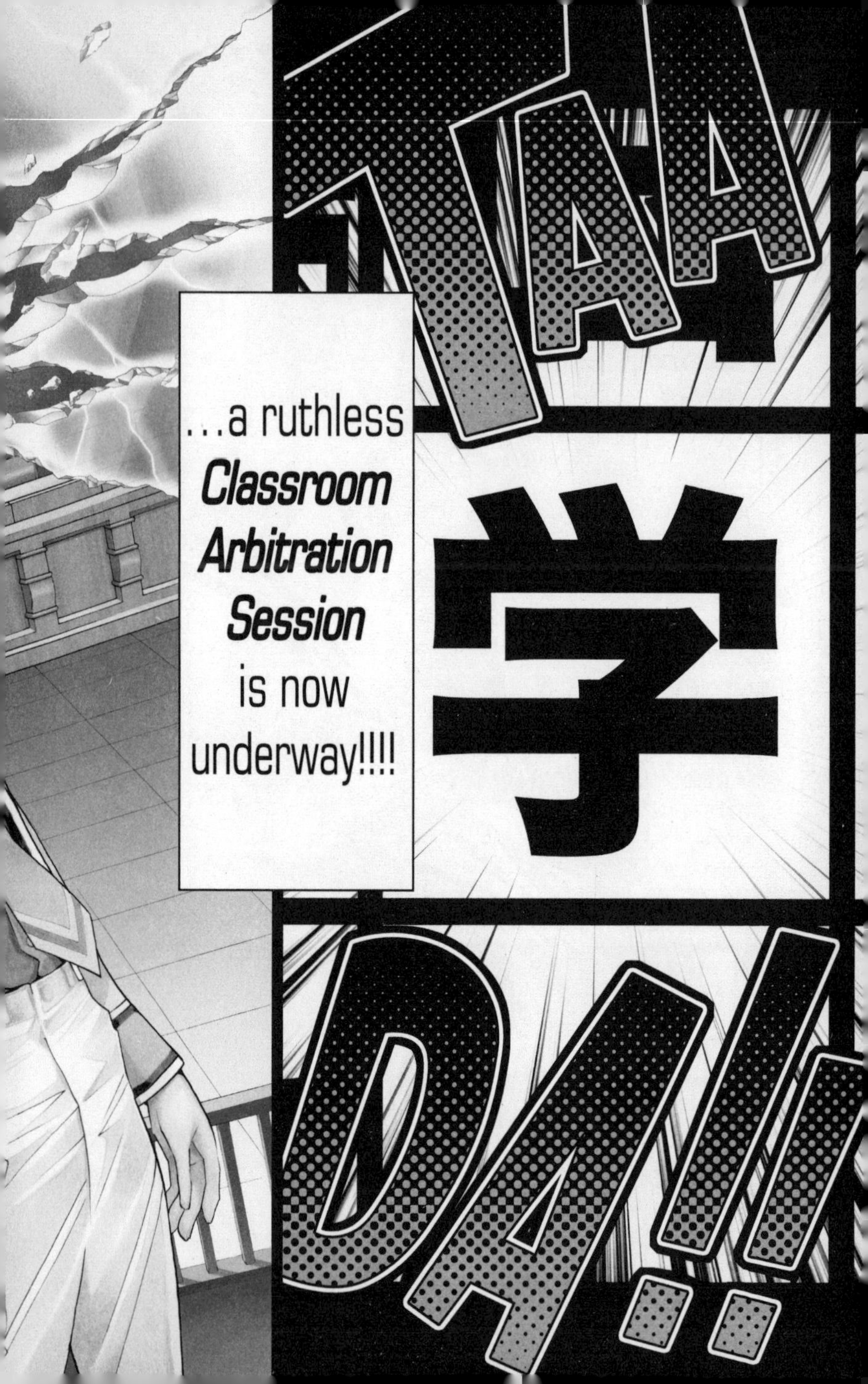

DAAAAN
学
DAN!!
...a ruthless *Classroom Arbitration Session* is now underway!!!!

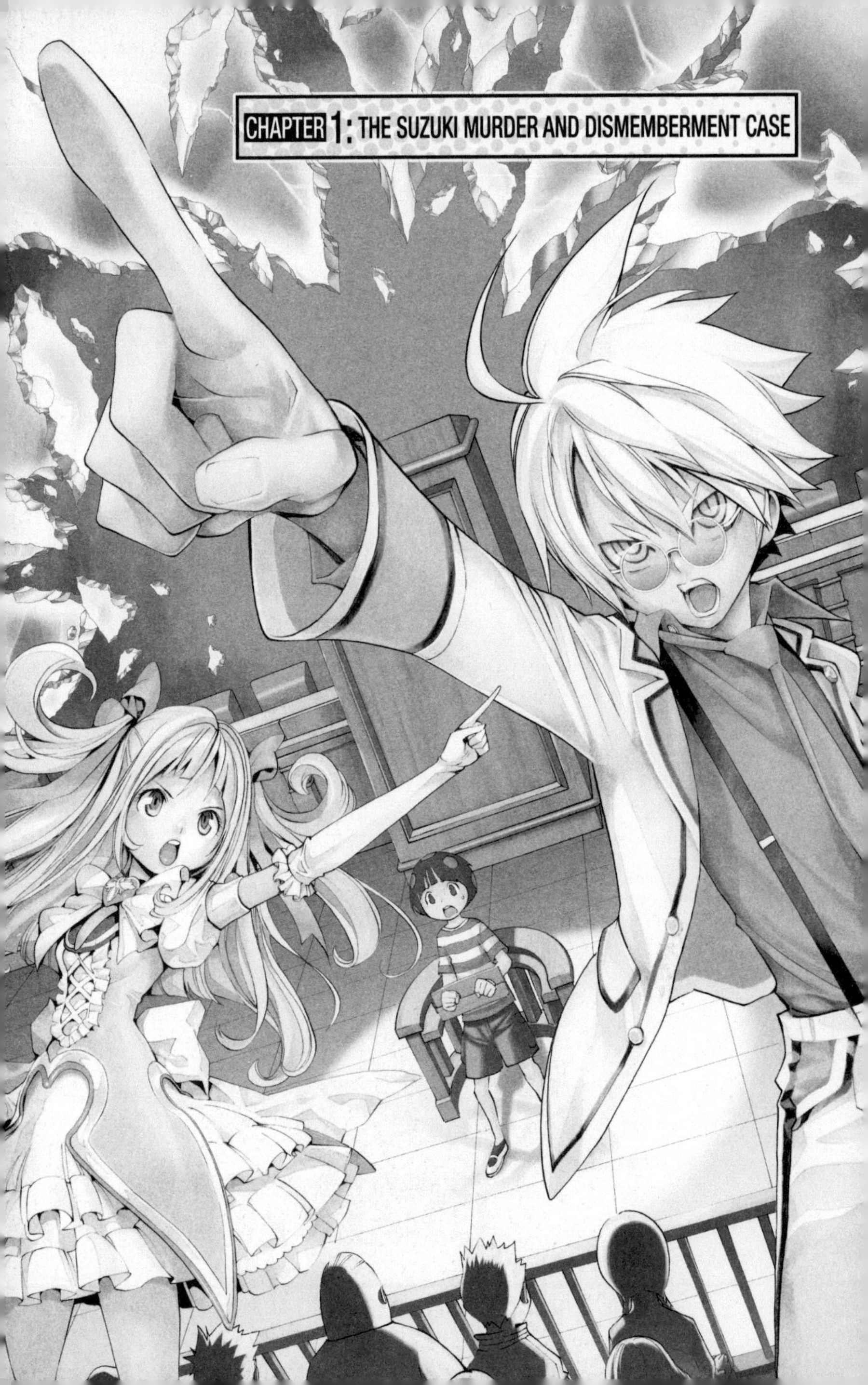
CHAPTER 1: THE SUZUKI MURDER AND DISMEMBERMENT CASE

School Judgment
GAKKYU HOTEI

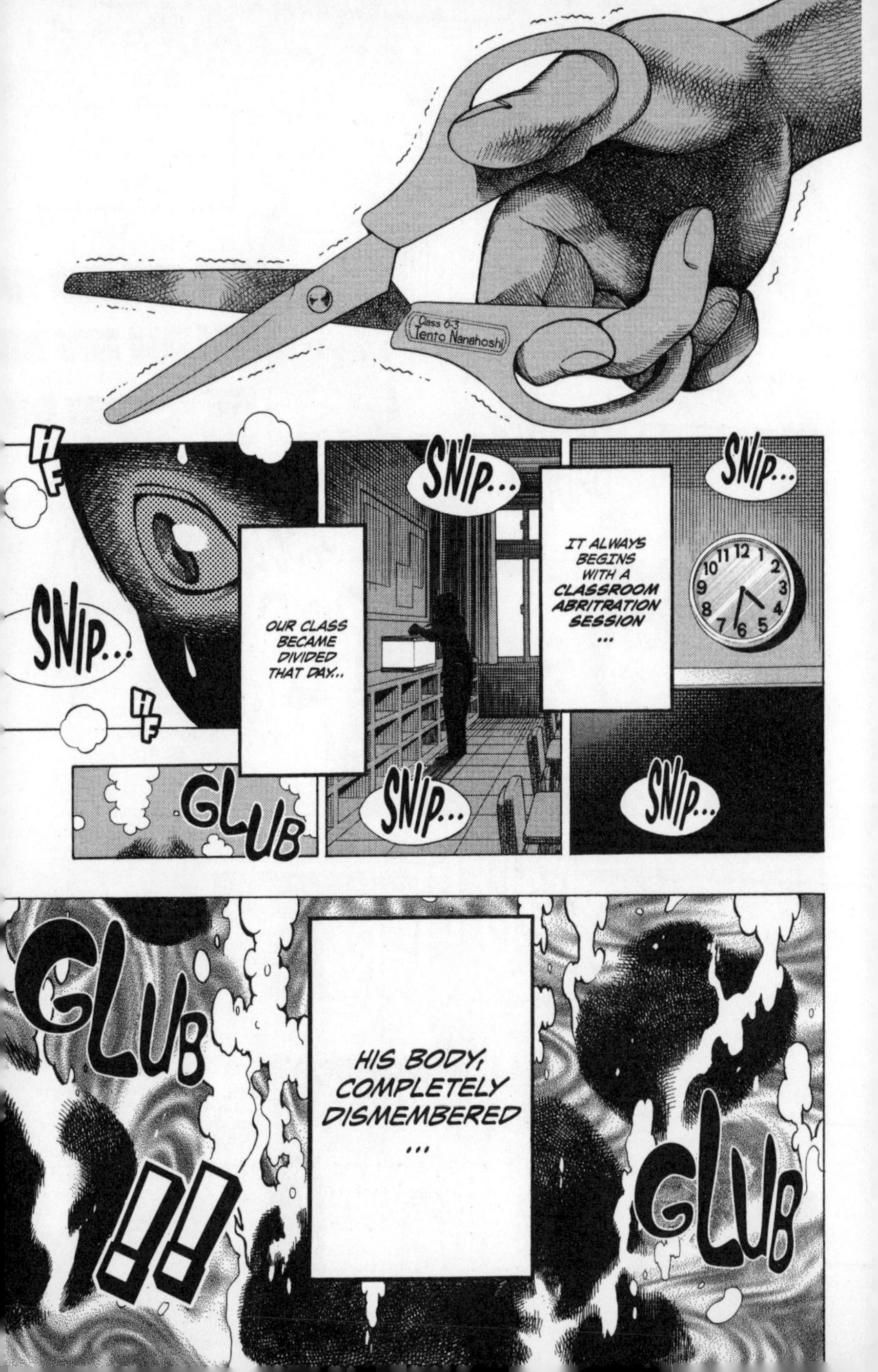

Class 6-3
Tento Nanahoshi
SNIP...
IT ALWAYS BEGINS WITH A CLASSROOM ABRITRATION SESSION ...
SNIP...
SNIP...
OUR CLASS BECAME DIVIDED THAT DAY...
SNIP...
HF
SNIP...
HF
GLUB
GLUB
HIS BODY, COMPLETELY DISMEMBERED ...
GLUB
!!

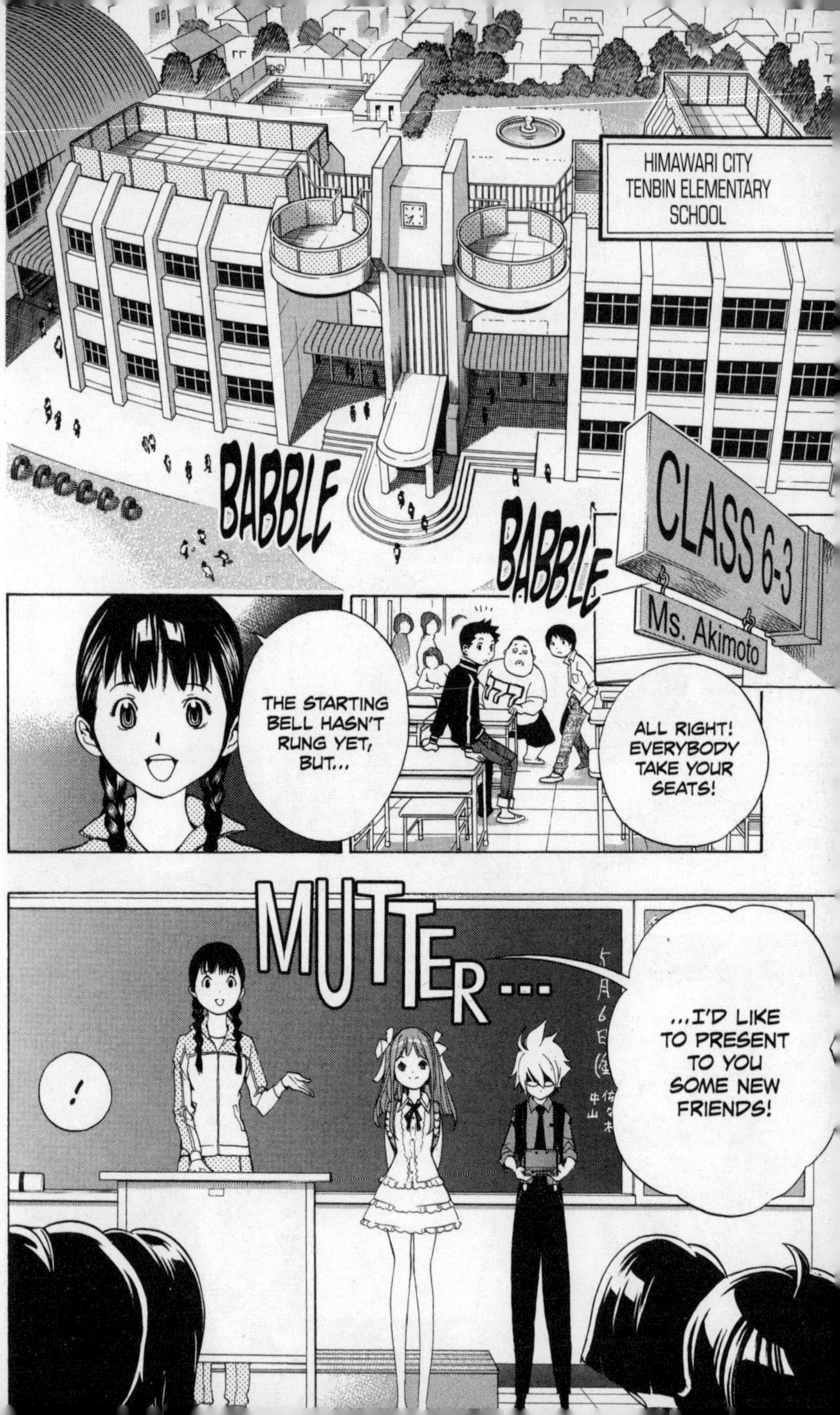
HIMAWARI CITY TENBIN ELEMENTARY SCHOOL
CLASS 6-3
Ms. Akimoto
BABBLE
BABBLE
ALL RIGHT! EVERYBODY TAKE YOUR SEATS!
THE STARTING BELL HASN'T RUNG YET, BUT...
...I'D LIKE TO PRESENT TO YOU SOME NEW FRIENDS!
MUTTER...
!

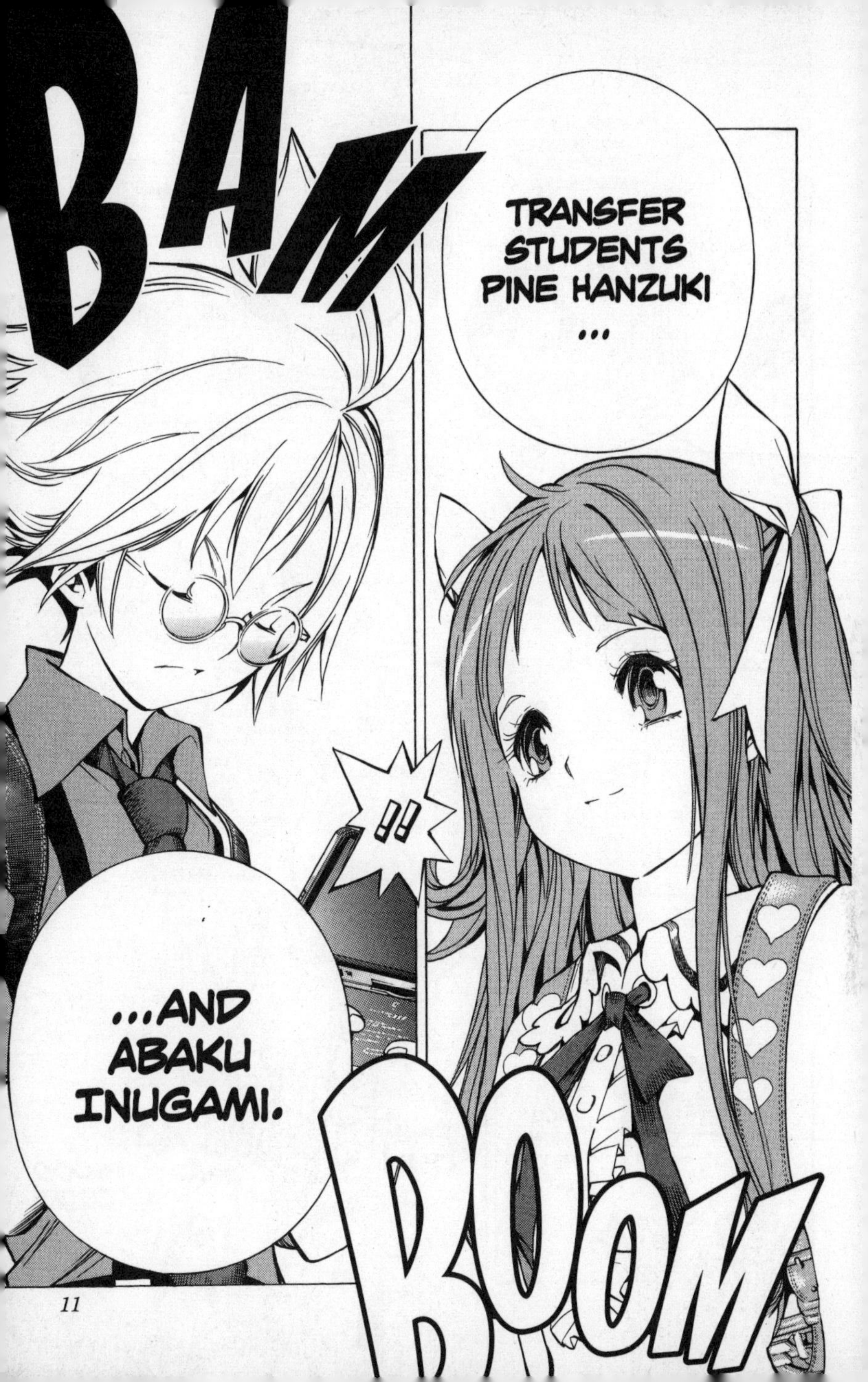
TRANSFER STUDENTS PINE HANZUKI ...
!!
BOOM
BAM
...AND ABAKU INUGAMI.

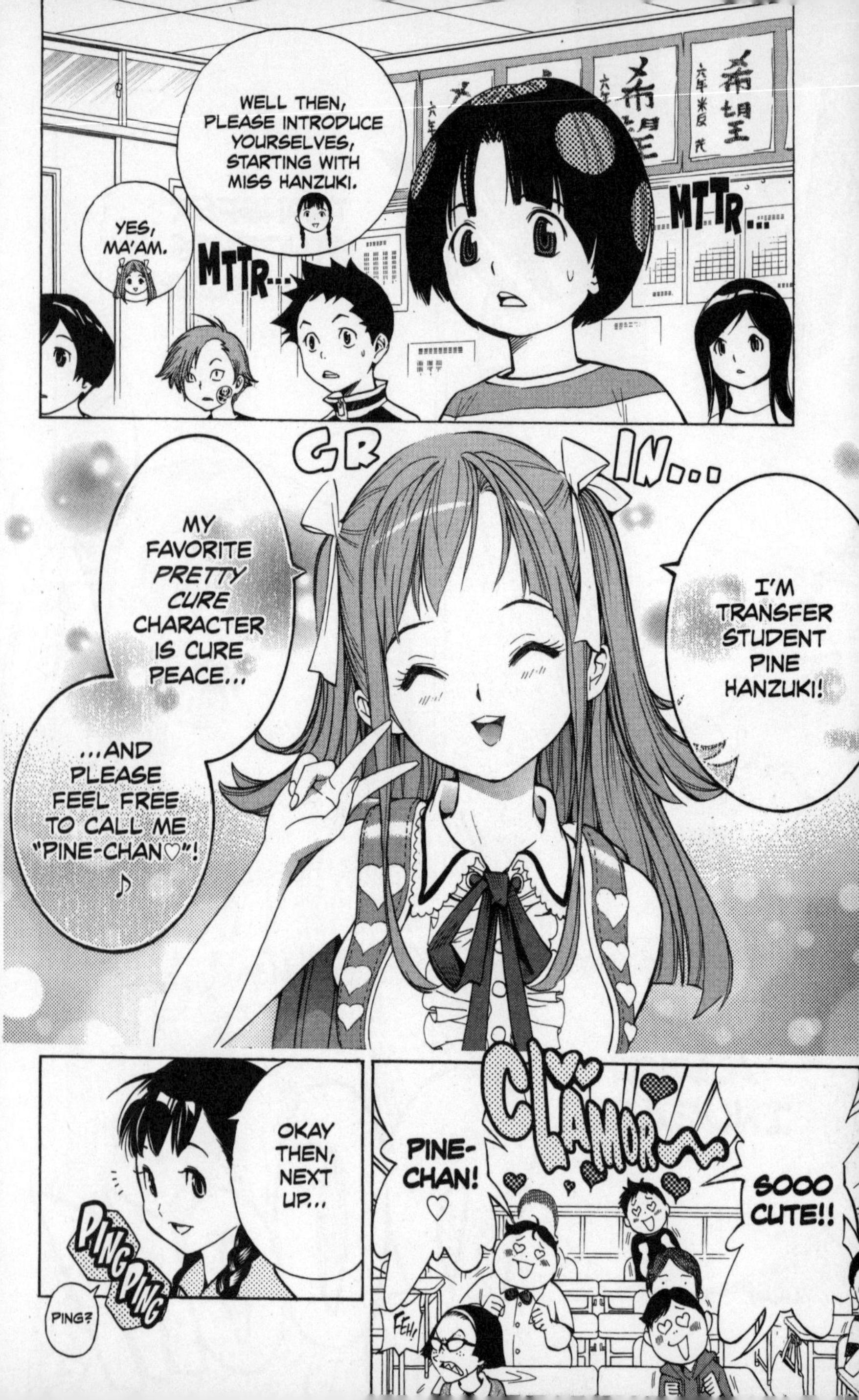
MTTR...
WELL THEN, PLEASE INTRODUCE YOURSELVES, STARTING WITH MISS HANZUKI.
YES, MA'AM.
MTTR...
GR IN...
I'M TRANSFER STUDENT PINE HANZUKI!
MY FAVORITE *PRETTY CURE* CHARACTER IS CURE PEACE...
...AND PLEASE FEEL FREE TO CALL ME "PINE-CHAN♡"! ♪
CLAMOR
SOOO CUTE!!
PINE-CHAN! ♡
FEH!
OKAY THEN, NEXT UP...
PING PING
PING?

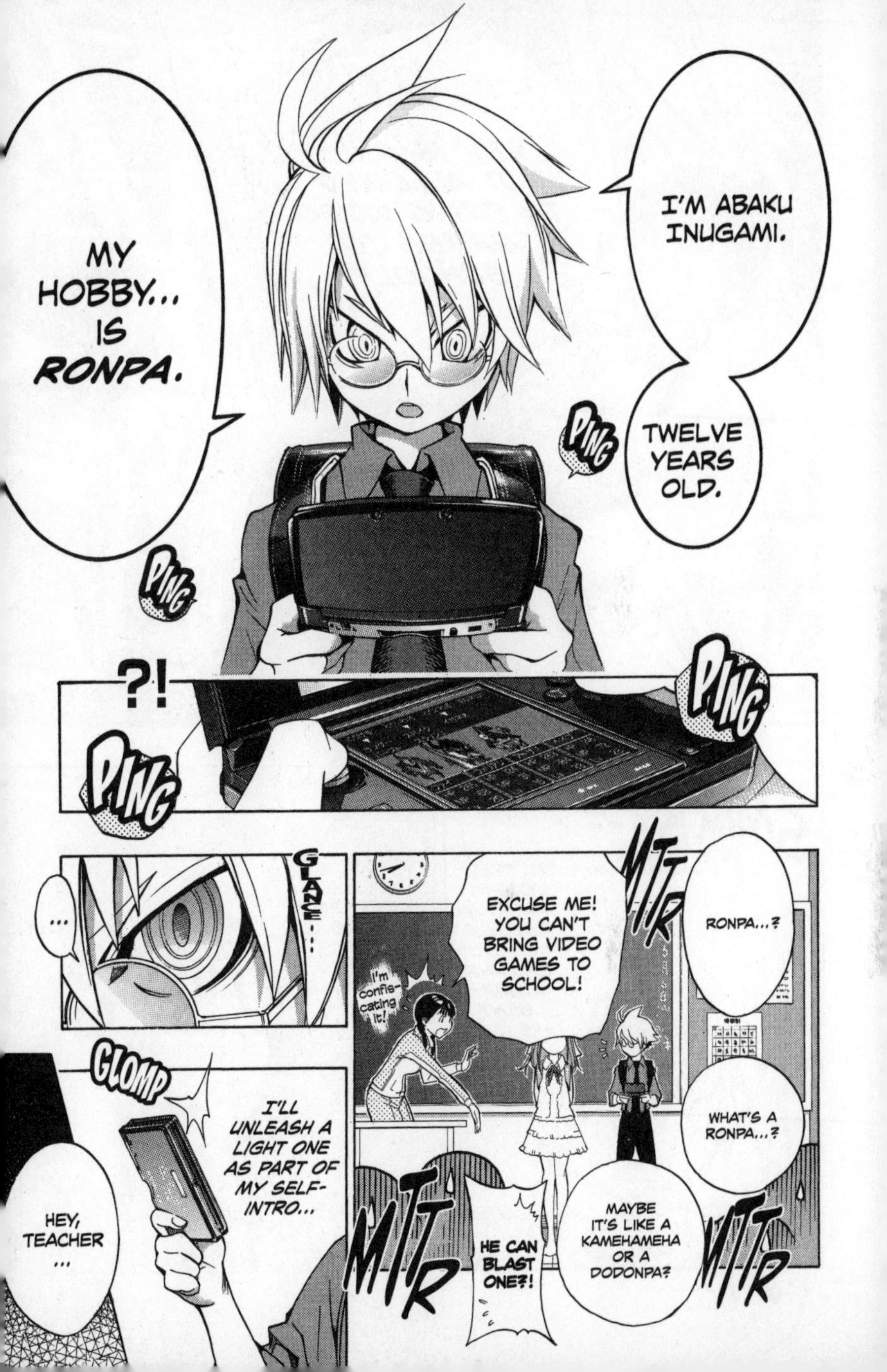

I'M ABAKU INUGAMI.
TWELVE YEARS OLD.
PING
MY HOBBY... IS RONPA.
PING
PING
?!
PING
MTTR
RONPA...?
EXCUSE ME! YOU CAN'T BRING VIDEO GAMES TO SCHOOL!
I'm confiscating it!
WHAT'S A RONPA...?
MAYBE IT'S LIKE A KAMEHAMEHA OR A DODONPA?
MTTR
HE CAN BLAST ONE?!
MTTR
GLANCE...
...
GLOMP
I'LL UNLEASH A LIGHT ONE AS PART OF MY SELF-INTRO...
HEY, TEACHER...

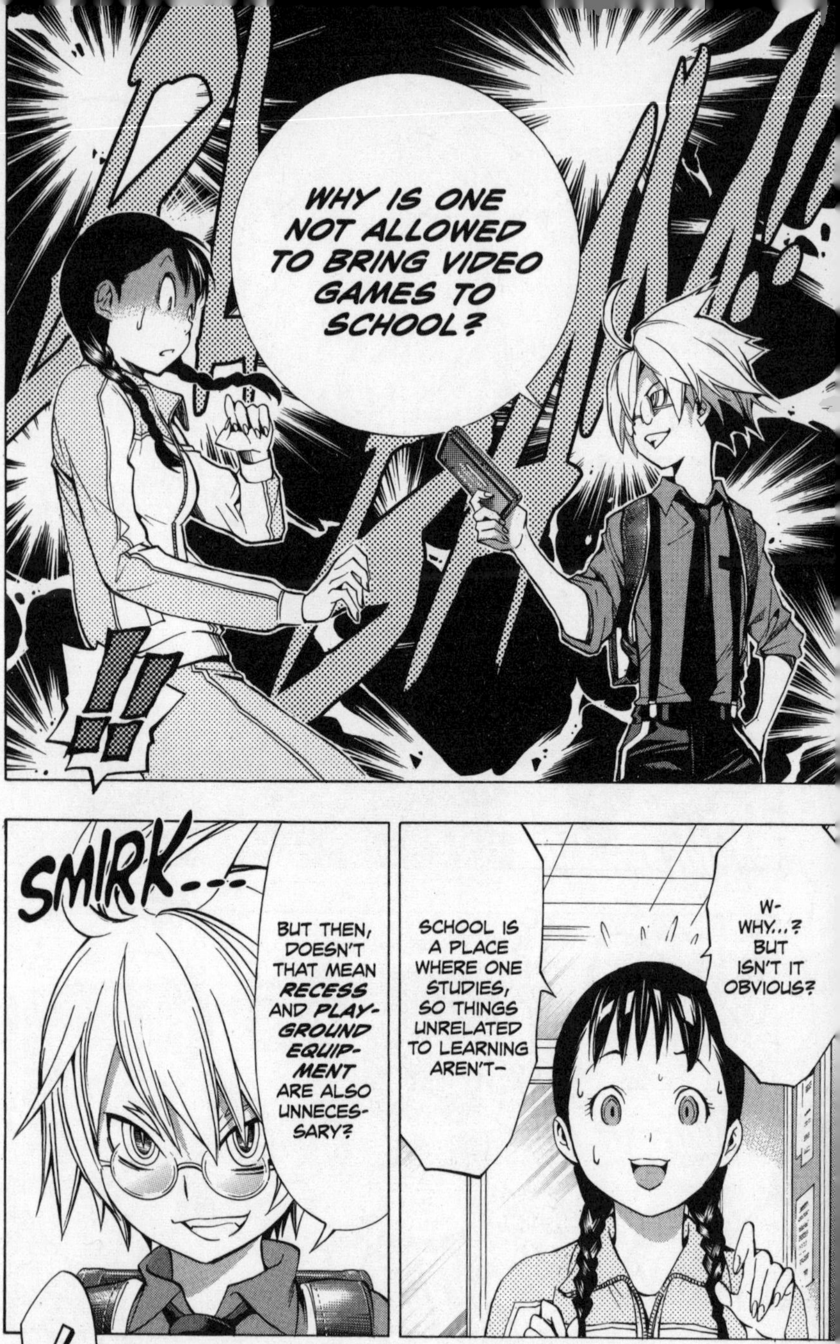

WHY IS ONE NOT ALLOWED TO BRING VIDEO GAMES TO SCHOOL?
!!
W- WHY...? BUT ISN'T IT OBVIOUS?
SCHOOL IS A PLACE WHERE ONE STUDIES, SO THINGS UNRELATED TO LEARNING AREN'T-
SMIRK...
BUT THEN, DOESN'T THAT MEAN *RECESS* AND *PLAYGROUND EQUIPMENT* ARE ALSO UNNECESSARY?
!

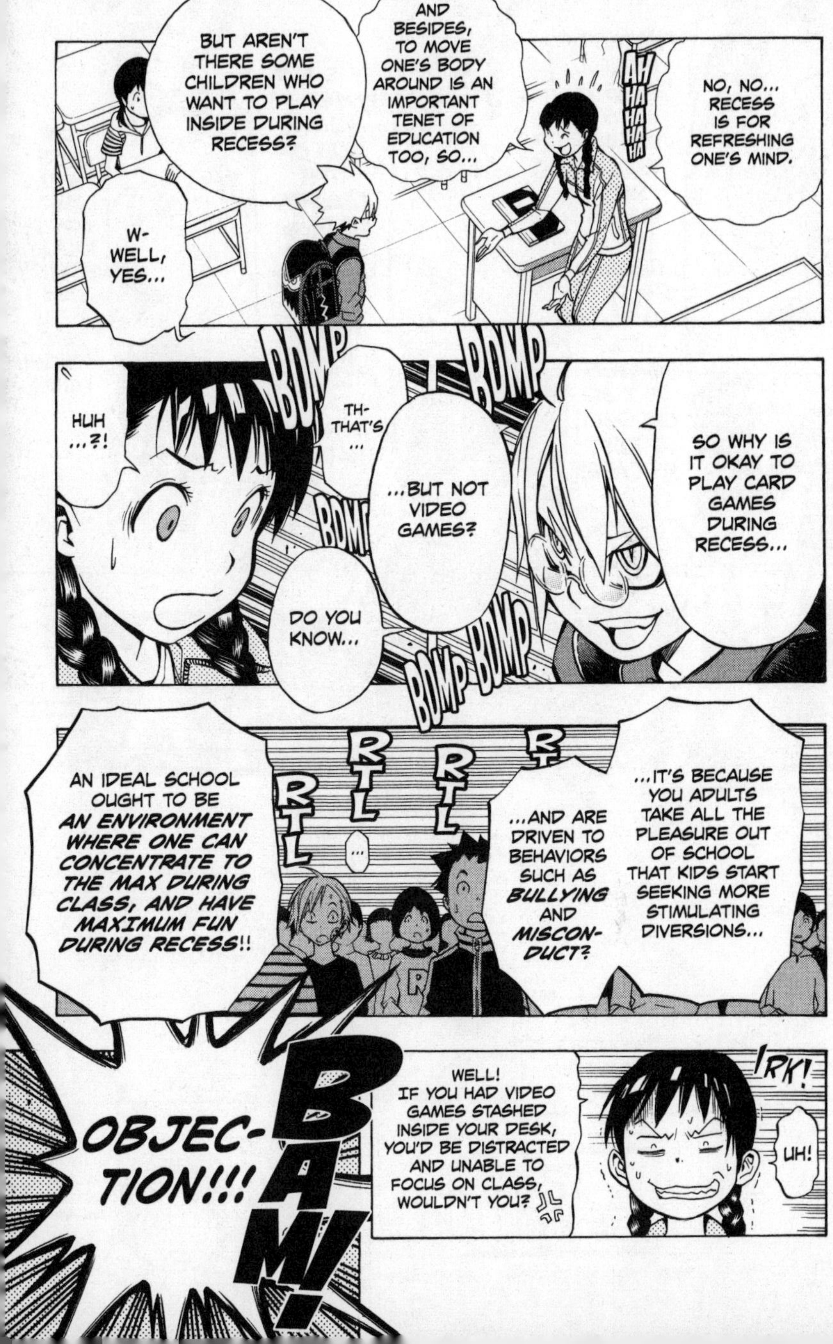
NO, NO... RECESS IS FOR REFRESHING ONE'S MIND.
AH HA HA HA HA
AND BESIDES, TO MOVE ONE'S BODY AROUND IS AN IMPORTANT TENET OF EDUCATION TOO, SO...
BUT AREN'T THERE SOME CHILDREN WHO WANT TO PLAY INSIDE DURING RECESS?
W-WELL, YES...
BOMP BOMP
SO WHY IS IT OKAY TO PLAY CARD GAMES DURING RECESS...
...BUT NOT VIDEO GAMES?
TH-THAT'S ...
HUH ...?!
BOMP
DO YOU KNOW...
BOMP BOMP
...IT'S BECAUSE YOU ADULTS TAKE ALL THE PLEASURE OUT OF SCHOOL THAT KIDS START SEEKING MORE STIMULATING DIVERSIONS...
...AND ARE DRIVEN TO BEHAVIORS SUCH AS *BULLYING* AND *MISCONDUCT*?
RTL RTL RTL RTL
...
AN IDEAL SCHOOL OUGHT TO BE *AN ENVIRONMENT WHERE ONE CAN CONCENTRATE TO THE MAX DURING CLASS, AND HAVE MAXIMUM FUN DURING RECESS*!!
UH!
IRK!
WELL! IF YOU HAD VIDEO GAMES STASHED INSIDE YOUR DESK, YOU'D BE DISTRACTED AND UNABLE TO FOCUS ON CLASS, WOULDN'T YOU?
OBJEC-TION!!!
BAM!

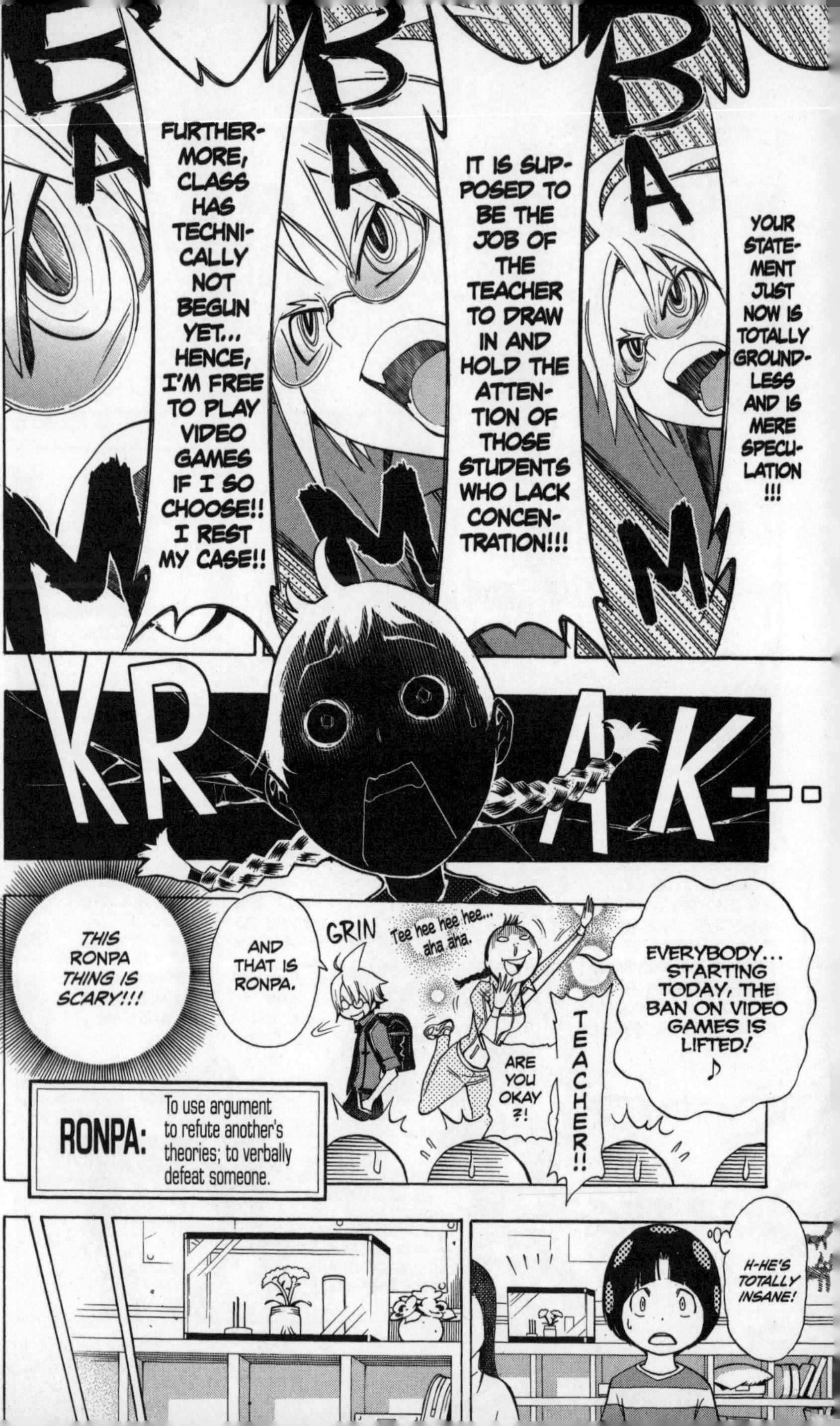
BAM
YOUR STATEMENT JUST NOW IS TOTALLY GROUNDLESS AND IS MERE SPECULATION!!!
BAM
IT IS SUPPOSED TO BE THE JOB OF THE TEACHER TO DRAW IN AND HOLD THE ATTENTION OF THOSE STUDENTS WHO LACK CONCENTRATION!!!
BAM
FURTHERMORE, CLASS HAS TECHNICALLY NOT BEGUN YET... HENCE, I'M FREE TO PLAY VIDEO GAMES IF I SO CHOOSE!! I REST MY CASE!!
KRAK...
EVERYBODY... STARTING TODAY, THE BAN ON VIDEO GAMES IS LIFTED! ♪
TEACHER!!
ARE YOU OKAY ?!
Tee hee hee hee... aha aha.
GRIN
AND THAT IS RONPA.
THIS RONPA THING IS SCARY!!!
RONPA: To use argument to refute another's theories; to verbally defeat someone.
H-HE'S TOTALLY INSANE!

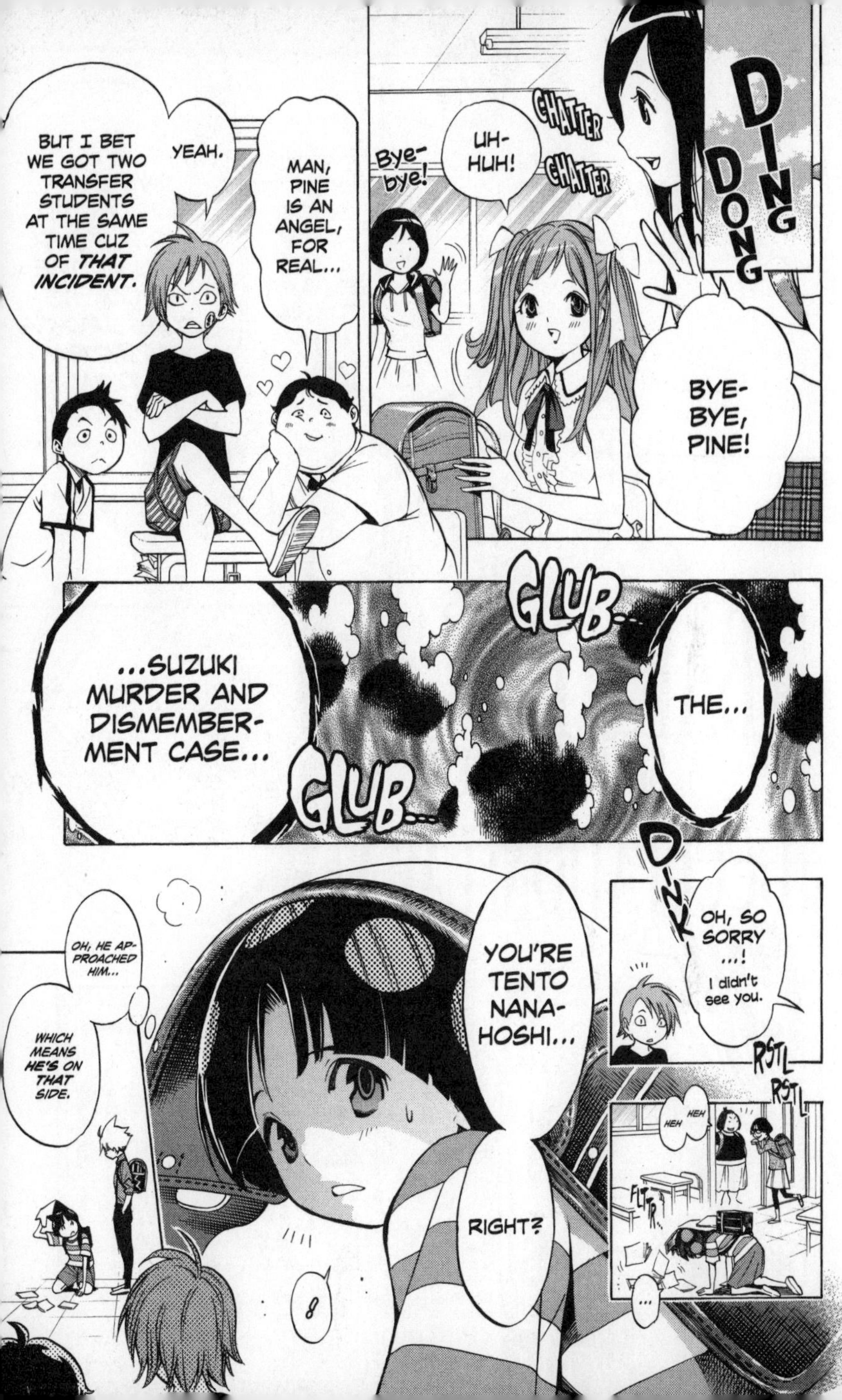
DING DONG
BYE-BYE, PINE!
CHATTER CHATTER
UH-HUH!
Bye-bye!
MAN, PINE IS AN ANGEL, FOR REAL...
YEAH.
BUT I BET WE GOT TWO TRANSFER STUDENTS AT THE SAME TIME CUZ OF *THAT INCIDENT*.
GLUB...
THE...
...SUZUKI MURDER AND DISMEMBERMENT CASE...
GLUB...
DINK
OH, SO SORRY...! I didn't see you.
RSTL RSTL
HEH HEH
FLTTR...
...
YOU'RE TENTO NANAHOSHI...
RIGHT?
OH, HE APPROACHED HIM...
WHICH MEANS HE'S ON THAT SIDE.

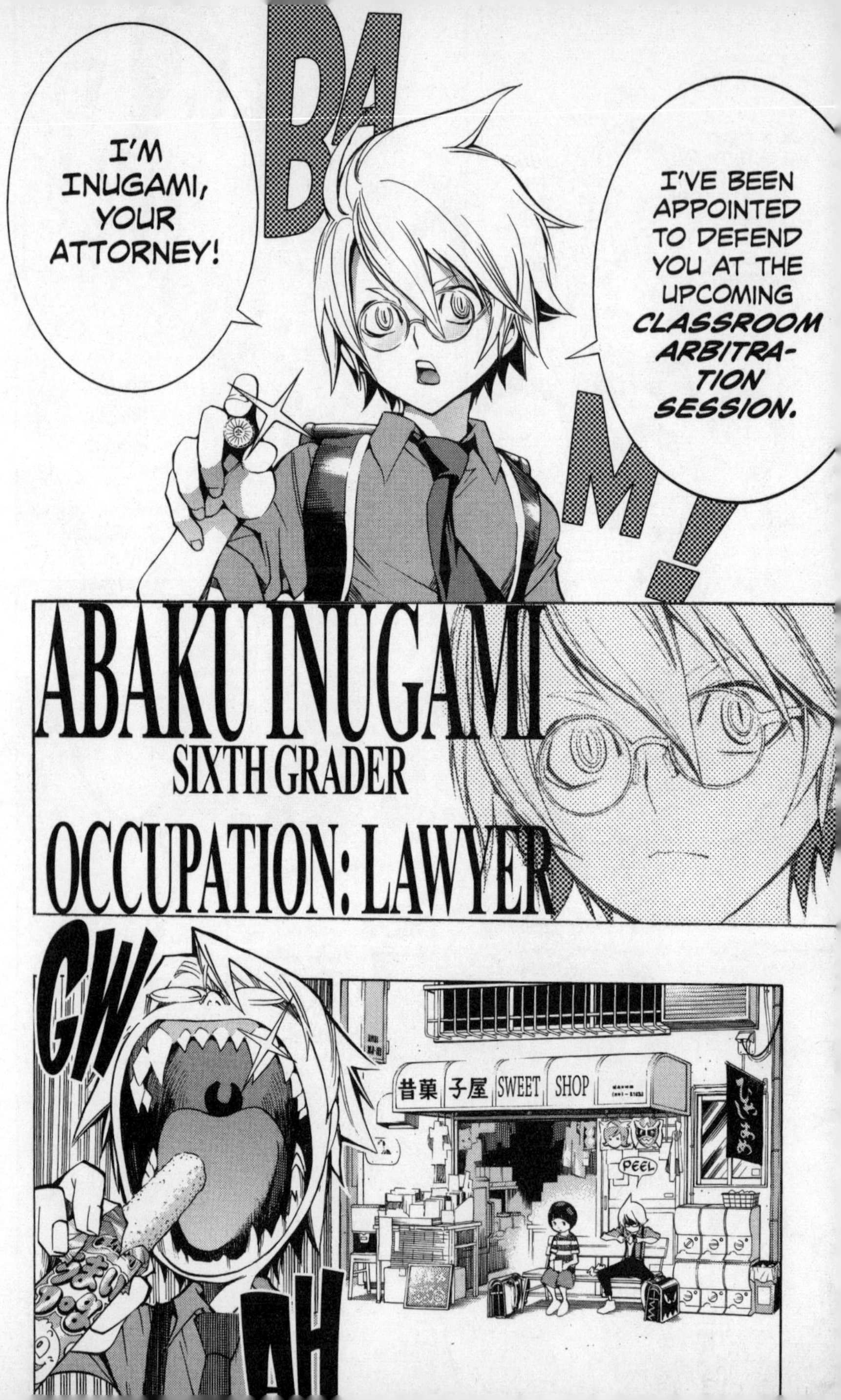
I'VE BEEN APPOINTED TO DEFEND YOU AT THE UPCOMING CLASSROOM ARBITRATION SESSION.
I'M INUGAMI, YOUR ATTORNEY!
BAM!
ABAKU INUGAMI
SIXTH GRADER
OCCUPATION: LAWYER
昔菓子屋 SWEET SHOP
PEEL
GWAH

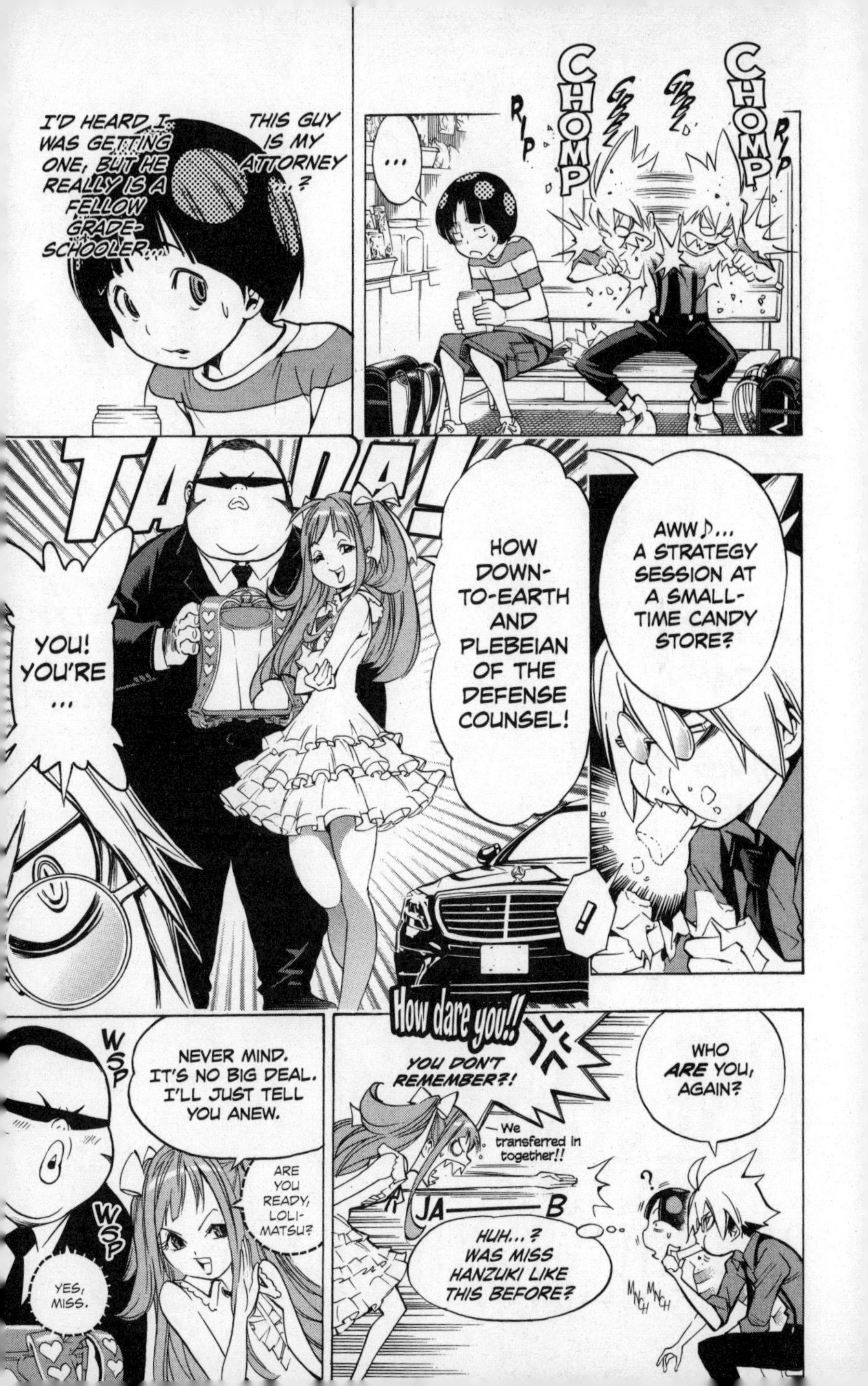
CHOMP
RIP
GRRL
GRRL
CHOMP
RIP
...
THIS GUY IS MY ATTORNEY...?
I'D HEARD I WAS GETTING ONE, BUT HE REALLY IS A FELLOW GRADE-SCHOOLER...
AWW♪... A STRATEGY SESSION AT A SMALL-TIME CANDY STORE?
!
TA-DA!
HOW DOWN-TO-EARTH AND PLEBEIAN OF THE DEFENSE COUNSEL!
YOU! YOU'RE ...
WHO ARE YOU, AGAIN?
How dare you!!
YOU DON'T REMEMBER?!
We transferred in together!!
JA——B
HUH...? WAS MISS HANZUKI LIKE THIS BEFORE?
MNCH MNCH
NEVER MIND. IT'S NO BIG DEAL. I'LL JUST TELL YOU ANEW.
WSP
WSP
ARE YOU READY, LOLI-MATSU?
YES, MISS.

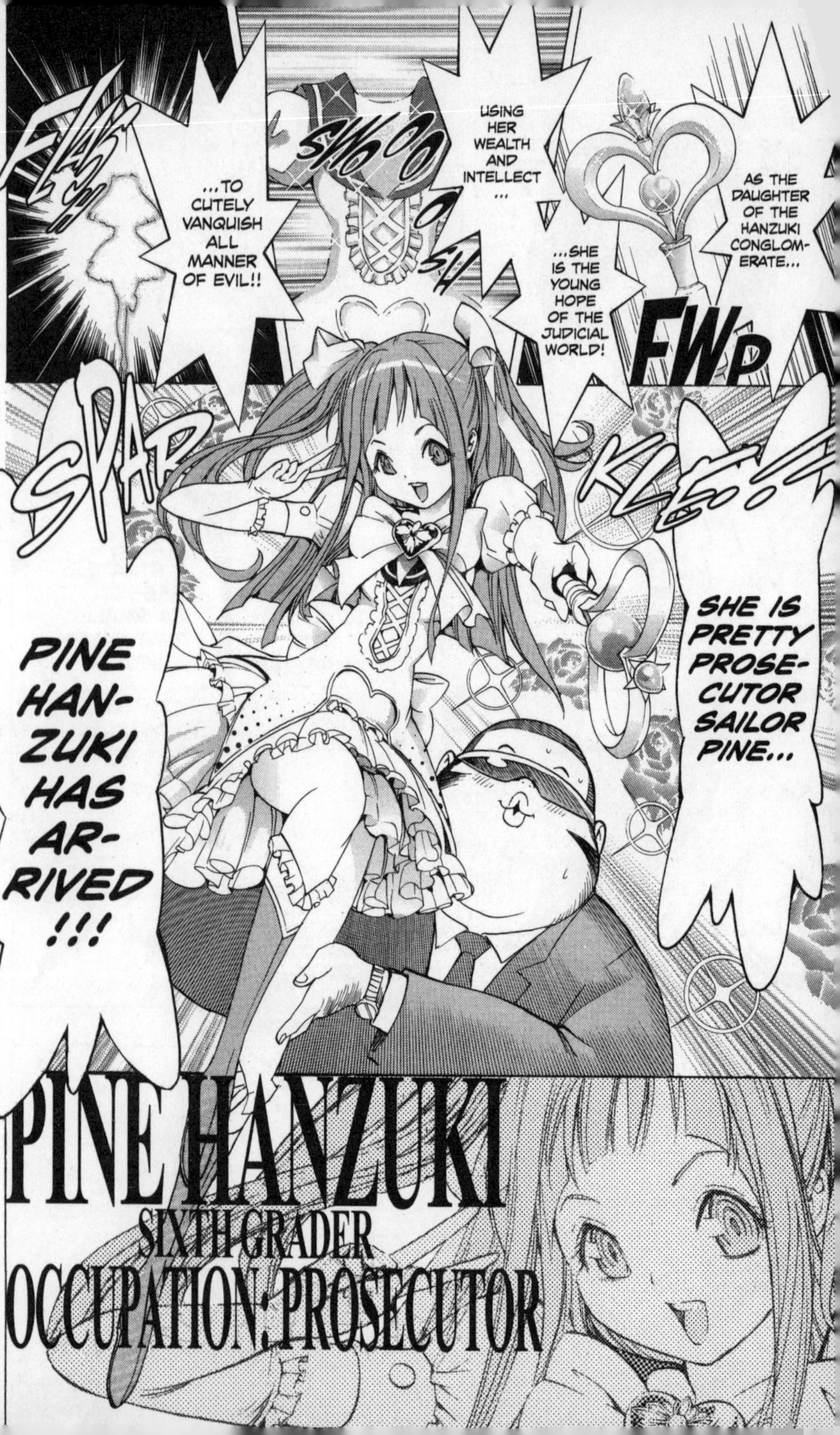
AS THE DAUGHTER OF THE HANZUKI CONGLOMERATE...
FWP
USING HER WEALTH AND INTELLECT...
...SHE IS THE YOUNG HOPE OF THE JUDICIAL WORLD!
...TO CUTELY VANQUISH ALL MANNER OF EVIL!!
SPAR
KLE...!!
SHE IS PRETTY PROSECUTOR SAILOR PINE...
PINE HANZUKI HAS ARRIVED!!!
PINE HANZUKI
SIXTH GRADER
OCCUPATION: PROSECUTOR

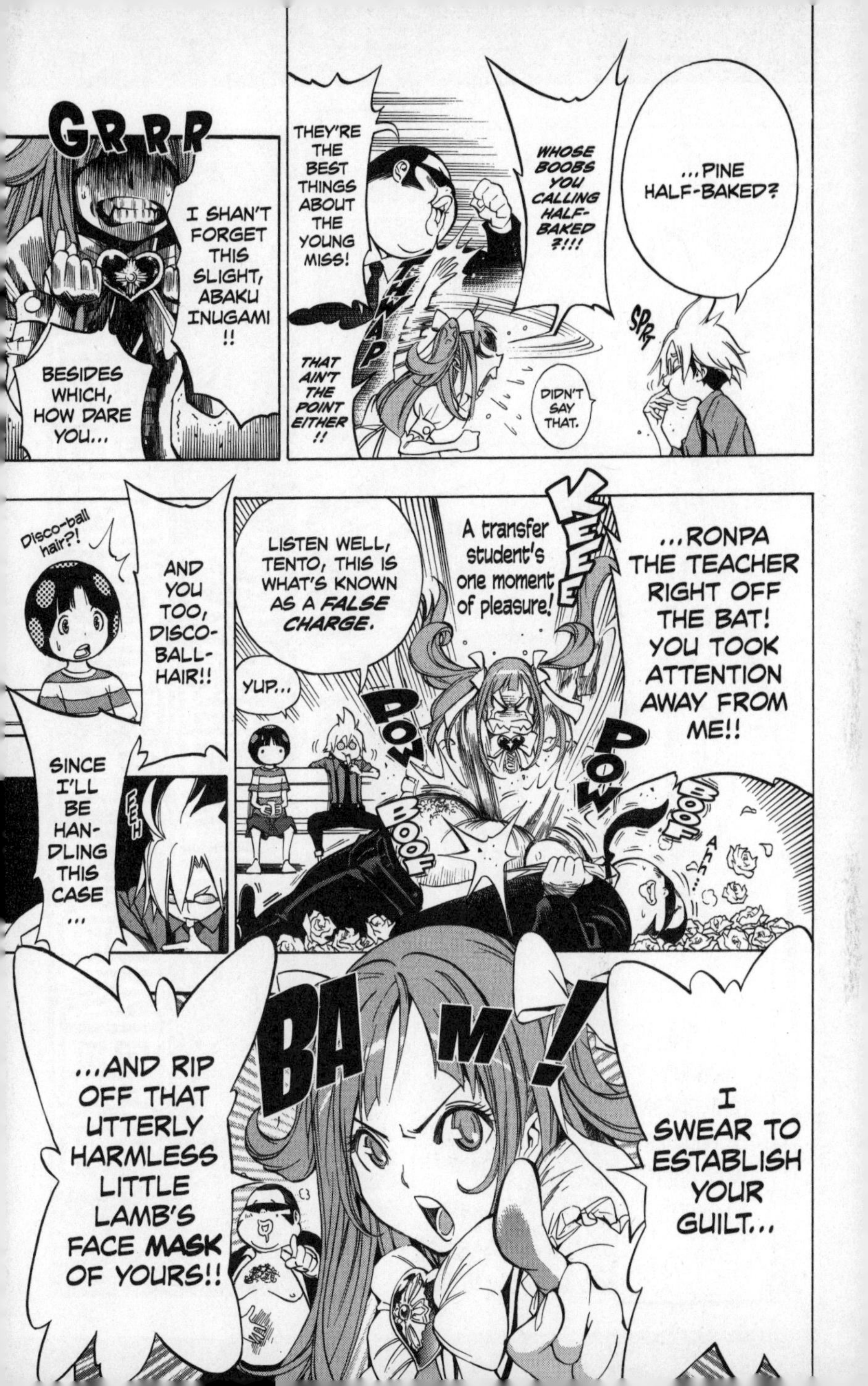
...PINE HALF-BAKED?
SPRT
DIDN'T SAY THAT.
WHOSE BOOBS YOU CALLING HALF-BAKED?!!!
THEY'RE THE BEST THINGS ABOUT THE YOUNG MISS!
THWAP
THAT AIN'T THE POINT EITHER!!
GRRR
I SHAN'T FORGET THIS SLIGHT, ABAKU INUGAMI!!
BESIDES WHICH, HOW DARE YOU...
...RONPA THE TEACHER RIGHT OFF THE BAT! YOU TOOK ATTENTION AWAY FROM ME!!
A transfer student's one moment of pleasure!
LISTEN WELL, TENTO, THIS IS WHAT'S KNOWN AS A FALSE CHARGE.
YUP...
POW
POW
BOOF
BOOF
AND YOU TOO, DISCO-BALL-HAIR!!
Disco-ball hair?!
SINCE I'LL BE HANDLING THIS CASE...
I SWEAR TO ESTABLISH YOUR GUILT...
BAM!
...AND RIP OFF THAT UTTERLY HARMLESS LITTLE LAMB'S FACE MASK OF YOURS!!

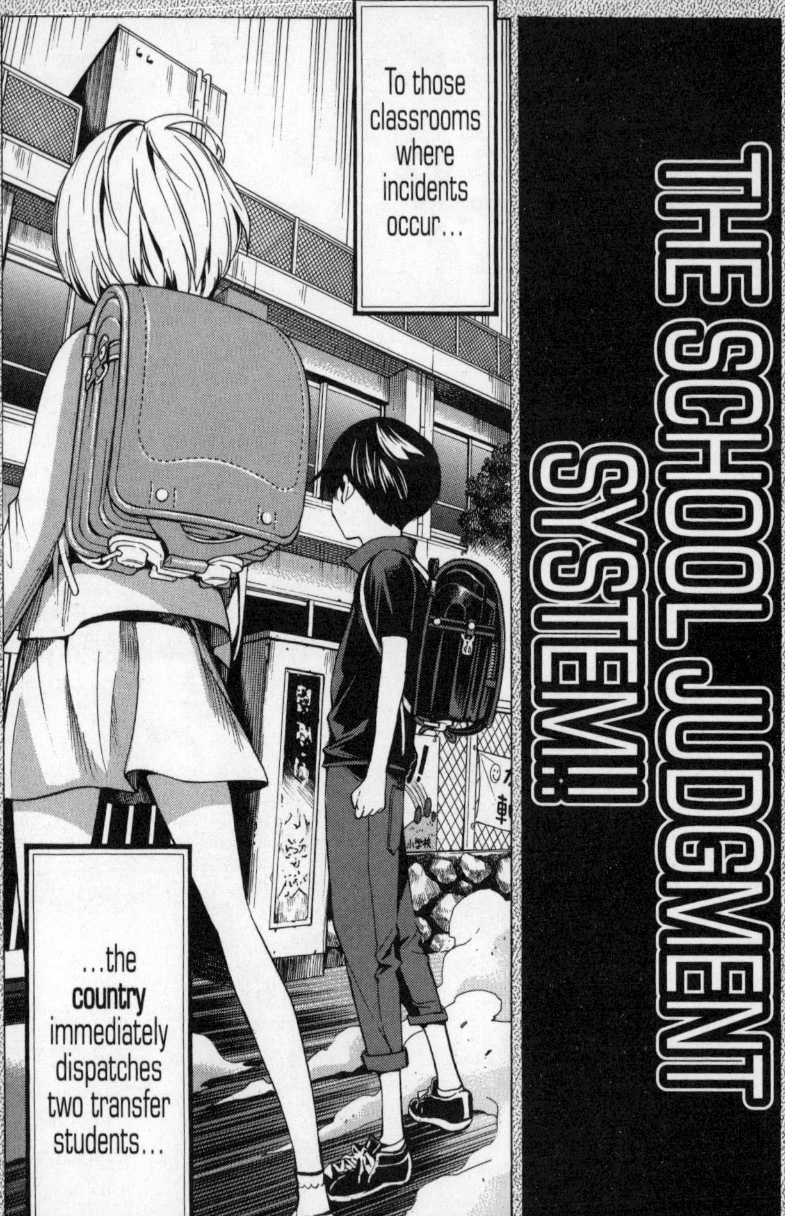
THE SCHOOL JUDGMENT SYSTEM!!
To those classrooms where incidents occur...
...the **country** immediately dispatches two transfer students...

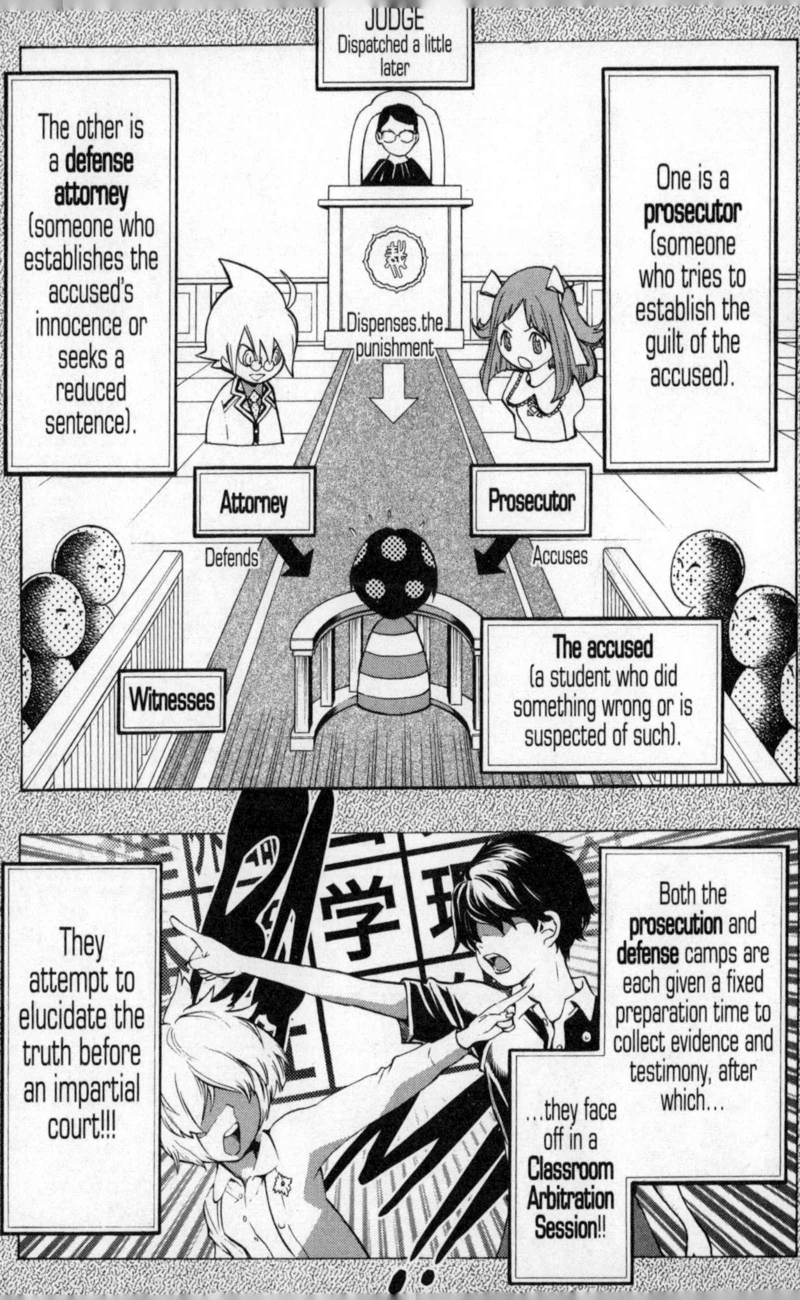
JUDGE
Dispatched a little later
One is a **prosecutor** (someone who tries to establish the guilt of the accused).
The other is a **defense attorney** (someone who establishes the accused's innocence or seeks a reduced sentence).
Dispenses.the punishment
Prosecutor
Attorney
Accuses
Defends
The accused
(a student who did something wrong or is suspected of such).
Witnesses
Both the **prosecution** and **defense** camps are each given a fixed preparation time to collect evidence and testimony, after which...
...they face off in a **Classroom Arbitration Session**!!
They attempt to elucidate the truth before an impartial court!!!

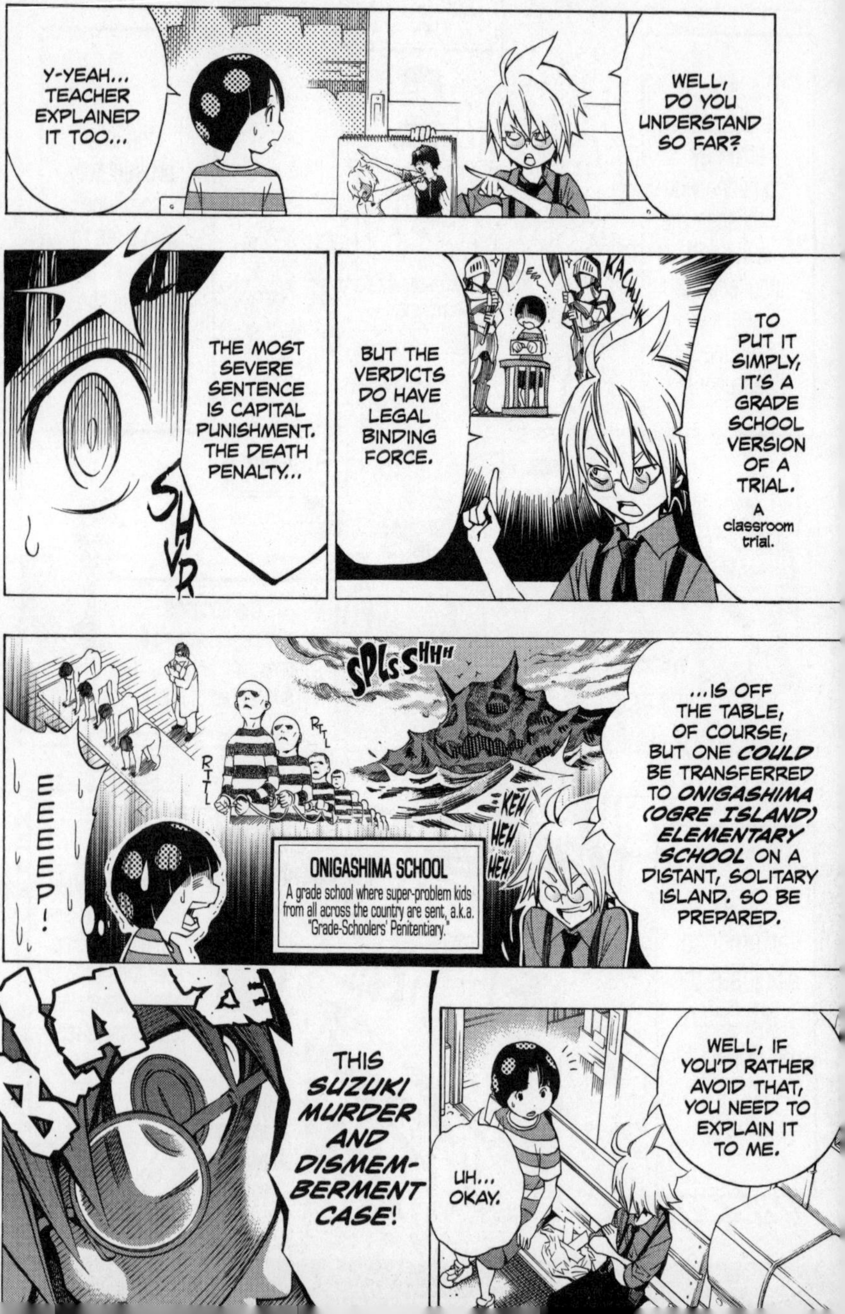
WELL, DO YOU UNDERSTAND SO FAR?
Y-YEAH... TEACHER EXPLAINED IT TOO...
KACHUNK
EEP
TO PUT IT SIMPLY, IT'S A GRADE SCHOOL VERSION OF A TRIAL.
A classroom trial.
BUT THE VERDICTS DO HAVE LEGAL BINDING FORCE.
THE MOST SEVERE SENTENCE IS CAPITAL PUNISHMENT. THE DEATH PENALTY...
SHVR
...IS OFF THE TABLE, OF COURSE, BUT ONE *COULD* BE TRANSFERRED TO *ONIGASHIMA (OGRE ISLAND) ELEMENTARY SCHOOL* ON A DISTANT, SOLITARY ISLAND. SO BE PREPARED.
KEH HEH HEH
SPLSSHHH
RTTL
RTTL
ONIGASHIMA SCHOOL
A grade school where super-problem kids from all across the country are sent, a.k.a. "Grade-Schoolers' Penitentiary."
EEEEEP!
WELL, IF YOU'D RATHER AVOID THAT, YOU NEED TO EXPLAIN IT TO ME.
UH... OKAY.
THIS *SUZUKI MURDER AND DISMEMBERMENT CASE*!
BLA

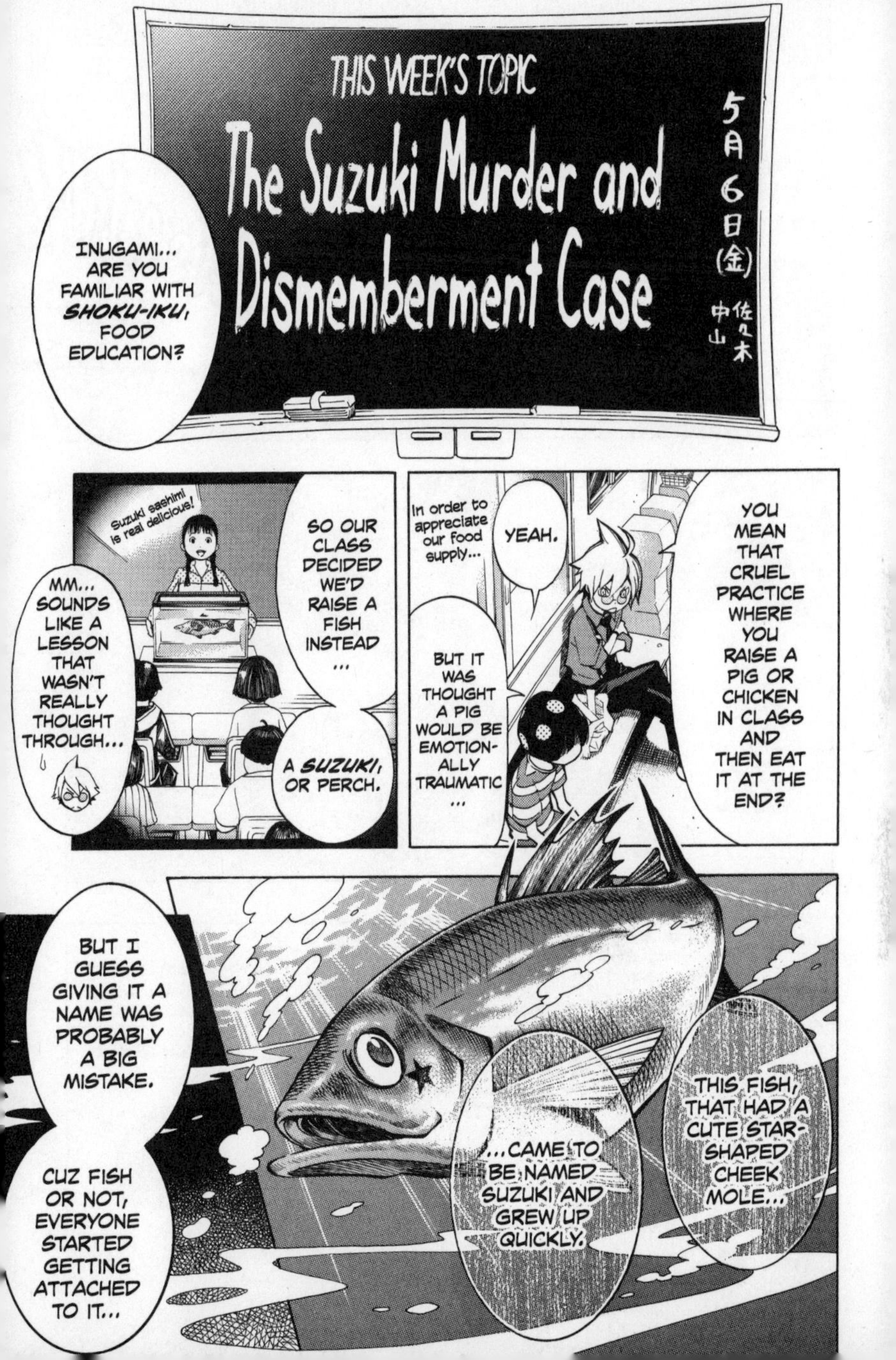
THIS WEEK'S TOPIC
The Suzuki Murder and Dismemberment Case
5月6日(金)
佐々木
中山
INUGAMI... ARE YOU FAMILIAR WITH SHOKU-IKU, FOOD EDUCATION?
YOU MEAN THAT CRUEL PRACTICE WHERE YOU RAISE A PIG OR CHICKEN IN CLASS AND THEN EAT IT AT THE END?
YEAH.
In order to appreciate our food supply...
BUT IT WAS THOUGHT A PIG WOULD BE EMOTION-ALLY TRAUMATIC...
SO OUR CLASS DECIDED WE'D RAISE A FISH INSTEAD...
Suzuki sashimi is real delicious!
A SUZUKI, OR PERCH.
MM... SOUNDS LIKE A LESSON THAT WASN'T REALLY THOUGHT THROUGH...
THIS FISH, THAT HAD A CUTE STAR-SHAPED CHEEK MOLE...
...CAME TO BE NAMED SUZUKI AND GREW UP QUICKLY.
BUT I GUESS GIVING IT A NAME WAS PROBABLY A BIG MISTAKE.
CUZ FISH OR NOT, EVERYONE STARTED GETTING ATTACHED TO IT...

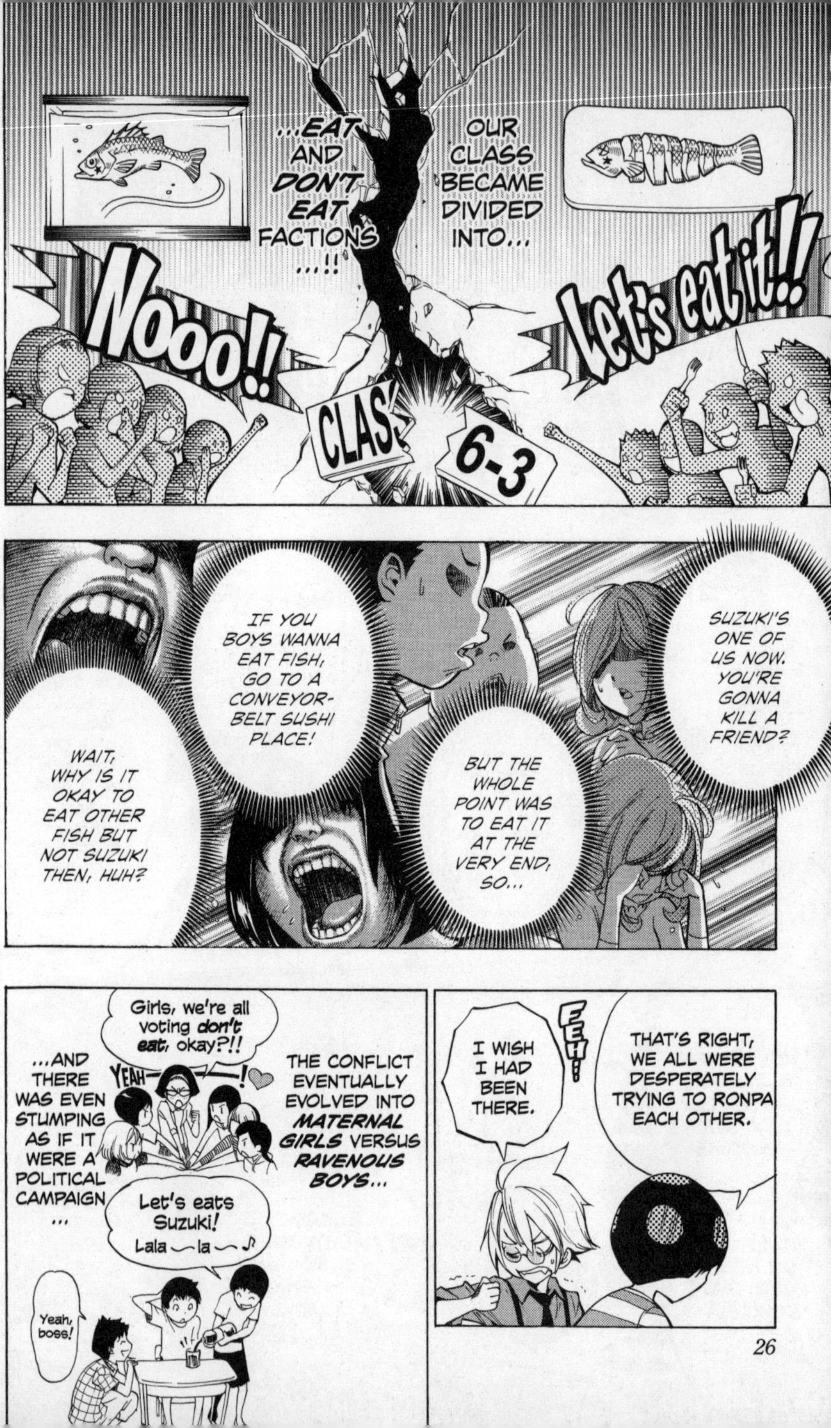
OUR CLASS BECAME DIVIDED INTO...
...EAT AND DON'T EAT FACTIONS...!!
Let's eat it!!
Nooo!!
CLAS 6-3
SUZUKI'S ONE OF US NOW. YOU'RE GONNA KILL A FRIEND?
IF YOU BOYS WANNA EAT FISH, GO TO A CONVEYOR-BELT SUSHI PLACE!
BUT THE WHOLE POINT WAS TO EAT IT AT THE VERY END, SO...
WAIT, WHY IS IT OKAY TO EAT OTHER FISH BUT NOT SUZUKI THEN, HUH?
THAT'S RIGHT, WE ALL WERE DESPERATELY TRYING TO RONPA EACH OTHER.
FEH!!
I WISH I HAD BEEN THERE.
THE CONFLICT EVENTUALLY EVOLVED INTO MATERNAL GIRLS VERSUS RAVENOUS BOYS...
Girls, we're all voting don't eat, okay?!!
YEAH—!
...AND THERE WAS EVEN STUMPING AS IF IT WERE A POLITICAL CAMPAIGN...
Let's eats Suzuki! Lala~la~♪
Yeah, boss!

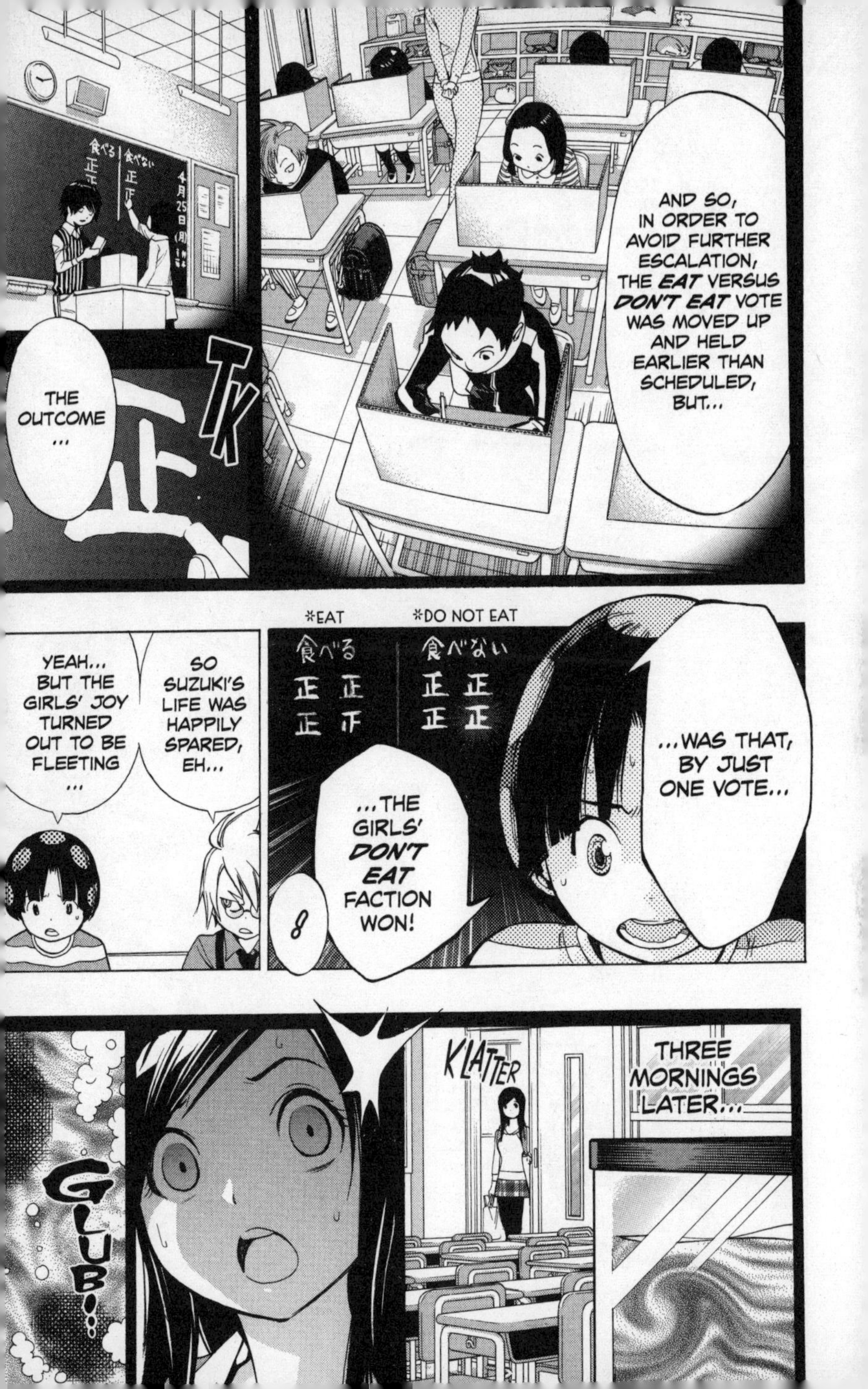
AND SO, IN ORDER TO AVOID FURTHER ESCALATION, THE *EAT* VERSUS *DON'T EAT* VOTE WAS MOVED UP AND HELD EARLIER THAN SCHEDULED, BUT...
TK
THE OUTCOME ...
*EAT
*DO NOT EAT
食べる
食べない
...WAS THAT, BY JUST ONE VOTE...
...THE GIRLS' *DON'T EAT* FACTION WON!
8
SO SUZUKI'S LIFE WAS HAPPILY SPARED, EH...
YEAH... BUT THE GIRLS' JOY TURNED OUT TO BE FLEETING ...
THREE MORNINGS LATER...
KLATTER
GLUB...

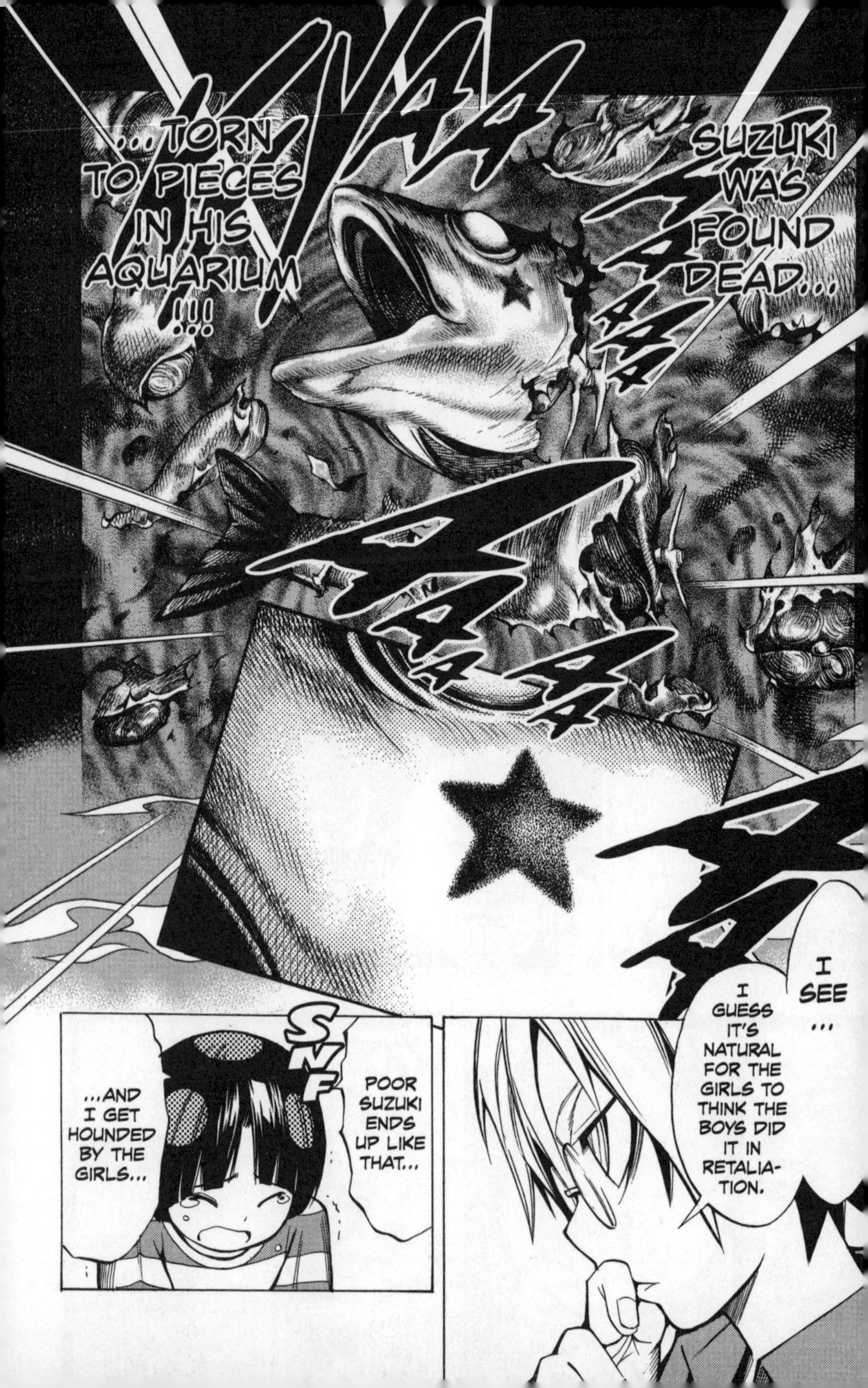

SUZUKI WAS FOUND DEAD...
...TORN TO PIECES IN HIS AQUARIUM!!!
I SEE...
I GUESS IT'S NATURAL FOR THE GIRLS TO THINK THE BOYS DID IT IN RETALIA-TION.
POOR SUZUKI ENDS UP LIKE THAT...
SNF
...AND I GET HOUNDED BY THE GIRLS...

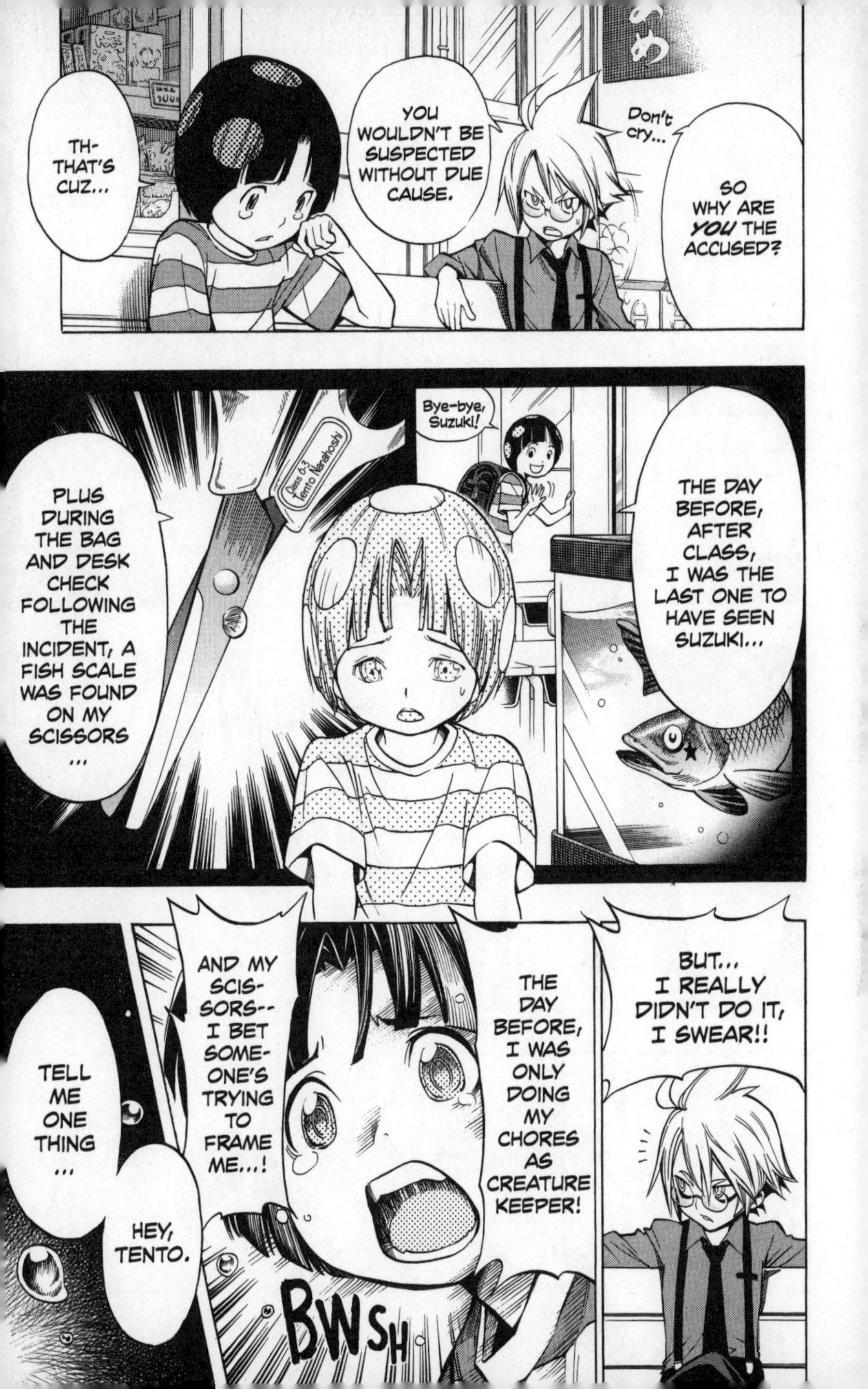
Don't cry...
SO WHY ARE *YOU* THE ACCUSED?
YOU WOULDN'T BE SUSPECTED WITHOUT DUE CAUSE.
TH-THAT'S CUZ...
THE DAY BEFORE, AFTER CLASS, I WAS THE LAST ONE TO HAVE SEEN SUZUKI...
Bye-bye, Suzuki!
Class 6-3 Tento Nanahoshi
PLUS DURING THE BAG AND DESK CHECK FOLLOWING THE INCIDENT, A FISH SCALE WAS FOUND ON MY SCISSORS...
BUT... I REALLY DIDN'T DO IT, I SWEAR!!
THE DAY BEFORE, I WAS ONLY DOING MY CHORES AS CREATURE KEEPER!
AND MY SCIS-SORS-- I BET SOME-ONE'S TRYING TO FRAME ME...!
HEY, TENTO.
TELL ME ONE THING...
BWSH

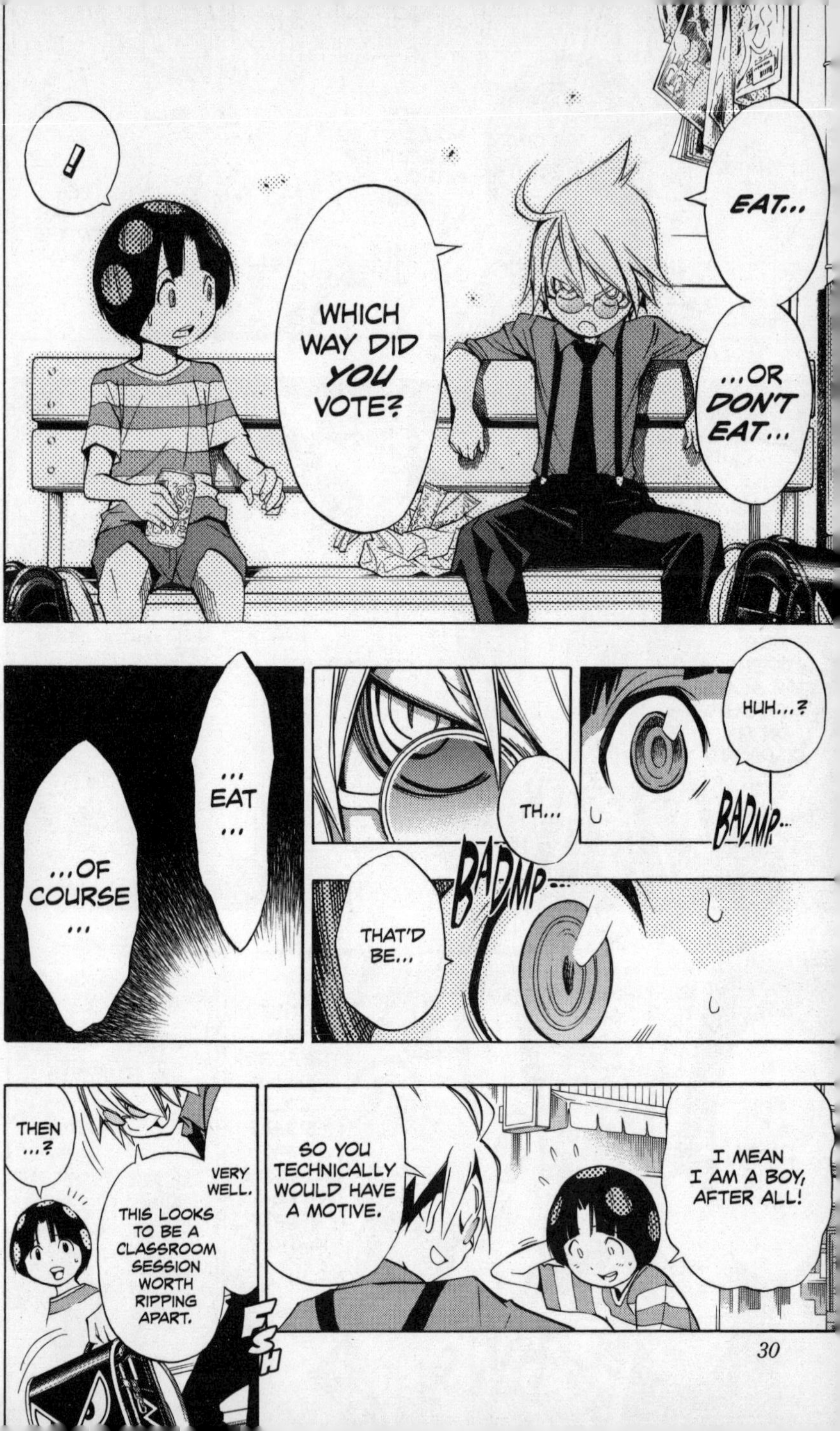
EAT...
...OR DON'T EAT...
WHICH WAY DID YOU VOTE?
!
HUH...?
BADMP...
TH...
THAT'D BE...
BADMP...
... EAT ...
...OF COURSE ...
I MEAN I AM A BOY, AFTER ALL!
SO YOU TECHNICALLY WOULD HAVE A MOTIVE.
VERY WELL.
THIS LOOKS TO BE A CLASSROOM SESSION WORTH RIPPING APART.
THEN ...?
FSH

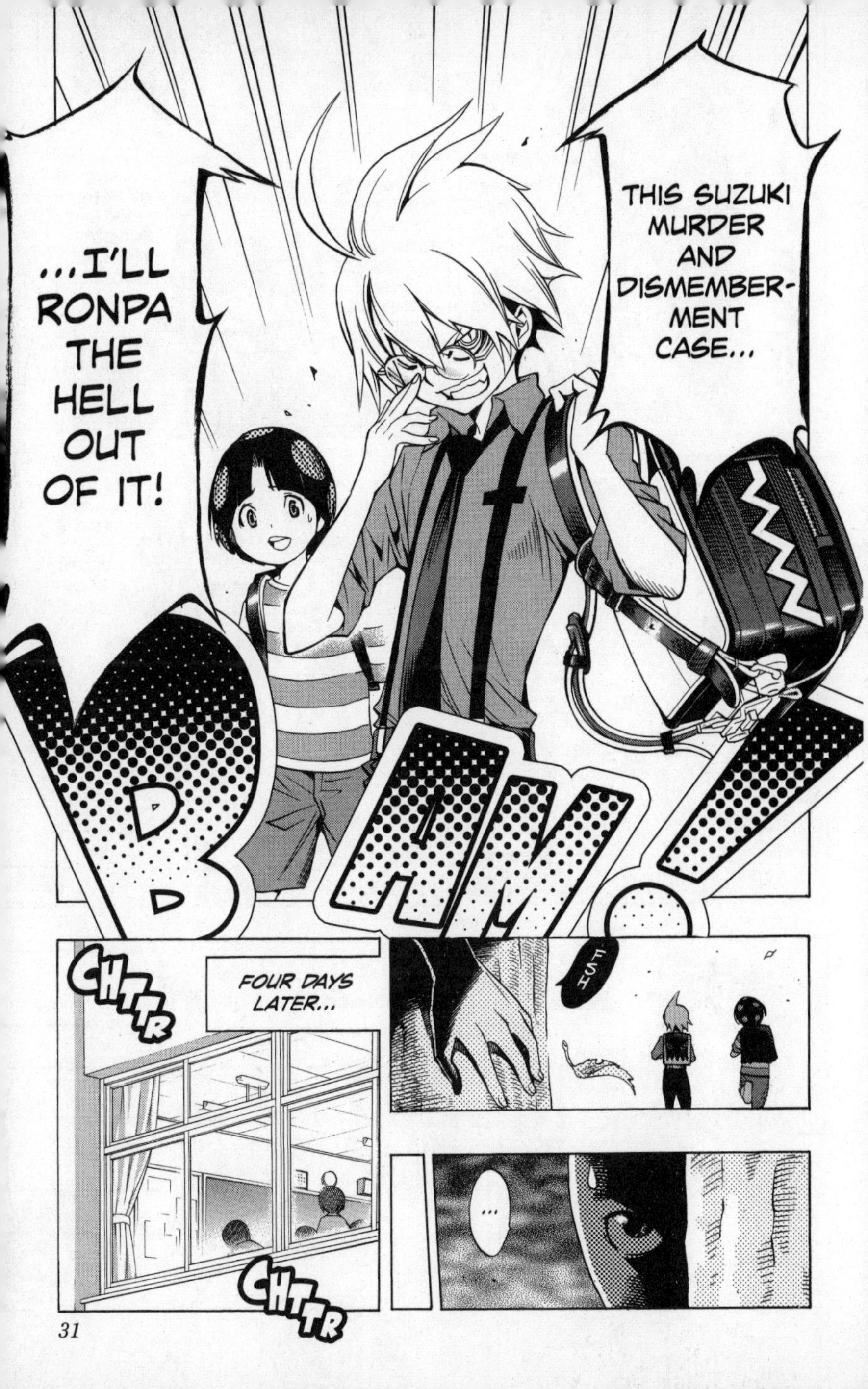

THIS SUZUKI MURDER AND DISMEMBER-MENT CASE...
...I'LL RONPA THE HELL OUT OF IT!
BAM!
FSH
...
CHTTR
FOUR DAYS LATER...
CHTTR

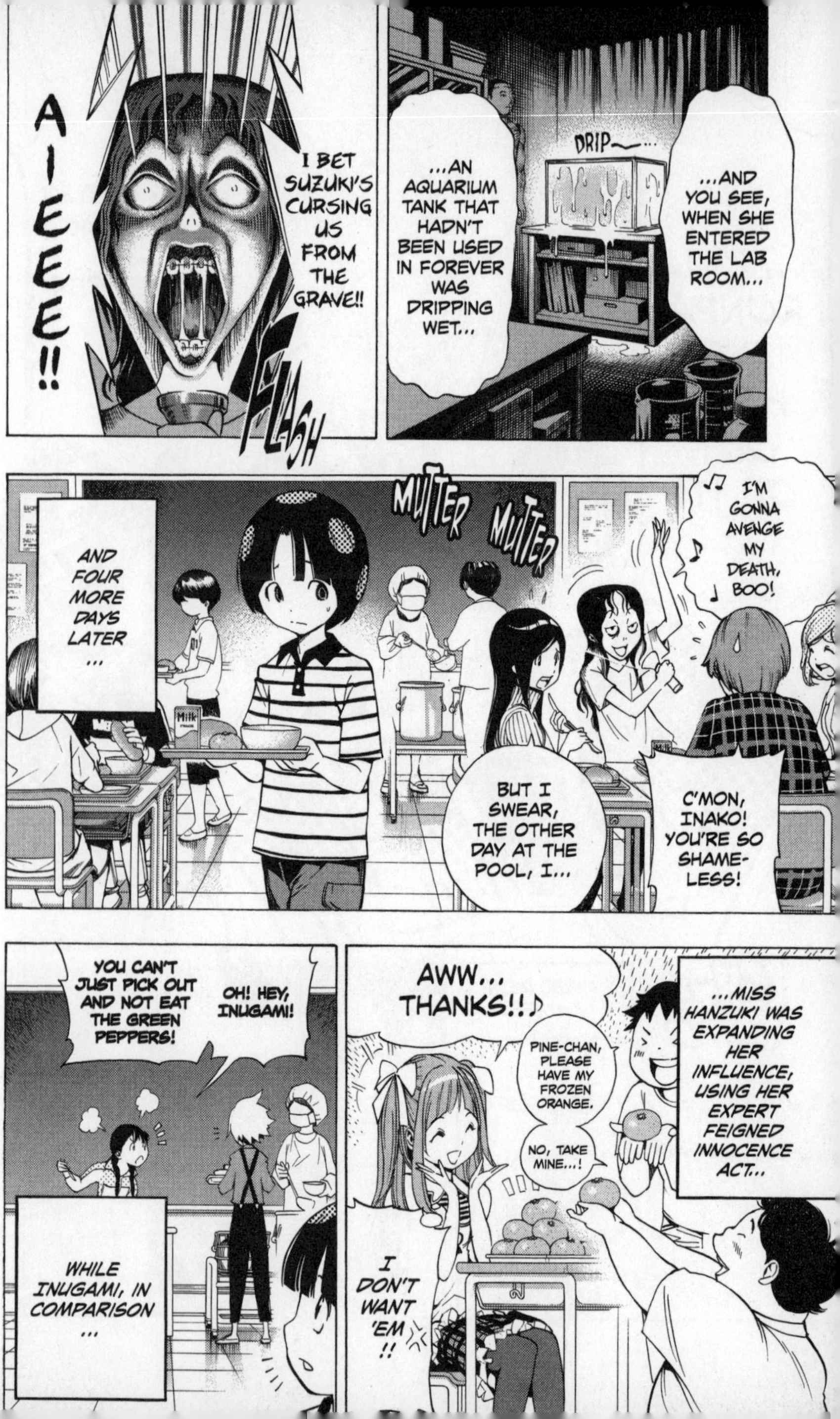
...AND YOU SEE, WHEN SHE ENTERED THE LAB ROOM...
DRIP~...
...AN AQUARIUM TANK THAT HADN'T BEEN USED IN FOREVER WAS DRIPPING WET...
I BET SUZUKI'S CURSING US FROM THE GRAVE!!
AIEEE!!
FLASH
♫ I'M GONNA AVENGE MY DEATH, BOO! ♪
MUTTER
MUTTER
AND FOUR MORE DAYS LATER...
C'MON, INAKO! YOU'RE SO SHAME-LESS!
BUT I SWEAR, THE OTHER DAY AT THE POOL, I...
AWW... THANKS!!♪
...MISS HANZUKI WAS EXPANDING HER INFLUENCE, USING HER EXPERT FEIGNED INNOCENCE ACT...
PINE-CHAN, PLEASE HAVE MY FROZEN ORANGE.
NO, TAKE MINE...!
I DON'T WANT 'EM!!
OH! HEY, INUGAMI!
YOU CAN'T JUST PICK OUT AND NOT EAT THE GREEN PEPPERS!
WHILE INUGAMI, IN COMPARISON...

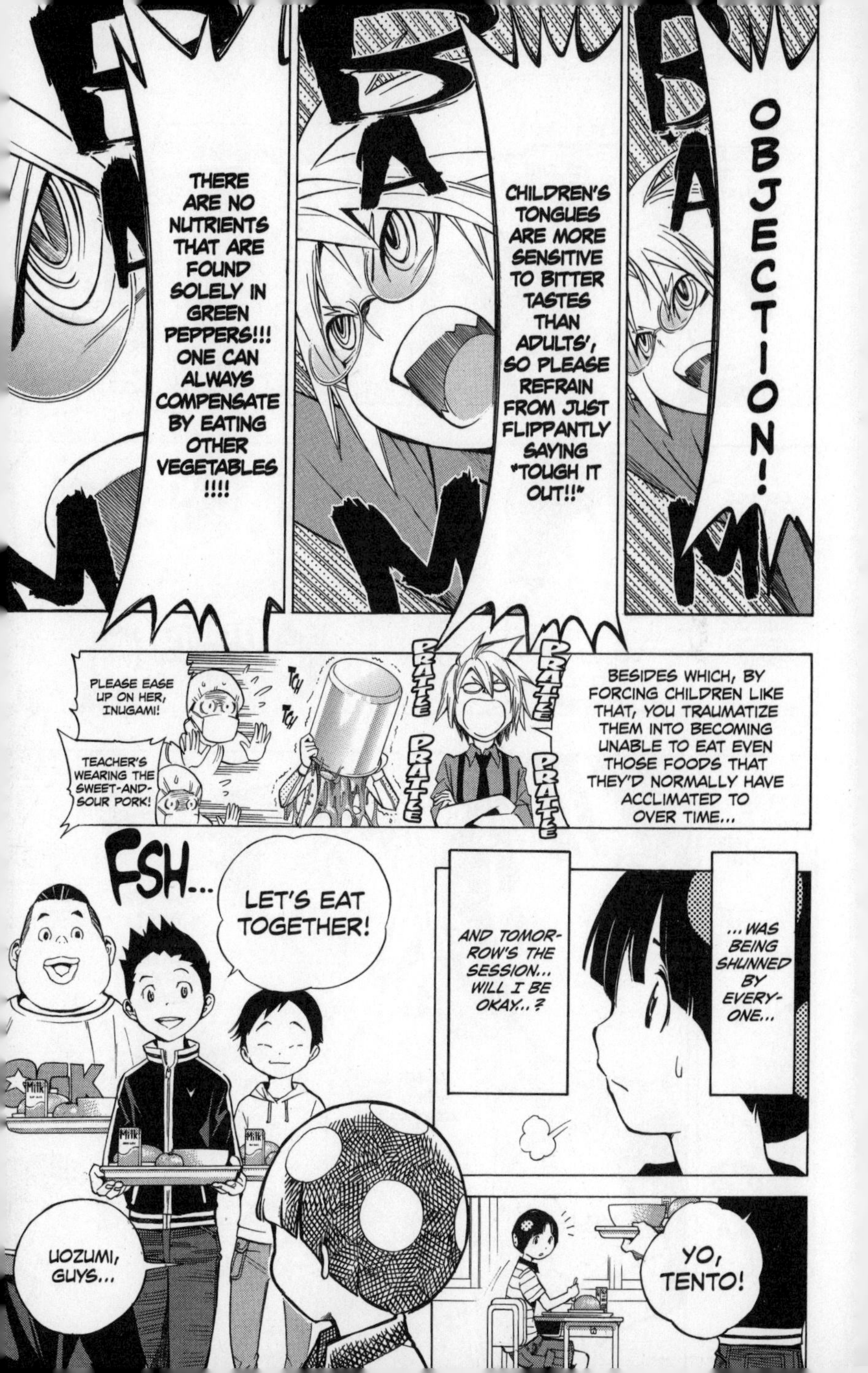
OBJECTION!
CHILDREN'S TONGUES ARE MORE SENSITIVE TO BITTER TASTES THAN ADULTS', SO PLEASE REFRAIN FROM JUST FLIPPANTLY SAYING "TOUGH IT OUT!!"
THERE ARE NO NUTRIENTS THAT ARE FOUND SOLELY IN GREEN PEPPERS!!! ONE CAN ALWAYS COMPENSATE BY EATING OTHER VEGETABLES!!!!
BESIDES WHICH, BY FORCING CHILDREN LIKE THAT, YOU TRAUMATIZE THEM INTO BECOMING UNABLE TO EAT EVEN THOSE FOODS THAT THEY'D NORMALLY HAVE ACCLIMATED TO OVER TIME...
PRATTLE
PRATTLE
PRATTLE
PRATTLE
TCH
TCH
PLEASE EASE UP ON HER, INUGAMI!
TEACHER'S WEARING THE SWEET-AND-SOUR PORK!
...WAS BEING SHUNNED BY EVERY-ONE...
AND TOMOR-ROW'S THE SESSION... WILL I BE OKAY...?
YO, TENTO!
FSH...
LET'S EAT TOGETHER!
UOZUMI, GUYS...

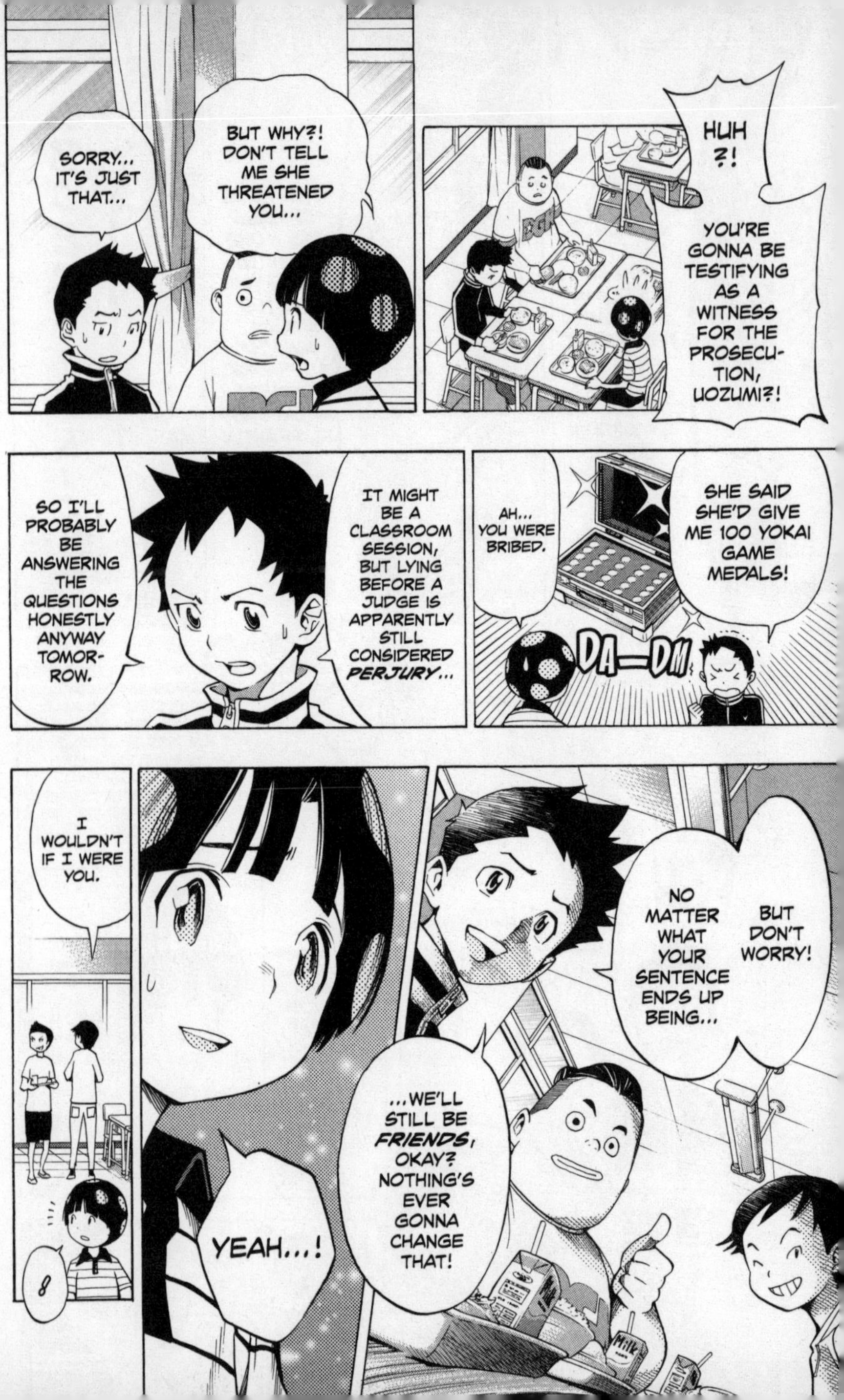
HUH ?!
YOU'RE GONNA BE TESTIFYING AS A WITNESS FOR THE PROSECUTION, UOZUMI?!
BUT WHY?! DON'T TELL ME SHE THREATENED YOU...
SORRY... IT'S JUST THAT...
SHE SAID SHE'D GIVE ME 100 YOKAI GAME MEDALS!
DA-DM
AH... YOU WERE BRIBED.
IT MIGHT BE A CLASSROOM SESSION, BUT LYING BEFORE A JUDGE IS APPARENTLY STILL CONSIDERED PERJURY...
SO I'LL PROBABLY BE ANSWERING THE QUESTIONS HONESTLY ANYWAY TOMORROW.
BUT DON'T WORRY!
NO MATTER WHAT YOUR SENTENCE ENDS UP BEING...
...WE'LL STILL BE FRIENDS, OKAY? NOTHING'S EVER GONNA CHANGE THAT!
YEAH...!
I WOULDN'T IF I WERE YOU.

READ THIS WAY

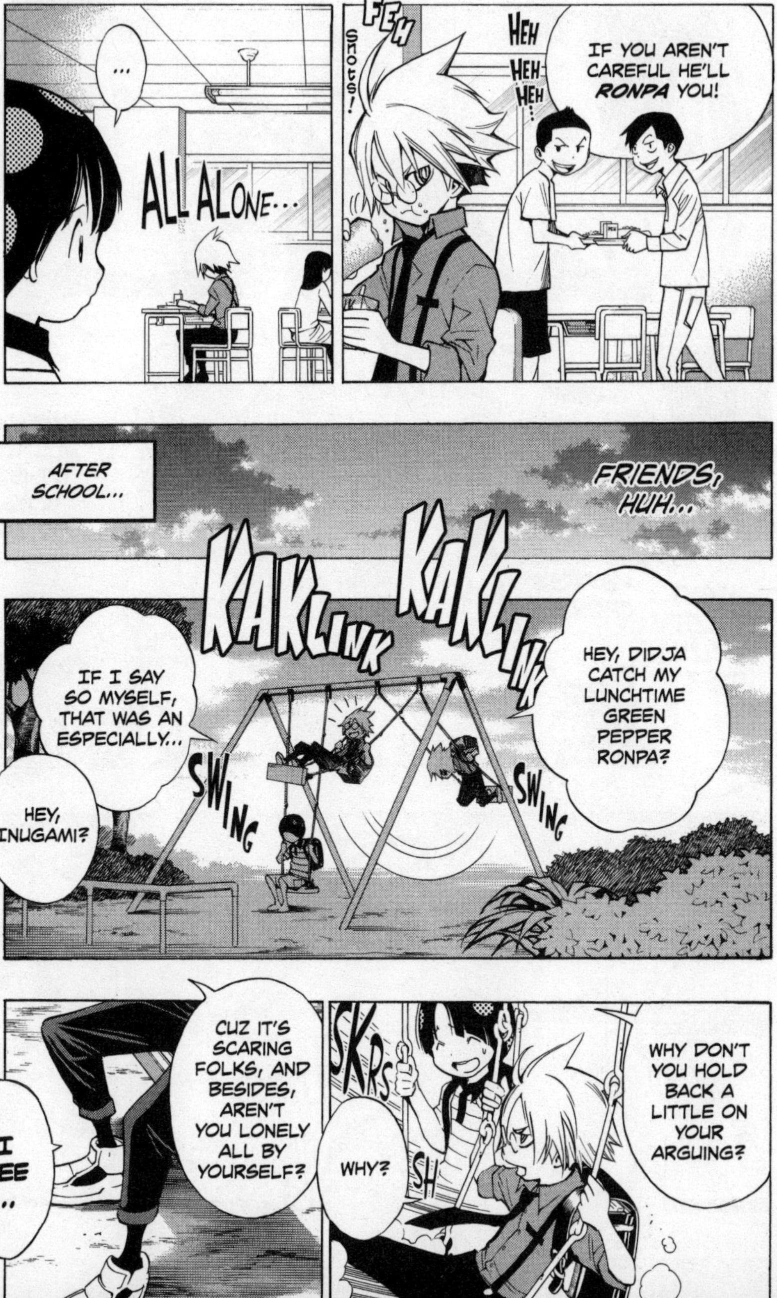
FEH
Snorts!
HEH HEH HEH
IF YOU AREN'T CAREFUL HE'LL *RONPA* YOU!
...
ALL ALONE...
FRIENDS, HUH...
AFTER SCHOOL...
KAKLINK
KAKLINK
HEY, DIDJA CATCH MY LUNCHTIME GREEN PEPPER RONPA?
SWING
IF I SAY SO MYSELF, THAT WAS AN ESPECIALLY...
HEY, INUGAMI?
SWING
WHY DON'T YOU HOLD BACK A LITTLE ON YOUR ARGUING?
SKRS
WHY?
SH
CUZ IT'S SCARING FOLKS, AND BESIDES, AREN'T YOU LONELY ALL BY YOURSELF?
I SEE...

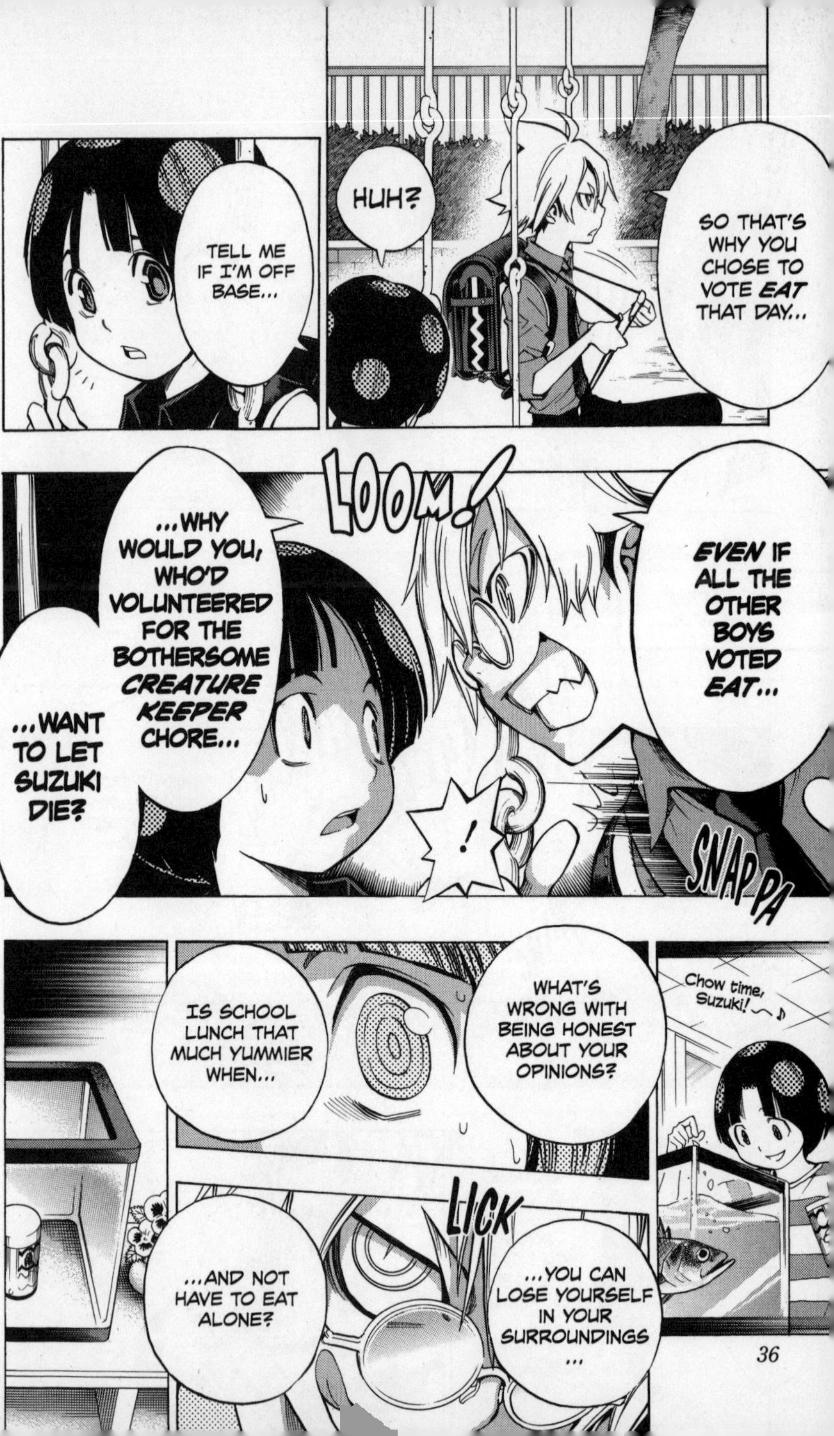
SO THAT'S WHY YOU CHOSE TO VOTE *EAT* THAT DAY...
HUH?
TELL ME IF I'M OFF BASE...
EVEN IF ALL THE OTHER BOYS VOTED *EAT*...
LOOM!
...WHY WOULD YOU, WHO'D VOLUNTEERED FOR THE BOTHERSOME *CREATURE KEEPER* CHORE...
...WANT TO LET SUZUKI DIE?
!
SNAP PA
Chow time, Suzuki! ♪
WHAT'S WRONG WITH BEING HONEST ABOUT YOUR OPINIONS?
IS SCHOOL LUNCH THAT MUCH YUMMIER WHEN...
LICK
...YOU CAN LOSE YOURSELF IN YOUR SURROUNDINGS ...
...AND NOT HAVE TO EAT ALONE?

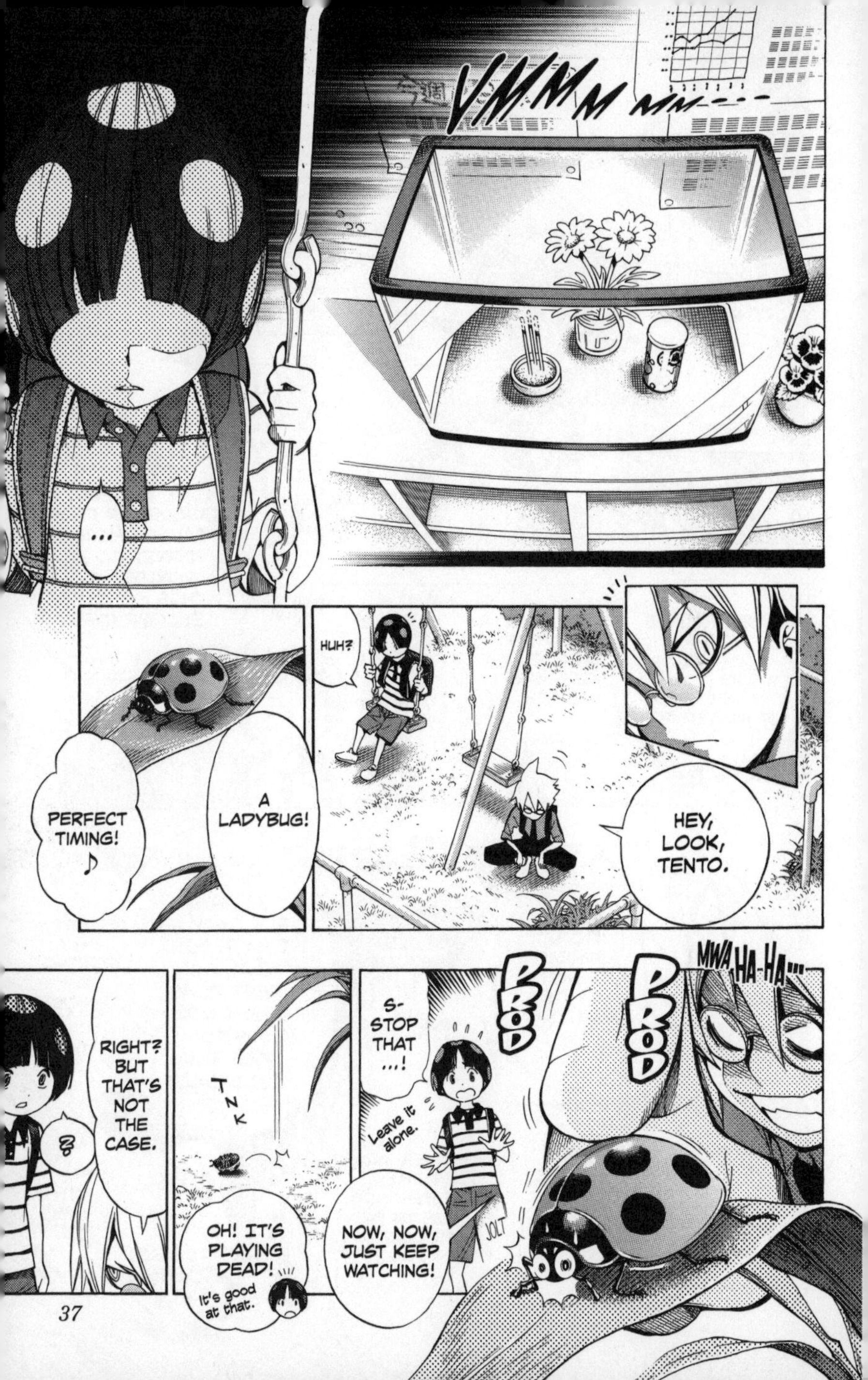
VMMM MM MM---
...
HEY, LOOK, TENTO.
HUH?
A LADYBUG!
PERFECT TIMING! ♪
MWA HA-HA...
PROD
PROD
S-STOP THAT...!
Leave it alone.
JOLT
NOW, NOW, JUST KEEP WATCHING!
TNK
OH! IT'S PLAYING DEAD!
It's good at that.
RIGHT? BUT THAT'S NOT THE CASE.
?

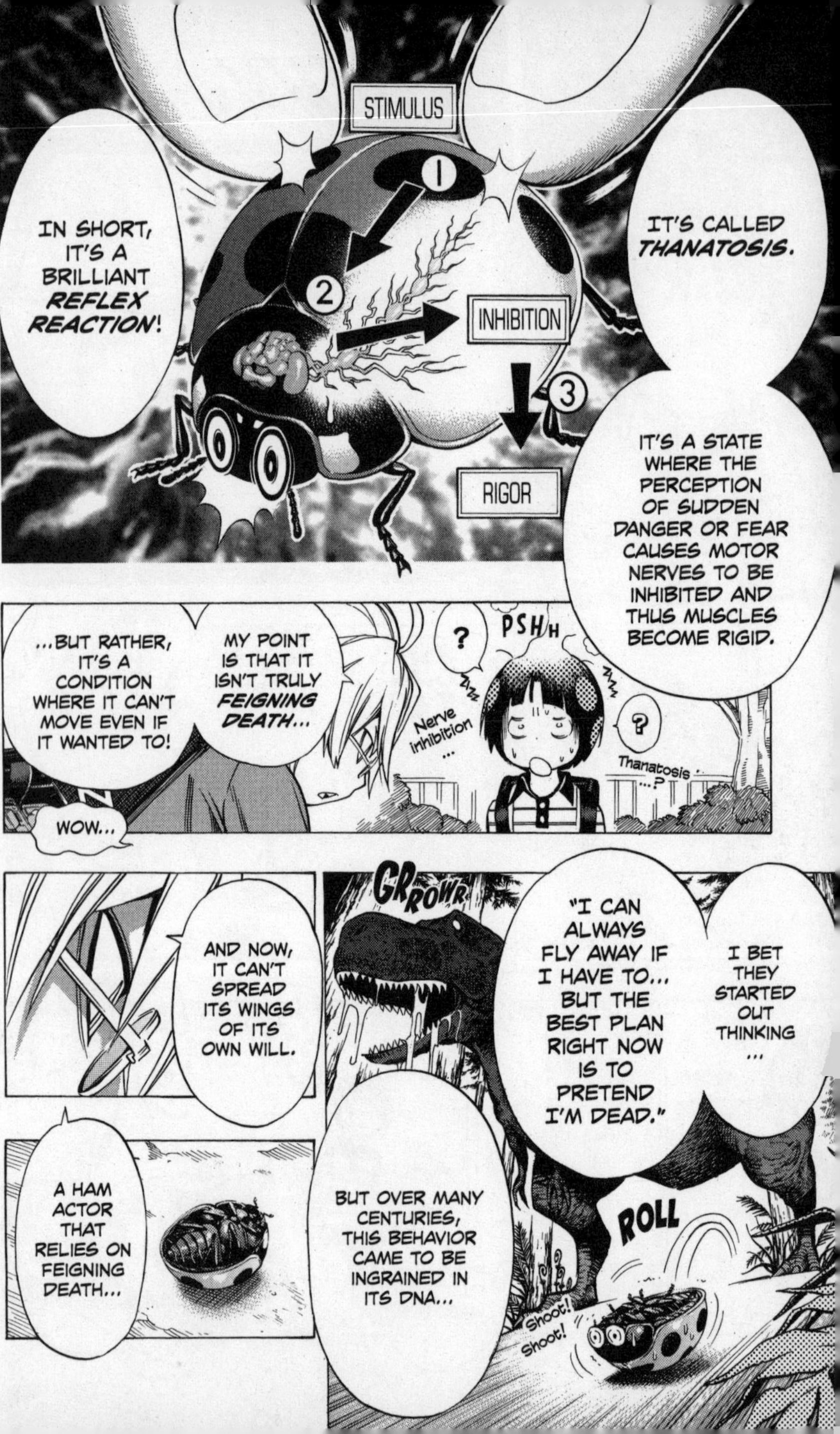
IT'S CALLED *THANATOSIS*.
IT'S A STATE WHERE THE PERCEPTION OF SUDDEN DANGER OR FEAR CAUSES MOTOR NERVES TO BE INHIBITED AND THUS MUSCLES BECOME RIGID.
STIMULUS
1
2
INHIBITION
3
RIGOR
IN SHORT, IT'S A BRILLIANT *REFLEX REACTION*!
PSHHH
?
Nerve inhibition ...
?
Thanatosis ...?
MY POINT IS THAT IT ISN'T TRULY *FEIGNING DEATH*...
...BUT RATHER, IT'S A CONDITION WHERE IT CAN'T MOVE EVEN IF IT WANTED TO!
WOW...
GRROWR
I BET THEY STARTED OUT THINKING ...
"I CAN ALWAYS FLY AWAY IF I HAVE TO... BUT THE BEST PLAN RIGHT NOW IS TO PRETEND I'M DEAD."
ROLL
Shoot! Shoot!
BUT OVER MANY CENTURIES, THIS BEHAVIOR CAME TO BE INGRAINED IN ITS DNA...
AND NOW, IT CAN'T SPREAD ITS WINGS OF ITS OWN WILL.
A HAM ACTOR THAT RELIES ON FEIGNING DEATH...

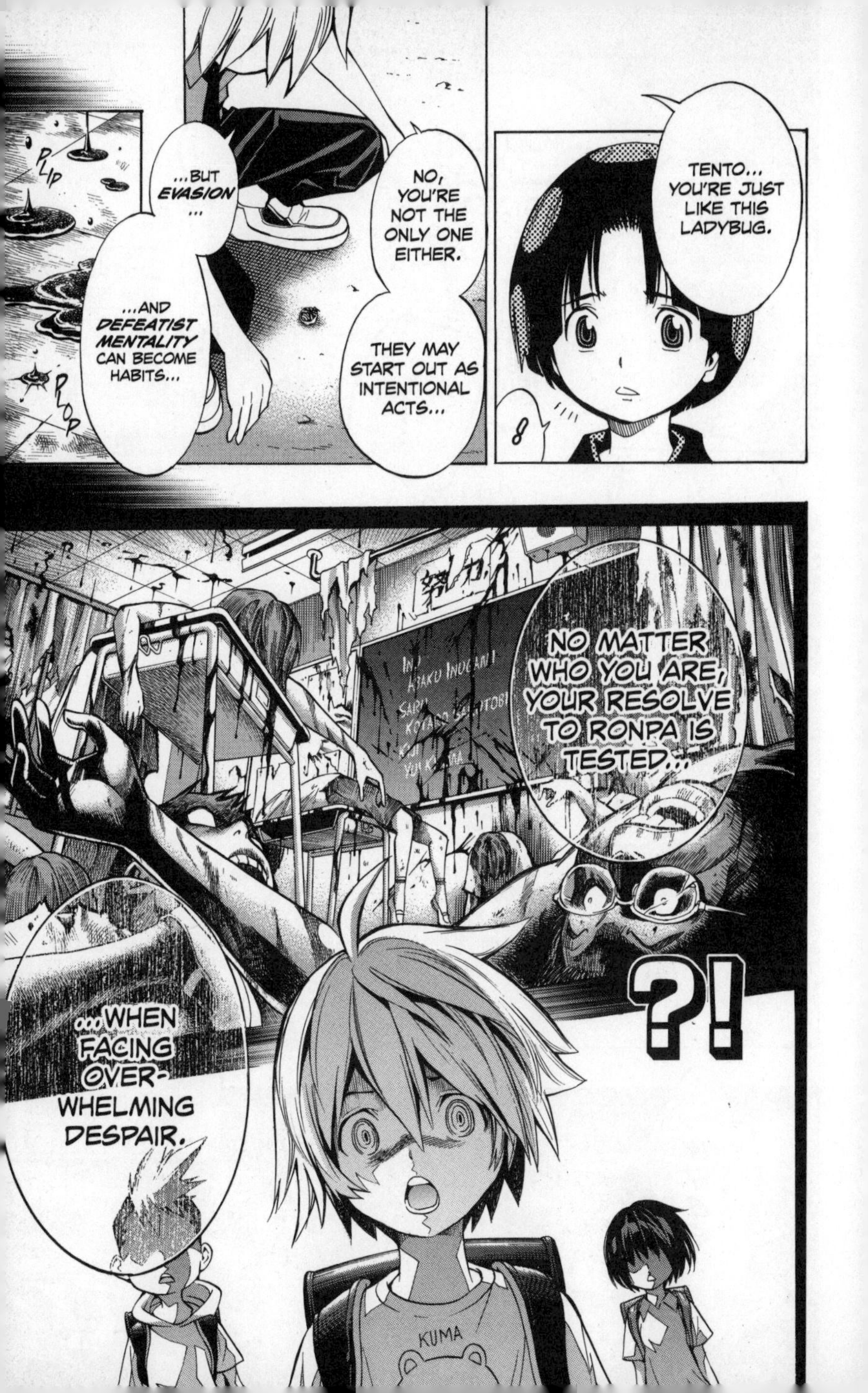
TENTO... YOU'RE JUST LIKE THIS LADYBUG.
NO, YOU'RE NOT THE ONLY ONE EITHER.
THEY MAY START OUT AS INTENTIONAL ACTS...
...BUT EVASION ...
...AND DEFEATIST MENTALITY CAN BECOME HABITS...
PLIP
PLOP
NO MATTER WHO YOU ARE, YOUR RESOLVE TO RONPA IS TESTED...
?!
...WHEN FACING OVER-WHELMING DESPAIR.
KUMA

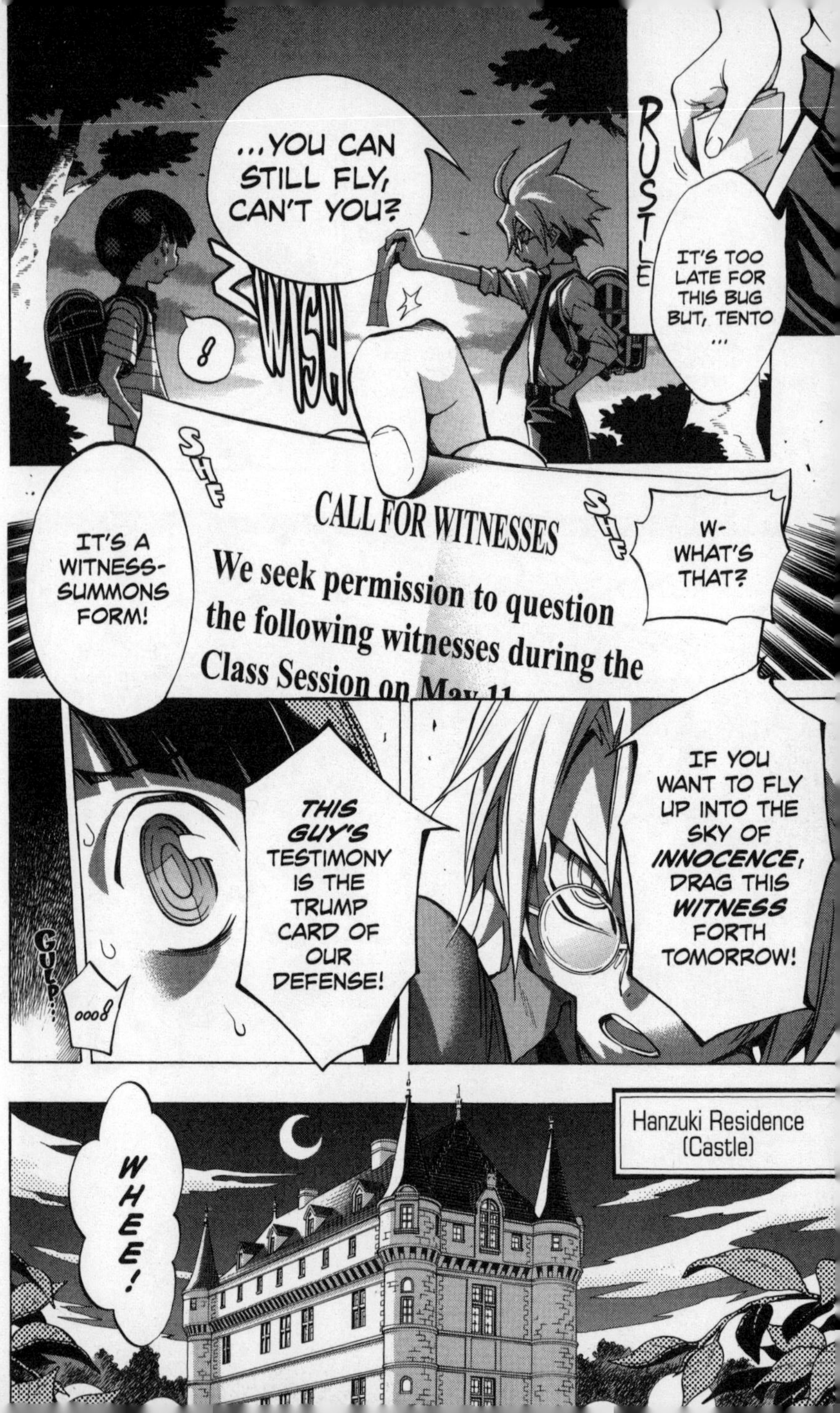
RUSTLE
IT'S TOO LATE FOR THIS BUG BUT, TENTO ...
...YOU CAN STILL FLY, CAN'T YOU?
ZWISH
!
SHF
SHF
W-WHAT'S THAT?
IT'S A WITNESS-SUMMONS FORM!
CALL FOR WITNESSES
We seek permission to question the following witnesses during the Class Session on May 11
IF YOU WANT TO FLY UP INTO THE SKY OF *INNOCENCE*, DRAG THIS *WITNESS* FORTH TOMORROW!
THIS GUY'S TESTIMONY IS THE TRUMP CARD OF OUR DEFENSE!
GULP...
ooo!
Hanzuki Residence (Castle)
WHEE!

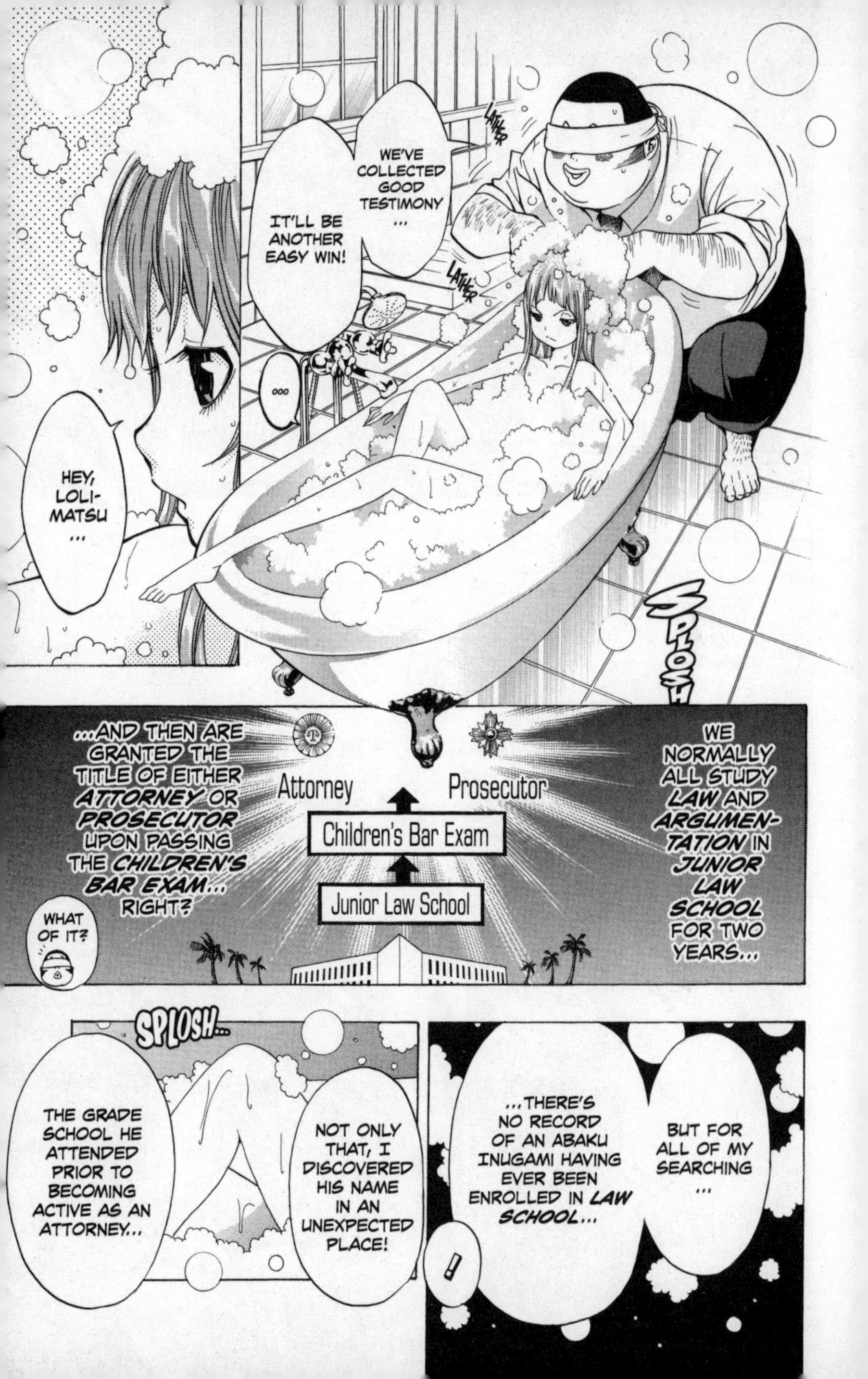
LATHER
WE'VE COLLECTED GOOD TESTIMONY...
IT'LL BE ANOTHER EASY WIN!
LATHER
...
SPLOSH
HEY, LOLI-MATSU...
WE NORMALLY ALL STUDY LAW AND ARGUMENTATION IN JUNIOR LAW SCHOOL FOR TWO YEARS...
Prosecutor
Attorney
Children's Bar Exam
Junior Law School
...AND THEN ARE GRANTED THE TITLE OF EITHER ATTORNEY OR PROSECUTOR UPON PASSING THE CHILDREN'S BAR EXAM... RIGHT?
WHAT OF IT?
BUT FOR ALL OF MY SEARCHING...
...THERE'S NO RECORD OF AN ABAKU INUGAMI HAVING EVER BEEN ENROLLED IN LAW SCHOOL...
!
SPLOSH...
NOT ONLY THAT, I DISCOVERED HIS NAME IN AN UNEXPECTED PLACE!
THE GRADE SCHOOL HE ATTENDED PRIOR TO BECOMING ACTIVE AS AN ATTORNEY...

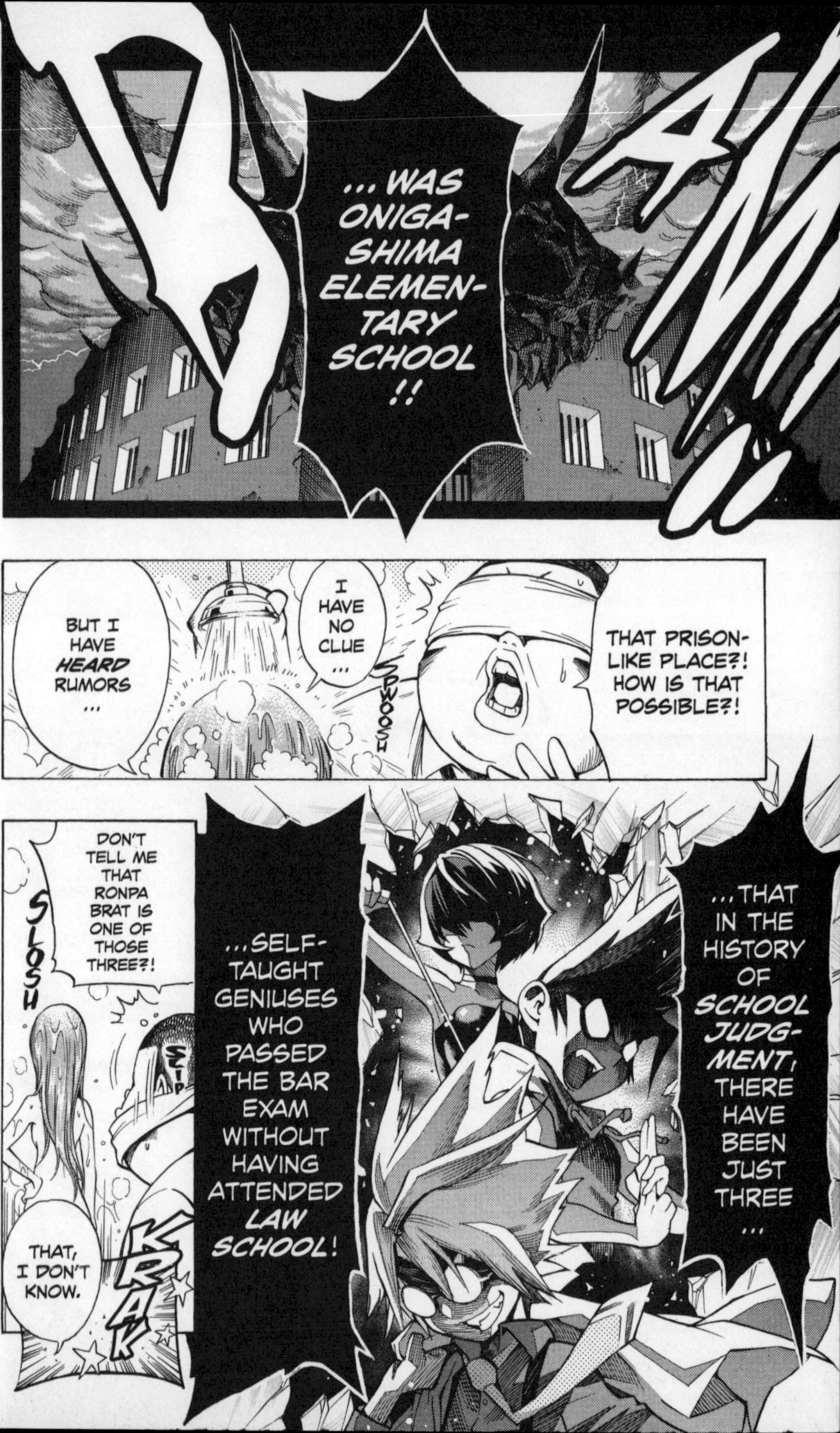

...WAS ONIGA-SHIMA ELEMEN-TARY SCHOOL!!
THAT PRISON-LIKE PLACE?! HOW IS THAT POSSIBLE?!
SPWOOSH
I HAVE NO CLUE...
BUT I HAVE HEARD RUMORS...
...THAT IN THE HISTORY OF SCHOOL JUDGMENT, THERE HAVE BEEN JUST THREE...
...SELF-TAUGHT GENIUSES WHO PASSED THE BAR EXAM WITHOUT HAVING ATTENDED LAW SCHOOL!
DON'T TELL ME THAT RONPA BRAT IS ONE OF THOSE THREE?!
SLOSH
KRAAK
THAT, I DON'T KNOW.

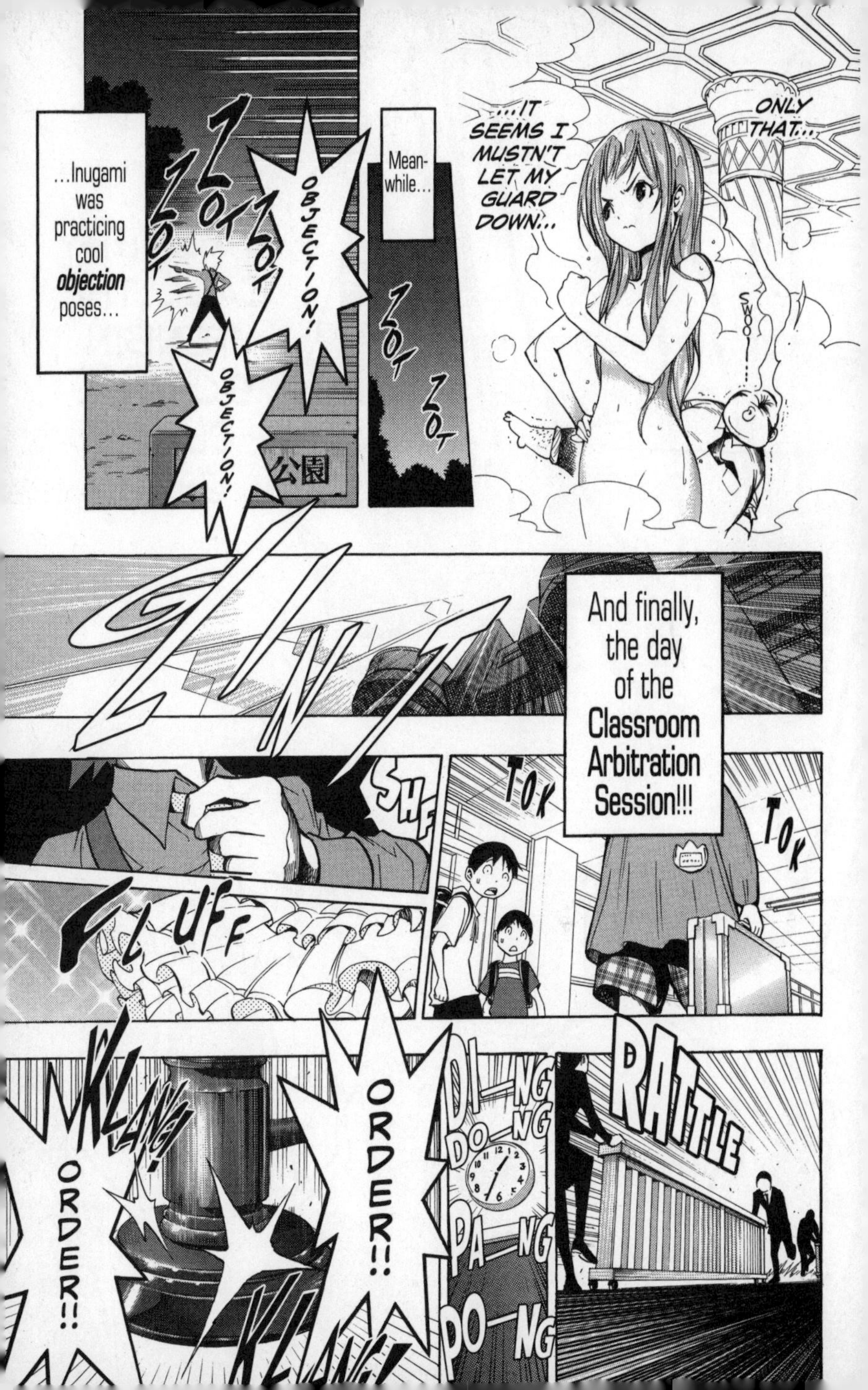

ONLY THAT...
...IT SEEMS I MUSTN'T LET MY GUARD DOWN...
SWOO!...
Mean-while...
ZOT
ZOT
...Inugami was practicing cool ***objection*** poses...
OBJECTION!
ZOT ZOT ZOT ZOT
OBJECTION!
GLINT
And finally, the day of the Classroom Arbitration Session!!!
TOK
TOK
SHF
FLUFF
RATTLE
DING DONG
PANG PONG
ORDER!!
KLANG!
ORDER!!
KLANG!

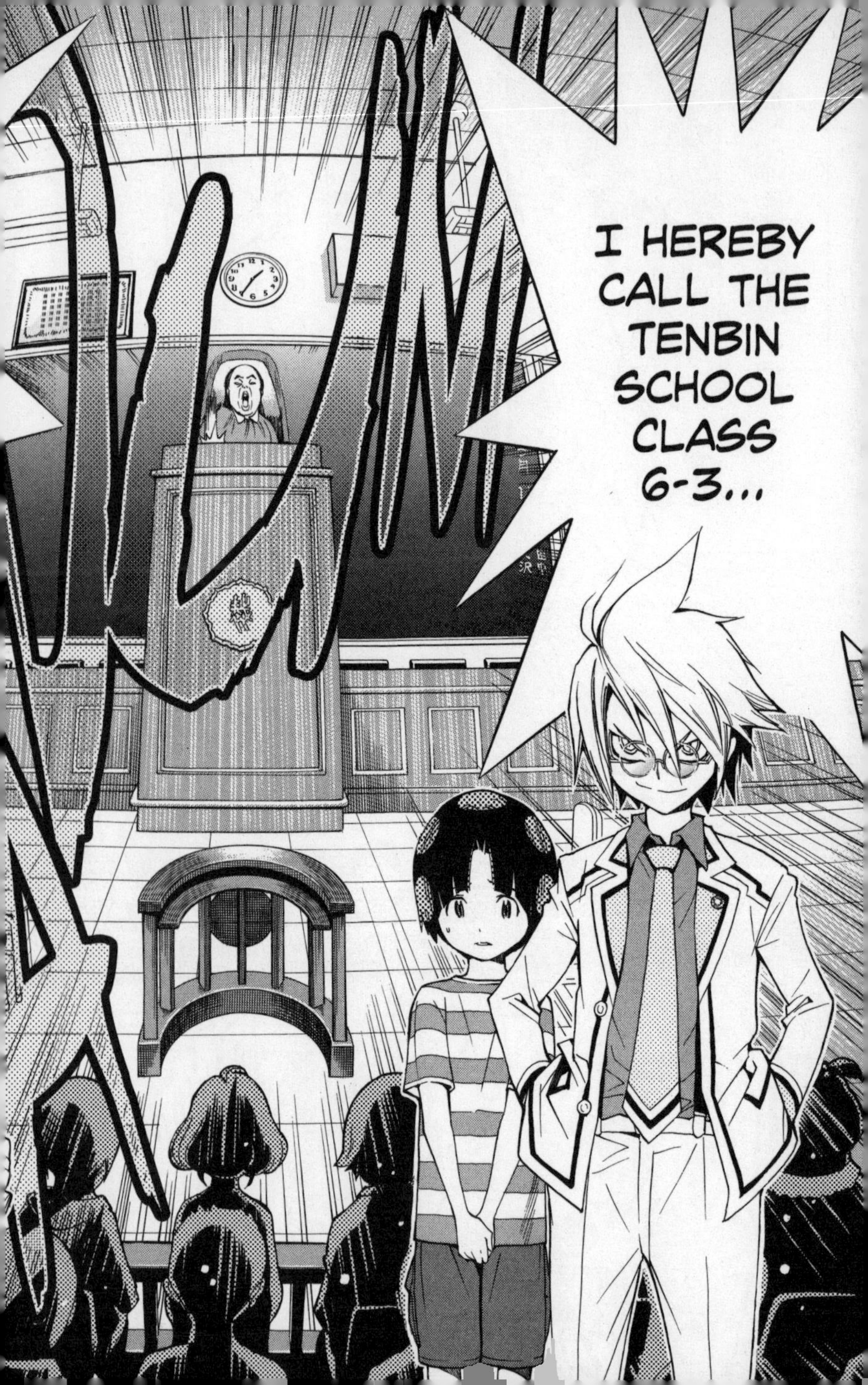
I HEREBY CALL THE TENBIN SCHOOL CLASS 6-3...

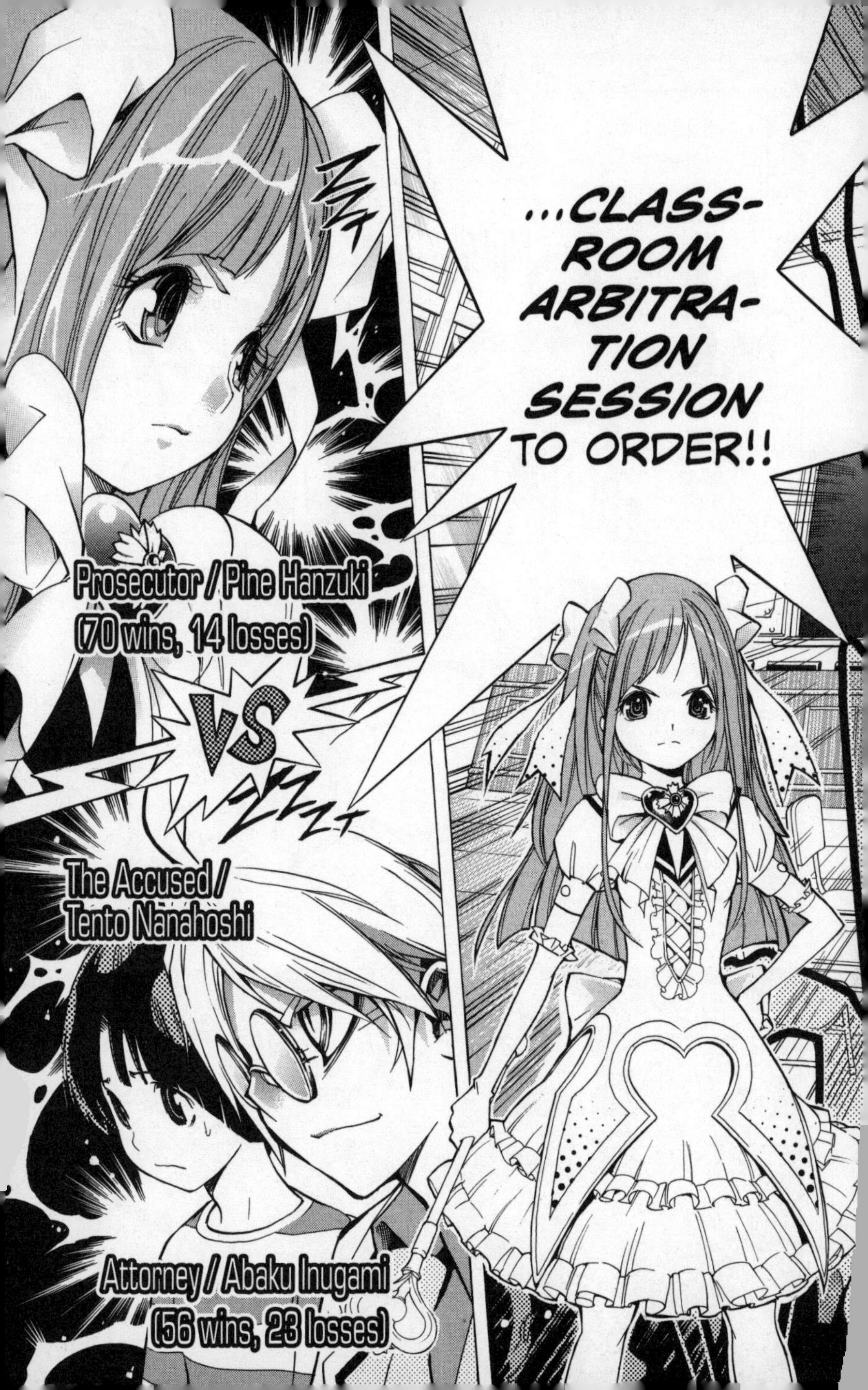
...CLASS-ROOM ARBITRATION SESSION TO ORDER!!
Prosecutor / Pine Hanzuki (70 wins, 14 losses)
VS
The Accused / Tento Nanahoshi
Attorney / Abaku Inugami (56 wins, 23 losses)

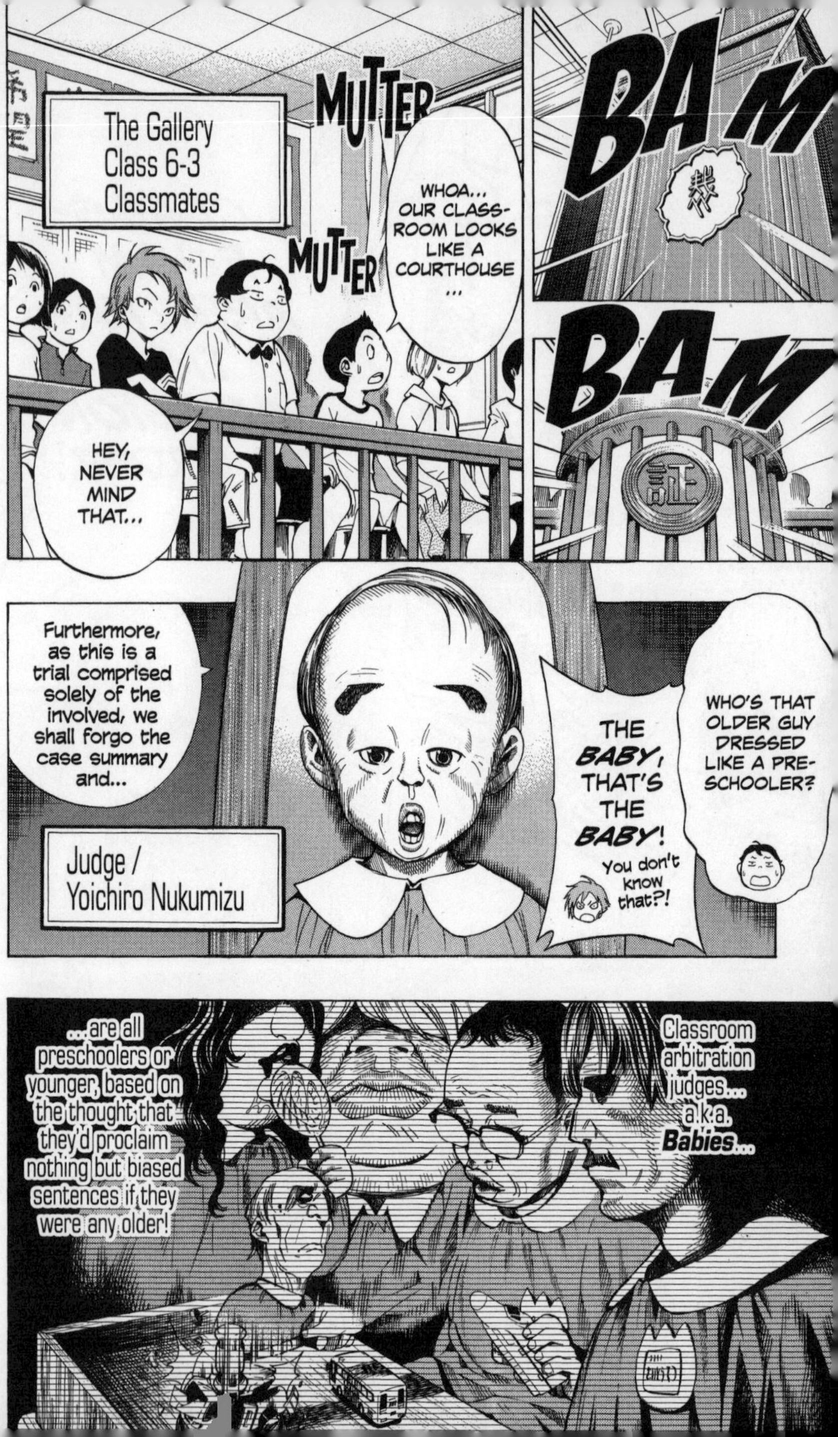
BAM
裁
BAM
証
MUTTER
WHOA... OUR CLASS-ROOM LOOKS LIKE A COURTHOUSE ...
The Gallery Class 6-3 Classmates
MUTTER
HEY, NEVER MIND THAT...
WHO'S THAT OLDER GUY DRESSED LIKE A PRE-SCHOOLER?
THE *BABY*, THAT'S THE *BABY*!
You don't know that?!
Furthermore, as this is a trial comprised solely of the involved, we shall forgo the case summary and...
Judge / Yoichiro Nukumizu
Classroom arbitration judges... a.k.a. **Babies**...
...are all preschoolers or younger, based on the thought that they'd proclaim nothing but biased sentences if they were any older!

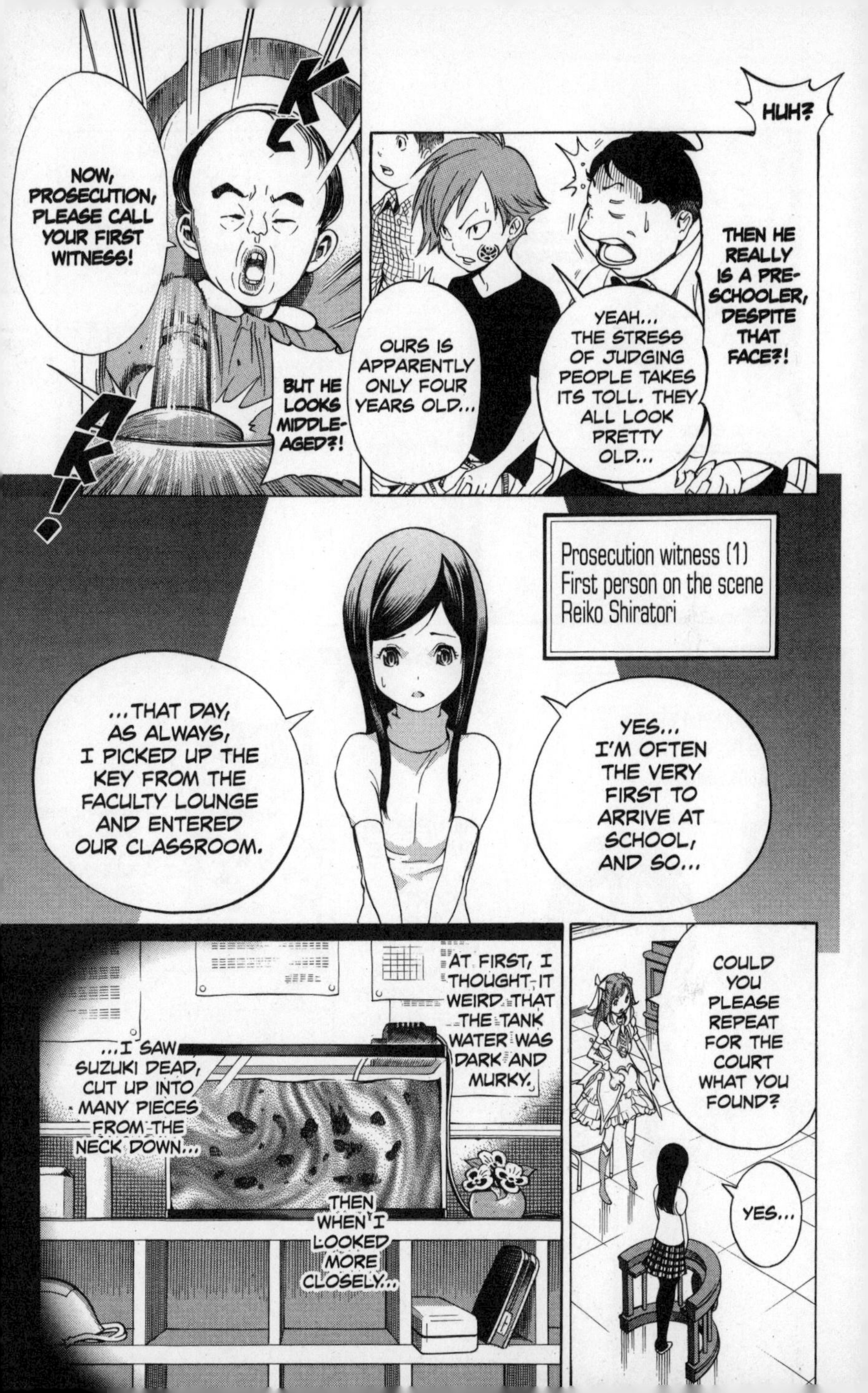
HUH?
THEN HE REALLY IS A PRE-SCHOOLER, DESPITE THAT FACE?!
YEAH... THE STRESS OF JUDGING PEOPLE TAKES ITS TOLL. THEY ALL LOOK PRETTY OLD...
OURS IS APPARENTLY ONLY FOUR YEARS OLD...
BUT HE LOOKS MIDDLE-AGED?!
NOW, PROSECUTION, PLEASE CALL YOUR FIRST WITNESS!
KLAK!
Prosecution witness (1)
First person on the scene
Reiko Shiratori
YES... I'M OFTEN THE VERY FIRST TO ARRIVE AT SCHOOL, AND SO...
...THAT DAY, AS ALWAYS, I PICKED UP THE KEY FROM THE FACULTY LOUNGE AND ENTERED OUR CLASSROOM.
COULD YOU PLEASE REPEAT FOR THE COURT WHAT YOU FOUND?
YES...
AT FIRST, I THOUGHT IT WEIRD THAT THE TANK WATER WAS DARK AND MURKY.
THEN WHEN I LOOKED MORE CLOSELY...
...I SAW SUZUKI DEAD, CUT UP INTO MANY PIECES FROM THE NECK DOWN...

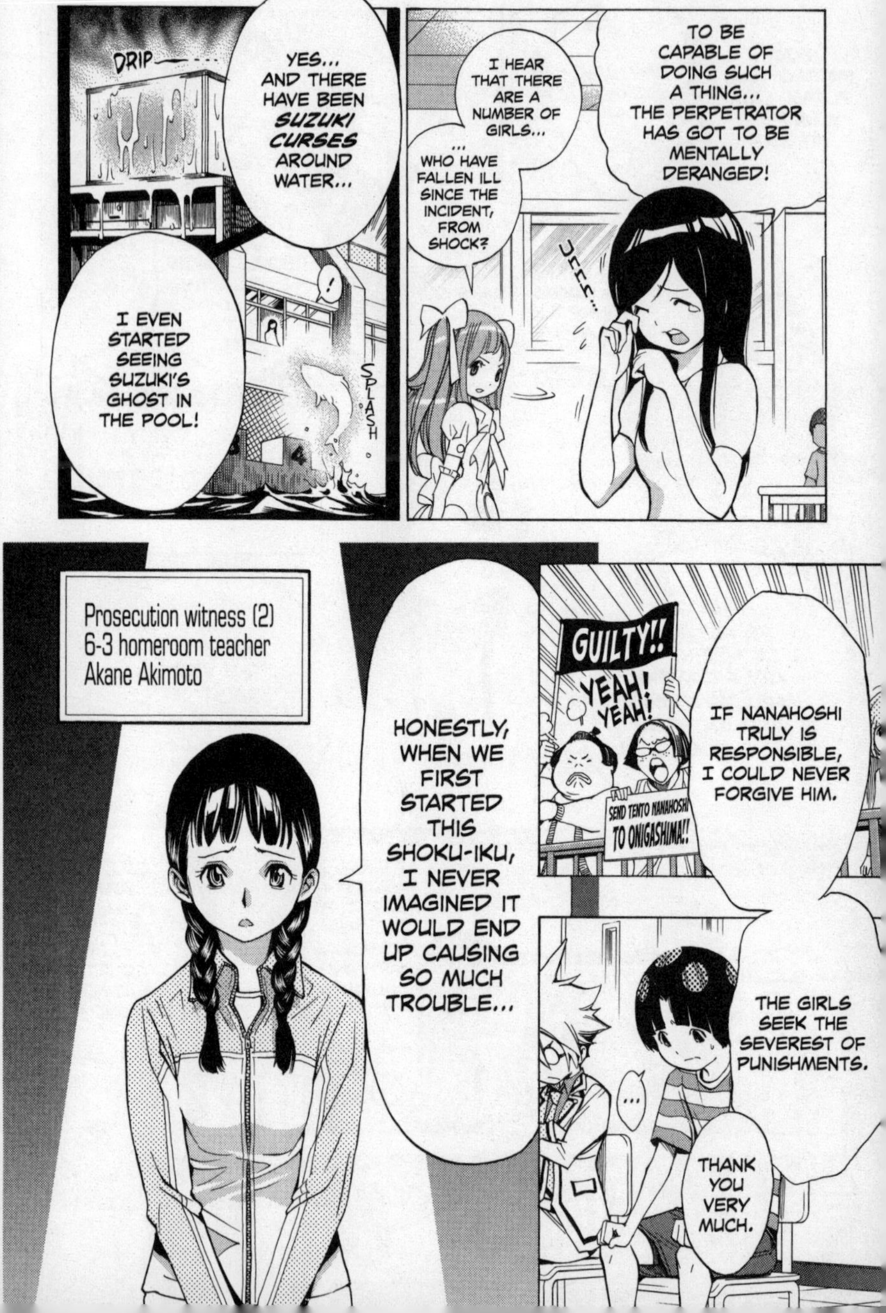
TO BE CAPABLE OF DOING SUCH A THING... THE PERPETRATOR HAS GOT TO BE MENTALLY DERANGED!
Urrr...
I HEAR THAT THERE ARE A NUMBER OF GIRLS...
...WHO HAVE FALLEN ILL SINCE THE INCIDENT, FROM SHOCK?
YES... AND THERE HAVE BEEN SUZUKI CURSES AROUND WATER...
DRIP
I EVEN STARTED SEEING SUZUKI'S GHOST IN THE POOL!
!
SPLASH
GUILTY!!
YEAH! YEAH!
SEND TENTO NANAHOSHI TO ONIGASHIMA!!
IF NANAHOSHI TRULY IS RESPONSIBLE, I COULD NEVER FORGIVE HIM.
THE GIRLS SEEK THE SEVEREST OF PUNISHMENTS.
...
THANK YOU VERY MUCH.
Prosecution witness (2) 6-3 homeroom teacher Akane Akimoto
HONESTLY, WHEN WE FIRST STARTED THIS SHOKU-IKU, I NEVER IMAGINED IT WOULD END UP CAUSING SO MUCH TROUBLE...

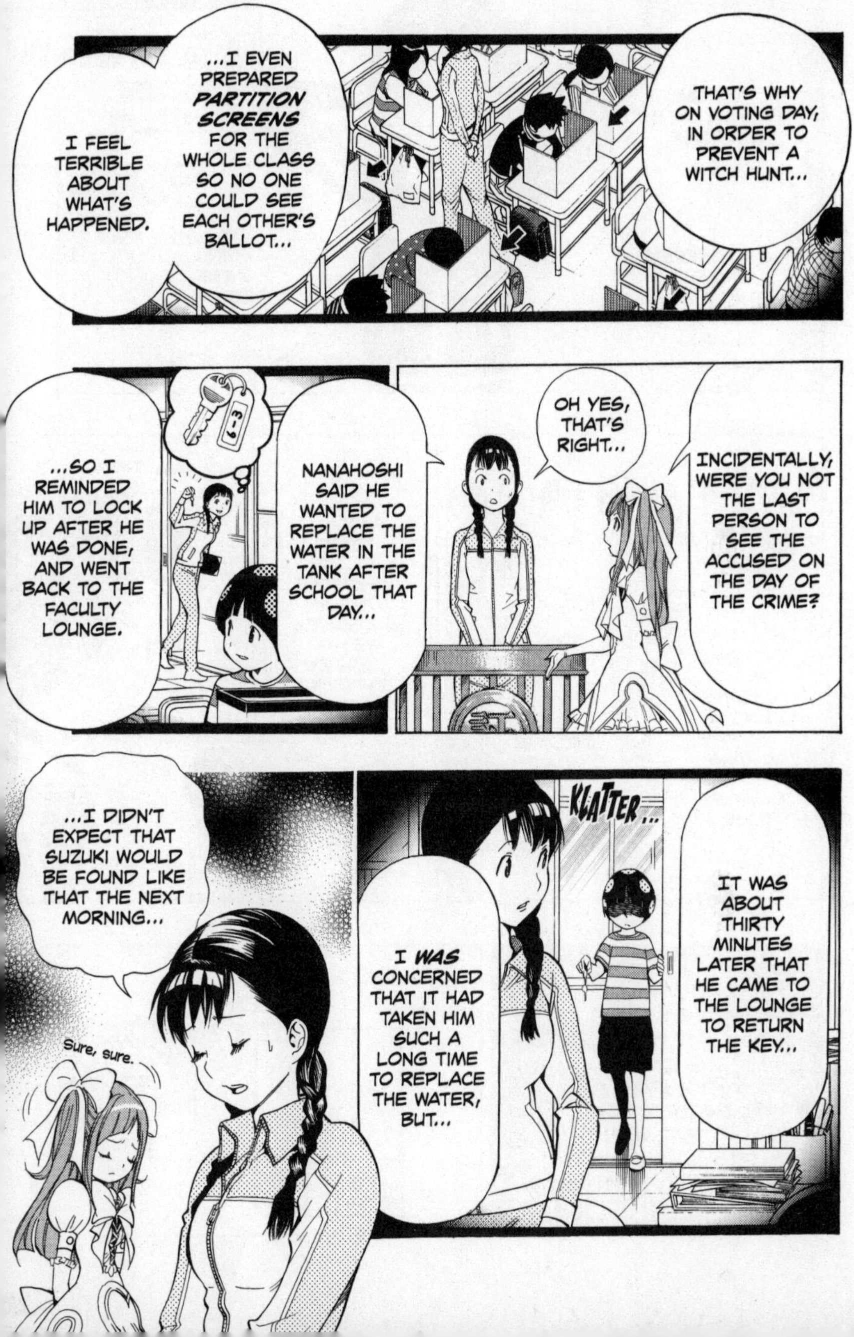
THAT'S WHY ON VOTING DAY, IN ORDER TO PREVENT A WITCH HUNT...
...I EVEN PREPARED PARTITION SCREENS FOR THE WHOLE CLASS SO NO ONE COULD SEE EACH OTHER'S BALLOT...
I FEEL TERRIBLE ABOUT WHAT'S HAPPENED.
INCIDENTALLY, WERE YOU NOT THE LAST PERSON TO SEE THE ACCUSED ON THE DAY OF THE CRIME?
OH YES, THAT'S RIGHT...
NANAHOSHI SAID HE WANTED TO REPLACE THE WATER IN THE TANK AFTER SCHOOL THAT DAY...
6-3
...SO I REMINDED HIM TO LOCK UP AFTER HE WAS DONE, AND WENT BACK TO THE FACULTY LOUNGE.
KLATTER...
IT WAS ABOUT THIRTY MINUTES LATER THAT HE CAME TO THE LOUNGE TO RETURN THE KEY...
I WAS CONCERNED THAT IT HAD TAKEN HIM SUCH A LONG TIME TO REPLACE THE WATER, BUT...
...I DIDN'T EXPECT THAT SUZUKI WOULD BE FOUND LIKE THAT THE NEXT MORNING...
Sure, sure.

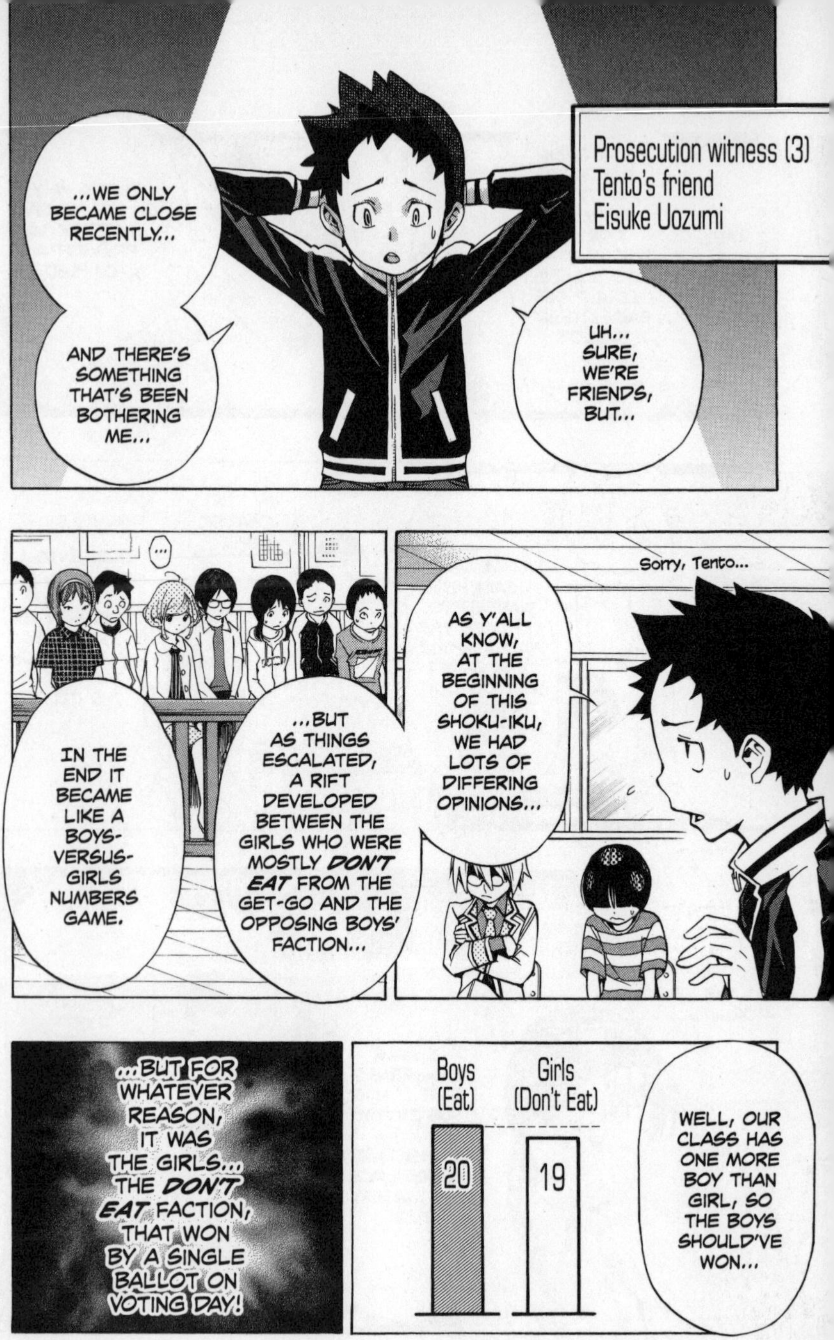
Prosecution witness (3) Tento's friend Eisuke Uozumi
UH... SURE, WE'RE FRIENDS, BUT...
...WE ONLY BECAME CLOSE RECENTLY...
AND THERE'S SOMETHING THAT'S BEEN BOTHERING ME...
Sorry, Tento...
AS Y'ALL KNOW, AT THE BEGINNING OF THIS SHOKU-IKU, WE HAD LOTS OF DIFFERING OPINIONS...
...BUT AS THINGS ESCALATED, A RIFT DEVELOPED BETWEEN THE GIRLS WHO WERE MOSTLY *DON'T EAT* FROM THE GET-GO AND THE OPPOSING BOYS' FACTION...
...
IN THE END IT BECAME LIKE A BOYS-VERSUS-GIRLS NUMBERS GAME.
Boys (Eat)
Girls (Don't Eat)
20
19
WELL, OUR CLASS HAS ONE MORE BOY THAN GIRL, SO THE BOYS SHOULD'VE WON...
...BUT FOR WHATEVER REASON, IT WAS THE GIRLS... THE *DON'T EAT* FACTION, THAT WON BY A SINGLE BALLOT ON VOTING DAY!

READ THIS WAY

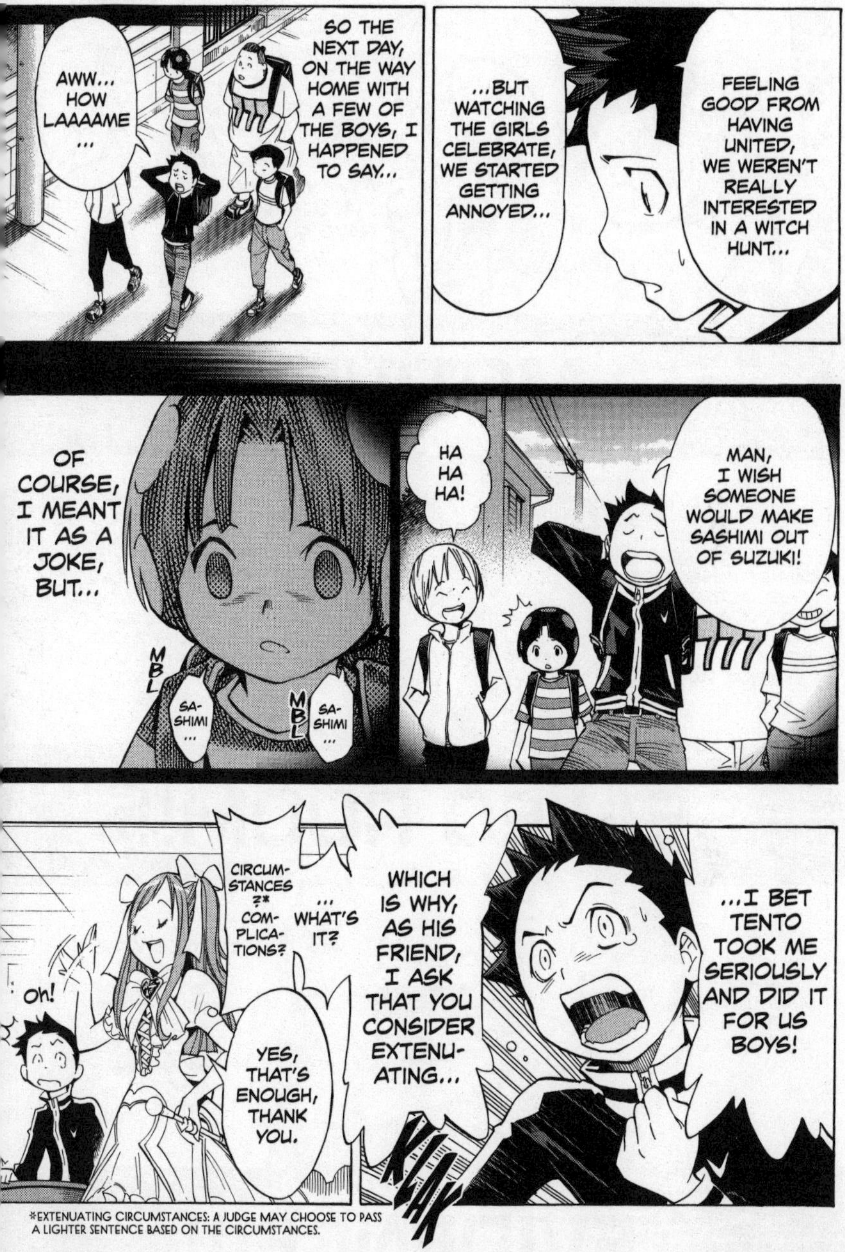
FEELING GOOD FROM HAVING UNITED, WE WEREN'T REALLY INTERESTED IN A WITCH HUNT...
...BUT WATCHING THE GIRLS CELEBRATE, WE STARTED GETTING ANNOYED...
SO THE NEXT DAY, ON THE WAY HOME WITH A FEW OF THE BOYS, I HAPPENED TO SAY...
AWW... HOW LAAAAME...
MAN, I WISH SOMEONE WOULD MAKE SASHIMI OUT OF SUZUKI!
HA HA HA!
OF COURSE, I MEANT IT AS A JOKE, BUT...
MBL
SA-SHIMI...
MBL
SA-SHIMI...
...I BET TENTO TOOK ME SERIOUSLY AND DID IT FOR US BOYS!
WHICH IS WHY, AS HIS FRIEND, I ASK THAT YOU CONSIDER EXTENU-ATING...
KYAH
...WHAT'S IT?
CIRCUM-STANCES?* COM-PLICA-TIONS?
YES, THAT'S ENOUGH, THANK YOU.
Oh!

*EXTENUATING CIRCUMSTANCES: A JUDGE MAY CHOOSE TO PASS A LIGHTER SENTENCE BASED ON THE CIRCUMSTANCES.

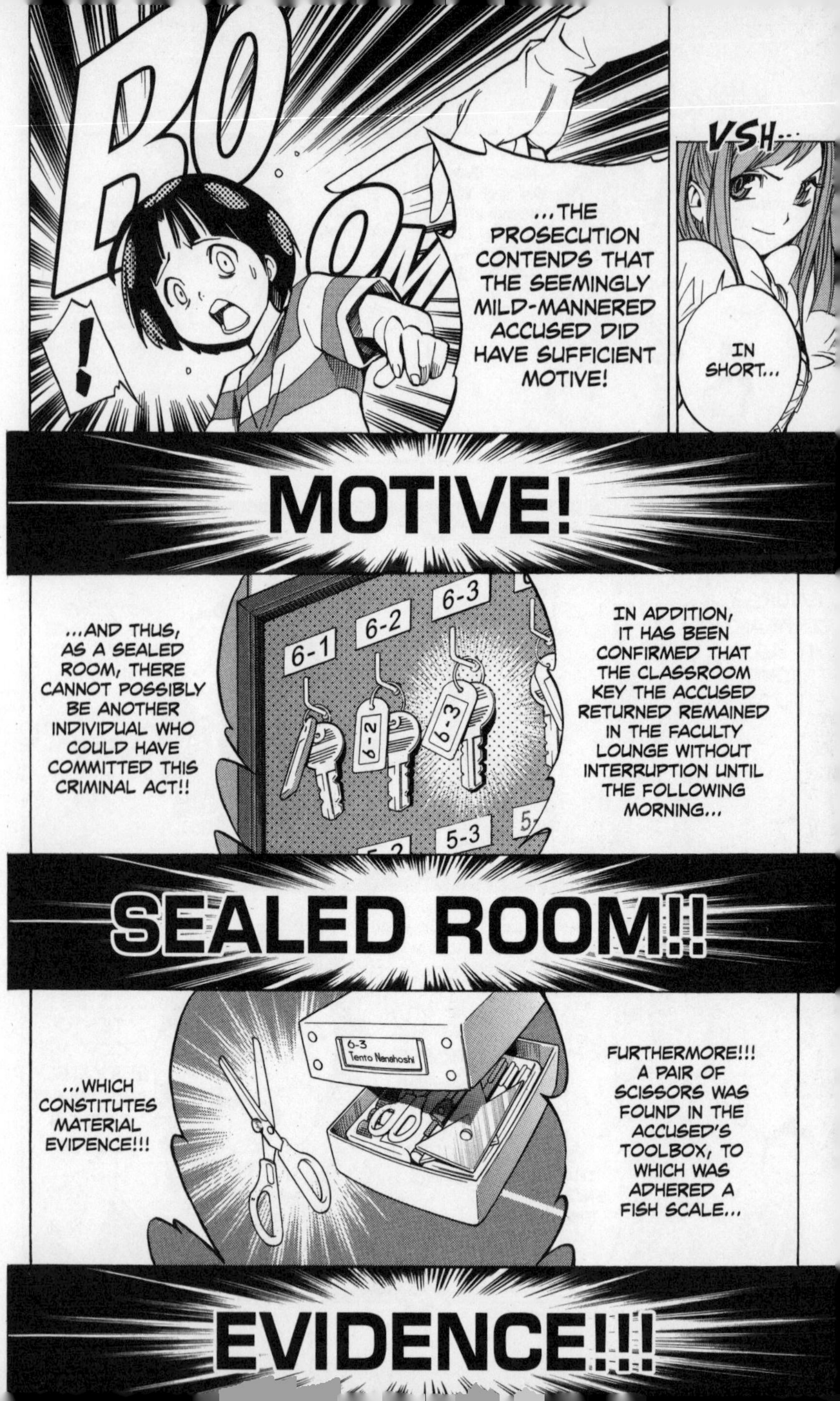
VSH...
IN SHORT...
BOOM
!
...THE PROSECUTION CONTENDS THAT THE SEEMINGLY MILD-MANNERED ACCUSED DID HAVE SUFFICIENT MOTIVE!
MOTIVE!
IN ADDITION, IT HAS BEEN CONFIRMED THAT THE CLASSROOM KEY THE ACCUSED RETURNED REMAINED IN THE FACULTY LOUNGE WITHOUT INTERRUPTION UNTIL THE FOLLOWING MORNING...
6-1
6-2
6-3
5-3
...AND THUS, AS A SEALED ROOM, THERE CANNOT POSSIBLY BE ANOTHER INDIVIDUAL WHO COULD HAVE COMMITTED THIS CRIMINAL ACT!!
SEALED ROOM!!
FURTHERMORE!!! A PAIR OF SCISSORS WAS FOUND IN THE ACCUSED'S TOOLBOX, TO WHICH WAS ADHERED A FISH SCALE...
6-3 Tento Nanahoshi
...WHICH CONSTITUTES MATERIAL EVIDENCE!!!
EVIDENCE!!!

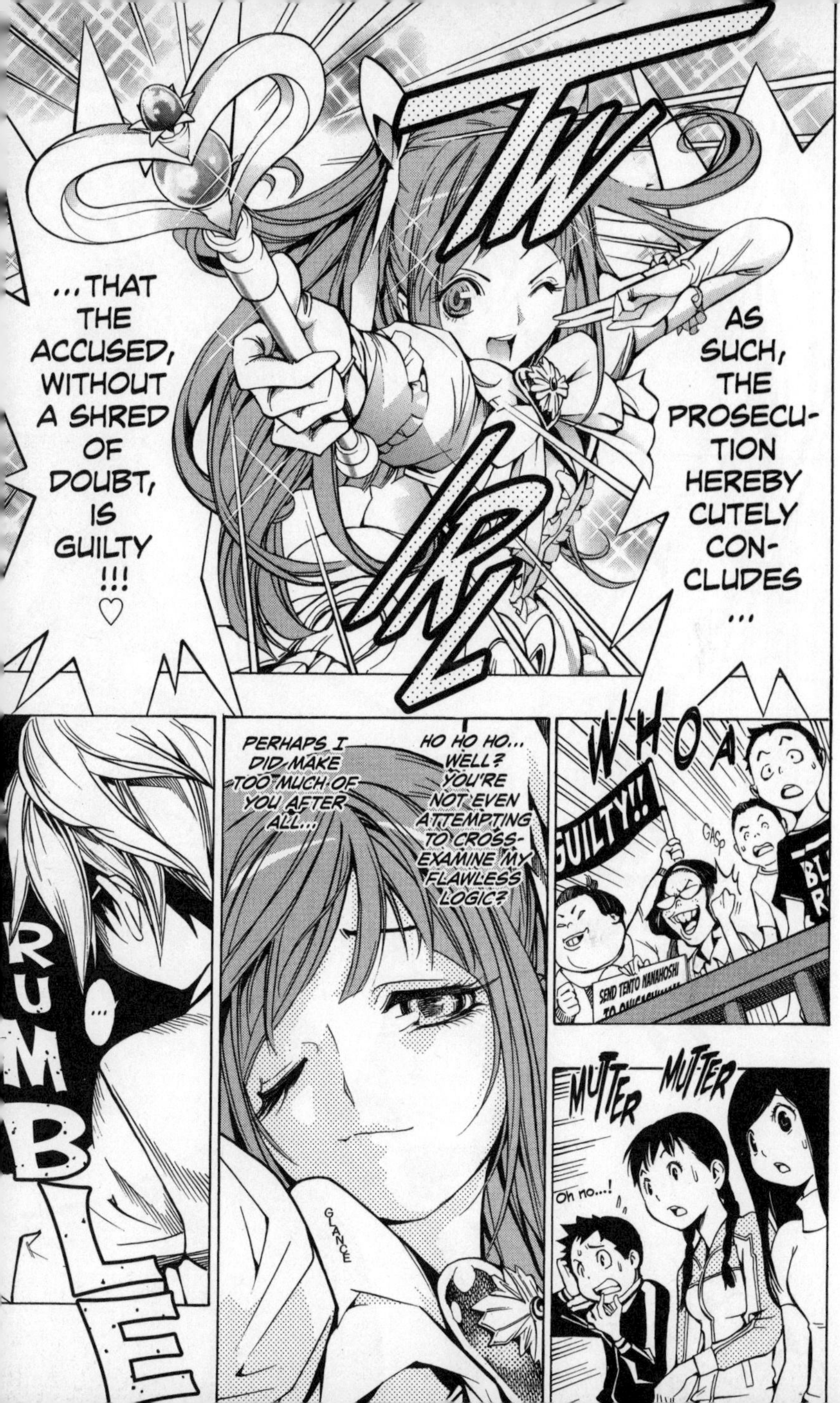
AS SUCH, THE PROSECUTION HEREBY CUTELY CONCLUDES...
TWIRL
...THAT THE ACCUSED, WITHOUT A SHRED OF DOUBT, IS GUILTY!!! ♡
WHOA
GUILTY!!
GASP
SEND TENTO NANAHOSHI
MUTTER MUTTER
Oh no...!
HO HO HO... WELL? YOU'RE NOT EVEN ATTEMPTING TO CROSS-EXAMINE MY FLAWLESS LOGIC?
PERHAPS I DID MAKE TOO MUCH OF YOU AFTER ALL...
GLANCE
RUMBLE
...

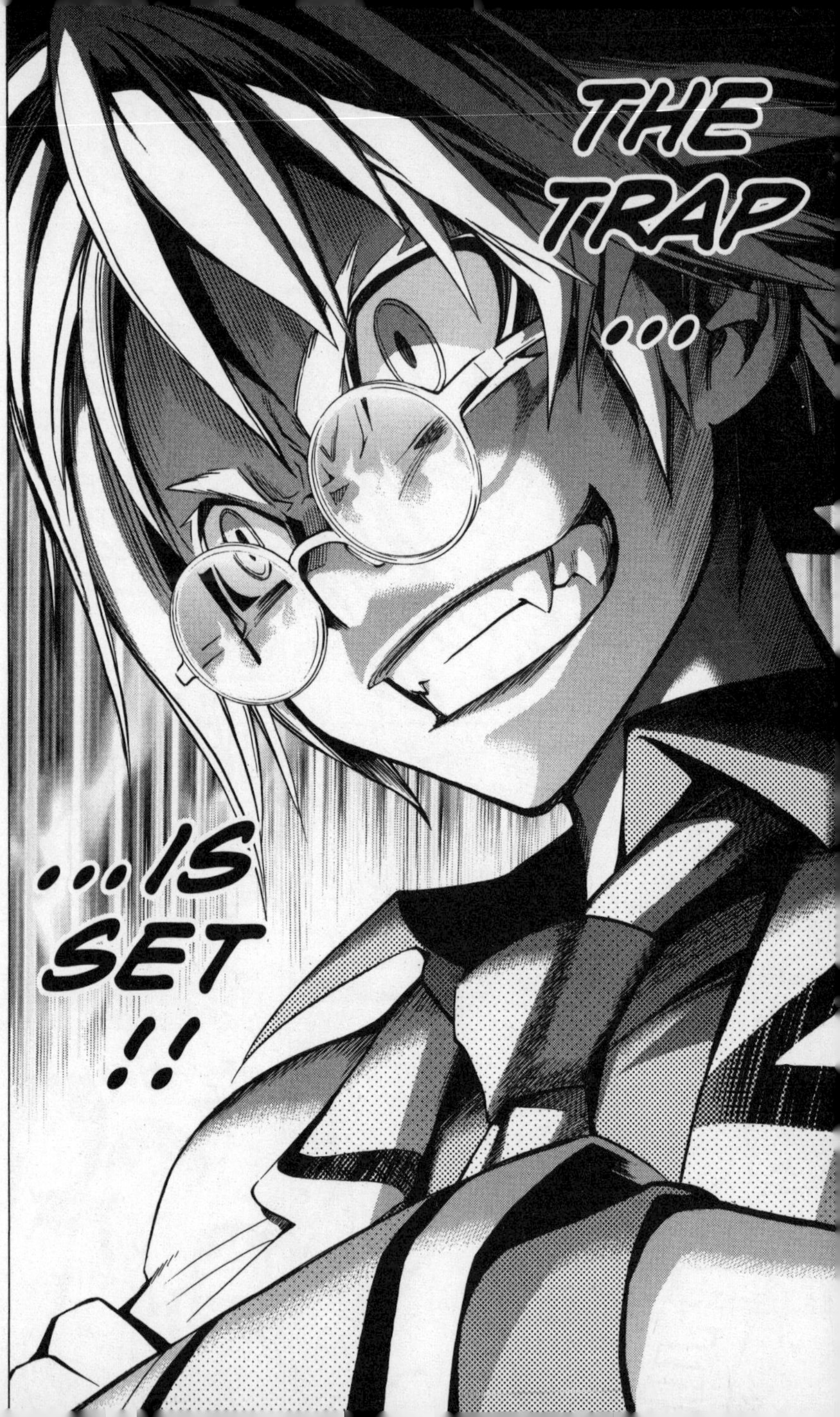
THE TRAP...
...IS SET!!

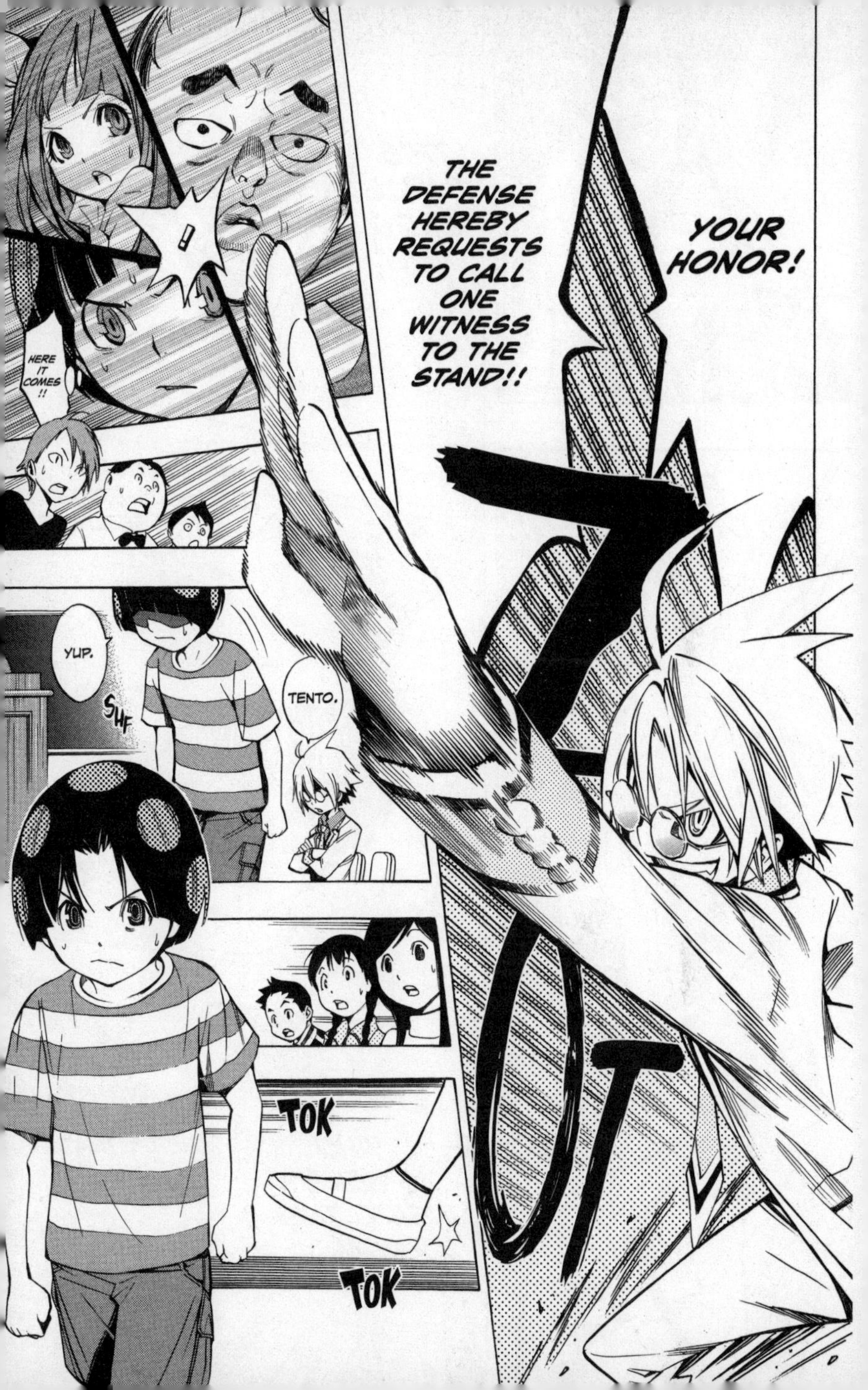
YOUR HONOR!
THE DEFENSE HEREBY REQUESTS TO CALL ONE WITNESS TO THE STAND!!
!
HERE IT COMES!!
TENTO.
YUP.
SHF
TOK
TOK

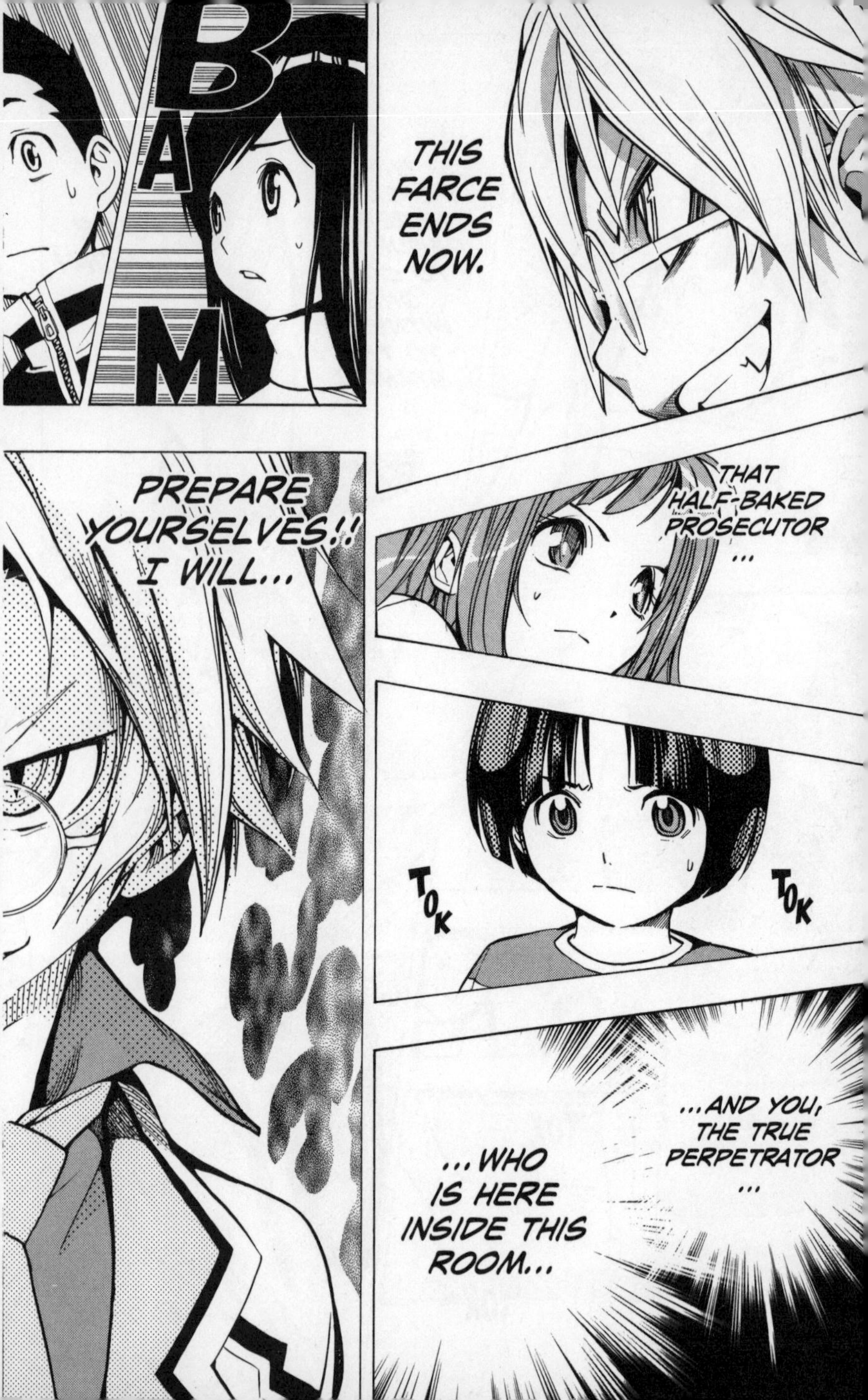
THIS FARCE ENDS NOW.
BAM
THAT HALF-BAKED PROSECUTOR...
TOK
TOK
...AND YOU, THE TRUE PERPETRATOR...
...WHO IS HERE INSIDE THIS ROOM...
PREPARE YOURSELVES!! I WILL...

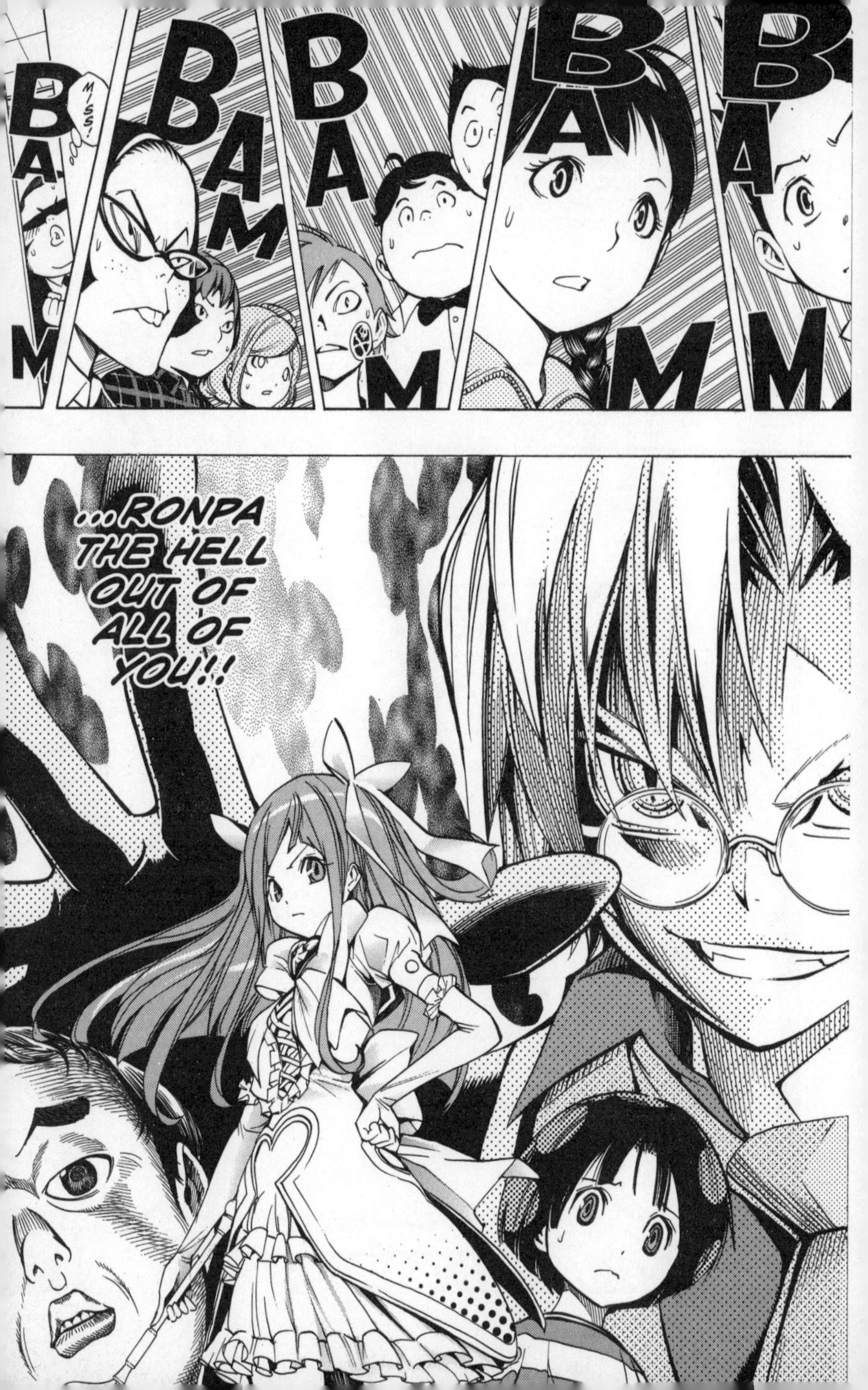
BAMM
BAMM
BAM
BAM
MISS!
BAM
...RONPA THE HELL OUT OF ALL OF YOU!!

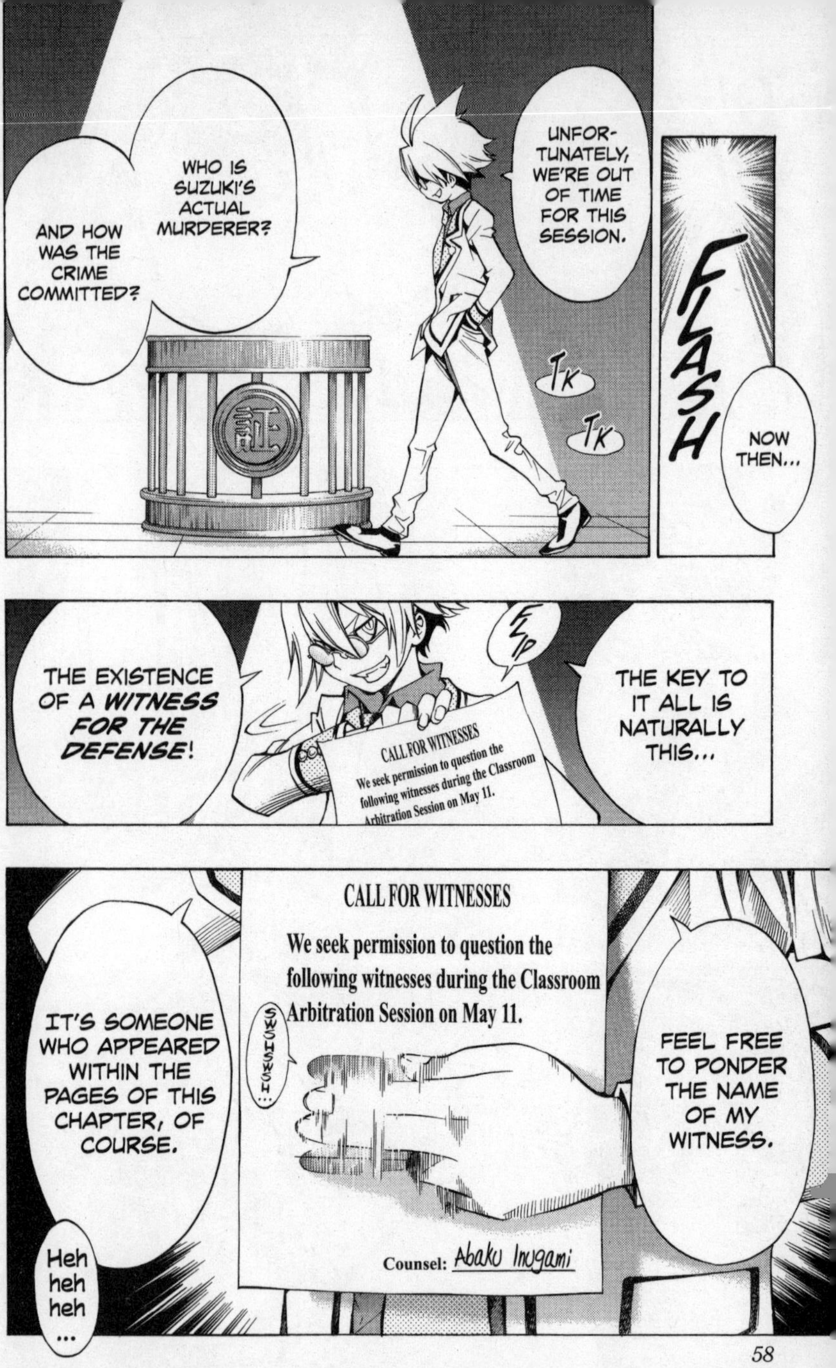
FLASH
NOW THEN...
UNFORTUNATELY, WE'RE OUT OF TIME FOR THIS SESSION.
TK
TK
WHO IS SUZUKI'S ACTUAL MURDERER?
AND HOW WAS THE CRIME COMMITTED?
FLIP
THE KEY TO IT ALL IS NATURALLY THIS...
CALL FOR WITNESSES
We seek permission to question the following witnesses during the Classroom Arbitration Session on May 11.
THE EXISTENCE OF A *WITNESS FOR THE DEFENSE*!
FEEL FREE TO PONDER THE NAME OF MY WITNESS.
CALL FOR WITNESSES
We seek permission to question the following witnesses during the Classroom Arbitration Session on May 11.
Counsel: Abaku Inugami
SWISH SWISH...
IT'S SOMEONE WHO APPEARED WITHIN THE PAGES OF THIS CHAPTER, OF COURSE.
Heh heh heh...

READ THIS WAY

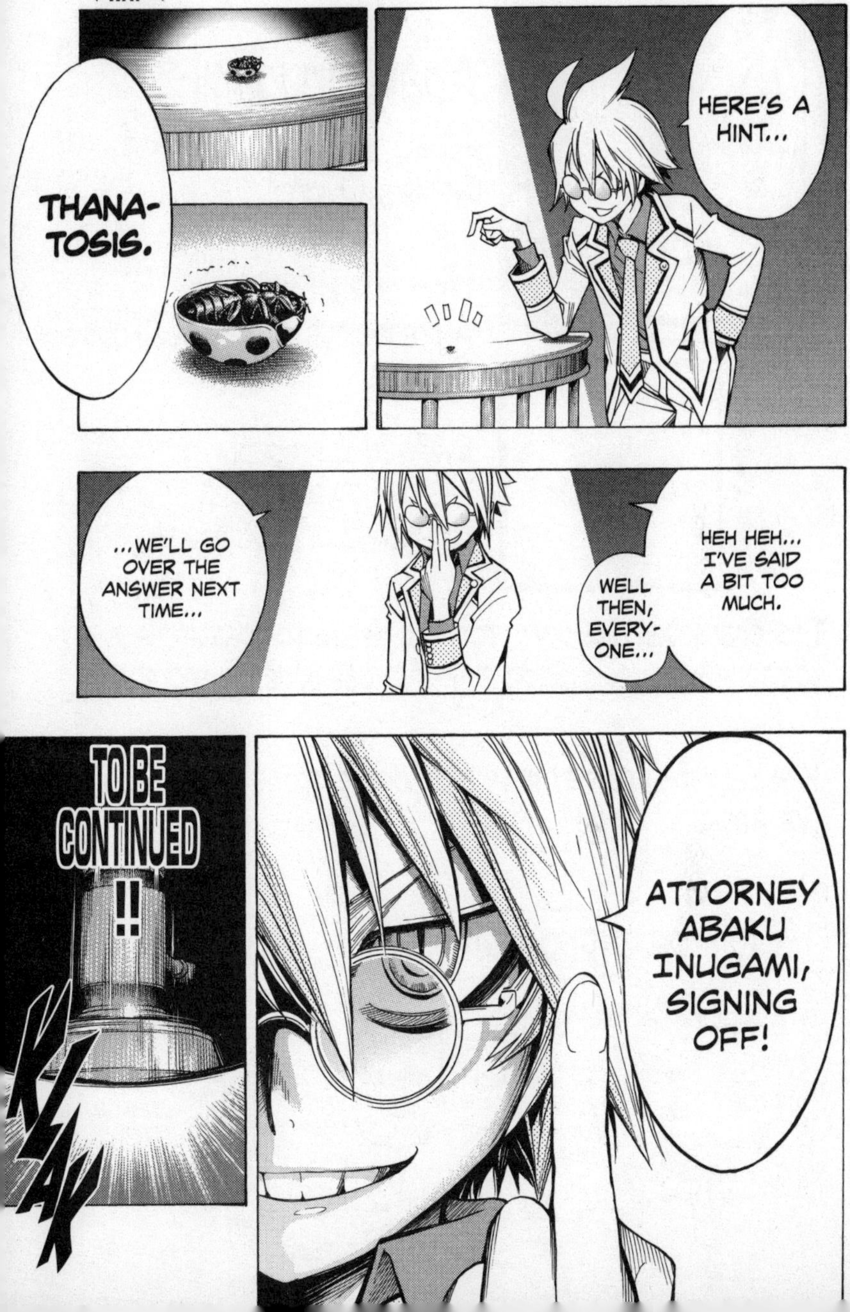

HERE'S A HINT...
THANA-TOSIS.
HEH HEH... I'VE SAID A BIT TOO MUCH.
WELL THEN, EVERY-ONE...
...WE'LL GO OVER THE ANSWER NEXT TIME...
ATTORNEY ABAKU INUGAMI, SIGNING OFF!
TO BE CONTINUED!!
KLAK

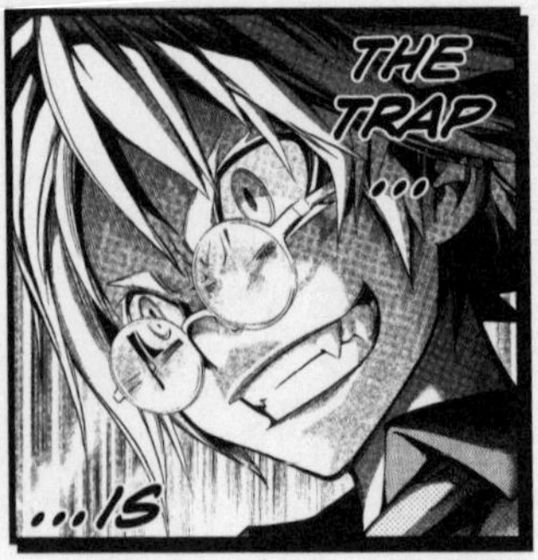
THE TRAP ...
...IS

(Obata's final version)

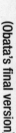

Abaku Inugami

Height: 5 ft.
Dislikes: Children
(first through third graders)

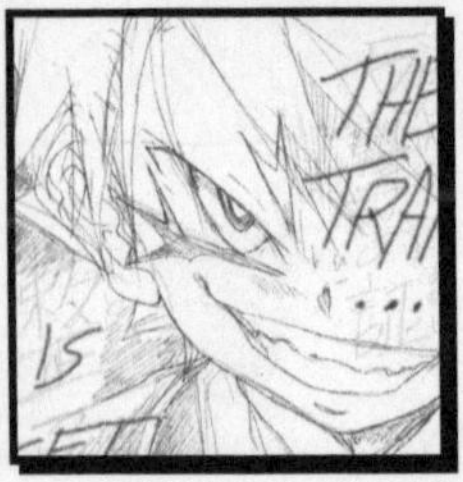

(Enoki's draft version)

Main character.
A precocious child whose hobby is ronpa.

Every adult probably has one or two ronpa they failed or left undone...

This character was born from the desire to create someone who could dispel any of those lingering regrets.

However, if I one day have a child who grows to be sassy like Abaku...

...it'll be a problem.

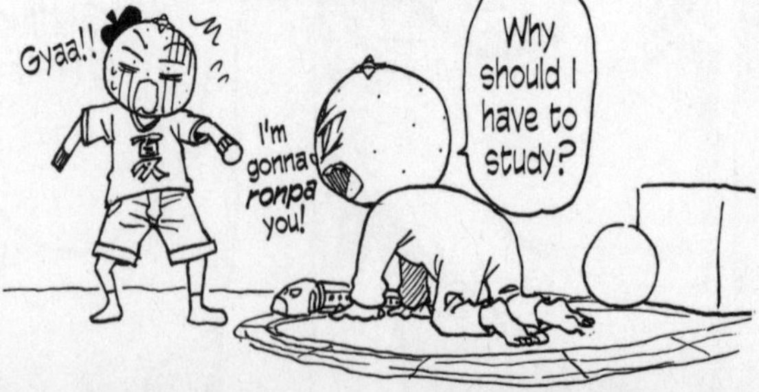
Why should I have to study?
I'm gonna *ronpa* you!
Gyaa!!

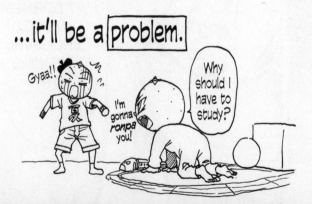

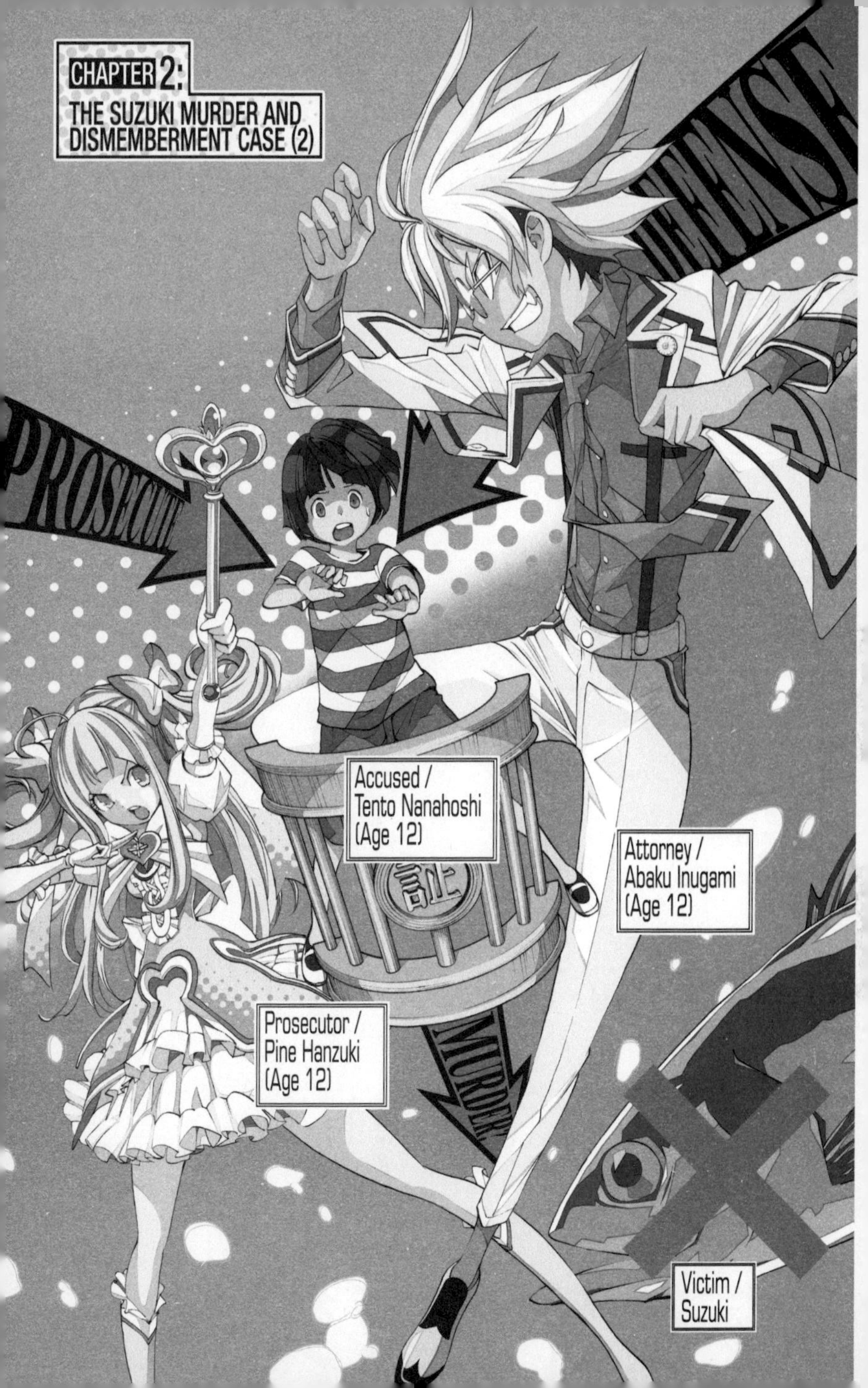
CHAPTER 2:
THE SUZUKI MURDER AND DISMEMBERMENT CASE (2)
Accused / Tento Nanahoshi (Age 12)
Attorney / Abaku Inugami (Age 12)
Prosecutor / Pine Hanzuki (Age 12)
Victim / Suzuki

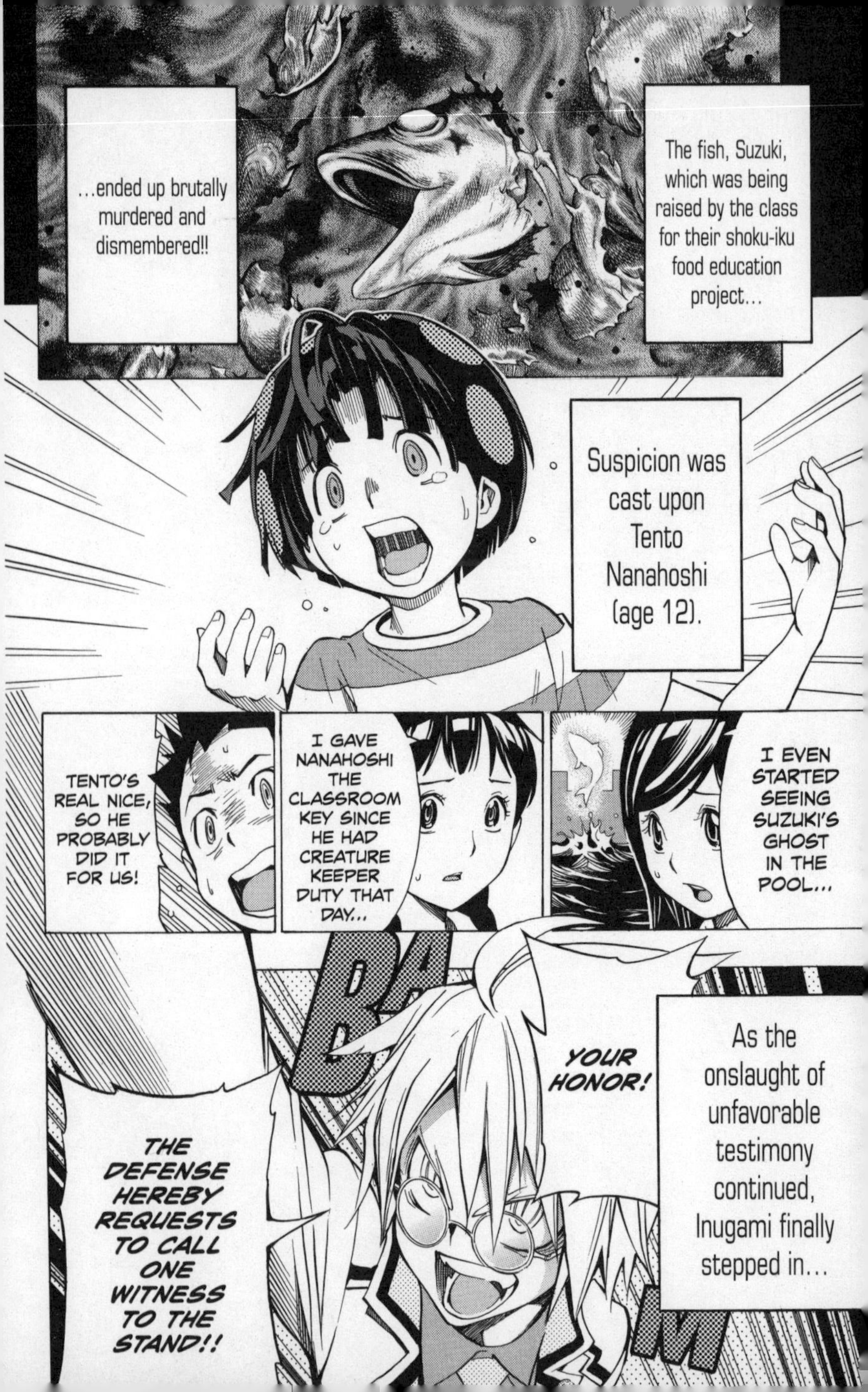
The fish, Suzuki, which was being raised by the class for their shoku-iku food education project…
…ended up brutally murdered and dismembered!!
Suspicion was cast upon Tento Nanahoshi (age 12).
I EVEN STARTED SEEING SUZUKI'S GHOST IN THE POOL…
I GAVE NANAHOSHI THE CLASSROOM KEY SINCE HE HAD CREATURE KEEPER DUTY THAT DAY…
TENTO'S REAL NICE, SO HE PROBABLY DID IT FOR US!
As the onslaught of unfavorable testimony continued, Inugami finally stepped in…
BAM
YOUR HONOR!
THE DEFENSE HEREBY REQUESTS TO CALL ONE WITNESS TO THE STAND!!

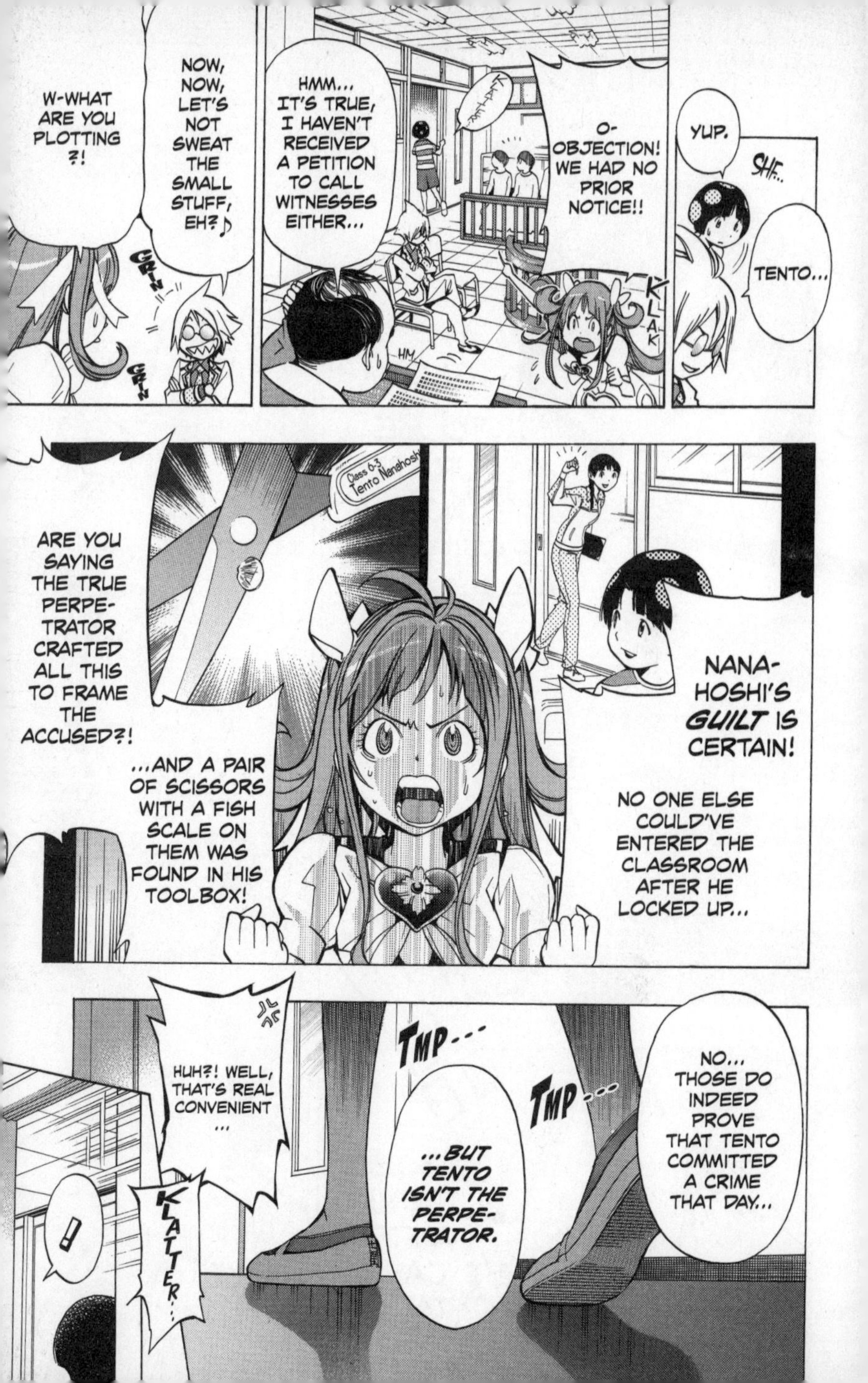
YUP.
SHF...
TENTO...
O-OBJECTION! WE HAD NO PRIOR NOTICE!!
KLAK
KLATTER
HMM... IT'S TRUE, I HAVEN'T RECEIVED A PETITION TO CALL WITNESSES EITHER...
HM
NOW, NOW, LET'S NOT SWEAT THE SMALL STUFF, EH?♪
GRIN
GRIN
W-WHAT ARE YOU PLOTTING?!
NANA-HOSHI'S GUILT IS CERTAIN!
NO ONE ELSE COULD'VE ENTERED THE CLASSROOM AFTER HE LOCKED UP...
...AND A PAIR OF SCISSORS WITH A FISH SCALE ON THEM WAS FOUND IN HIS TOOLBOX!
Class 6-3 Tento Nanahoshi
ARE YOU SAYING THE TRUE PERPE-TRATOR CRAFTED ALL THIS TO FRAME THE ACCUSED?!
NO... THOSE DO INDEED PROVE THAT TENTO COMMITTED A CRIME THAT DAY...
TMP...
TMP...
...BUT TENTO ISN'T THE PERPE-TRATOR.
HUH?! WELL, THAT'S REAL CONVENIENT...
KLATTER...
!

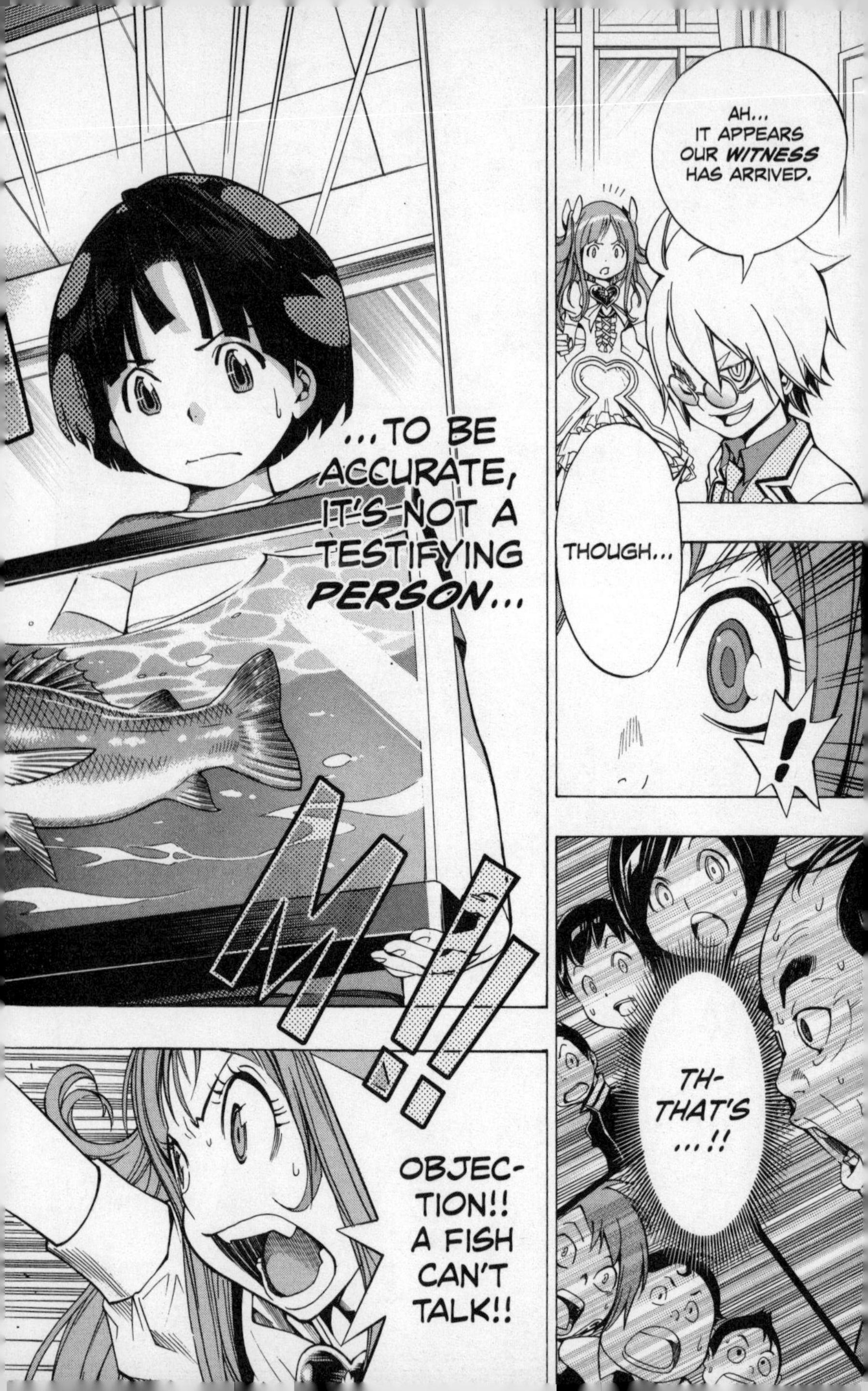
AH... IT APPEARS OUR ***WITNESS*** HAS ARRIVED.
THOUGH...
!
...TO BE ACCURATE, IT'S NOT A TESTIFYING ***PERSON***...
M!!
TH-THAT'S ...!!
OBJECTION!! A FISH CAN'T TALK!!

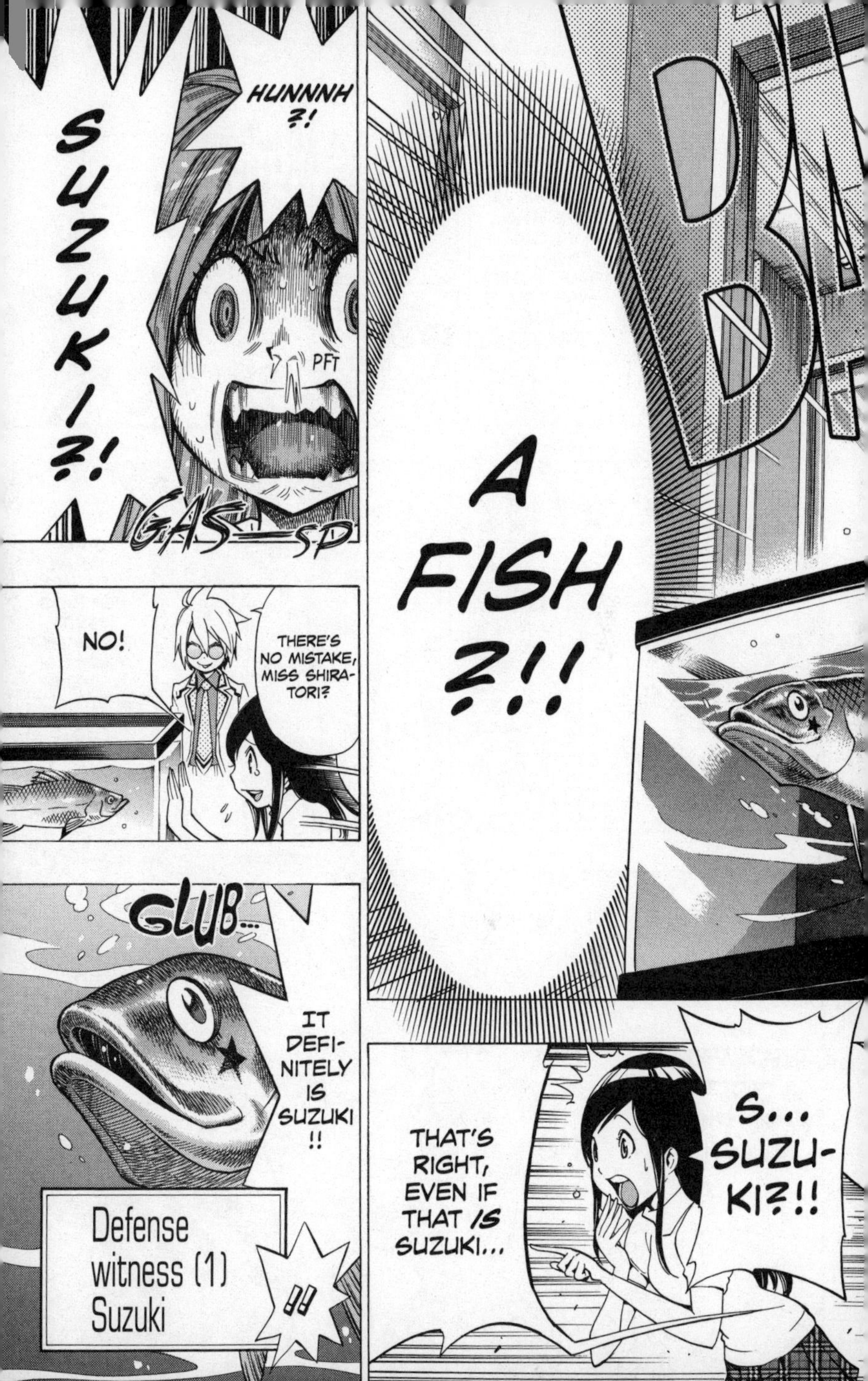
A FISH ?!!
HUNNNH ?!
SUZUKI ?!
GAS—SP
PFT
THERE'S NO MISTAKE, MISS SHIRATORI?
NO!
S... SUZUKI?!!
THAT'S RIGHT, EVEN IF THAT *IS* SUZUKI...
GLUB...
IT DEFINITELY IS SUZUKI !!
!!
Defense witness (1) Suzuki

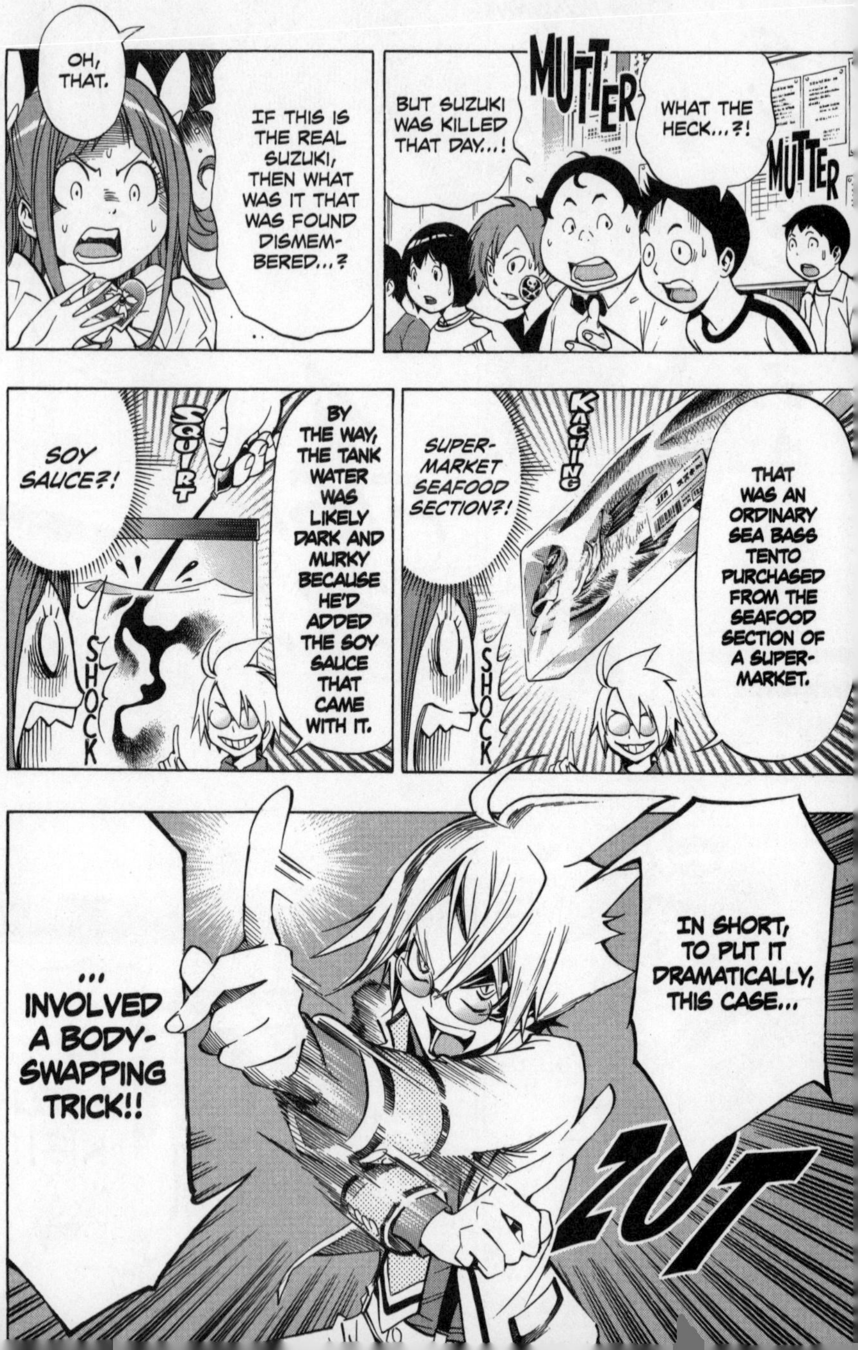
WHAT THE HECK...?!
MUTTER
MUTTER
BUT SUZUKI WAS KILLED THAT DAY...!
IF THIS IS THE REAL SUZUKI, THEN WHAT WAS IT THAT WAS FOUND DISMEMBERED...?
OH, THAT.
THAT WAS AN ORDINARY SEA BASS TENTO PURCHASED FROM THE SEAFOOD SECTION OF A SUPERMARKET.
KACHING
SUPERMARKET SEAFOOD SECTION?!
SHOCK
BY THE WAY, THE TANK WATER WAS LIKELY DARK AND MURKY BECAUSE HE'D ADDED THE SOY SAUCE THAT CAME WITH IT.
SQUIRT
SOY SAUCE?!
SHOCK
IN SHORT, TO PUT IT DRAMATICALLY, THIS CASE...
...INVOLVED A BODY-SWAPPING TRICK!!
ZUT

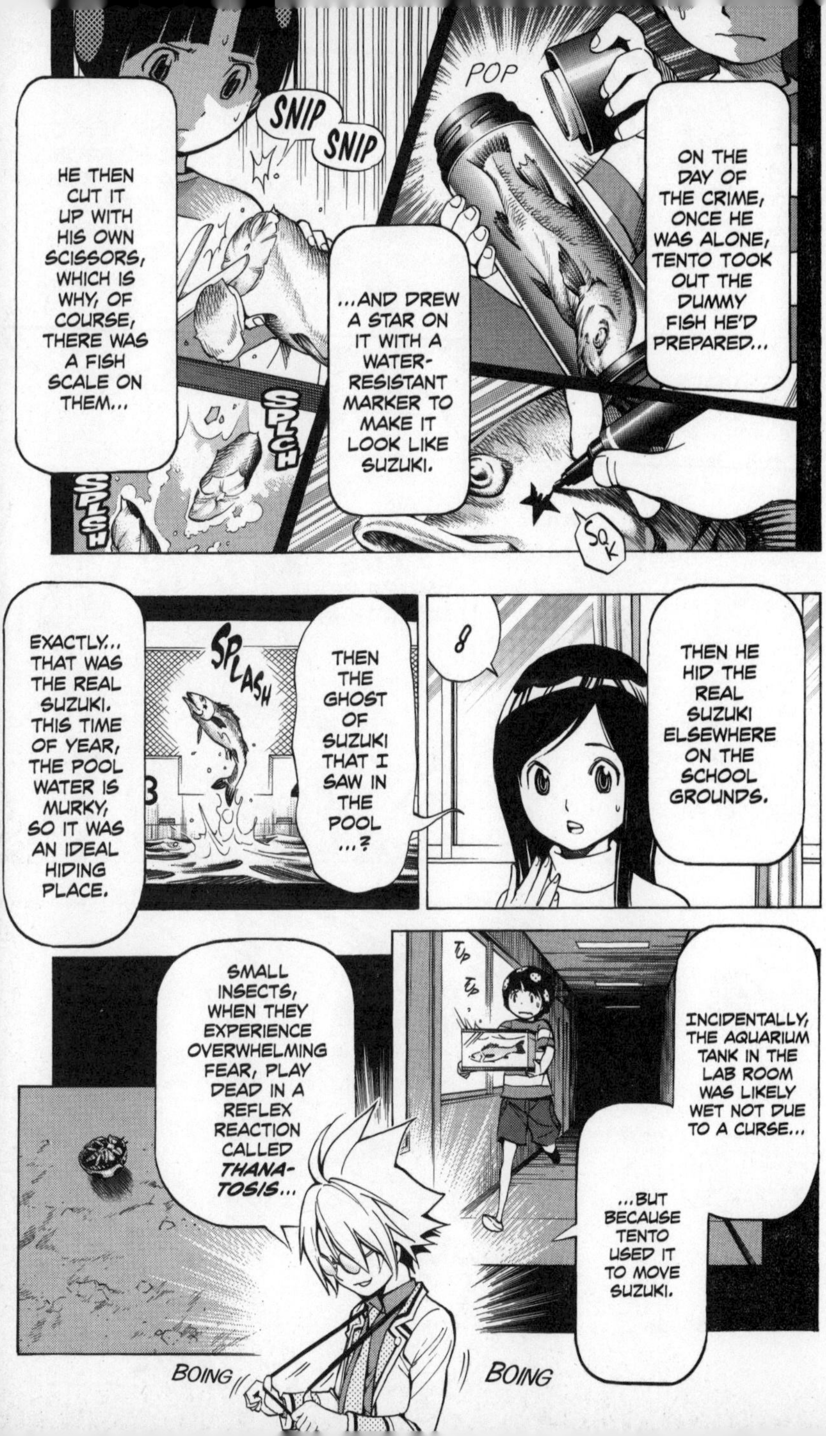
ON THE DAY OF THE CRIME, ONCE HE WAS ALONE, TENTO TOOK OUT THE DUMMY FISH HE'D PREPARED...
POP
...AND DREW A STAR ON IT WITH A WATER-RESISTANT MARKER TO MAKE IT LOOK LIKE SUZUKI.
SQK
HE THEN CUT IT UP WITH HIS OWN SCISSORS, WHICH IS WHY, OF COURSE, THERE WAS A FISH SCALE ON THEM...
SNIP
SNIP
SPLSH
SPLSH
THEN HE HID THE REAL SUZUKI ELSEWHERE ON THE SCHOOL GROUNDS.
THEN THE GHOST OF SUZUKI THAT I SAW IN THE POOL ...?
SPLASH
EXACTLY... THAT WAS THE REAL SUZUKI. THIS TIME OF YEAR, THE POOL WATER IS MURKY, SO IT WAS AN IDEAL HIDING PLACE.
INCIDENTALLY, THE AQUARIUM TANK IN THE LAB ROOM WAS LIKELY WET NOT DUE TO A CURSE...
TUP
TUP
...BUT BECAUSE TENTO USED IT TO MOVE SUZUKI.
SMALL INSECTS, WHEN THEY EXPERIENCE OVERWHELMING FEAR, PLAY DEAD IN A REFLEX REACTION CALLED *THANATOSIS*...
BOING
BOING

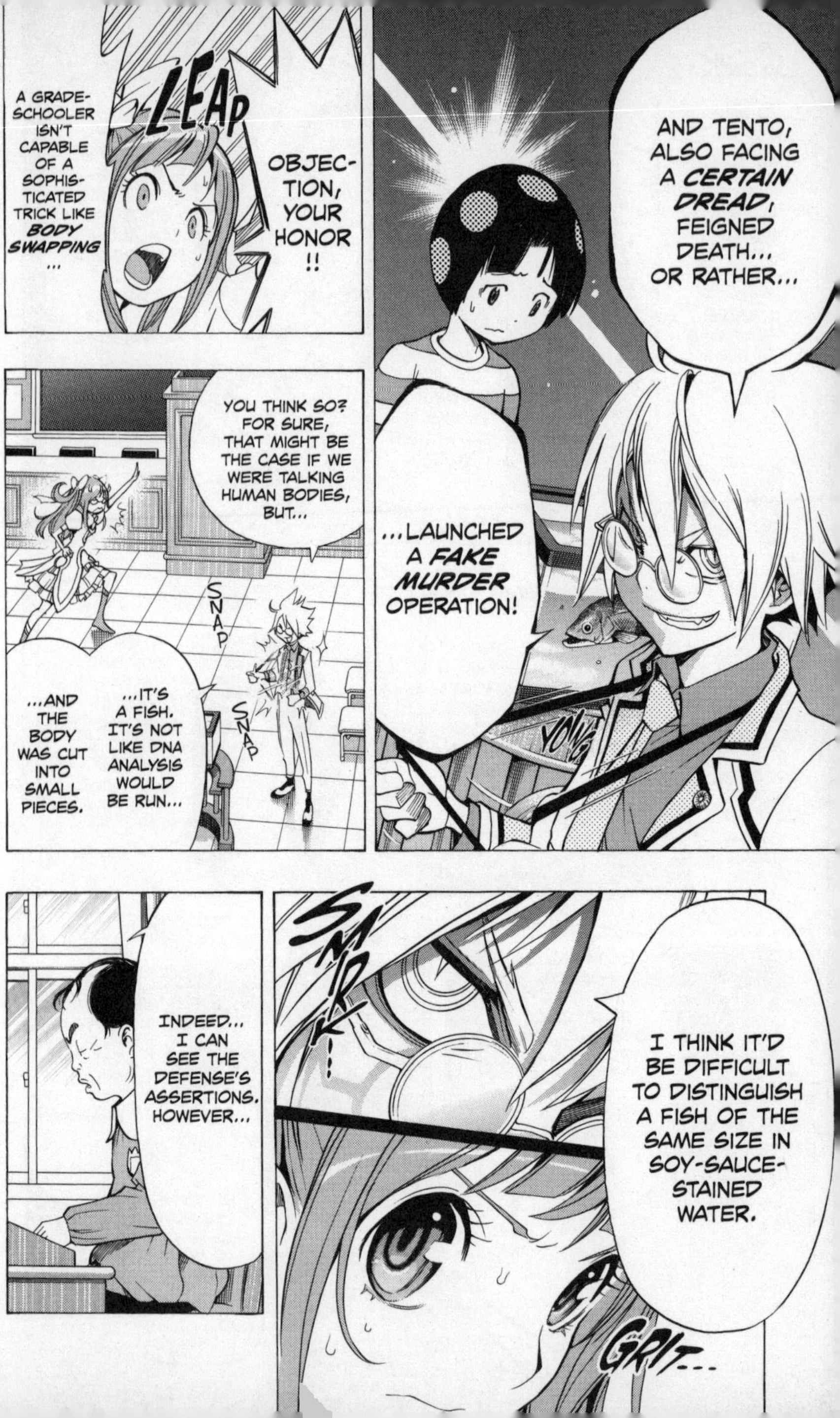
AND TENTO, ALSO FACING A *CERTAIN DREAD*, FEIGNED DEATH... OR RATHER...
...LAUNCHED A *FAKE MURDER* OPERATION!
LEAP
OBJECTION, YOUR HONOR!!
A GRADE-SCHOOLER ISN'T CAPABLE OF A SOPHISTICATED TRICK LIKE *BODY SWAPPING*...
YOU THINK SO? FOR SURE, THAT MIGHT BE THE CASE IF WE WERE TALKING HUMAN BODIES, BUT...
SNAP
SNAP
...IT'S A FISH. IT'S NOT LIKE DNA ANALYSIS WOULD BE RUN...
...AND THE BODY WAS CUT INTO SMALL PIECES.
I THINK IT'D BE DIFFICULT TO DISTINGUISH A FISH OF THE SAME SIZE IN SOY-SAUCE-STAINED WATER.
SMIRK!
GRIT...
INDEED... I CAN SEE THE DEFENSE'S ASSERTIONS. HOWEVER...

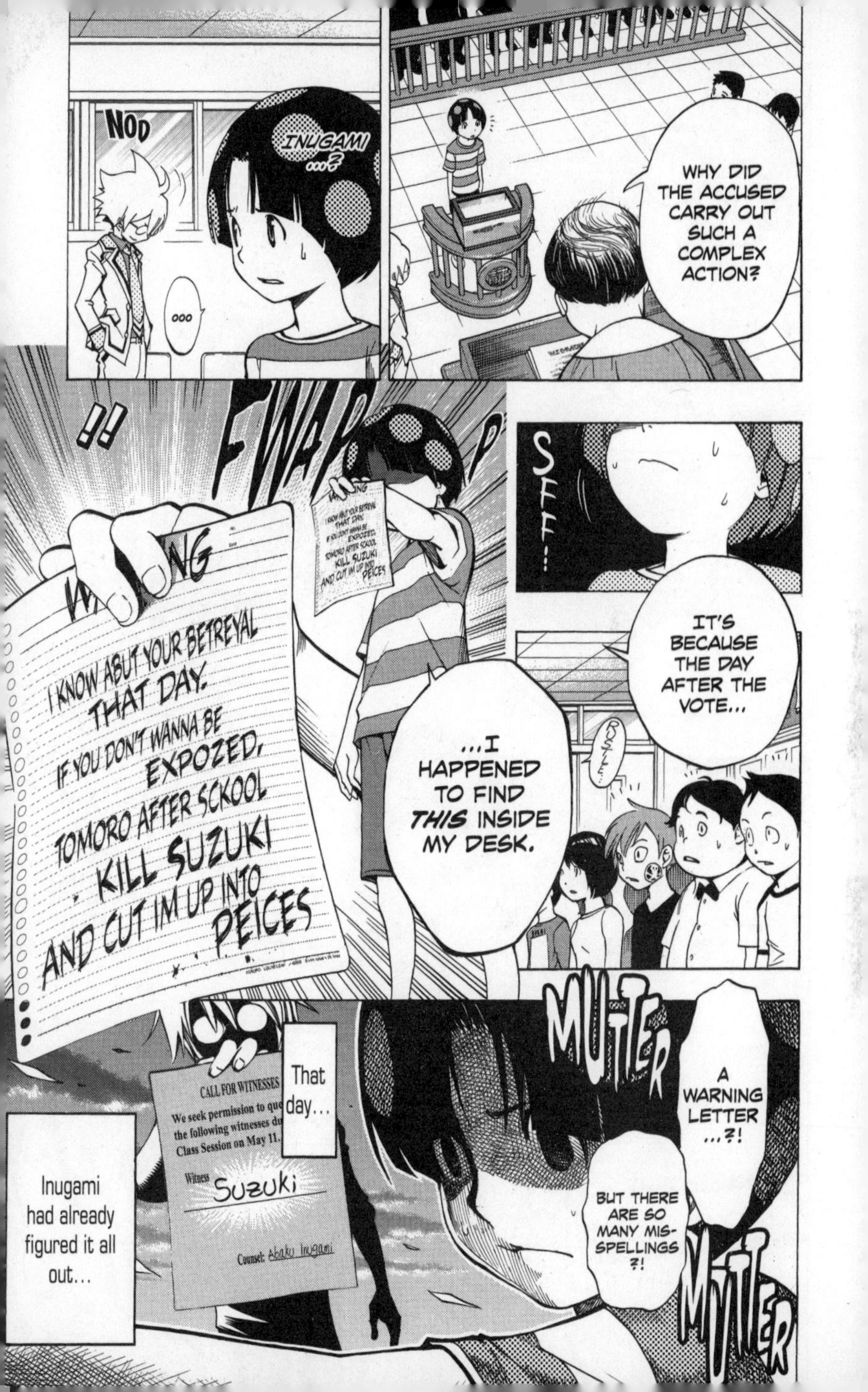
WHY DID THE ACCUSED CARRY OUT SUCH A COMPLEX ACTION?
NOD
INUGAMI ...?
ooo
SFF...
IT'S BECAUSE THE DAY AFTER THE VOTE...
RUSTLE
...I HAPPENED TO FIND THIS INSIDE MY DESK.
!!
FWAP
I KNOW ABUT YOUR BETREYAL THAT DAY.
IF YOU DON'T WANNA BE EXPOZED,
TOMORO AFTER SCKOOL
KILL SUZUKI
AND CUT IM UP INTO PEICES
MUTTER
A WARNING LETTER ...?!
BUT THERE ARE SO MANY MIS-SPELLINGS ?!
MUTTER
That day...
CALL FOR WITNESSES
Witness Suzuki
Counsel: Abaku Inugami
Inugami had already figured it all out...

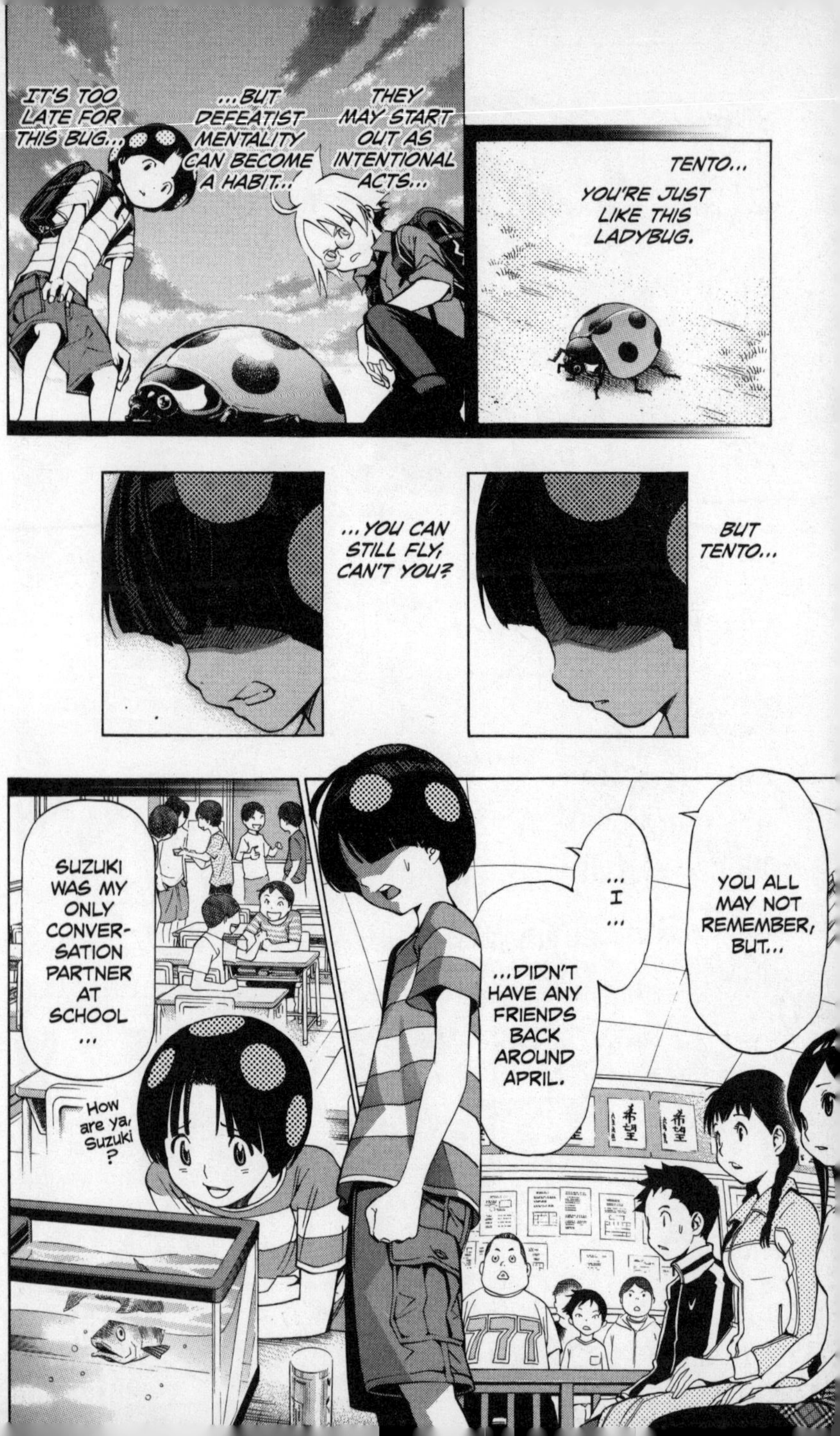
TENTO...
YOU'RE JUST LIKE THIS LADYBUG.
THEY MAY START OUT AS INTENTIONAL ACTS...
...BUT DEFEATIST MENTALITY CAN BECOME A HABIT...
IT'S TOO LATE FOR THIS BUG...
BUT TENTO...
...YOU CAN STILL FLY, CAN'T YOU?
YOU ALL MAY NOT REMEMBER, BUT...
... I ...
...DIDN'T HAVE ANY FRIENDS BACK AROUND APRIL.
SUZUKI WAS MY ONLY CONVER-SATION PARTNER AT SCHOOL ...
How are ya, Suzuki?

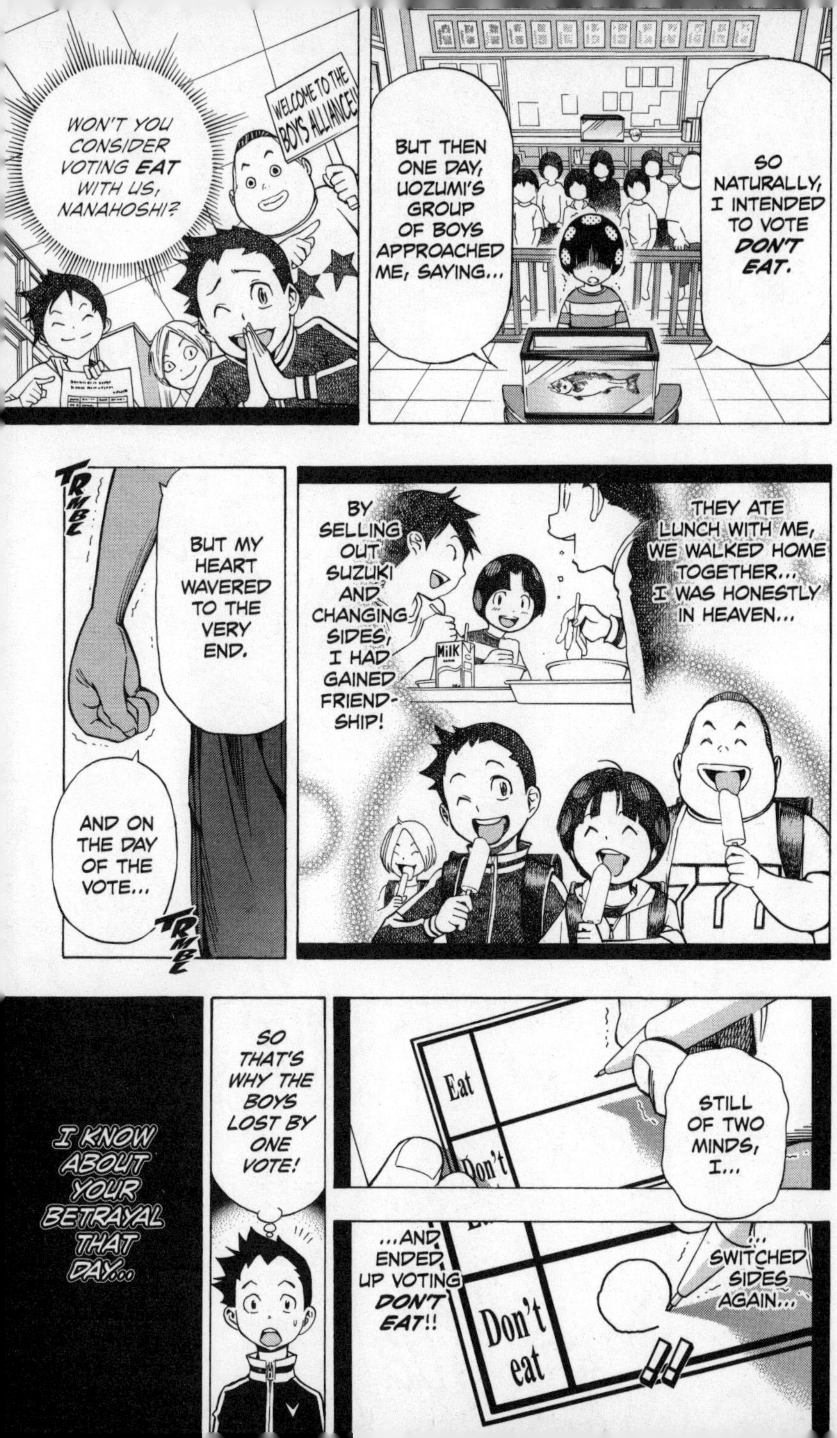
SO NATURALLY, I INTENDED TO VOTE DON'T EAT.
BUT THEN ONE DAY, UOZUMI'S GROUP OF BOYS APPROACHED ME, SAYING...
WELCOME TO THE BOYS ALLIANCE!!
WON'T YOU CONSIDER VOTING EAT WITH US, NANAHOSHI?
THEY ATE LUNCH WITH ME, WE WALKED HOME TOGETHER... I WAS HONESTLY IN HEAVEN...
BY SELLING OUT SUZUKI AND CHANGING SIDES, I HAD GAINED FRIEND-SHIP!
MILK
TRMBL
BUT MY HEART WAVERED TO THE VERY END.
AND ON THE DAY OF THE VOTE...
TRMBL
Eat
Don't
STILL OF TWO MINDS, I...
...SWITCHED SIDES AGAIN...
...AND ENDED UP VOTING DON'T EAT!!
Don't eat
SO THAT'S WHY THE BOYS LOST BY ONE VOTE!
I KNOW ABOUT YOUR BETRAYAL THAT DAY...

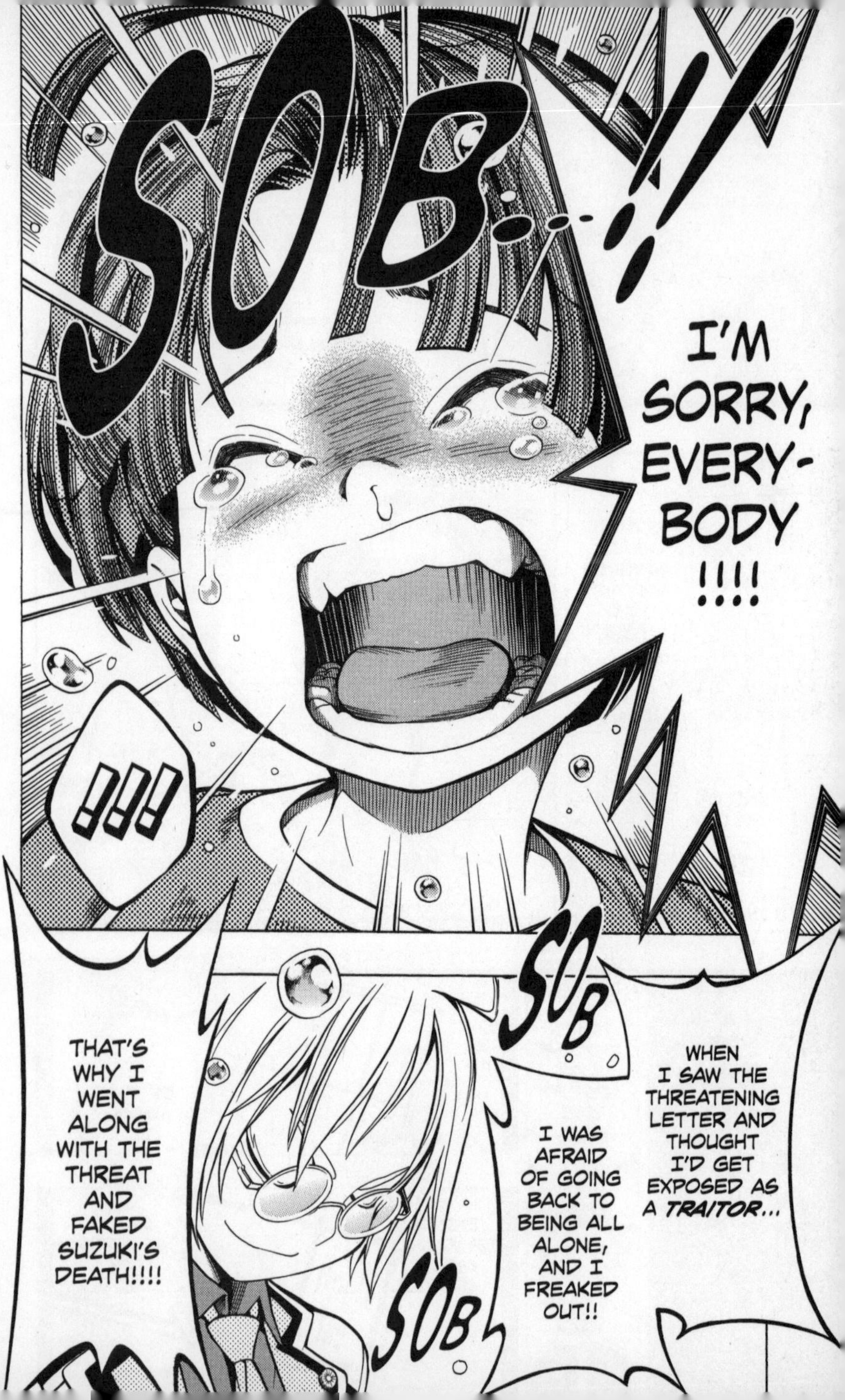
SOB...!!
I'M SORRY, EVERY-BODY!!!!
!!!
SOB
WHEN I SAW THE THREATENING LETTER AND THOUGHT I'D GET EXPOSED AS A *TRAITOR*...
I WAS AFRAID OF GOING BACK TO BEING ALL ALONE, AND I FREAKED OUT!!
THAT'S WHY I WENT ALONG WITH THE THREAT AND FAKED SUZUKI'S DEATH!!!!
SOB

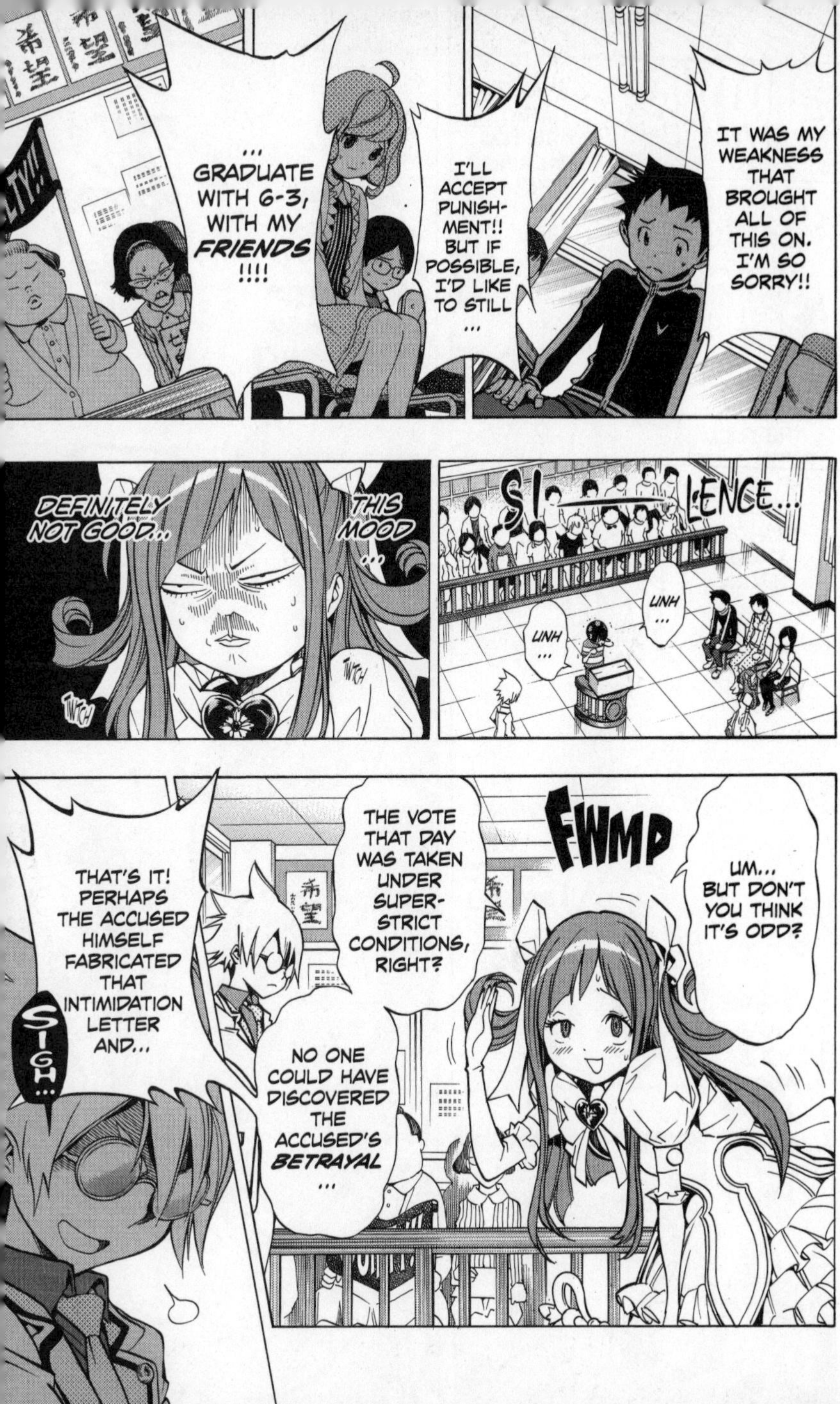
IT WAS MY WEAKNESS THAT BROUGHT ALL OF THIS ON. I'M SO SORRY!!
I'LL ACCEPT PUNISHMENT!! BUT IF POSSIBLE, I'D LIKE TO STILL ...
... GRADUATE WITH 6-3, WITH MY *FRIENDS* !!!!
SI... LENCE...
UNH ...
UNH ...
THIS MOOD ...
DEFINITELY NOT GOOD...
TWITCH
TWITCH
UM... BUT DON'T YOU THINK IT'S ODD?
FWMP
THE VOTE THAT DAY WAS TAKEN UNDER SUPER-STRICT CONDITIONS, RIGHT?
NO ONE COULD HAVE DISCOVERED THE ACCUSED'S *BETRAYAL* ...
THAT'S IT! PERHAPS THE ACCUSED HIMSELF FABRICATED THAT INTIMIDATION LETTER AND...
SIGH...

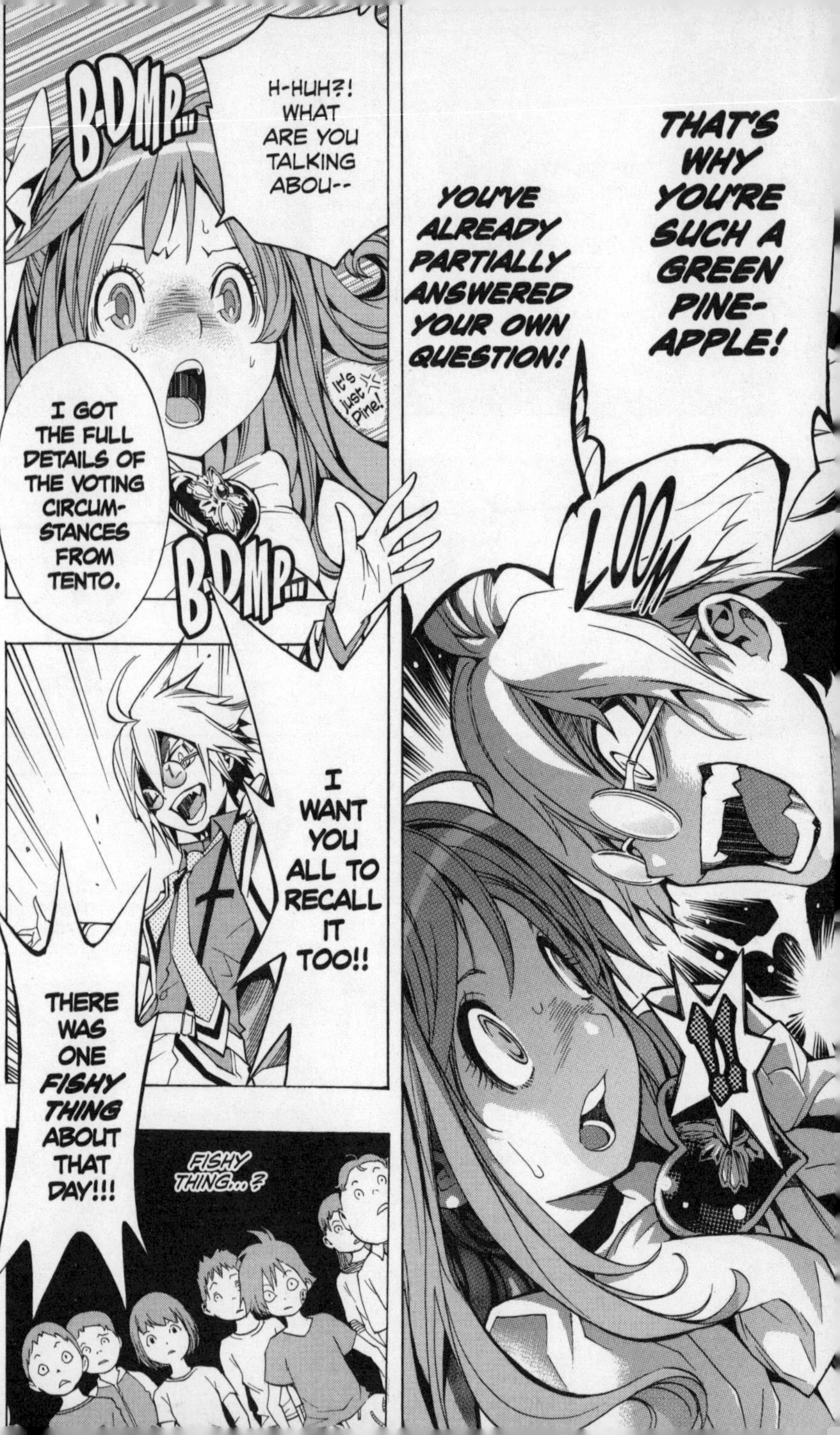
THAT'S WHY YOU'RE SUCH A GREEN PINE-APPLE!
YOU'VE ALREADY PARTIALLY ANSWERED YOUR OWN QUESTION!
LOOM
H-HUH?! WHAT ARE YOU TALKING ABOU--
B-DMP...
It's just Pine!
I GOT THE FULL DETAILS OF THE VOTING CIRCUM-STANCES FROM TENTO.
B-DMP...
I WANT YOU ALL TO RECALL IT TOO!!
THERE WAS ONE FISHY THING ABOUT THAT DAY!!!
FISHY THING...?

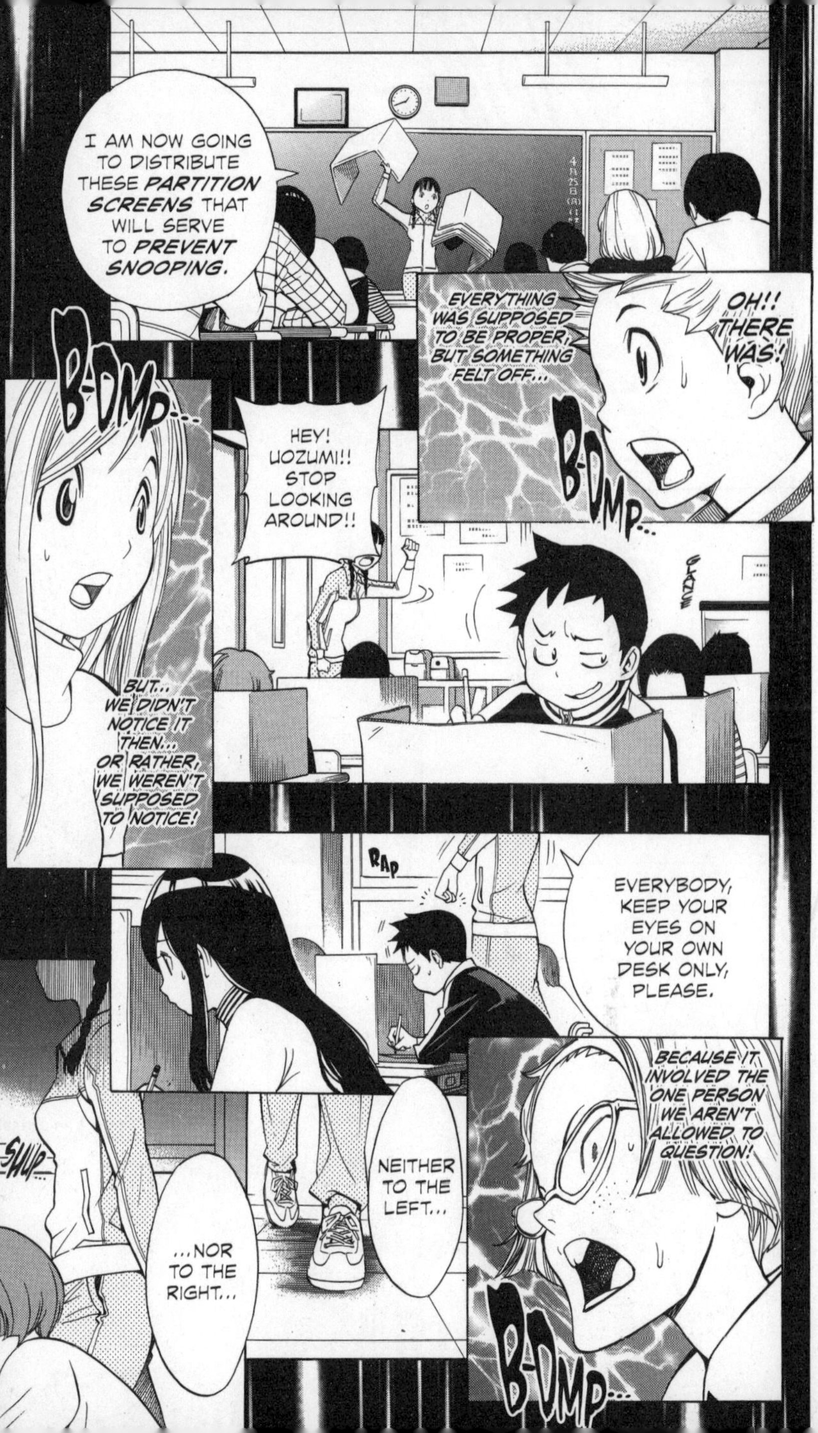
I AM NOW GOING TO DISTRIBUTE THESE *PARTITION SCREENS* THAT WILL SERVE TO *PREVENT SNOOPING*.
OH!! THERE WAS!
EVERYTHING WAS SUPPOSED TO BE PROPER, BUT SOMETHING FELT OFF...
B-DMP...
GLANCE
HEY! UOZUMI!! STOP LOOKING AROUND!!
B-DMP...
BUT... WE DIDN'T NOTICE IT THEN... OR RATHER, WE WEREN'T SUPPOSED TO NOTICE!
EVERYBODY, KEEP YOUR EYES ON YOUR OWN DESK ONLY, PLEASE.
RAP
BECAUSE IT INVOLVED THE ONE PERSON WE AREN'T ALLOWED TO QUESTION!
B-DMP...
NEITHER TO THE LEFT...
...NOR TO THE RIGHT...
SHUP...

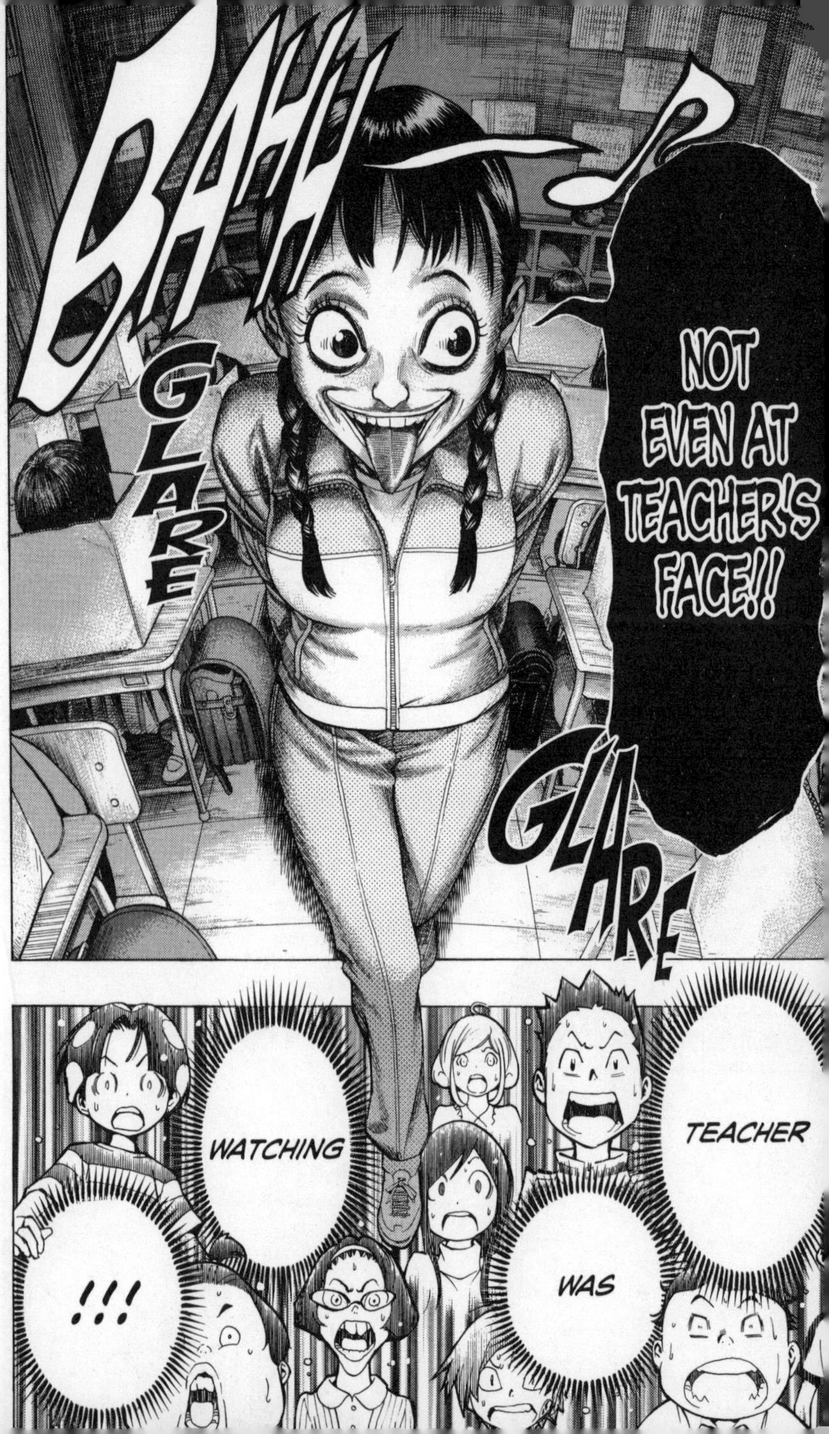
BAHH♪
NOT EVEN AT TEACHER'S FACE!!
GLARE
GLARE
TEACHER
WAS
WATCHING
!!!

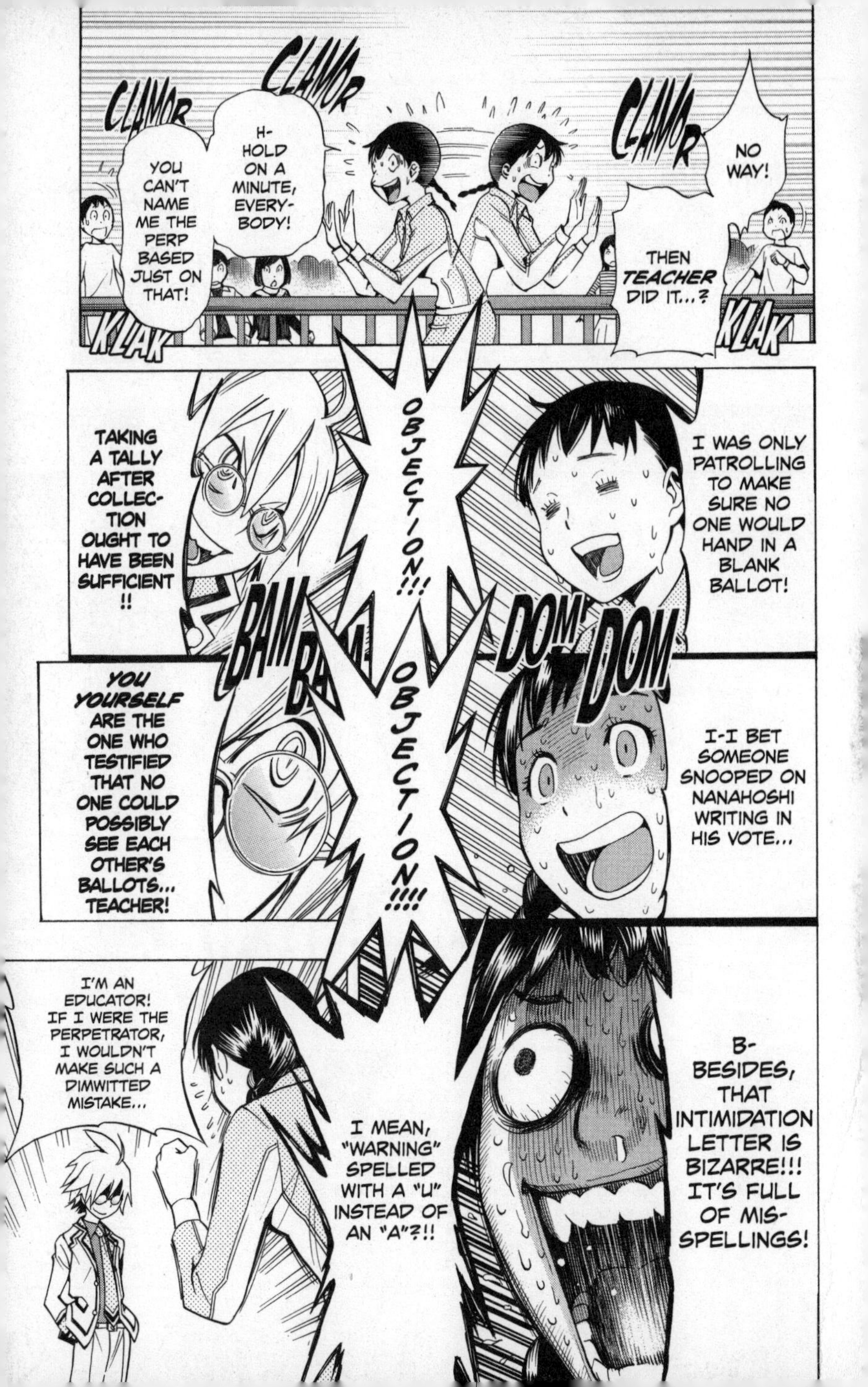
NO WAY!
CLAMOR
THEN *TEACHER* DID IT...?
KLAK
H-HOLD ON A MINUTE, EVERYBODY!
CLAMOR
YOU CAN'T NAME ME THE PERP BASED JUST ON THAT!
CLAMOR
KLAK
I WAS ONLY PATROLLING TO MAKE SURE NO ONE WOULD HAND IN A BLANK BALLOT!
DOM DOM
OBJECTION!!!
TAKING A TALLY AFTER COLLECTION OUGHT TO HAVE BEEN SUFFICIENT!!
BAM
I-I BET SOMEONE SNOOPED ON NANAHOSHI WRITING IN HIS VOTE...
OBJECTION!!!!
YOU YOURSELF ARE THE ONE WHO TESTIFIED THAT NO ONE COULD POSSIBLY SEE EACH OTHER'S BALLOTS... TEACHER!
B-BESIDES, THAT INTIMIDATION LETTER IS BIZARRE!!! IT'S FULL OF MIS-SPELLINGS!
I MEAN, "WARNING" SPELLED WITH A "U" INSTEAD OF AN "A"?!!
I'M AN EDUCATOR! IF I WERE THE PERPETRATOR, I WOULDN'T MAKE SUCH A DIMWITTED MISTAKE...

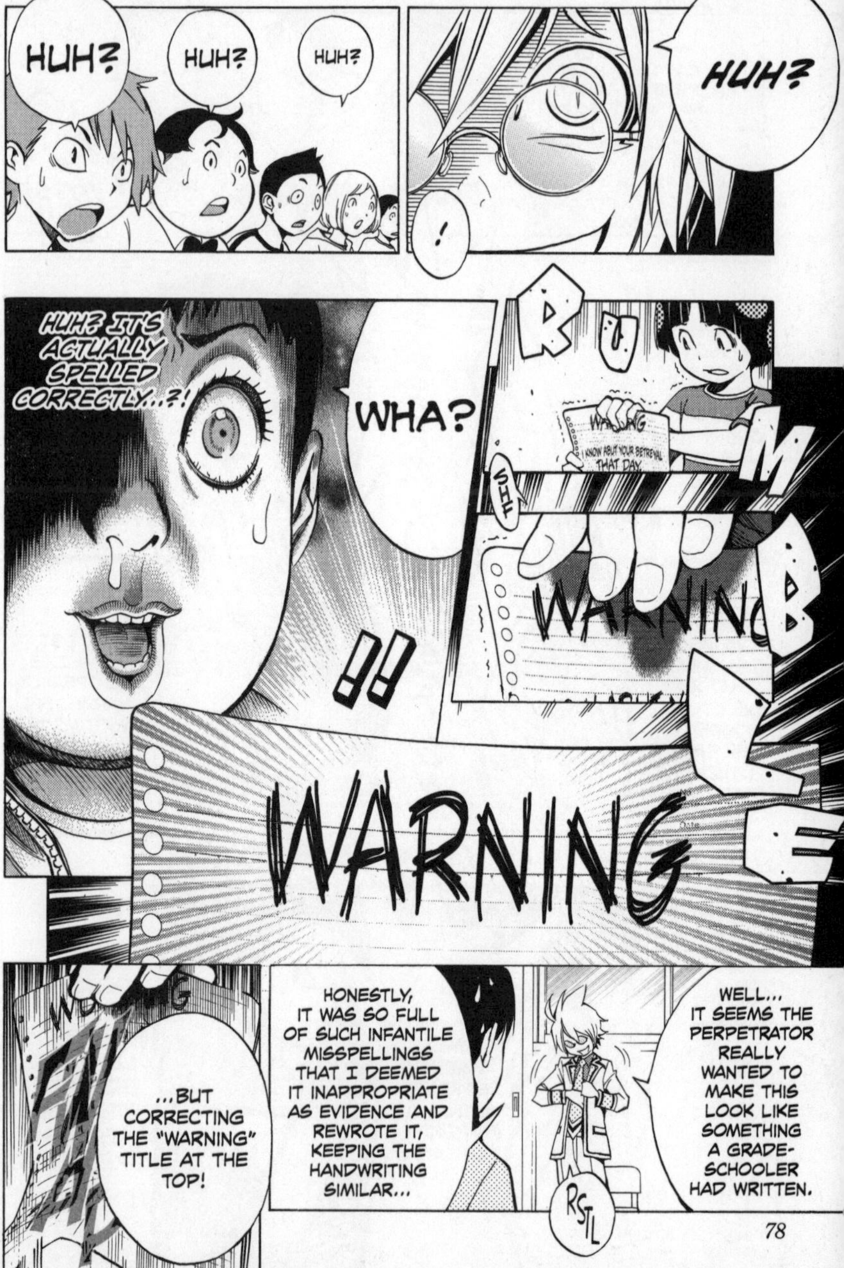
HUH?
!
HUH?
HUH?
HUH?
RUMBLE
WARNING
I KNOW ABUT YOUR BETREYAL THAT DAY
SHF
WARNING
WHA?
HUH? IT'S ACTUALLY SPELLED CORRECTLY...?!
!!
WARNING
WELL... IT SEEMS THE PERPETRATOR REALLY WANTED TO MAKE THIS LOOK LIKE SOMETHING A GRADE-SCHOOLER HAD WRITTEN.
RSTL
HONESTLY, IT WAS SO FULL OF SUCH INFANTILE MISSPELLINGS THAT I DEEMED IT INAPPROPRIATE AS EVIDENCE AND REWROTE IT, KEEPING THE HANDWRITING SIMILAR...
...BUT CORRECTING THE "WARNING" TITLE AT THE TOP!

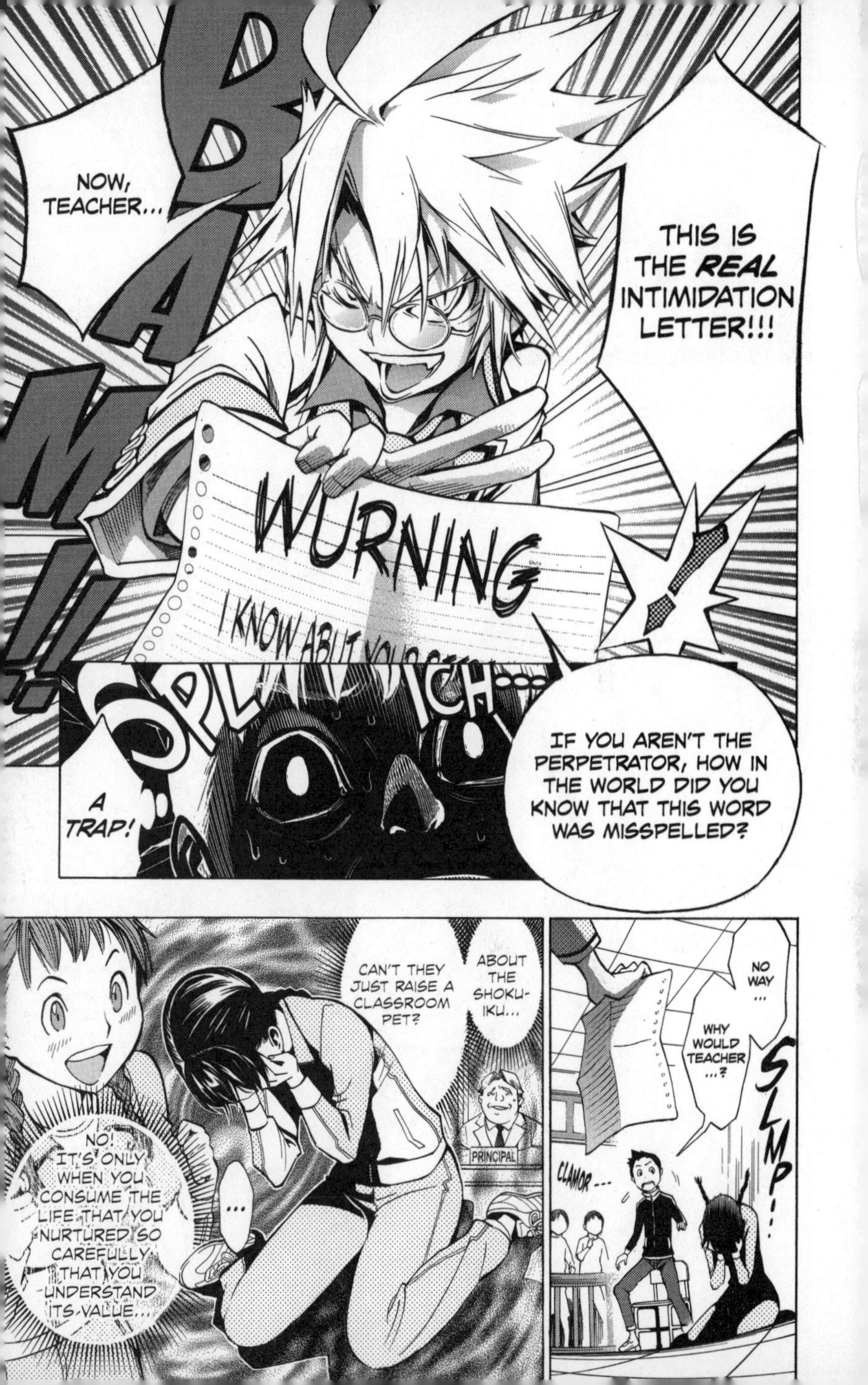
BAM!!
NOW, TEACHER...
THIS IS THE *REAL* INTIMIDATION LETTER!!!
WURNING
IF YOU AREN'T THE PERPETRATOR, HOW IN THE WORLD DID YOU KNOW THAT THIS WORD WAS MISSPELLED?
A TRAP!
NO WAY...
WHY WOULD TEACHER...?
SLMP!
CLAMOR...
ABOUT THE SHOKU-IKU...
CAN'T THEY JUST RAISE A CLASSROOM PET?
PRINCIPAL
NO! IT'S ONLY WHEN YOU CONSUME THE LIFE THAT YOU NURTURED SO CAREFULLY THAT YOU UNDERSTAND ITS VALUE...
...

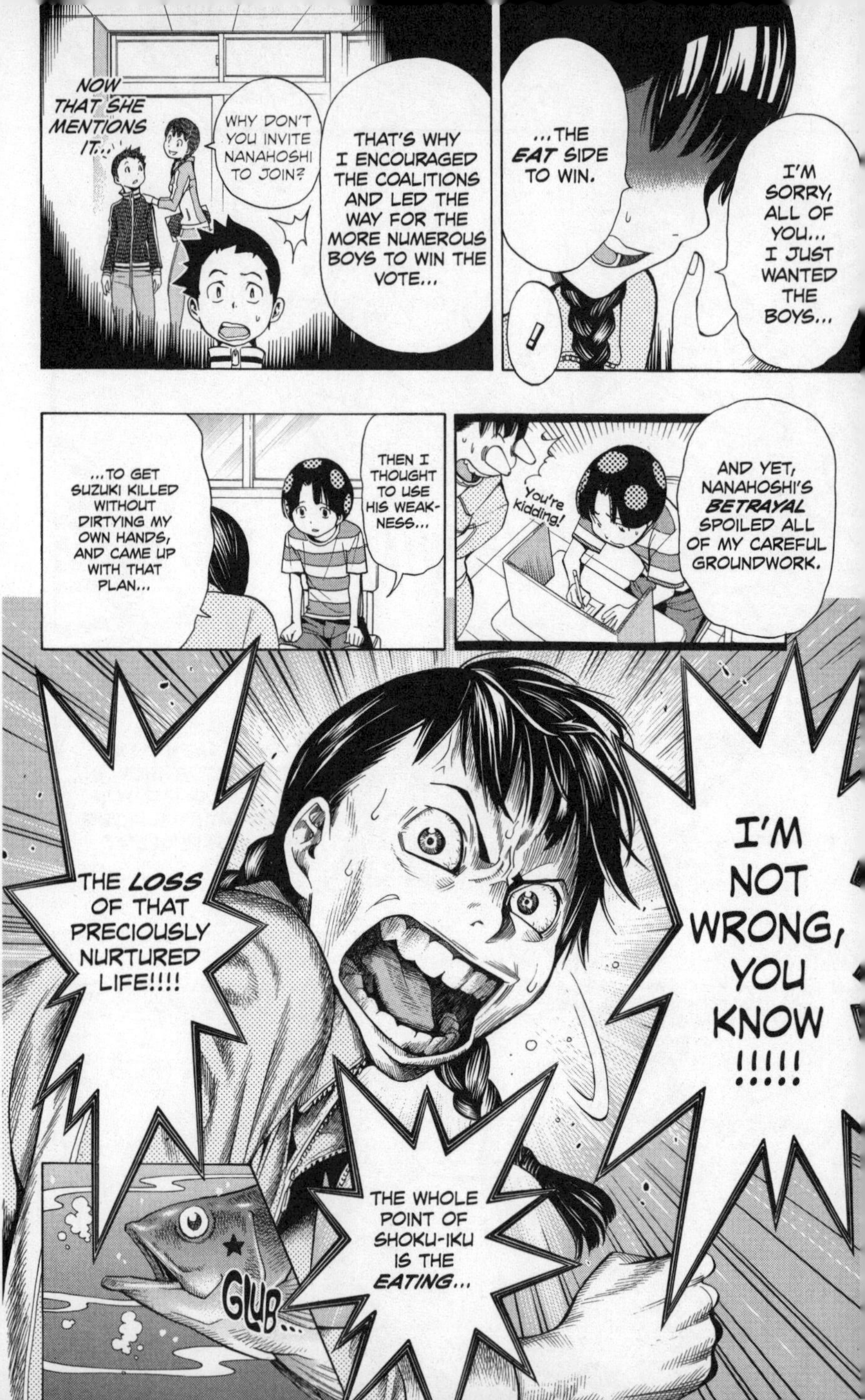
I'M SORRY, ALL OF YOU... I JUST WANTED THE BOYS...
...THE *EAT* SIDE TO WIN.
!
THAT'S WHY I ENCOURAGED THE COALITIONS AND LED THE WAY FOR THE MORE NUMEROUS BOYS TO WIN THE VOTE...
WHY DON'T YOU INVITE NANAHOSHI TO JOIN?
NOW THAT SHE MENTIONS IT...
AND YET, NANAHOSHI'S *BETRAYAL* SPOILED ALL OF MY CAREFUL GROUNDWORK.
You're kidding!
THEN I THOUGHT TO USE HIS WEAKNESS...
...TO GET SUZUKI KILLED WITHOUT DIRTYING MY OWN HANDS, AND CAME UP WITH THAT PLAN...
I'M NOT WRONG, YOU KNOW!!!!!
THE *LOSS* OF THAT PRECIOUSLY NURTURED LIFE!!!!
THE WHOLE POINT OF SHOKU-IKU IS THE *EATING*...
GLUB...

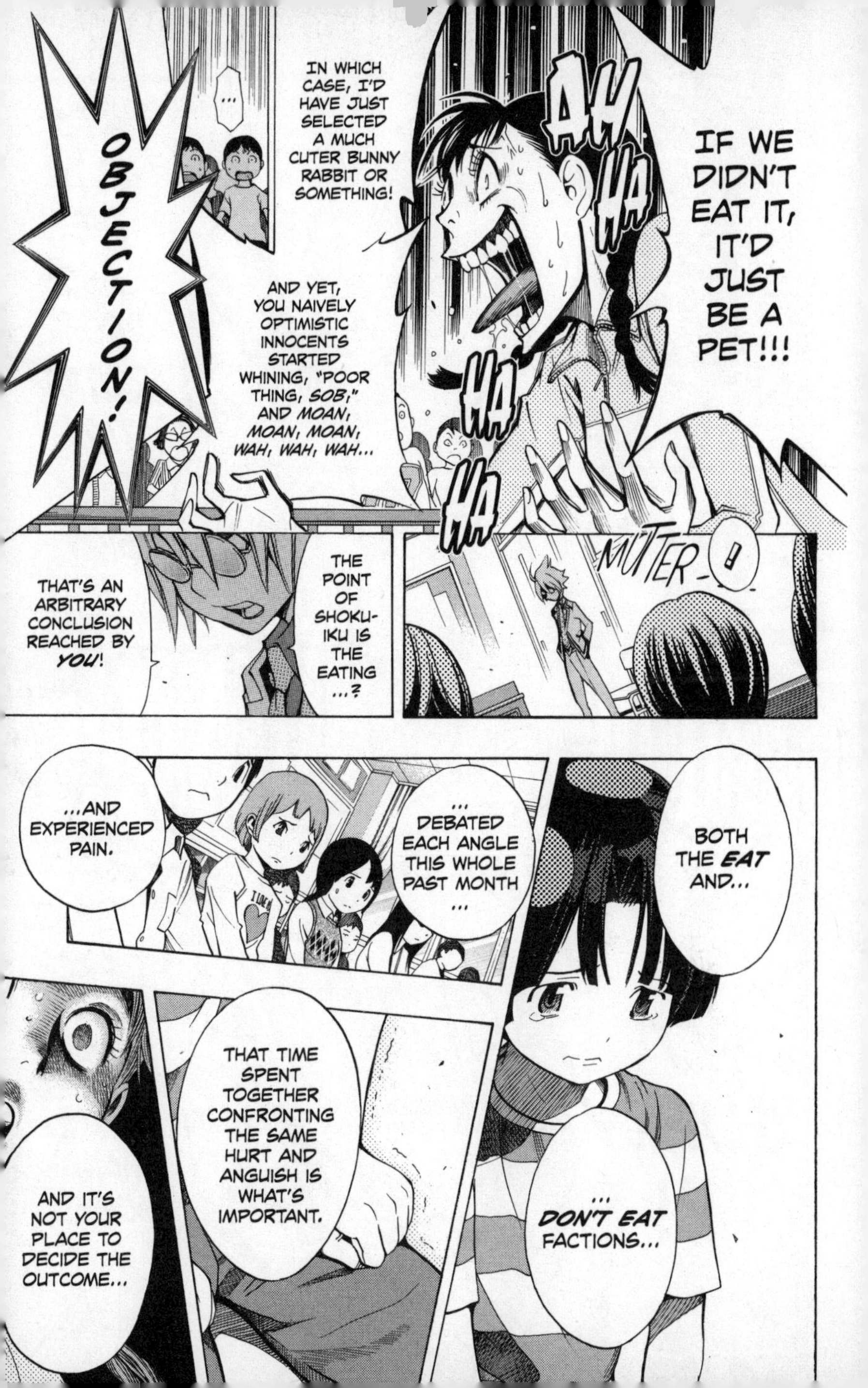
IF WE DIDN'T EAT IT, IT'D JUST BE A PET!!!
AH HA HA HA
IN WHICH CASE, I'D HAVE JUST SELECTED A MUCH CUTER BUNNY RABBIT OR SOMETHING!
AND YET, YOU NAIVELY OPTIMISTIC INNOCENTS STARTED WHINING, "POOR THING, *SOB*," AND *MOAN, MOAN, MOAN, WAH, WAH, WAH*...
...
OBJECTION!
MUTTER
!
THE POINT OF SHOKU-IKU IS THE EATING ...?
THAT'S AN ARBITRARY CONCLUSION REACHED BY *YOU*!
BOTH THE *EAT* AND...
... *DON'T EAT* FACTIONS...
... DEBATED EACH ANGLE THIS WHOLE PAST MONTH ...
...AND EXPERIENCED PAIN.
THAT TIME SPENT TOGETHER CONFRONTING THE SAME HURT AND ANGUISH IS WHAT'S IMPORTANT.
AND IT'S NOT YOUR PLACE TO DECIDE THE OUTCOME...

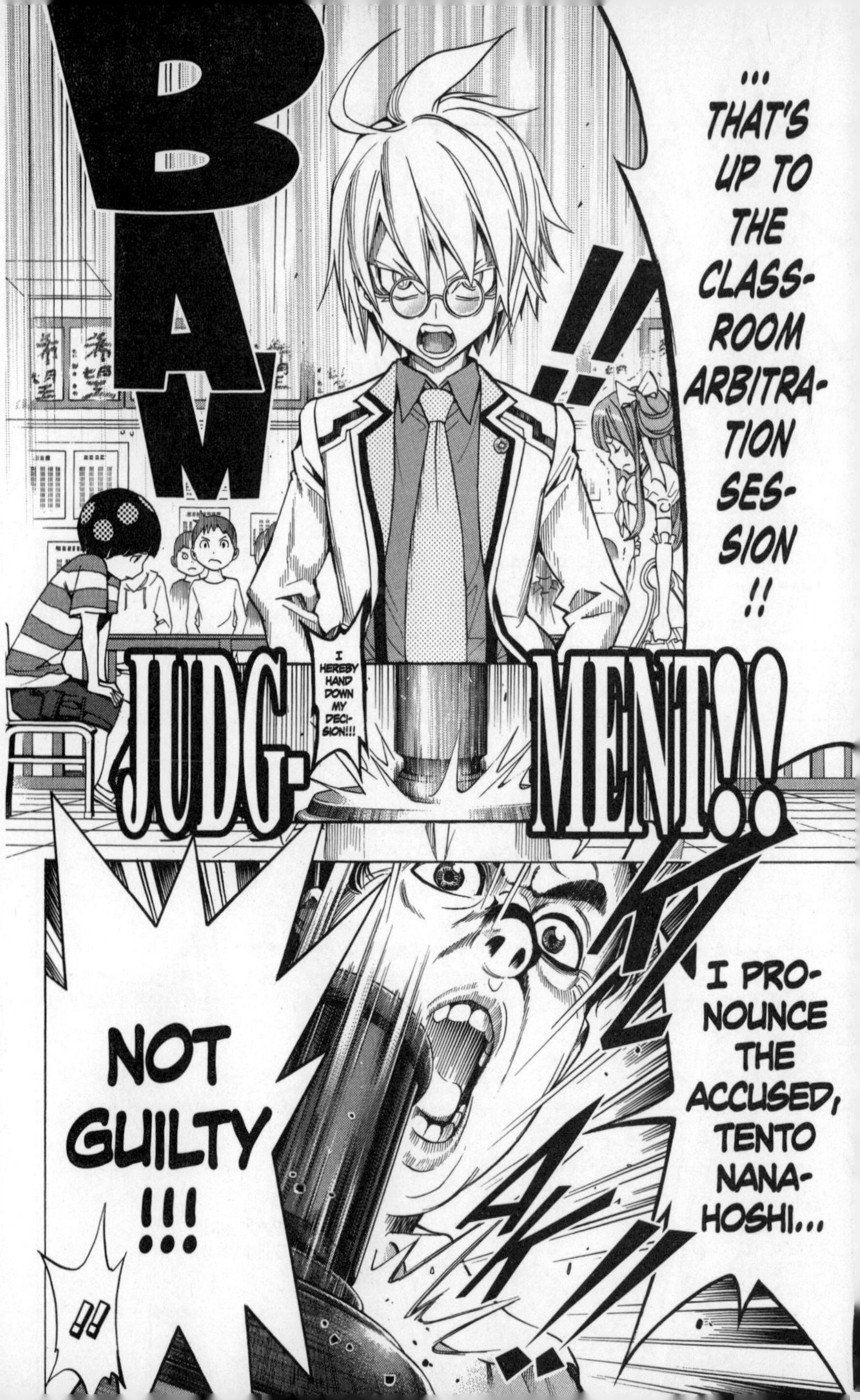

BAM
!!
...THAT'S UP TO THE CLASS-ROOM ARBITRA-TION SES-SION!!
JUDG-MENT!!
I HEREBY HAND DOWN MY DECI-SION!!!
I PRO-NOUNCE THE ACCUSED, TENTO NANA-HOSHI...
NOT GUILTY!!!
!!
K
A
K
...

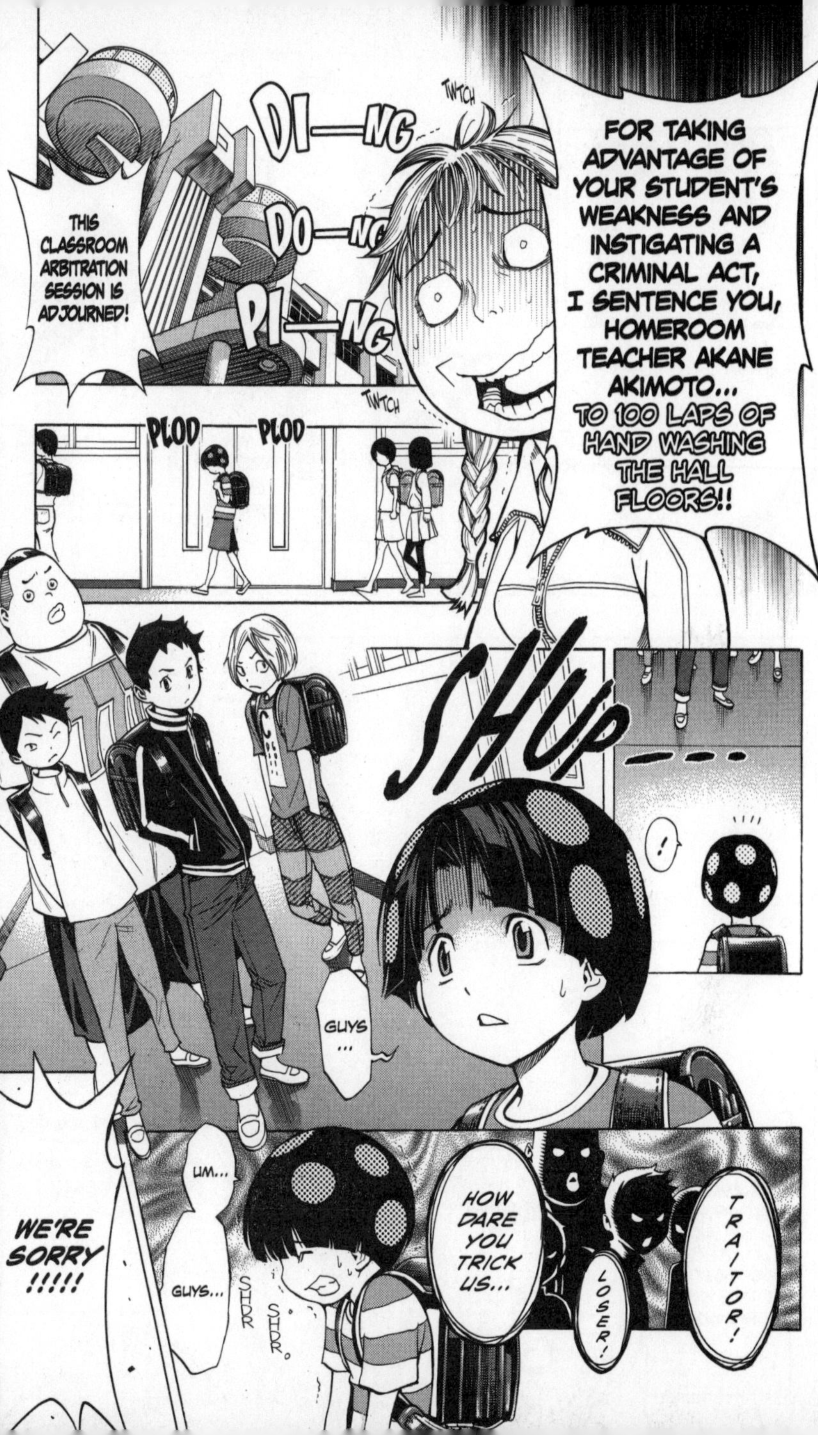
TWITCH
FOR TAKING ADVANTAGE OF YOUR STUDENT'S WEAKNESS AND INSTIGATING A CRIMINAL ACT, I SENTENCE YOU, HOMEROOM TEACHER AKANE AKIMOTO... TO 100 LAPS OF HAND WASHING THE HALL FLOORS!!
DI—NG
DO—NG
PI—NG
THIS CLASSROOM ARBITRATION SESSION IS ADJOURNED!
TWITCH
PLOD PLOD
SHUP
!
GUYS...
TRAITOR!
LOSER!
HOW DARE YOU TRICK US...
UM...
GUYS...
SHDR SHDR
WE'RE SORRY!!!!!

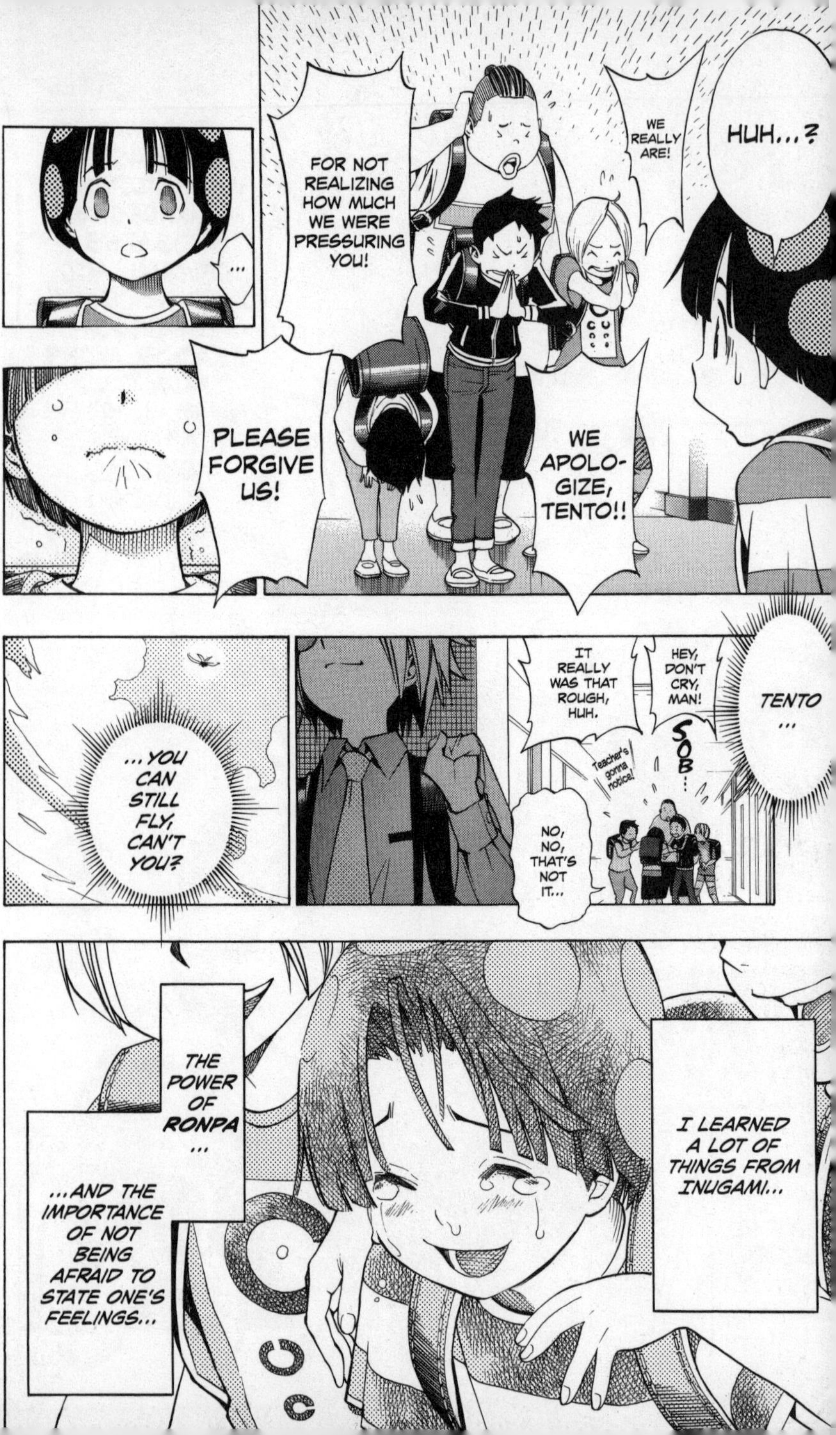
HUH...?
WE REALLY ARE!
FOR NOT REALIZING HOW MUCH WE WERE PRESSURING YOU!
WE APOLOGIZE, TENTO!!
PLEASE FORGIVE US!
...
TENTO ...
HEY, DON'T CRY, MAN!
IT REALLY WAS THAT ROUGH, HUH.
SOB...
Teacher's gonna notice!
NO, NO, THAT'S NOT IT...
...YOU CAN STILL FLY, CAN'T YOU?
I LEARNED A LOT OF THINGS FROM INUGAMI...
THE POWER OF RONPA ...
...AND THE IMPORTANCE OF NOT BEING AFRAID TO STATE ONE'S FEELINGS...

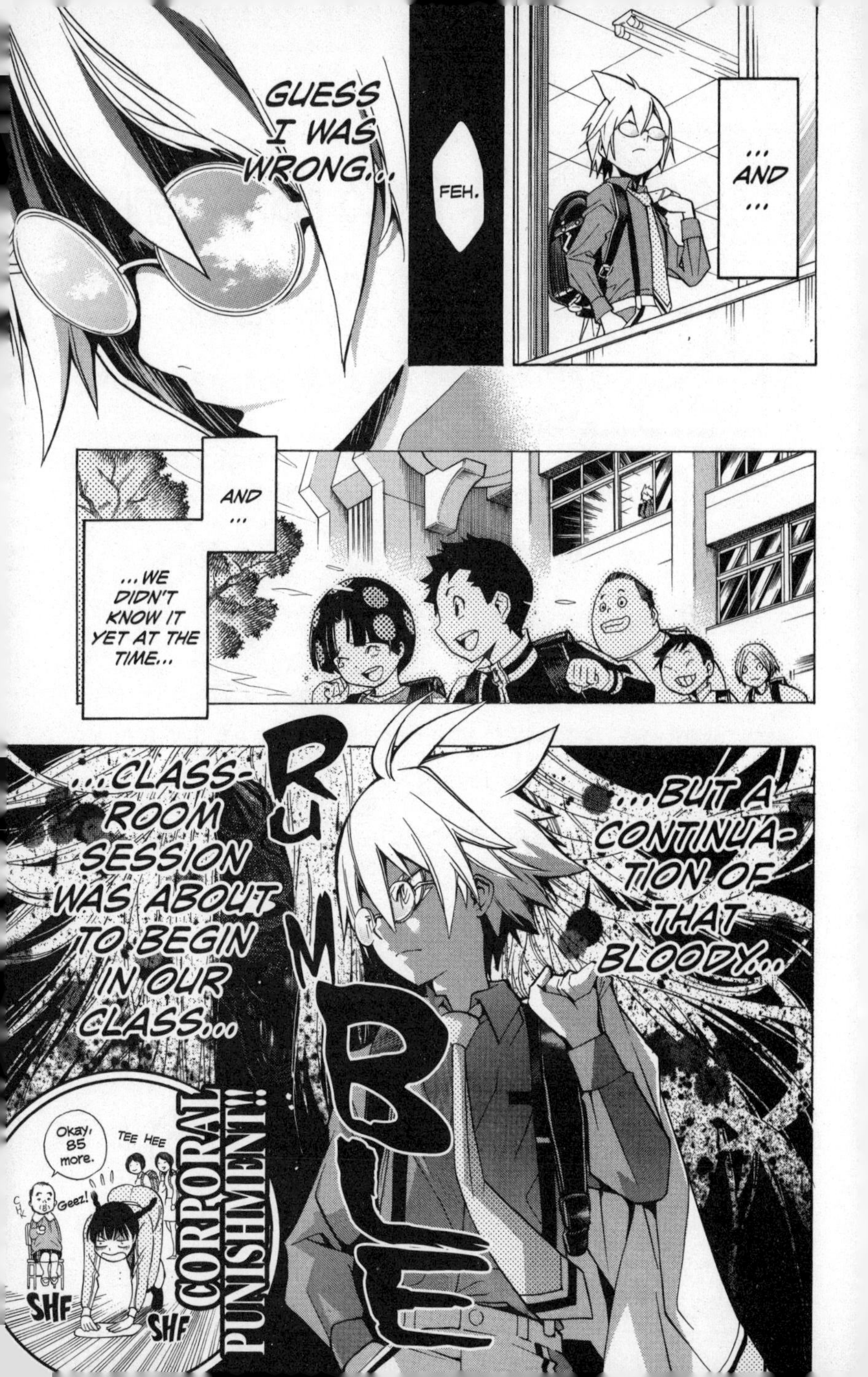
... AND ...
FEH.
GUESS I WAS WRONG...
AND ...
...WE DIDN'T KNOW IT YET AT THE TIME...
...BUT A CONTINUATION OF THAT BLOODY...
RUMBLE
...CLASSROOM SESSION WAS ABOUT TO BEGIN IN OUR CLASS...
CORPORAL PUNISHMENT!!
TEE HEE
Okay, 85 more.
Geez!
SHF
SHF

(Obata's final version)

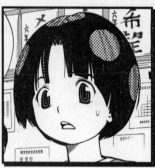

Tento Nanahoshi

Height: 4 ft. 8 in.
Dislikes: Silly arguments

He has a Watson-like presence.

(Enoki's draft version)

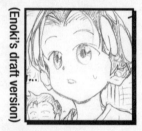

He was born with the spots in his hair, which is his most distinctive trait.

If he had been born in a different era, he probably would've been deemed an ill omen and immediately abandoned on some mountaintop.

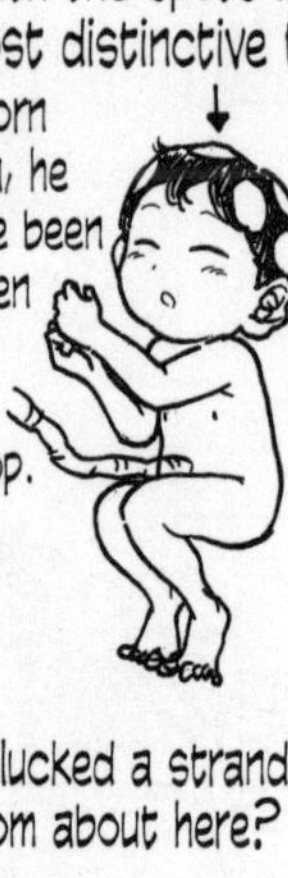

By the way, if Tento were to shave his head,

← this is how he'd look.

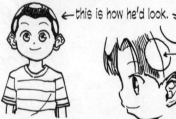

But say you plucked a strand of hair from about here?

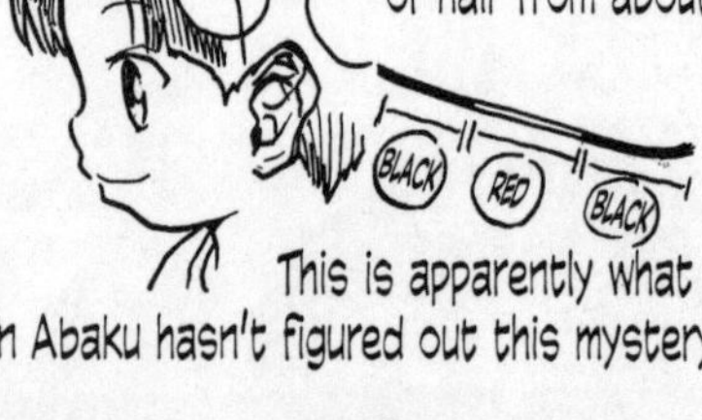

BLACK
RED
BLACK

This is apparently what it looks like.

It's said that even Abaku hasn't figured out this mystery yet.

☆School Judgment Backstory ①

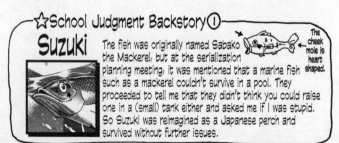

Suzuki

The fish was originally named Sabako the Mackerel, but at the serialization planning meeting, it was mentioned that a marine fish such as a mackerel couldn't survive in a pool. They proceeded to tell me that they didn't think you could raise one in a (small) tank either and asked me if I was stupid. So Suzuki was reimagined as a Japanese perch and survived without further issues.

← The cheek mole is heart shaped.

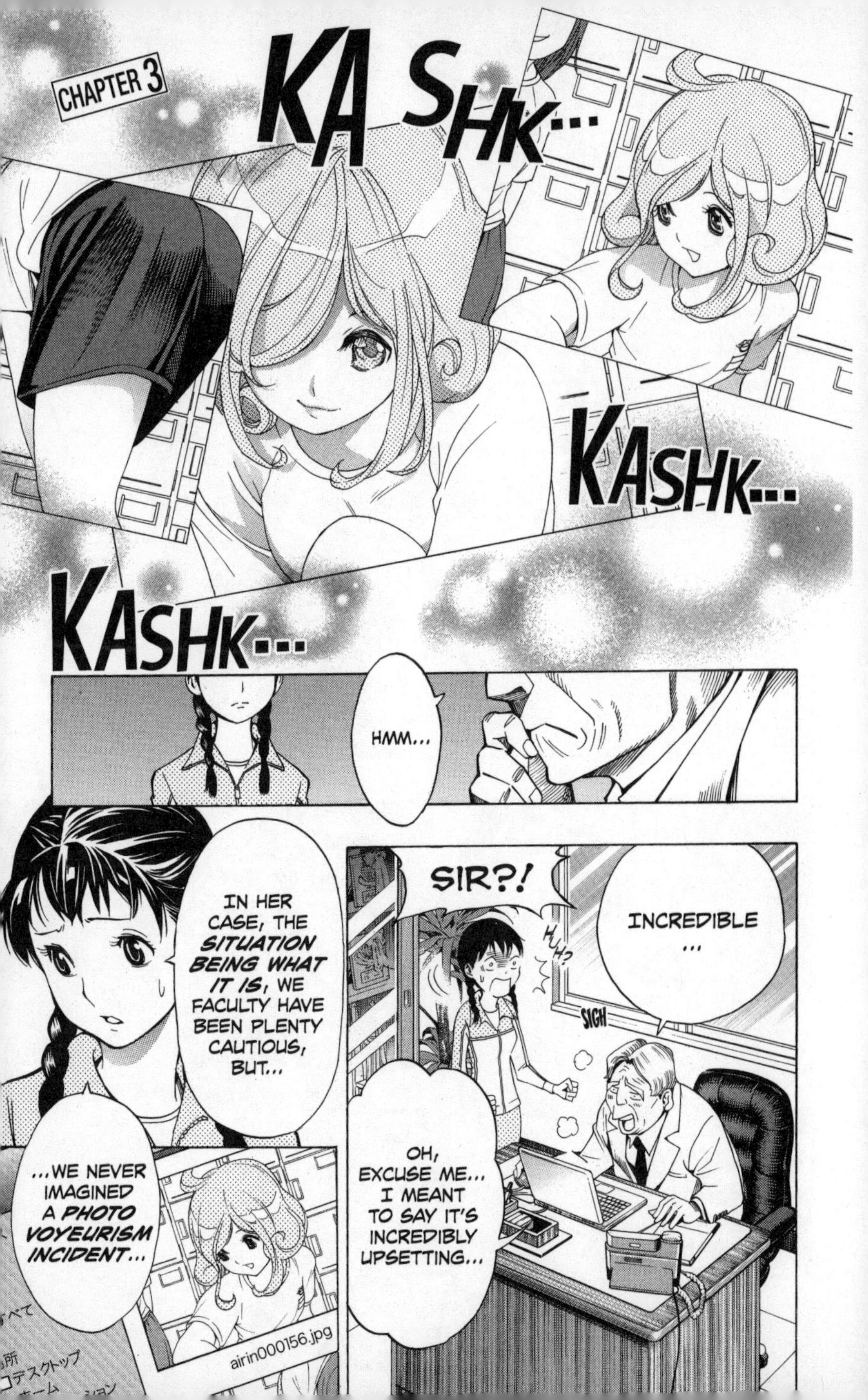
CHAPTER 3
KA SHK...
KASHK...
KASHK...
HMM...
INCREDIBLE ...
SIR?!
HUH?
SIGH
OH, EXCUSE ME... I MEANT TO SAY IT'S INCREDIBLY UPSETTING...
IN HER CASE, THE SITUATION BEING WHAT IT IS, WE FACULTY HAVE BEEN PLENTY CAUTIOUS, BUT...
...WE NEVER IMAGINED A PHOTO VOYEURISM INCIDENT...
airin000156.jpg

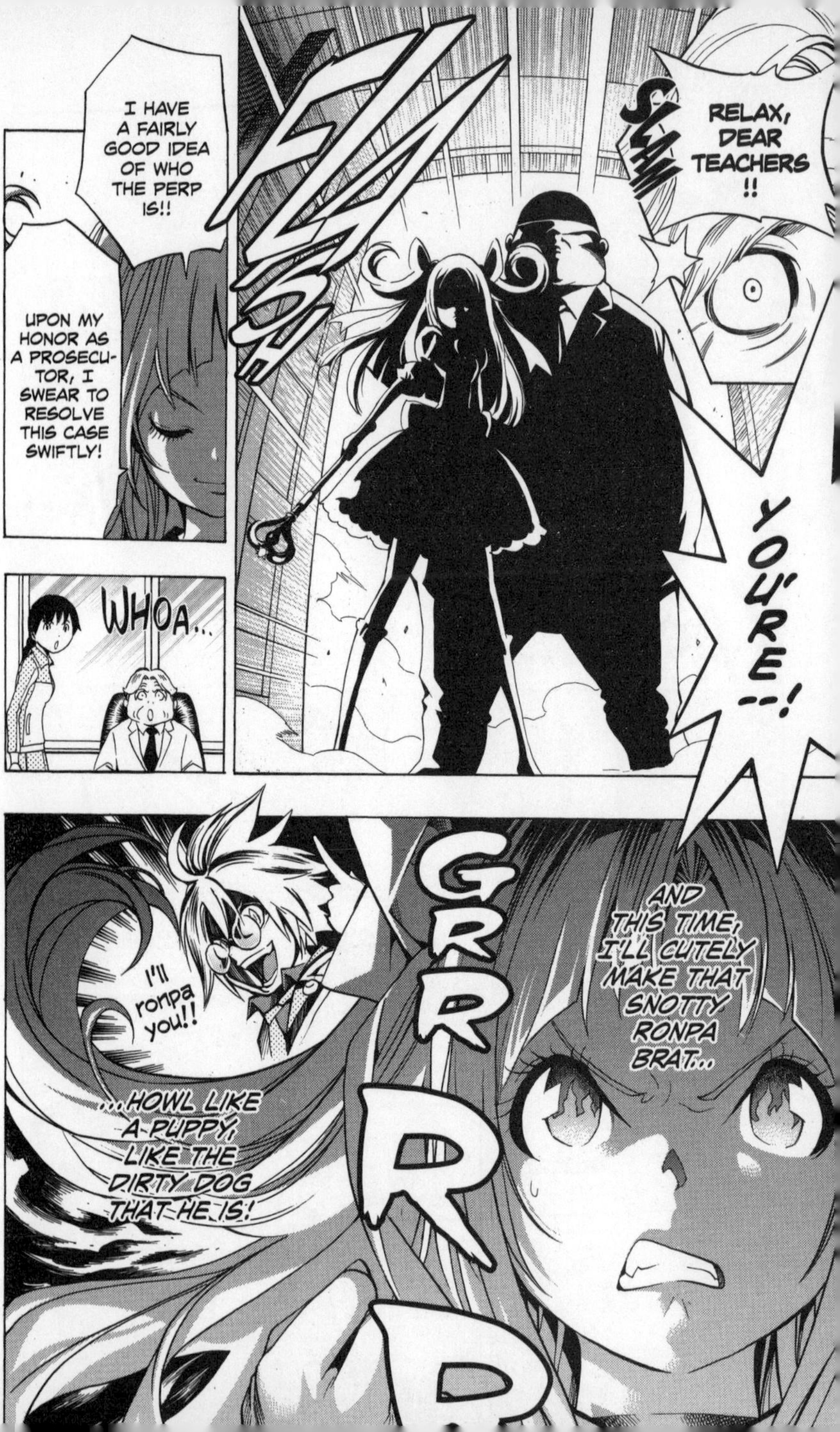
SLAM
RELAX, DEAR TEACHERS!!
YOU'RE--!
I HAVE A FAIRLY GOOD IDEA OF WHO THE PERP IS!!
UPON MY HONOR AS A PROSECUTOR, I SWEAR TO RESOLVE THIS CASE SWIFTLY!
WHOA...
AND THIS TIME, I'LL CUTELY MAKE THAT SNOTTY RONPA BRAT...
I'll ronpa you!!
...HOWL LIKE A PUPPY, LIKE THE DIRTY DOG THAT HE IS!
GRRRR

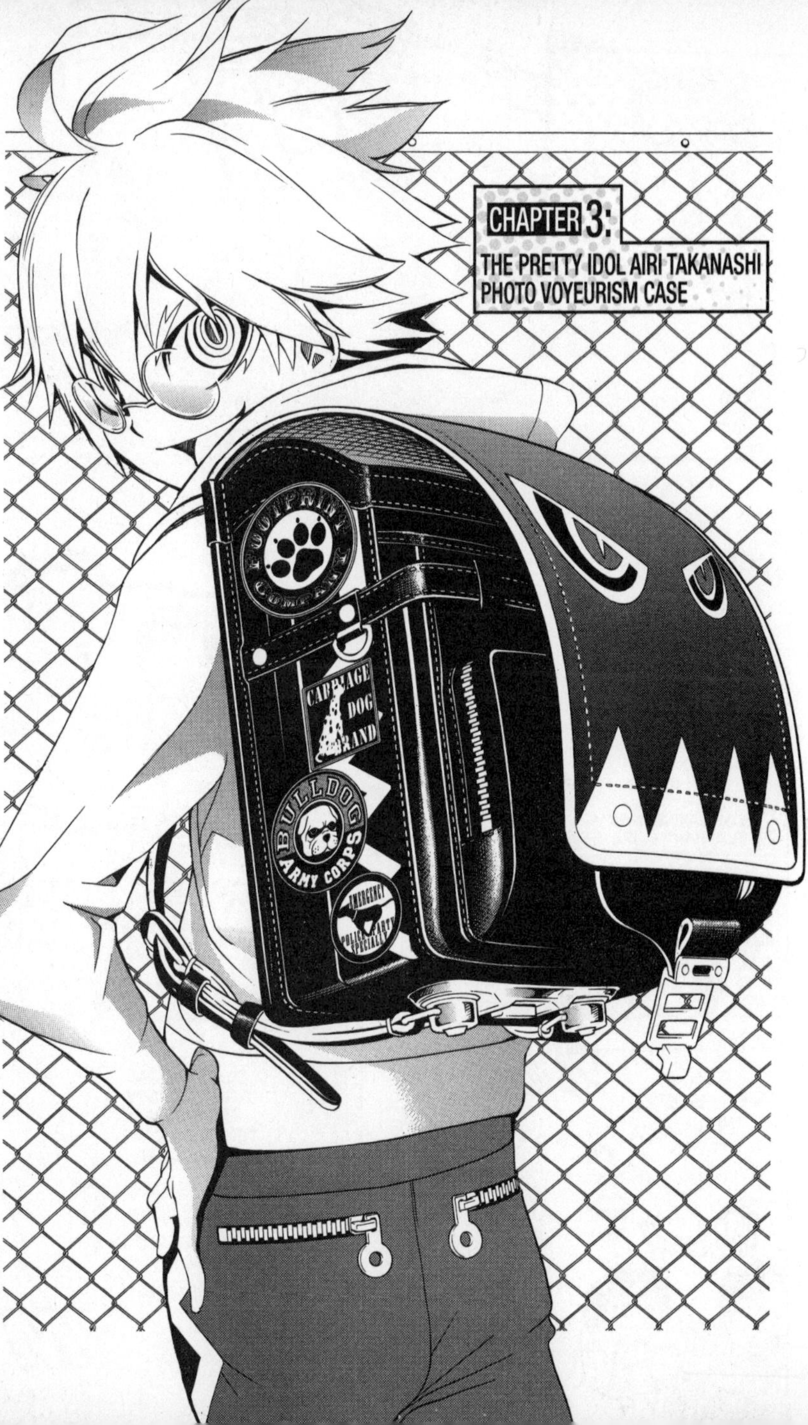
CHAPTER 3:
THE PRETTY IDOL AIRI TAKANASHI PHOTO VOYEURISM CASE
FOOTPRINT COMPANY
BULLDOG ARMY CORPS

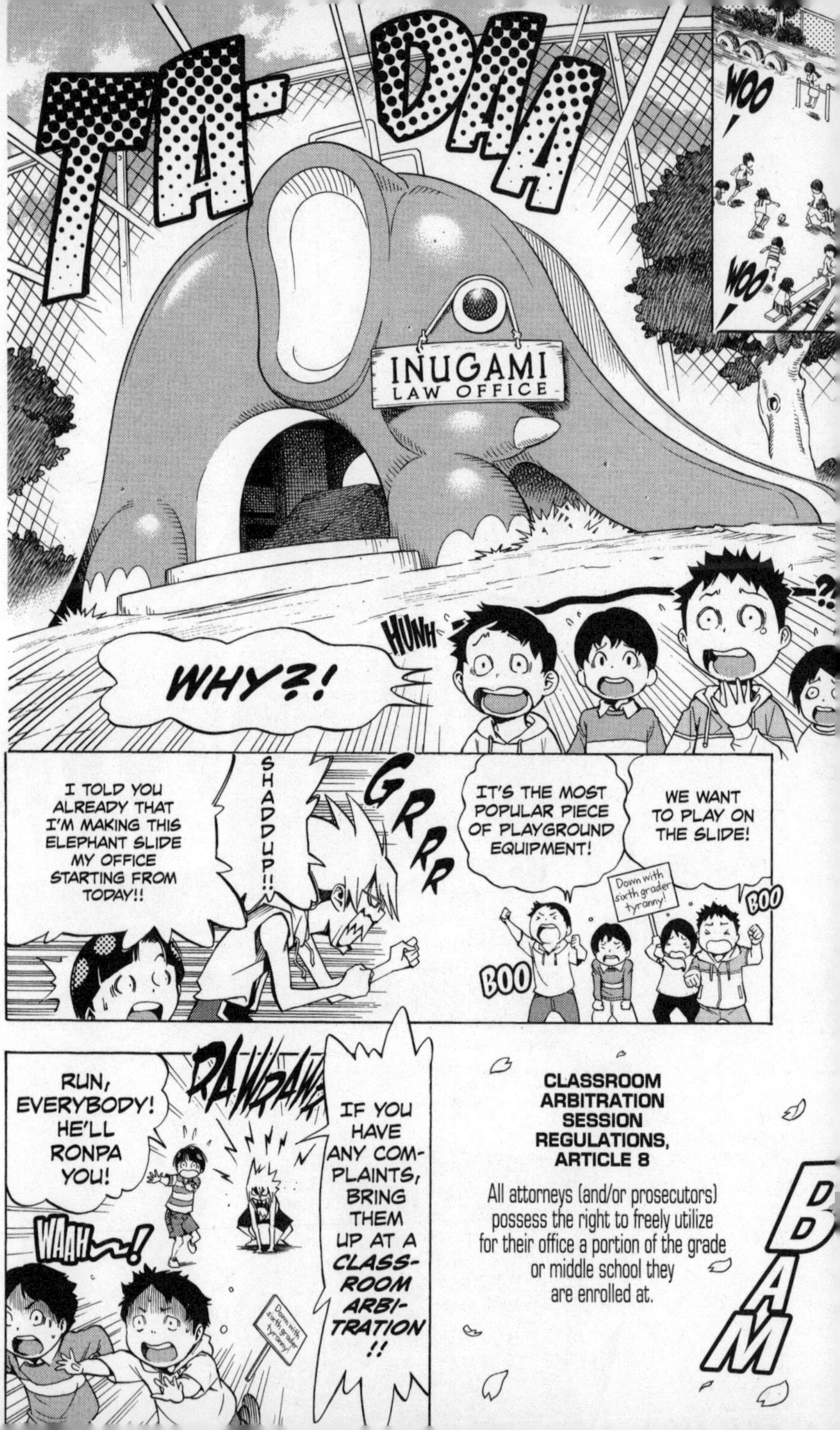
WOO
WOO
TA-DAA
INUGAMI
LAW OFFICE
HUNH—??
WHY?!
WE WANT TO PLAY ON THE SLIDE!
IT'S THE MOST POPULAR PIECE OF PLAYGROUND EQUIPMENT!
Down with sixth grader tyranny!
BOO
BOO
GRRR
SHADDUP!!
I TOLD YOU ALREADY THAT I'M MAKING THIS ELEPHANT SLIDE MY OFFICE STARTING FROM TODAY!!
CLASSROOM ARBITRATION SESSION REGULATIONS, ARTICLE 8
All attorneys (and/or prosecutors) possess the right to freely utilize for their office a portion of the grade or middle school they are enrolled at.
BAM
IF YOU HAVE ANY COM-PLAINTS, BRING THEM UP AT A CLASS-ROOM ARBI-TRATION!!
DAWDAW
RUN, EVERYBODY! HE'LL RONPA YOU!
WAAH~!
Down with sixth grader tyranny!

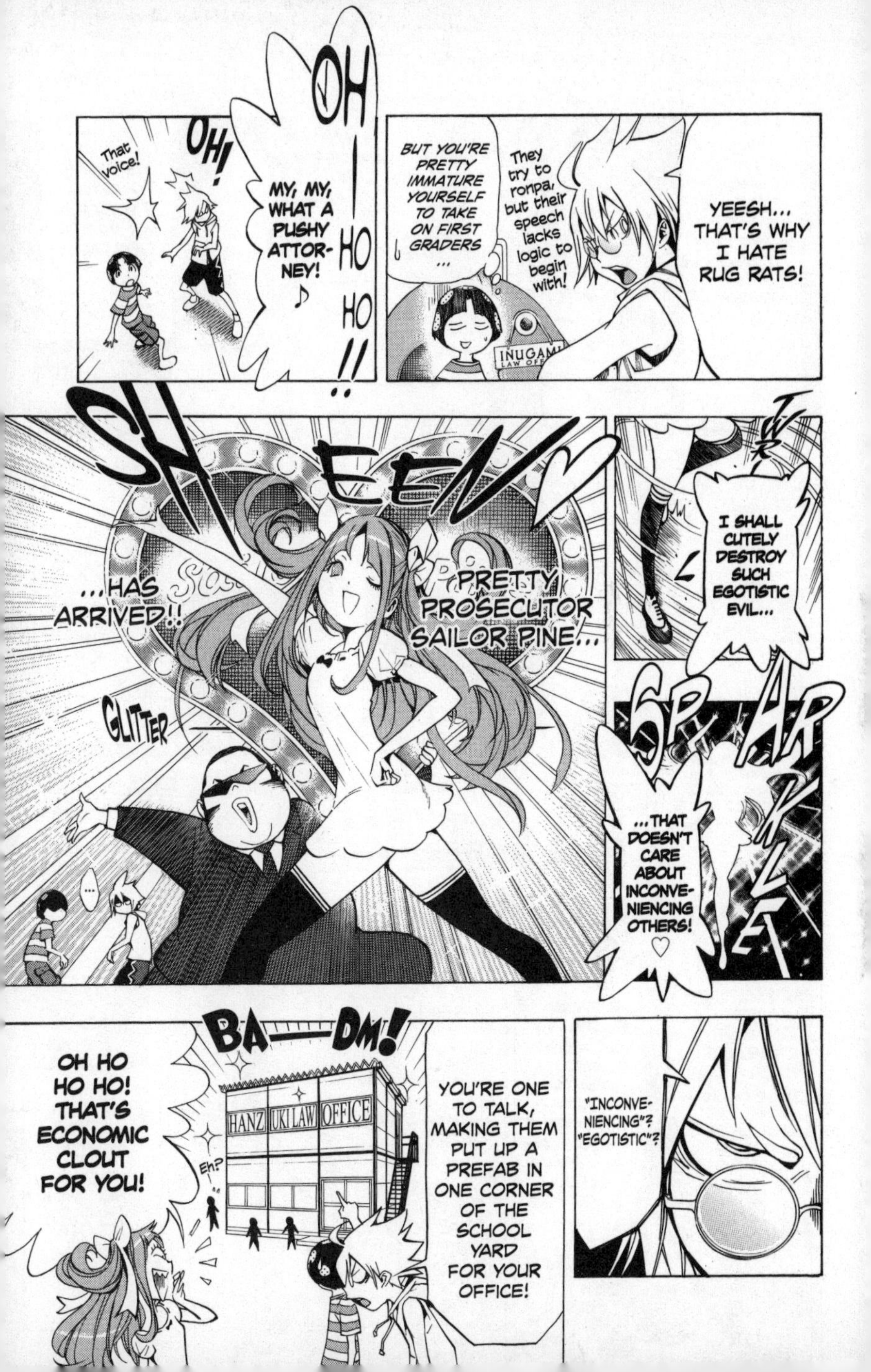
YEESH... THAT'S WHY I HATE RUG RATS!
They try to ronpa, but their speech lacks logic to begin with!
BUT YOU'RE PRETTY IMMATURE YOURSELF TO TAKE ON FIRST GRADERS ...
INUGAMI LAW OFF
OH HO HO HO!!
MY, MY, WHAT A PUSHY ATTORNEY! ♪
OH!
That voice!
I SHALL CUTELY DESTROY SUCH EGOTISTIC EVIL...
SPARKLE
...THAT DOESN'T CARE ABOUT INCONVENIENCING OTHERS! ♡
SHEEN
PRETTY PROSECUTOR SAILOR PINE...
...HAS ARRIVED!!
GLITTER
...
"INCONVENIENCING"? "EGOTISTIC"?
BA-DM!
YOU'RE ONE TO TALK, MAKING THEM PUT UP A PREFAB IN ONE CORNER OF THE SCHOOL YARD FOR YOUR OFFICE!
HANZUKI LAW OFFICE
OH HO HO HO! THAT'S ECONOMIC CLOUT FOR YOU!
Eh?

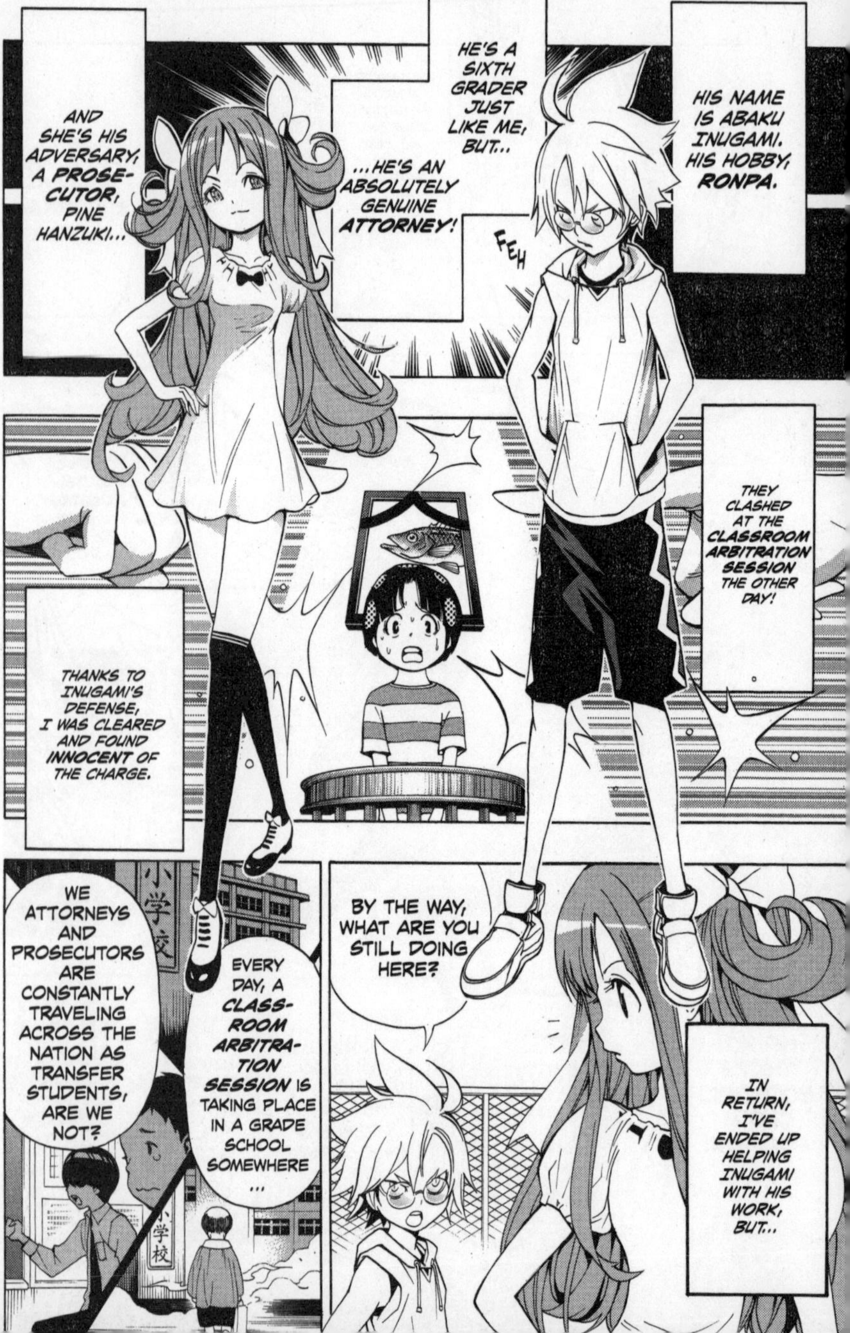
HIS NAME IS ABAKU INUGAMI. HIS HOBBY, RONPA.
FEH
HE'S A SIXTH GRADER JUST LIKE ME, BUT...
...HE'S AN ABSOLUTELY GENUINE ATTORNEY!
AND SHE'S HIS ADVERSARY, A PROSE-CUTOR, PINE HANZUKI...
THEY CLASHED AT THE CLASSROOM ARBITRATION SESSION THE OTHER DAY!
THANKS TO INUGAMI'S DEFENSE, I WAS CLEARED AND FOUND INNOCENT OF THE CHARGE.
IN RETURN, I'VE ENDED UP HELPING INUGAMI WITH HIS WORK, BUT...
BY THE WAY, WHAT ARE YOU STILL DOING HERE?
小学校
WE ATTORNEYS AND PROSECUTORS ARE CONSTANTLY TRAVELING ACROSS THE NATION AS TRANSFER STUDENTS, ARE WE NOT?
EVERY DAY, A CLASS-ROOM ARBITRA-TION SESSION IS TAKING PLACE IN A GRADE SCHOOL SOMEWHERE...

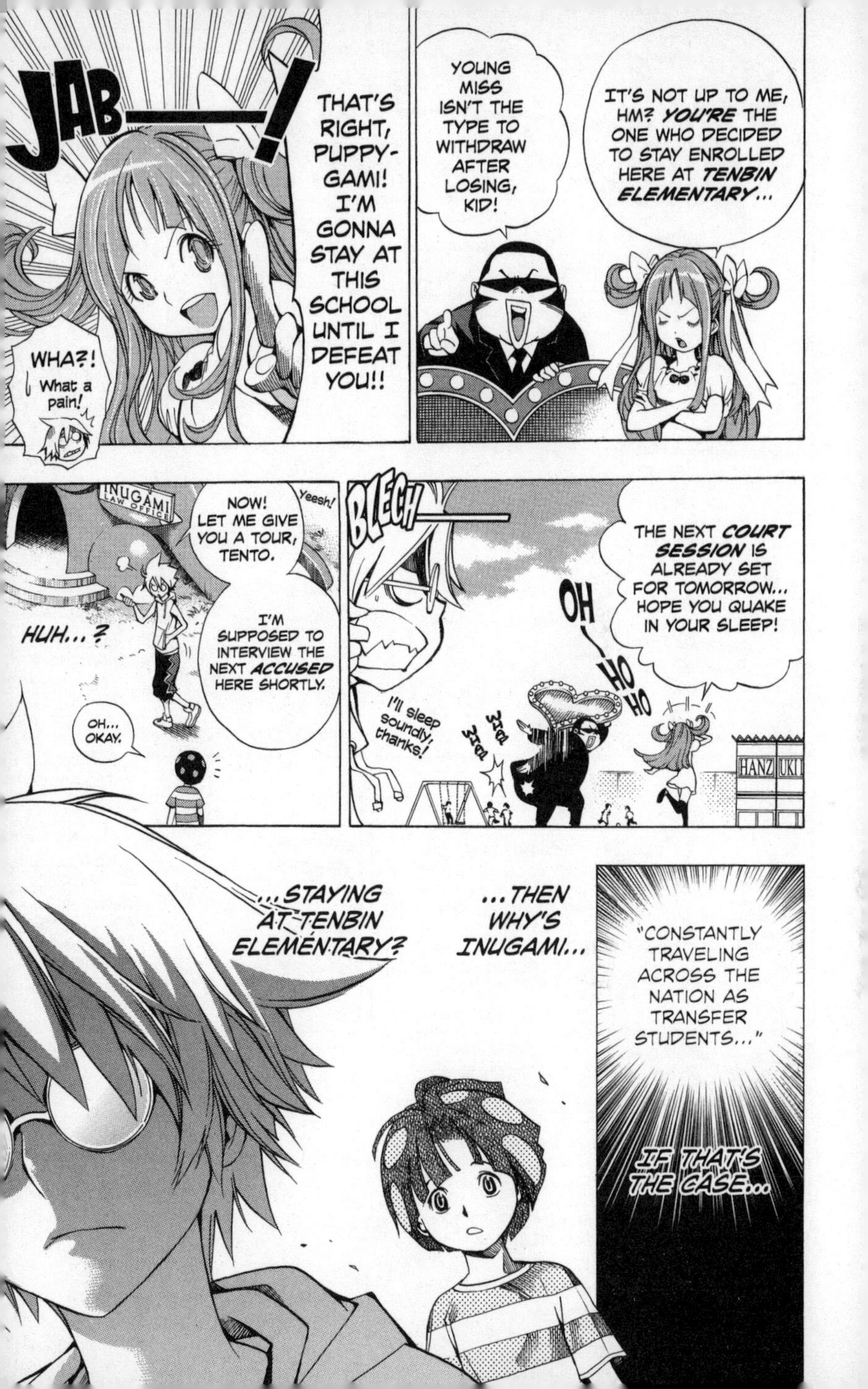

IT'S NOT UP TO ME, HM? YOU'RE THE ONE WHO DECIDED TO STAY ENROLLED HERE AT TENBIN ELEMENTARY...
YOUNG MISS ISN'T THE TYPE TO WITHDRAW AFTER LOSING, KID!
THAT'S RIGHT, PUPPY-GAMI! I'M GONNA STAY AT THIS SCHOOL UNTIL I DEFEAT YOU!!
JAB——!
WHA?! What a pain!
THE NEXT COURT SESSION IS ALREADY SET FOR TOMORROW... HOPE YOU QUAKE IN YOUR SLEEP!
OH-HO HO
BLECH
I'll sleep soundly, thanks!
Yeesh!
NOW! LET ME GIVE YOU A TOUR, TENTO.
INUGAMI LAW OFFICE
I'M SUPPOSED TO INTERVIEW THE NEXT ACCUSED HERE SHORTLY.
HUH...?
OH... OKAY.
"CONSTANTLY TRAVELING ACROSS THE NATION AS TRANSFER STUDENTS..."
IF THAT'S THE CASE...
...THEN WHY'S INUGAMI...
...STAYING AT TENBIN ELEMENTARY?

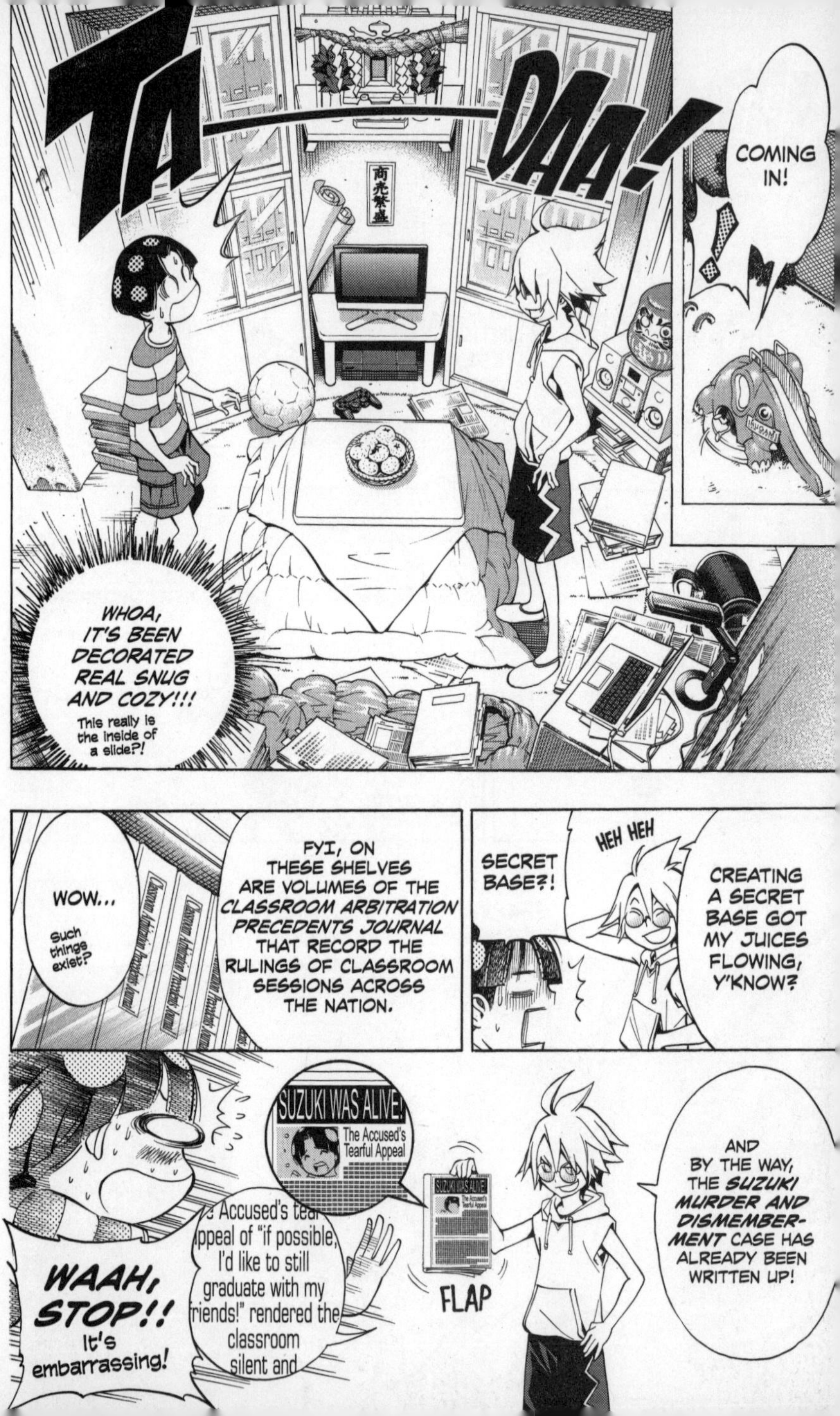

COMING IN!
!!
TA—DAA!
商売繁盛
WHOA, IT'S BEEN DECORATED REAL SNUG AND COZY!!!
This really is the inside of a slide?!
HEH HEH
CREATING A SECRET BASE GOT MY JUICES FLOWING, Y'KNOW?
SECRET BASE?!
FYI, ON THESE SHELVES ARE VOLUMES OF THE *CLASSROOM ARBITRATION PRECEDENTS JOURNAL* THAT RECORD THE RULINGS OF CLASSROOM SESSIONS ACROSS THE NATION.
WOW...
Such things exist?
AND BY THE WAY, THE *SUZUKI MURDER AND DISMEMBERMENT* CASE HAS ALREADY BEEN WRITTEN UP!
FLAP
SUZUKI WAS ALIVE!
The Accused's Tearful Appeal
e Accused's tea ppeal of "if possible, I'd like to still graduate with my riends!" rendered the classroom silent and
WAAH, STOP!!
It's embarrassing!

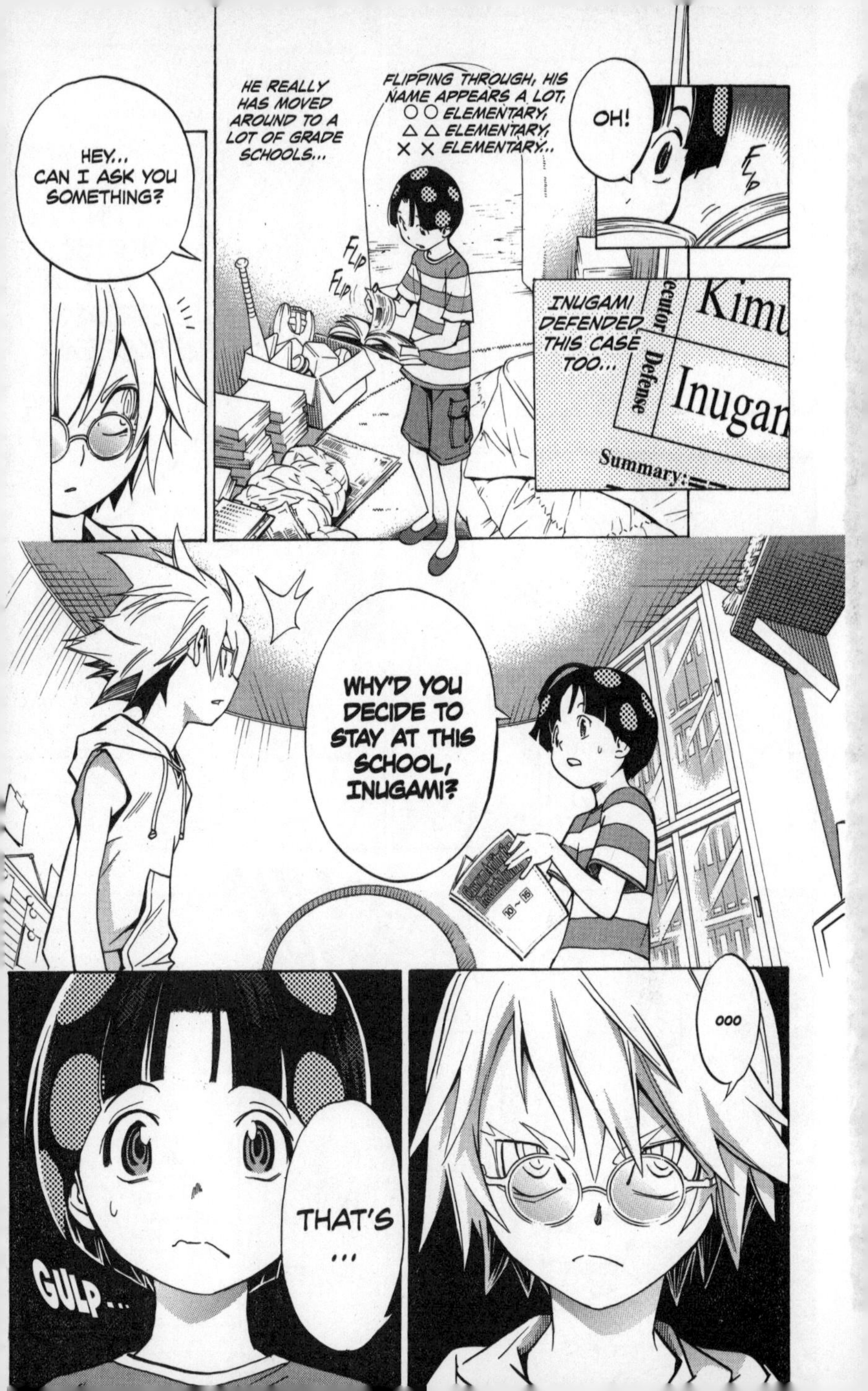
OH!
FLIP
INUGAMI DEFENDED THIS CASE TOO...
ecutor
Kimu
Defense
Inugan
Summary:
FLIPPING THROUGH, HIS NAME APPEARS A LOT, ○○ ELEMENTARY, △△ ELEMENTARY, ×× ELEMENTARY...
HE REALLY HAS MOVED AROUND TO A LOT OF GRADE SCHOOLS...
FLIP
FLIP
HEY... CAN I ASK YOU SOMETHING?
WHY'D YOU DECIDE TO STAY AT THIS SCHOOL, INUGAMI?
ooo
THAT'S ...
GULP...

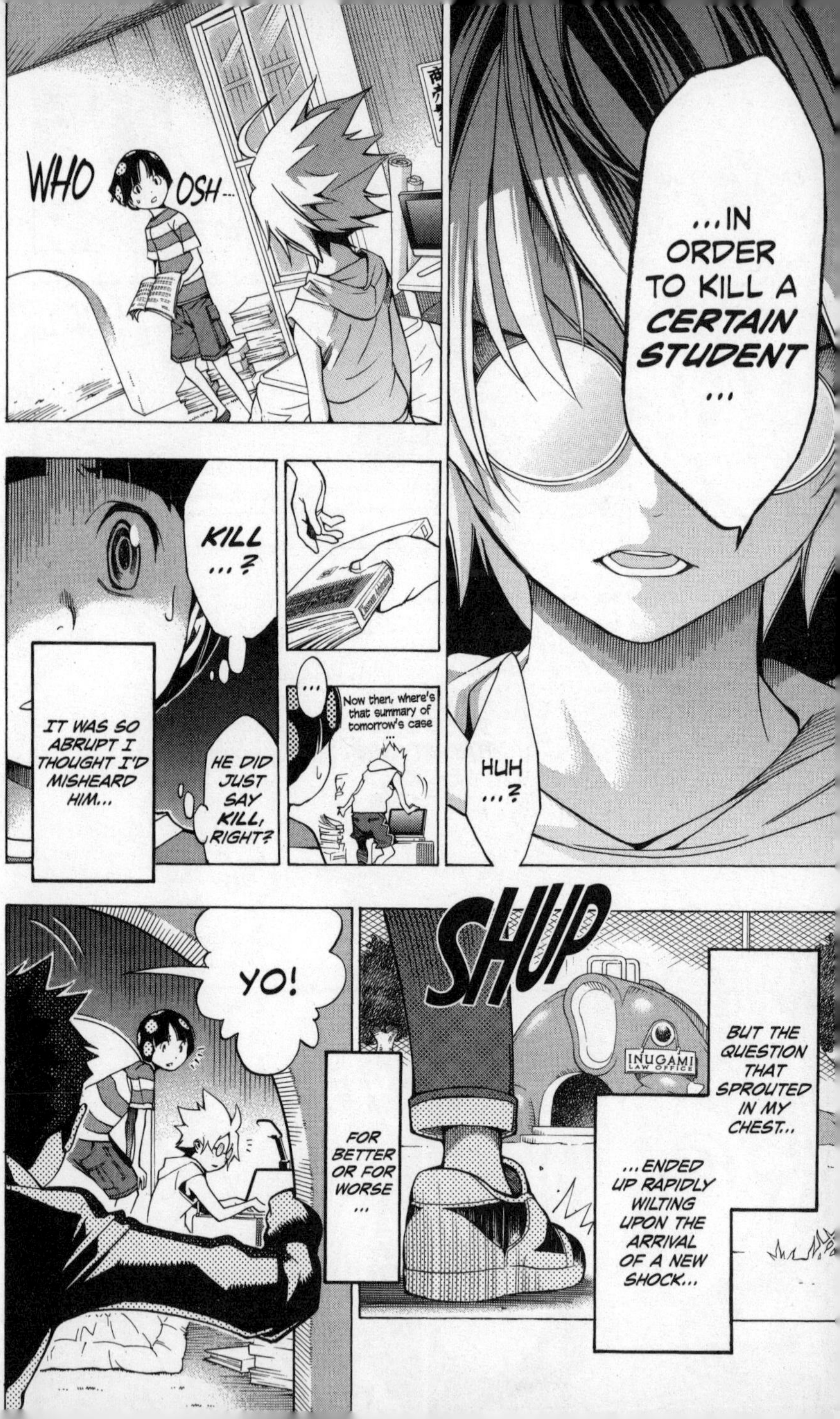
...IN ORDER TO KILL A CERTAIN STUDENT ...
HUH ...?
WHOOSH...
...
Now then, where's that summary of tomorrow's case ...
KILL ...?
HE DID JUST SAY KILL, RIGHT?
IT WAS SO ABRUPT I THOUGHT I'D MISHEARD HIM...
SHUP
INUGAMI LAW OFFICE
BUT THE QUESTION THAT SPROUTED IN MY CHEST...
...ENDED UP RAPIDLY WILTING UPON THE ARRIVAL OF A NEW SHOCK...
FOR BETTER OR FOR WORSE ...
YO!

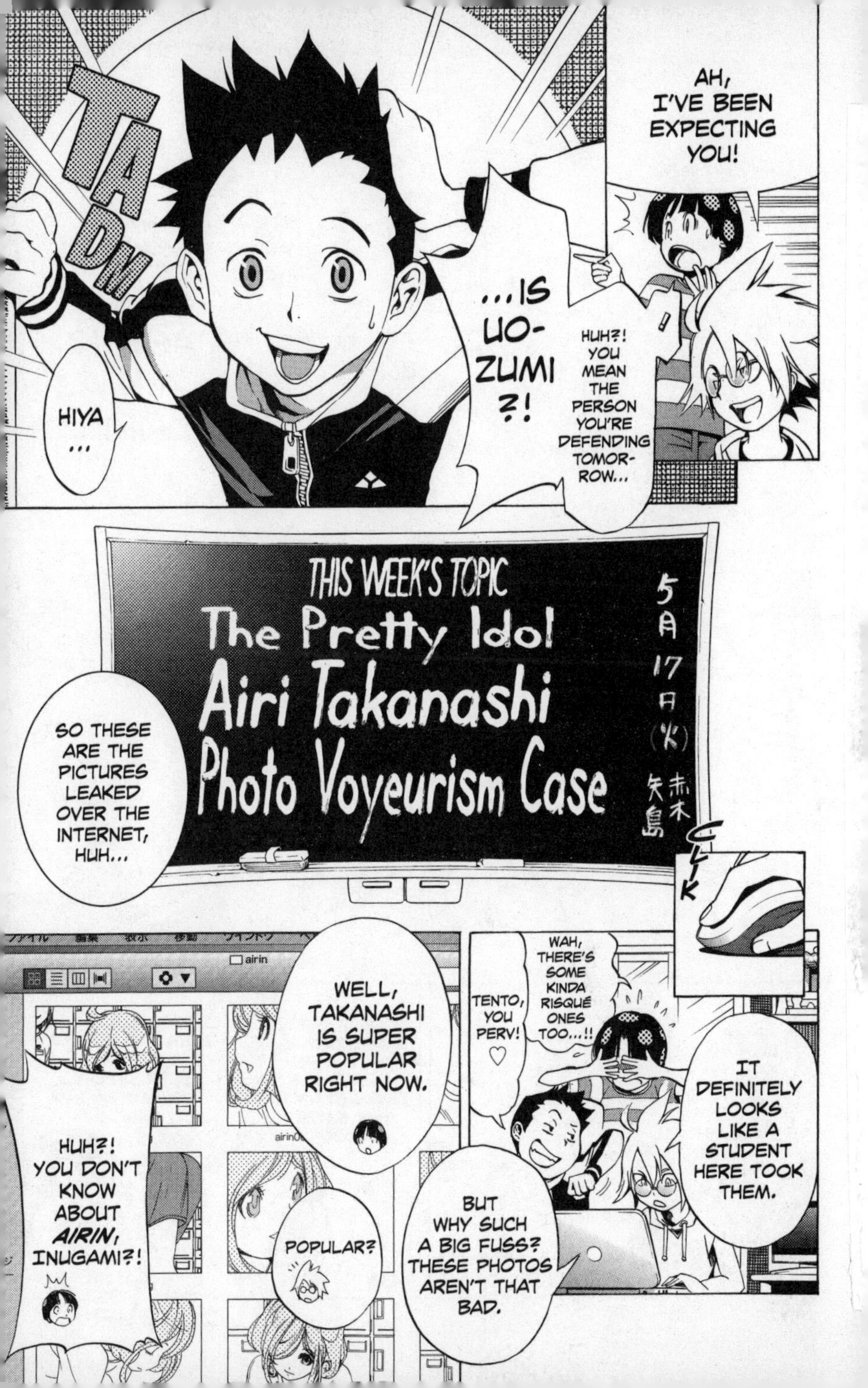
AH, I'VE BEEN EXPECTING YOU!
HUH?! YOU MEAN THE PERSON YOU'RE DEFENDING TOMORROW...
...IS UO-ZUMI?!
TA DM
HIYA...
THIS WEEK'S TOPIC
The Pretty Idol
Airi Takanashi
Photo Voyeurism Case
5月17日(火)
赤木
矢島
SO THESE ARE THE PICTURES LEAKED OVER THE INTERNET, HUH...
CLIK
WAH, THERE'S SOME KINDA RISQUÉ ONES TOO...!!
TENTO, YOU PERV! ♡
IT DEFINITELY LOOKS LIKE A STUDENT HERE TOOK THEM.
BUT WHY SUCH A BIG FUSS? THESE PHOTOS AREN'T THAT BAD.
airin
WELL, TAKANASHI IS SUPER POPULAR RIGHT NOW.
POPULAR?
HUH?! YOU DON'T KNOW ABOUT *AIRIN*, INUGAMI?!

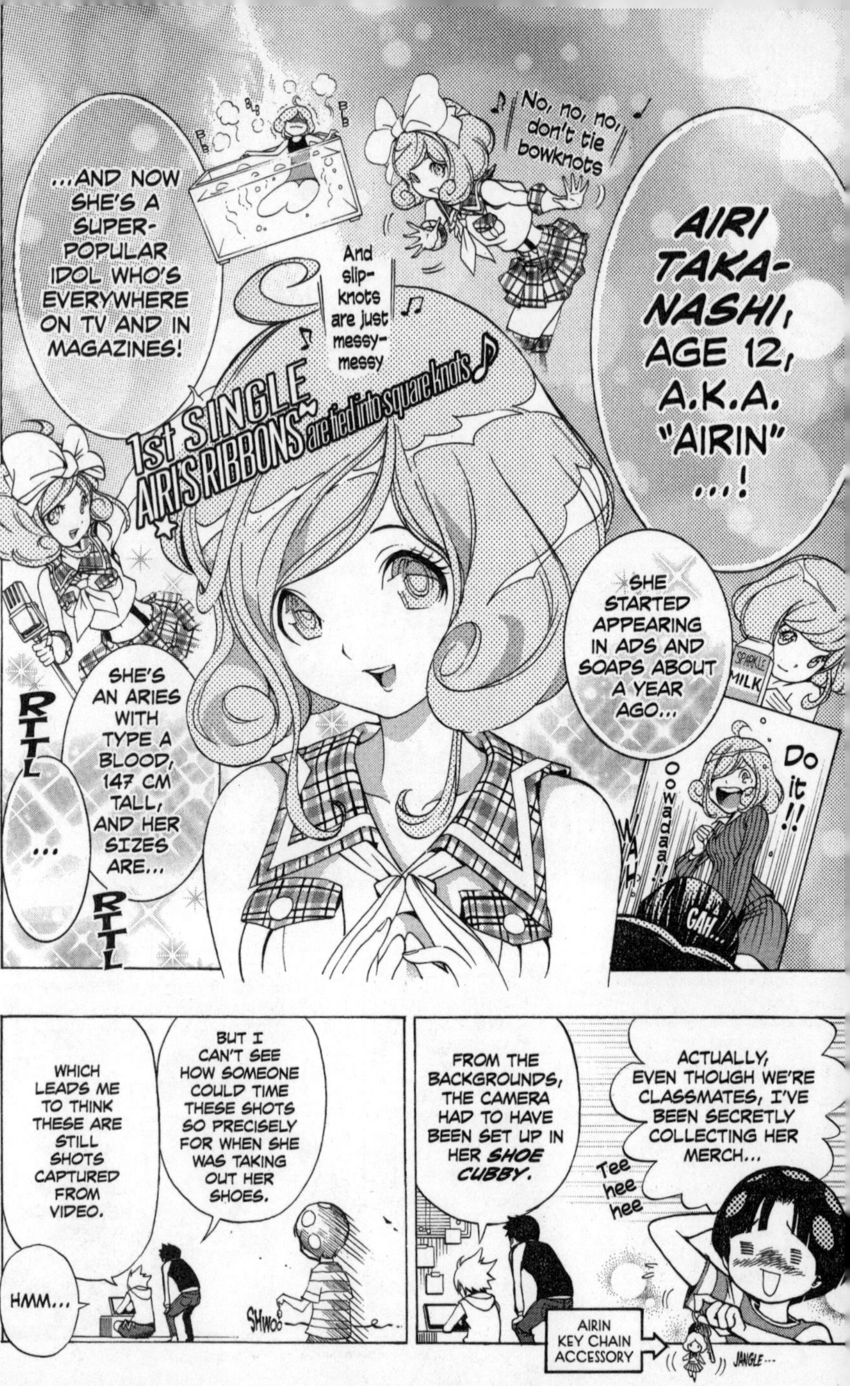
AIRI TAKANASHI, AGE 12, A.K.A. "AIRIN" ...!
No, no, no, don't tie bowknots
...AND NOW SHE'S A SUPER-POPULAR IDOL WHO'S EVERYWHERE ON TV AND IN MAGAZINES!
And slip-knots are just messy-messy
1st SINGLE AIRI'S RIBBONS are tied into square knots
SHE STARTED APPEARING IN ADS AND SOAPS ABOUT A YEAR AGO...
SPARKLE MILK
Do it!!
Oowadaaa!!
WAH
GAH...
SHE'S AN ARIES WITH TYPE A BLOOD, 147 CM TALL, AND HER SIZES ARE...
RTTL
...
RTTL
ACTUALLY, EVEN THOUGH WE'RE CLASSMATES, I'VE BEEN SECRETLY COLLECTING HER MERCH...
Tee hee hee
FROM THE BACKGROUNDS, THE CAMERA HAD TO HAVE BEEN SET UP IN HER *SHOE CUBBY*.
AIRIN KEY CHAIN ACCESSORY
JANGLE...
BUT I CAN'T SEE HOW SOMEONE COULD TIME THESE SHOTS SO PRECISELY FOR WHEN SHE WAS TAKING OUT HER SHOES.
WHICH LEADS ME TO THINK THESE ARE STILL SHOTS CAPTURED FROM VIDEO.
HMM...
SHWOO

READ THIS WAY

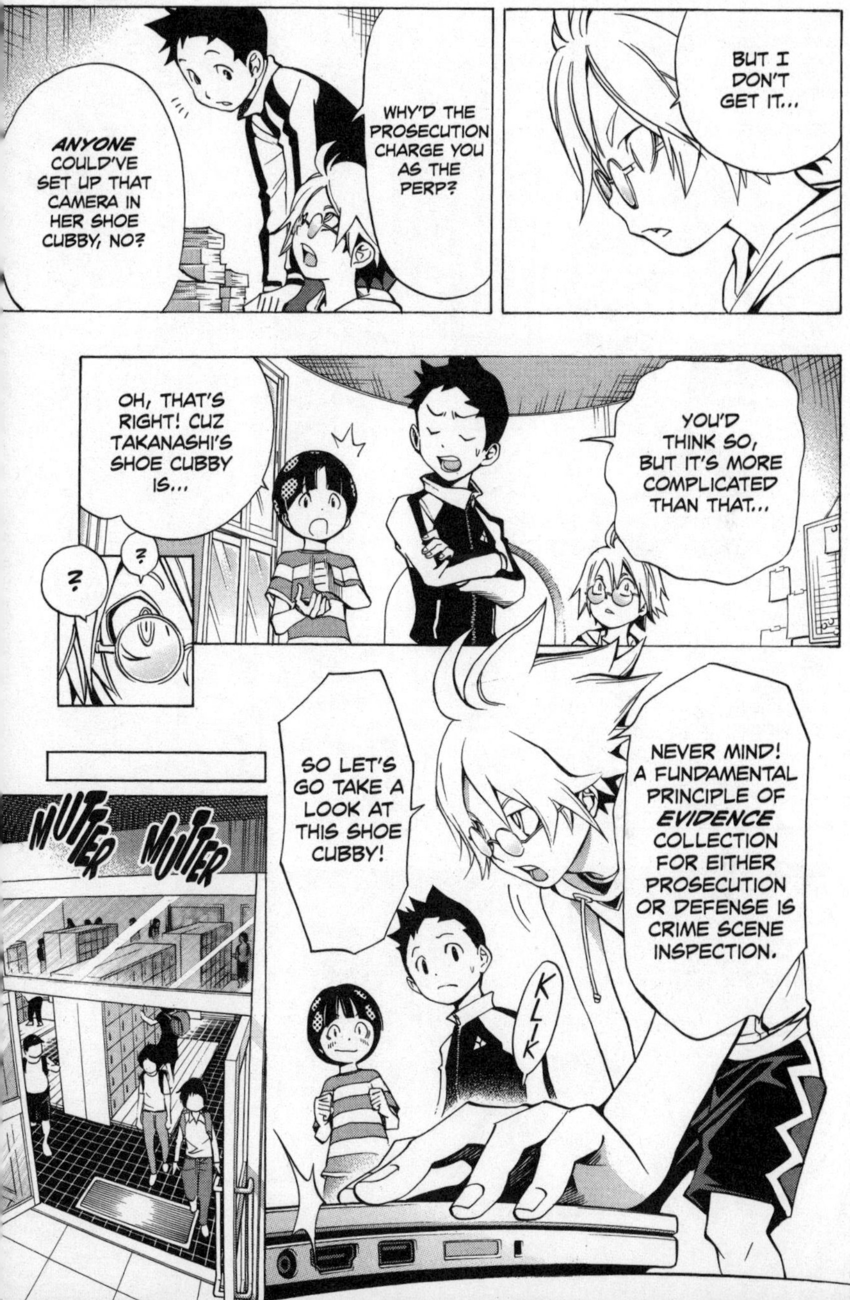
BUT I DON'T GET IT...
WHY'D THE PROSECUTION CHARGE YOU AS THE PERP?
ANYONE COULD'VE SET UP THAT CAMERA IN HER SHOE CUBBY, NO?
YOU'D THINK SO, BUT IT'S MORE COMPLICATED THAN THAT...
OH, THAT'S RIGHT! CUZ TAKANASHI'S SHOE CUBBY IS...
?
?
NEVER MIND! A FUNDAMENTAL PRINCIPLE OF *EVIDENCE* COLLECTION FOR EITHER PROSECUTION OR DEFENSE IS CRIME SCENE INSPECTION.
SO LET'S GO TAKE A LOOK AT THIS SHOE CUBBY!
KLIK
MUTTER MUTTER

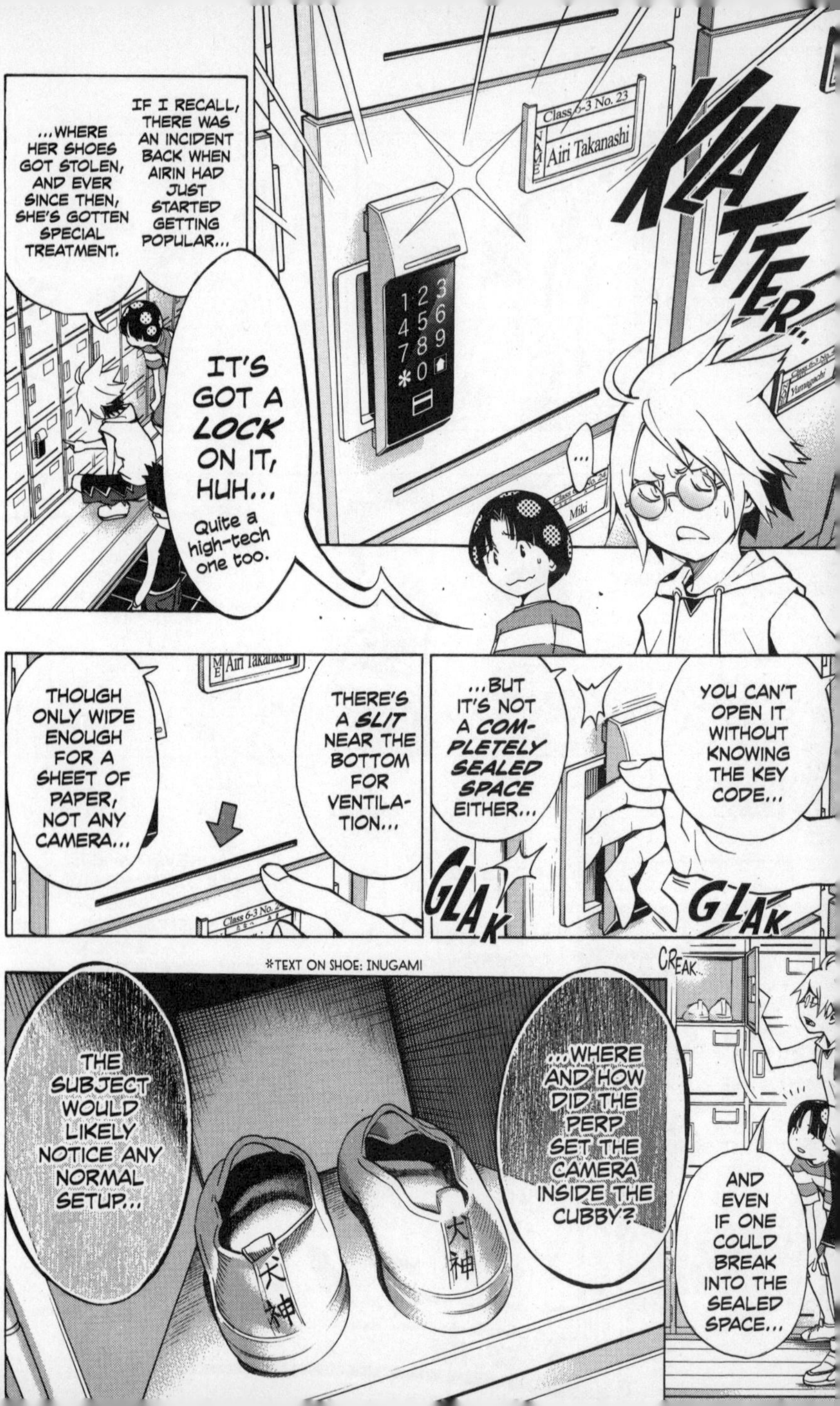
KLATTER...
Class 6-3 No. 23
NAME Airi Takanashi
...
IT'S GOT A LOCK ON IT, HUH... Quite a high-tech one too.
Miki
IF I RECALL, THERE WAS AN INCIDENT BACK WHEN AIRIN HAD JUST STARTED GETTING POPULAR...
...WHERE HER SHOES GOT STOLEN, AND EVER SINCE THEN, SHE'S GOTTEN SPECIAL TREATMENT.
YOU CAN'T OPEN IT WITHOUT KNOWING THE KEY CODE...
GLAK
GLAK
...BUT IT'S NOT A COMPLETELY SEALED SPACE EITHER...
Airi Takanashi
THERE'S A SLIT NEAR THE BOTTOM FOR VENTILATION...
THOUGH ONLY WIDE ENOUGH FOR A SHEET OF PAPER, NOT ANY CAMERA...
CREAK...
AND EVEN IF ONE COULD BREAK INTO THE SEALED SPACE...
...WHERE AND HOW DID THE PERP SET THE CAMERA INSIDE THE CUBBY?
THE SUBJECT WOULD LIKELY NOTICE ANY NORMAL SETUP...
大神
大神
*TEXT ON SHOE: INUGAMI

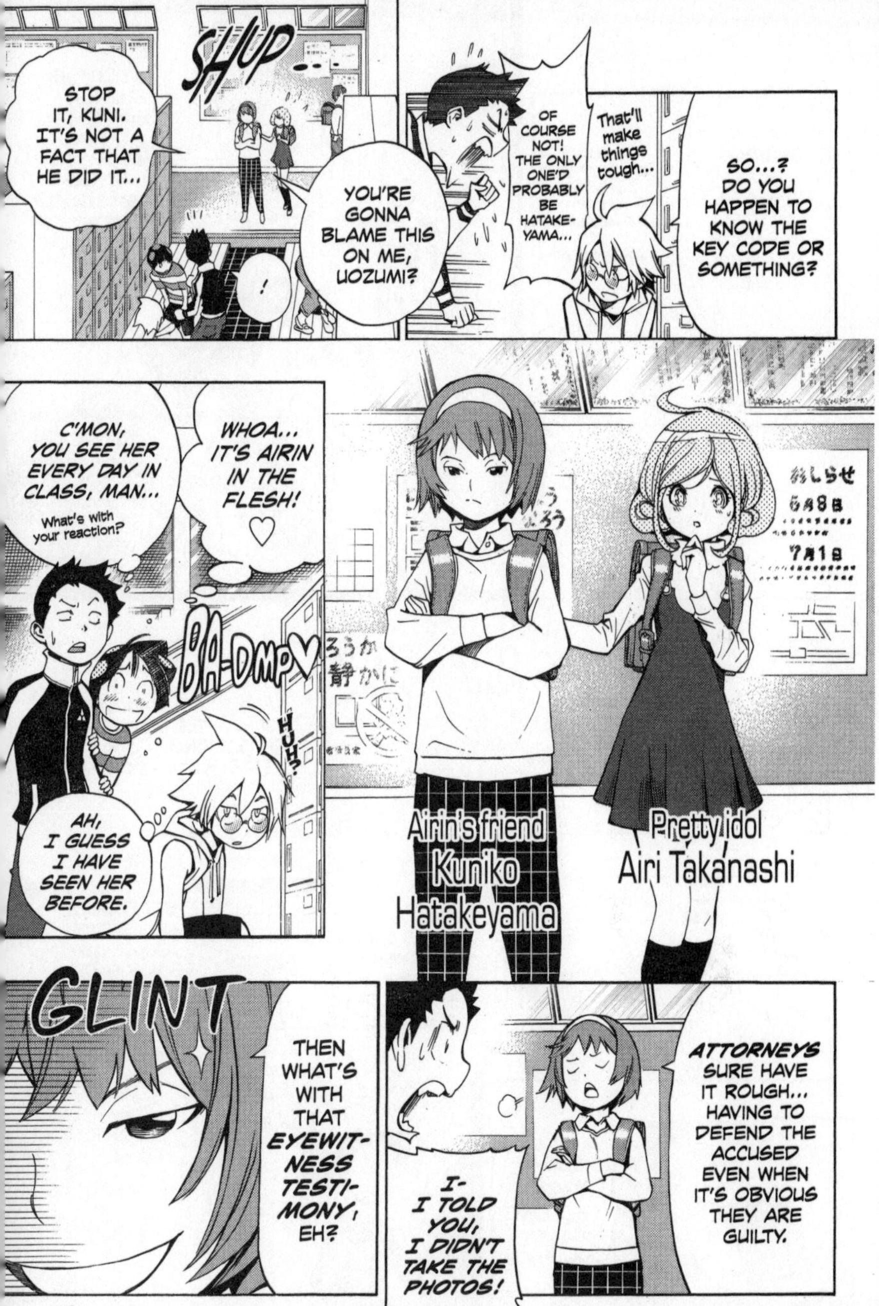
SO...? DO YOU HAPPEN TO KNOW THE KEY CODE OR SOMETHING?
That'll make things tough...
OF COURSE NOT! THE ONLY ONE'D PROBABLY BE HATAKEYAMA...
YOU'RE GONNA BLAME THIS ON ME, UOZUMI?
SHUP
!
STOP IT, KUNI. IT'S NOT A FACT THAT HE DID IT...
おしらせ
ろうか 静かに
Pretty idol Airi Takanashi
Airin's friend Kuniko Hatakeyama
WHOA... IT'S AIRIN IN THE FLESH! ♡
C'MON, YOU SEE HER EVERY DAY IN CLASS, MAN... What's with your reaction?
BA-DMP♥
HUH?
AH, I GUESS I HAVE SEEN HER BEFORE.
ATTORNEYS SURE HAVE IT ROUGH... HAVING TO DEFEND THE ACCUSED EVEN WHEN IT'S OBVIOUS THEY ARE GUILTY.
I- I TOLD YOU, I DIDN'T TAKE THE PHOTOS!
GLINT
THEN WHAT'S WITH THAT EYEWITNESS TESTIMONY, EH?

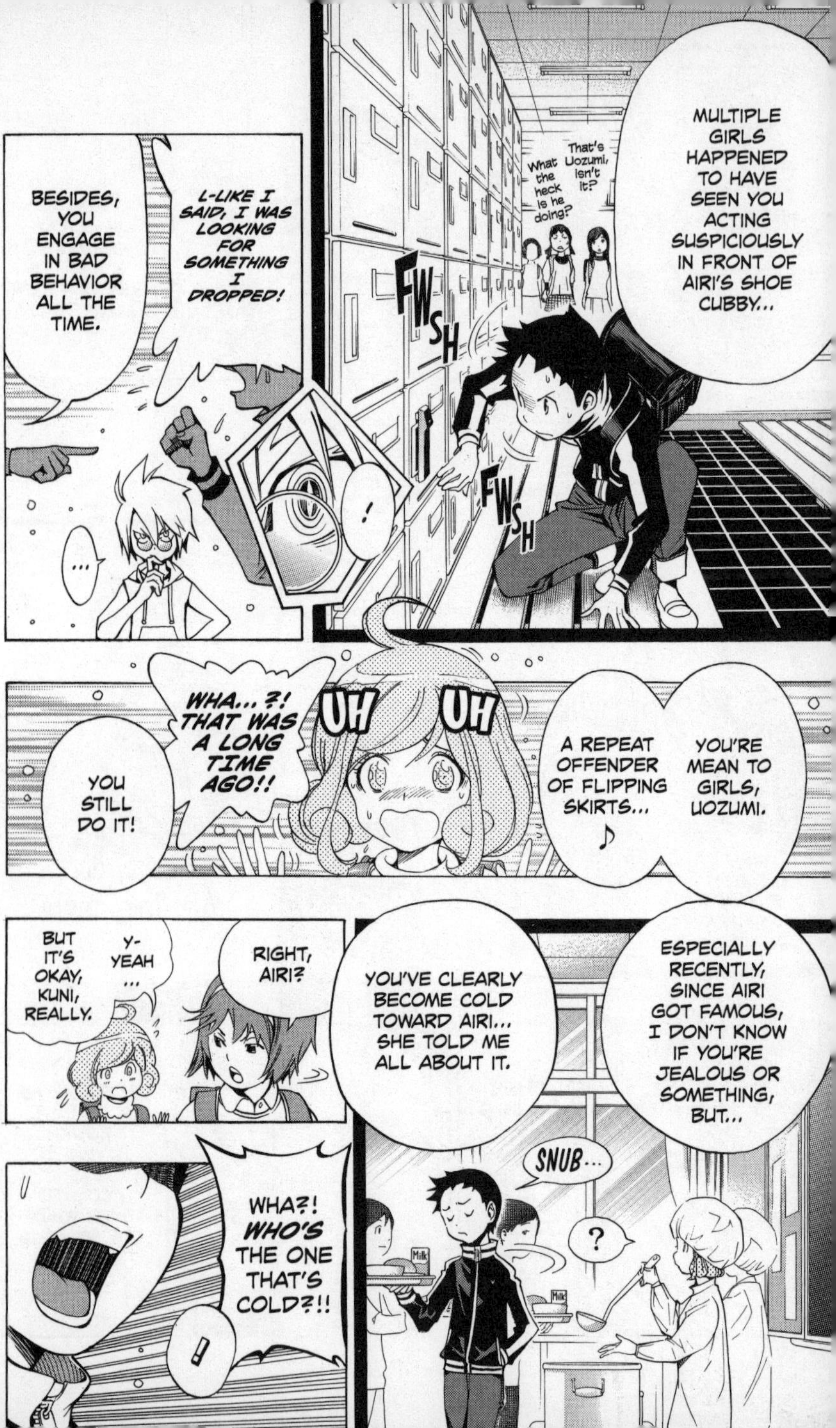
MULTIPLE GIRLS HAPPENED TO HAVE SEEN YOU ACTING SUSPICIOUSLY IN FRONT OF AIRI'S SHOE CUBBY...
That's Uozumi, isn't it?
What the heck is he doing?
FWSH
FWSH
!
L-LIKE I SAID, I WAS LOOKING FOR SOMETHING I DROPPED!
BESIDES, YOU ENGAGE IN BAD BEHAVIOR ALL THE TIME.
...
YOU'RE MEAN TO GIRLS, UOZUMI.
A REPEAT OFFENDER OF FLIPPING SKIRTS... ♪
UH UH
WHA...?! THAT WAS A LONG TIME AGO!!
YOU STILL DO IT!
ESPECIALLY RECENTLY, SINCE AIRI GOT FAMOUS, I DON'T KNOW IF YOU'RE JEALOUS OR SOMETHING, BUT...
YOU'VE CLEARLY BECOME COLD TOWARD AIRI... SHE TOLD ME ALL ABOUT IT.
SNUB...
?
Milk
Milk
RIGHT, AIRI?
Y-YEAH...
BUT IT'S OKAY, KUNI, REALLY.
WHA?! WHO'S THE ONE THAT'S COLD?!!
!

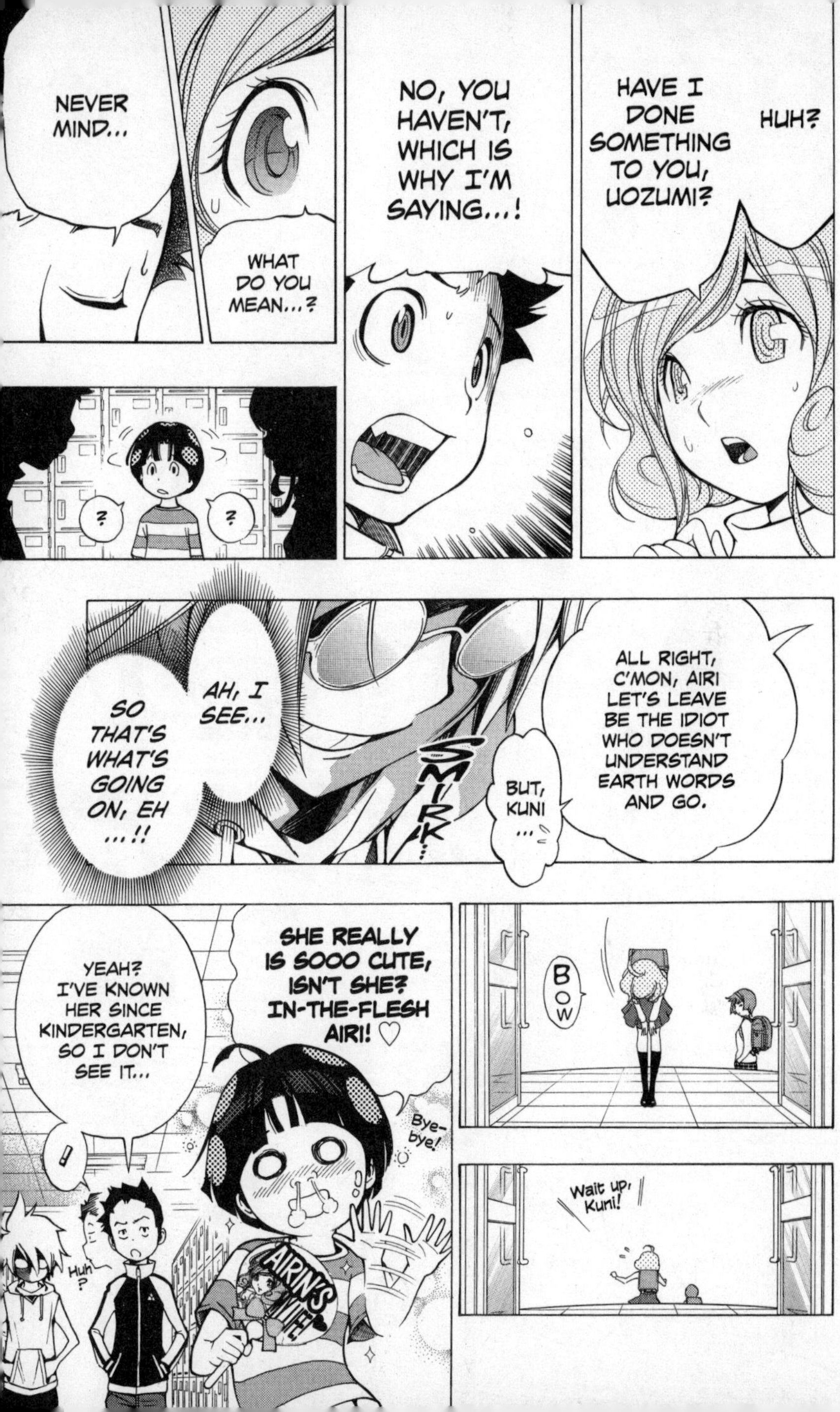
HUH?
HAVE I DONE SOMETHING TO YOU, UOZUMI?
NO, YOU HAVEN'T, WHICH IS WHY I'M SAYING...!
WHAT DO YOU MEAN...?
NEVER MIND...
?
?
ALL RIGHT, C'MON, AIRI LET'S LEAVE BE THE IDIOT WHO DOESN'T UNDERSTAND EARTH WORDS AND GO.
BUT, KUNI ...
SMIRK...
AH, I SEE...
SO THAT'S WHAT'S GOING ON, EH ...!!
BOW
Wait up, Kuni!
Bye-bye!
SHE REALLY IS SOOO CUTE, ISN'T SHE? IN-THE-FLESH AIRI! ♡
YEAH? I'VE KNOWN HER SINCE KINDERGARTEN, SO I DON'T SEE IT...
!
Huh?
AIRIN'S

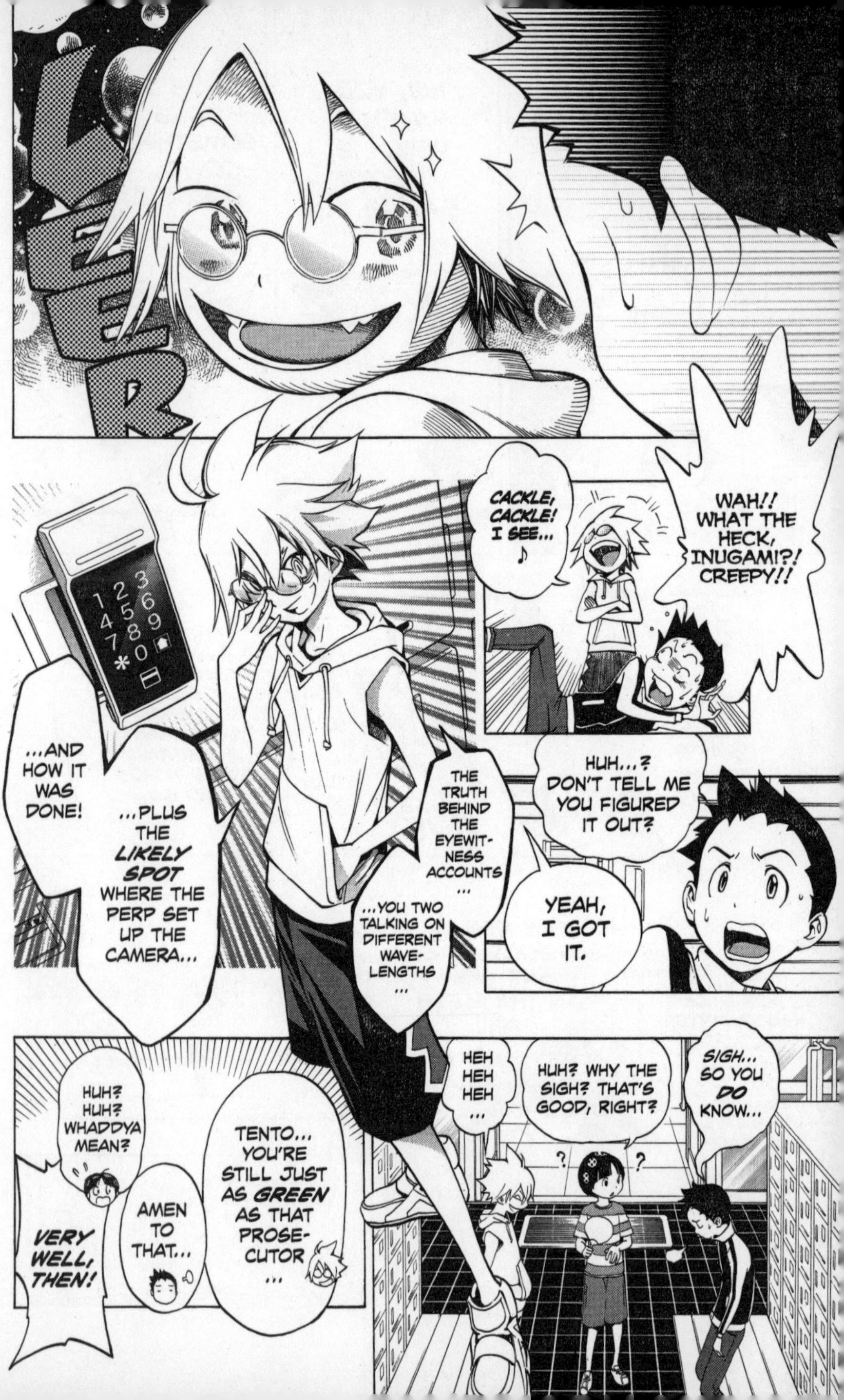
LEER
CACKLE, CACKLE! I SEE... ♪
WAH!! WHAT THE HECK, INUGAMI?! CREEPY!!
HUH...? DON'T TELL ME YOU FIGURED IT OUT?
YEAH, I GOT IT.
THE TRUTH BEHIND THE EYEWITNESS ACCOUNTS...
...YOU TWO TALKING ON DIFFERENT WAVELENGTHS...
...PLUS THE LIKELY SPOT WHERE THE PERP SET UP THE CAMERA...
...AND HOW IT WAS DONE!
SIGH... SO YOU DO KNOW...
HUH? WHY THE SIGH? THAT'S GOOD, RIGHT?
HEH HEH HEH...
TENTO... YOU'RE STILL JUST AS GREEN AS THAT PROSECUTOR...
AMEN TO THAT...
HUH? HUH? WHADDYA MEAN?
VERY WELL, THEN!

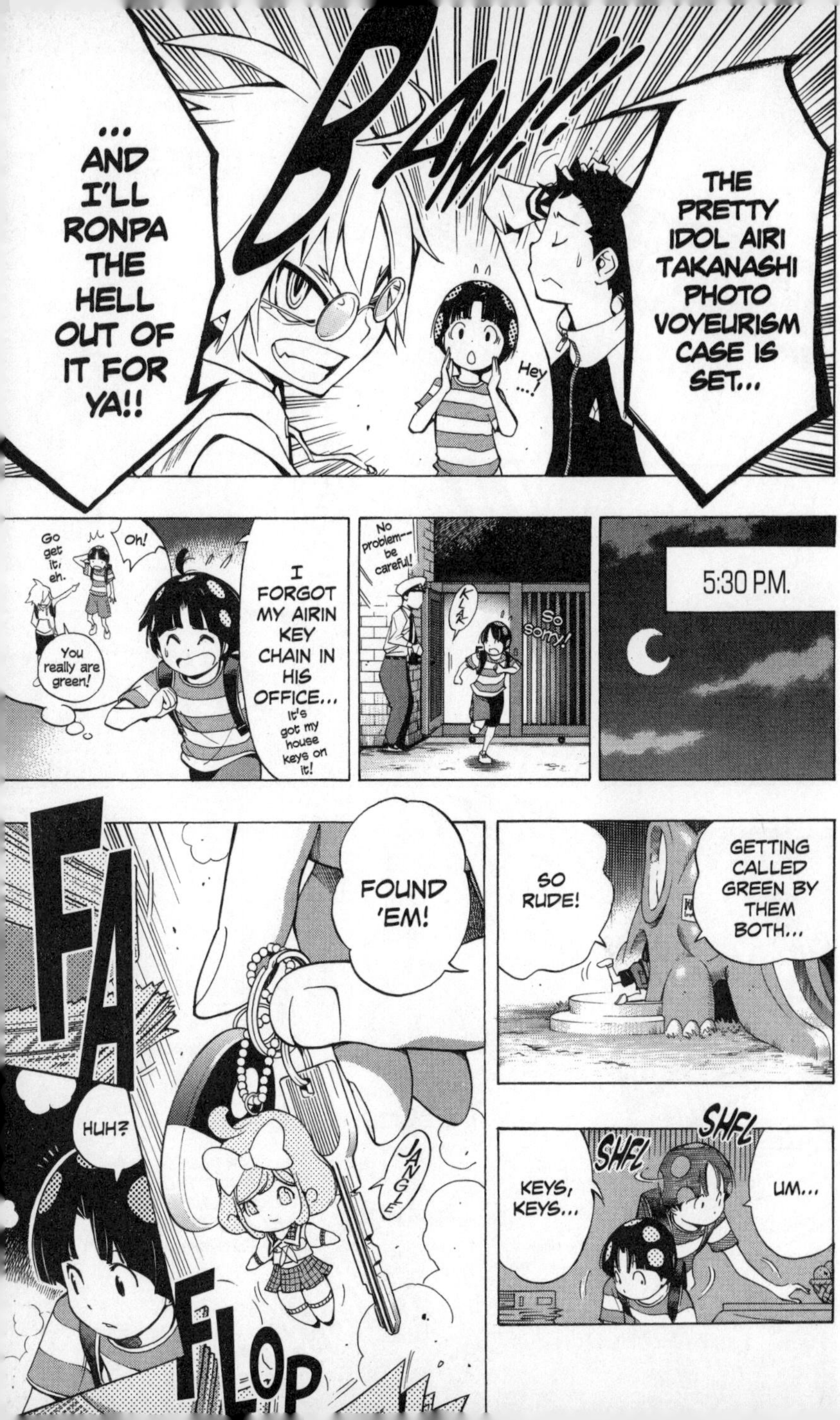
THE PRETTY IDOL AIRI TAKANASHI PHOTO VOYEURISM CASE IS SET...
BAM!!
Hey...!
... AND I'LL RONPA THE HELL OUT OF IT FOR YA!!
5:30 P.M.
No problem--be careful!
KLAK
So sorry!
I FORGOT MY AIRIN KEY CHAIN IN HIS OFFICE...
It's got my house keys on it!
Oh!
Go get it, eh.
You really are green!
GETTING CALLED GREEN BY THEM BOTH...
SO RUDE!
UM...
SHFL
SHFL
KEYS, KEYS...
FOUND 'EM!
JANGLE
FA
HUH?
FLOP

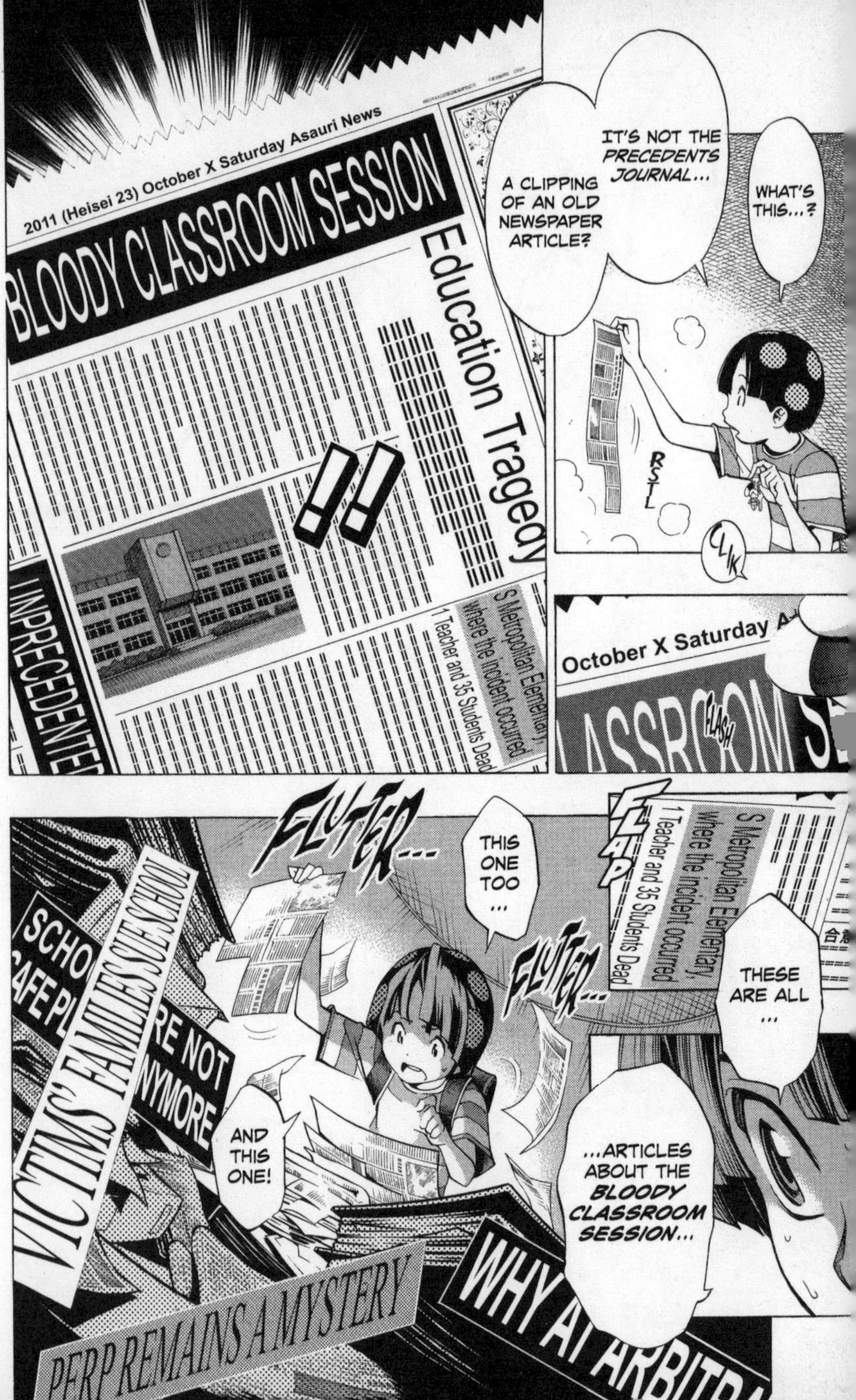
WHAT'S THIS...?
IT'S NOT THE PRECEDENTS JOURNAL...
A CLIPPING OF AN OLD NEWSPAPER ARTICLE?
RSTL
CLIK
October X Saturday A
ASSROOM S
FLASH
2011 (Heisei 23) October X Saturday Asauri News
BLOODY CLASSROOM SESSION
Education Tragedy
!!
S Metropolitan Elementary, where the incident occurred
1 Teacher and 35 Students Dead
UNPRECEDENTE
FLAP
S Metropolitan Elementary, where the incident occurred
1 Teacher and 35 Students Dead
THESE ARE ALL...
...ARTICLES ABOUT THE BLOODY CLASSROOM SESSION...
FLUTTER...
THIS ONE TOO...
FLUTTER...
AND THIS ONE!
SCHO
SAFE PL
RE NOT
NYMORE
VICTIMS' FAMILIES SUE SCHOOL
PERP REMAINS A MYSTERY
WHY AT ARBITRA

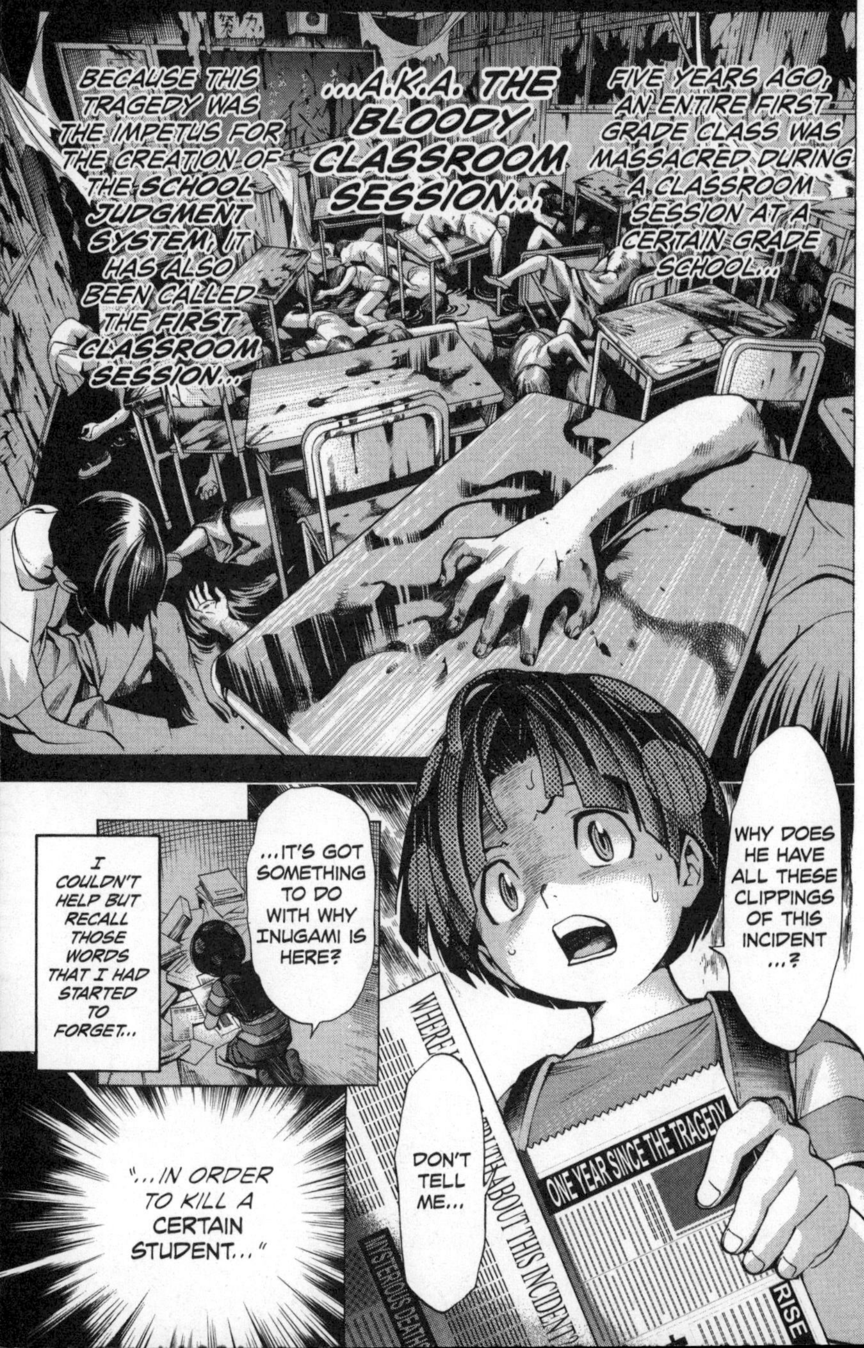
FIVE YEARS AGO, AN ENTIRE FIRST GRADE CLASS WAS MASSACRED DURING A CLASSROOM SESSION AT A CERTAIN GRADE SCHOOL...
...A.K.A. THE BLOODY CLASSROOM SESSION...
BECAUSE THIS TRAGEDY WAS THE IMPETUS FOR THE CREATION OF THE SCHOOL JUDGMENT SYSTEM, IT HAS ALSO BEEN CALLED THE FIRST CLASSROOM SESSION...
WHY DOES HE HAVE ALL THESE CLIPPINGS OF THIS INCIDENT ...?
...IT'S GOT SOMETHING TO DO WITH WHY INUGAMI IS HERE?
I COULDN'T HELP BUT RECALL THOSE WORDS THAT I HAD STARTED TO FORGET...
ONE YEAR SINCE THE TRAGEDY
ABOUT THIS INCIDENT
DON'T TELL ME...
"...IN ORDER TO KILL A CERTAIN STUDENT..."

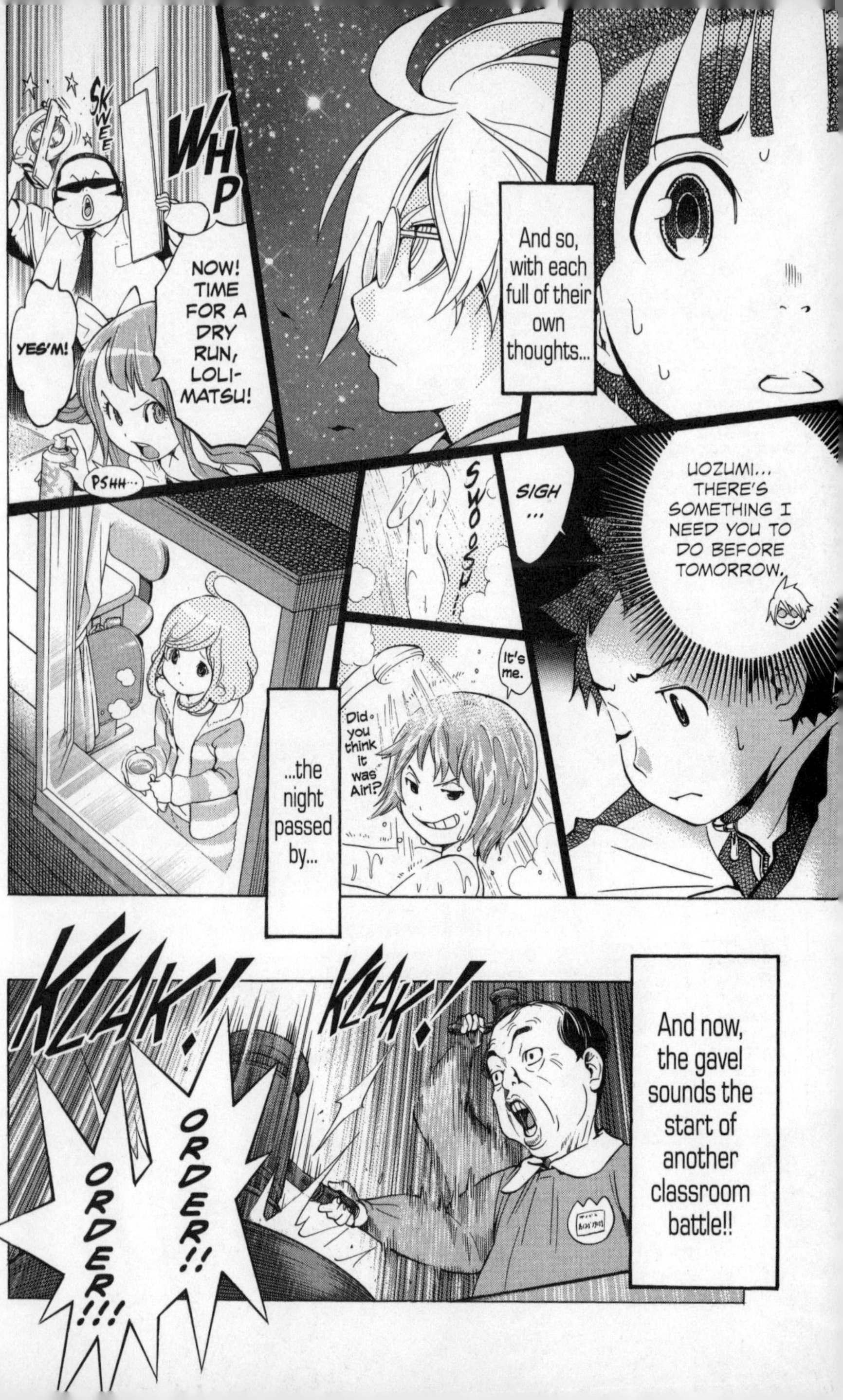
And so, with each full of their own thoughts...
SKWEEE
WHP
NOW! TIME FOR A DRY RUN, LOLI-MATSU!
YES'M!
PSHH...
UOZUMI... THERE'S SOMETHING I NEED YOU TO DO BEFORE TOMORROW.
SIGH...
SWOOSH!!
It's me.
Did you think it was Airi?
...the night passed by...
And now, the gavel sounds the start of another classroom battle!!
KLAK!
KLAK!
ORDER!!
ORDER!!!

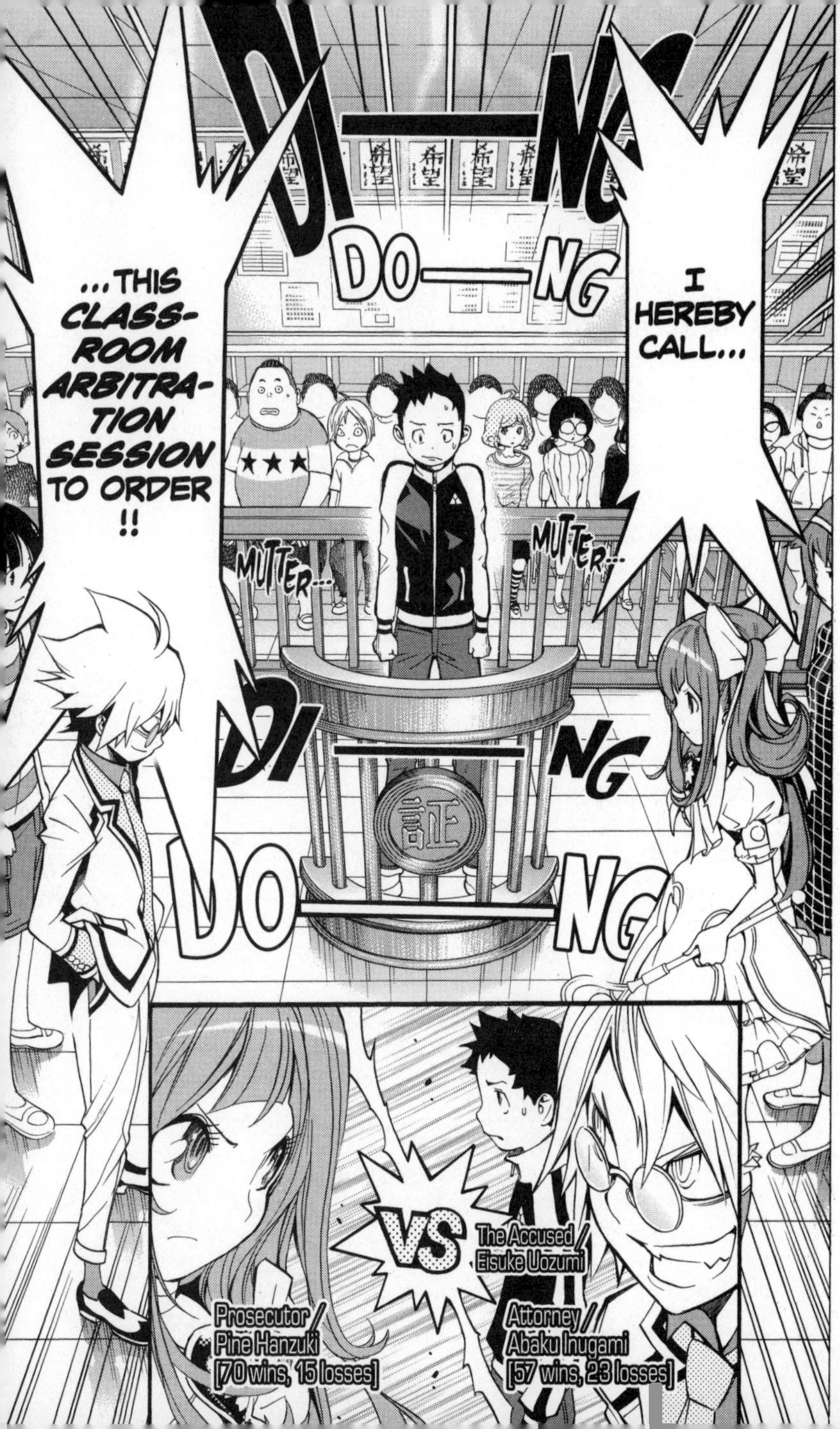
DI—NG
DO—NG
I HEREBY CALL...
...THIS CLASSROOM ARBITRATION SESSION TO ORDER!!
MUTTER...
MUTTER...
DI—NG
DO—NG
The Accused / Eisuke Uozumi
Attorney / Abaku Inugami [57 wins, 23 losses]
VS
Prosecutor / Pine Hanzuki [70 wins, 15 losses]

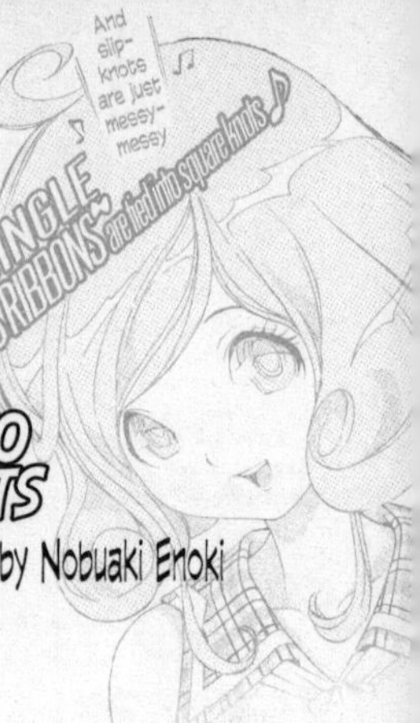
And slip-knots are just messy-messy
1st SINGLE
AIRI'S RIBBONS are tied into square knots

AIRI'S RIBBONS ARE TIED INTO SQUARE KNOTS

Lyrics & Music by Nobuaki Enoki

(Hug Hug Hug ♡ Hug Hug ♡ Hug Hug Hug Yeah) x 2

(Verse A)

Twilight street corner   Fake tears and gloom
"Why in the world are boys always so mean...?"
At the park after school   There was a shadow waiting
"Sorry," a sudden teary admission   I hate his honesty

(Verse B)

"He loves me," "he loves me not," "he loves me..."
Shall I entrust my feelings to flower petals?
Or should I not?   Endless soliloquy   Can't even ask Mommy
-- 'Cuz it's my first DOKI DOKI experience -- ...

(Chorus)

No, no, no, don't tie bowknots
And slipknots are just messy-messy
No, I tie it tight   Don't show it to anyone
My heart is tied into a square knot

(Verse C)

But now, he's about to undo it   See through and uncover
My hidden heart
Block it quietly   Don't tell anyone, darling
-- 'Cuz it's my DOKI DOKI experience -- ...

(Chorus)

No, no, no, don't tie bowknots
And slip knots are just messy-messy
Stored away forever   I shan't give it to anyone
My heart is tied into a square knot
He's tied it into a square knot

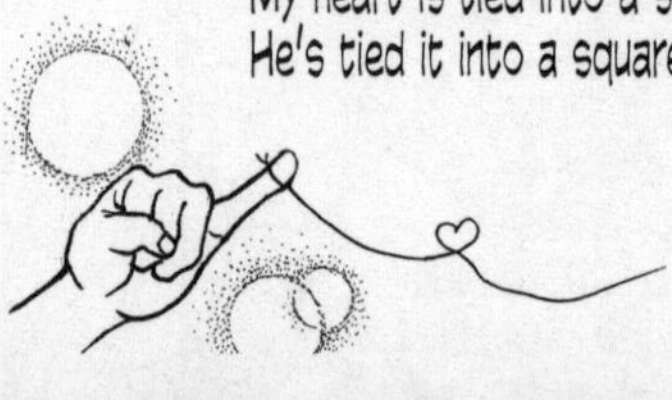

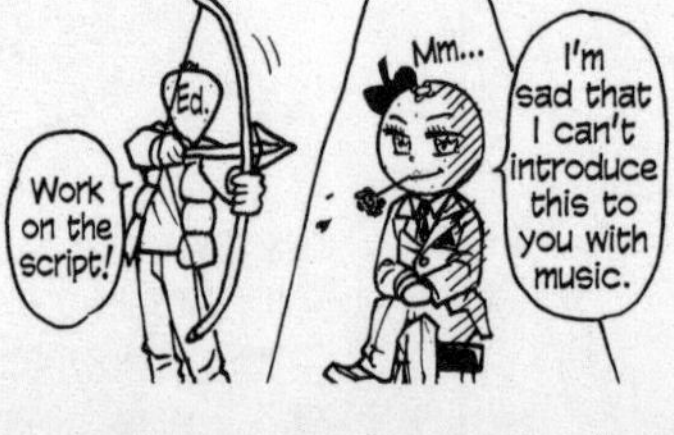
Mm...
I'm sad that I can't introduce this to you with music.
Ed.
Work on the script!

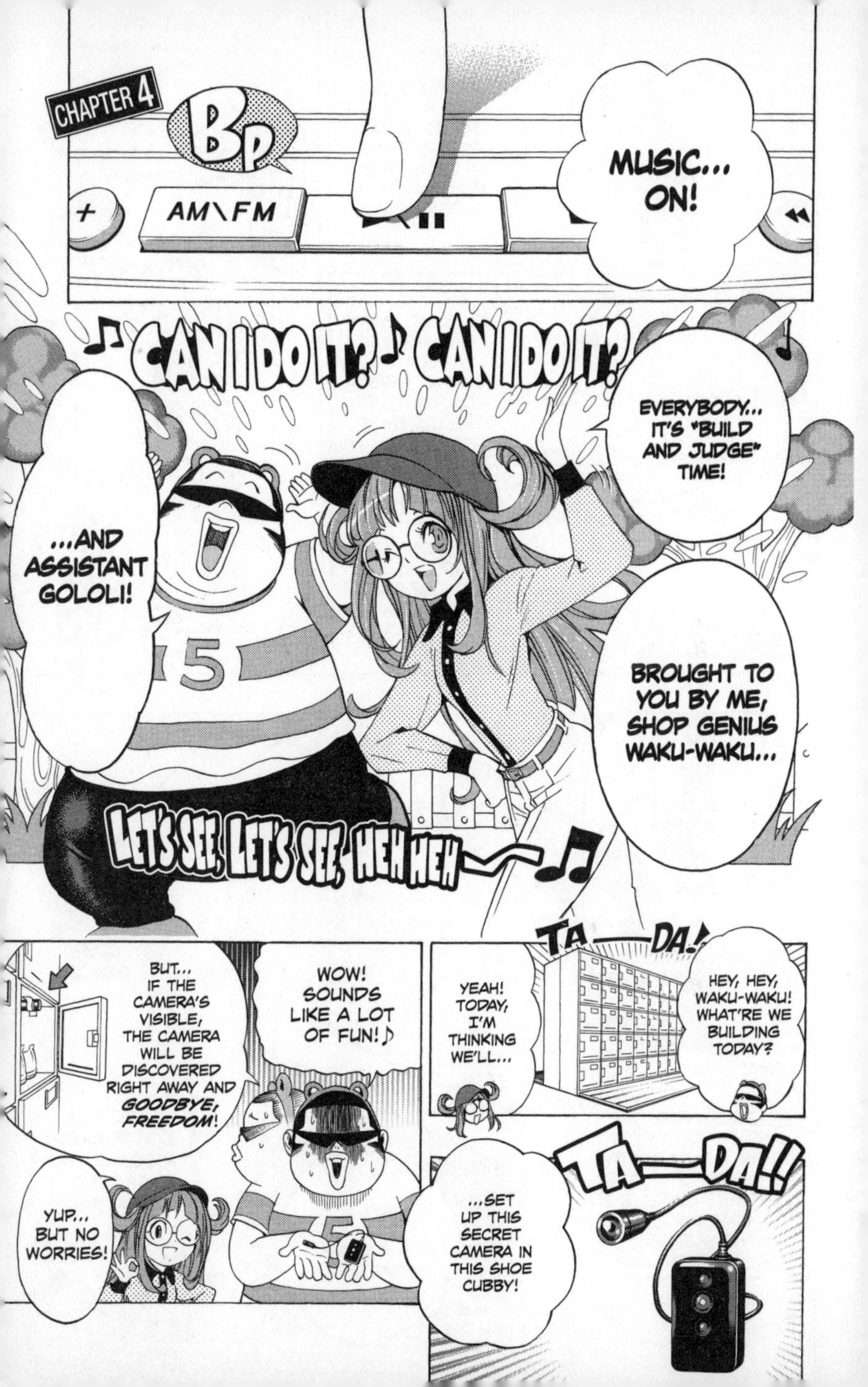
CHAPTER 4
MUSIC... ON!
Bp
AM\FM
♪ CAN I DO IT? ♪ CAN I DO IT? ♪
EVERYBODY... IT'S "BUILD AND JUDGE" TIME!
BROUGHT TO YOU BY ME, SHOP GENIUS WAKU-WAKU...
...AND ASSISTANT GOLOLI!
LET'S SEE, LET'S SEE, HEH HEH~♪
TA—DA!
HEY, HEY, WAKU-WAKU! WHAT'RE WE BUILDING TODAY?
YEAH! TODAY, I'M THINKING WE'LL...
TA—DA!!
...SET UP THIS SECRET CAMERA IN THIS SHOE CUBBY!
WOW! SOUNDS LIKE A LOT OF FUN!♪
BUT... IF THE CAMERA'S VISIBLE, THE CAMERA WILL BE DISCOVERED RIGHT AWAY AND *GOODBYE, FREEDOM*!
YUP... BUT NO WORRIES!

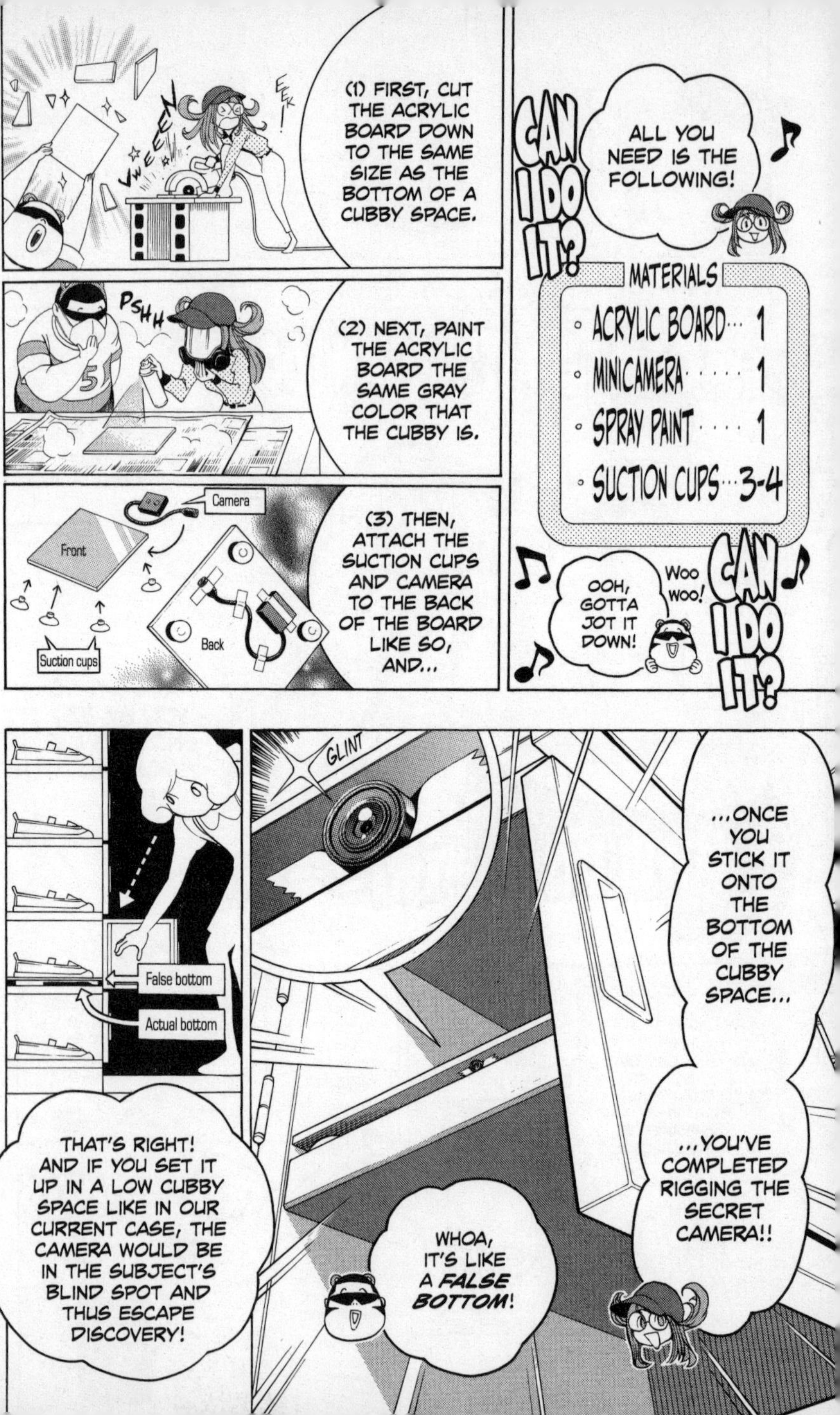
CAN I DO IT?
ALL YOU NEED IS THE FOLLOWING!
MATERIALS
ACRYLIC BOARD··· 1
MINICAMERA······ 1
SPRAY PAINT····· 1
SUCTION CUPS···3-4
OOH, GOTTA JOT IT DOWN!
Woo woo!
CAN I DO IT?
(1) FIRST, CUT THE ACRYLIC BOARD DOWN TO THE SAME SIZE AS THE BOTTOM OF A CUBBY SPACE.
EEK!
VWEEEN
(2) NEXT, PAINT THE ACRYLIC BOARD THE SAME GRAY COLOR THAT THE CUBBY IS.
PSHH
(3) THEN, ATTACH THE SUCTION CUPS AND CAMERA TO THE BACK OF THE BOARD LIKE SO, AND...
Camera
Front
Back
Suction cups
...ONCE YOU STICK IT ONTO THE BOTTOM OF THE CUBBY SPACE...
GLINT
...YOU'VE COMPLETED RIGGING THE SECRET CAMERA!!
WHOA, IT'S LIKE A *FALSE BOTTOM*!
False bottom
Actual bottom
THAT'S RIGHT! AND IF YOU SET IT UP IN A LOW CUBBY SPACE LIKE IN OUR CURRENT CASE, THE CAMERA WOULD BE IN THE SUBJECT'S BLIND SPOT AND THUS ESCAPE DISCOVERY!

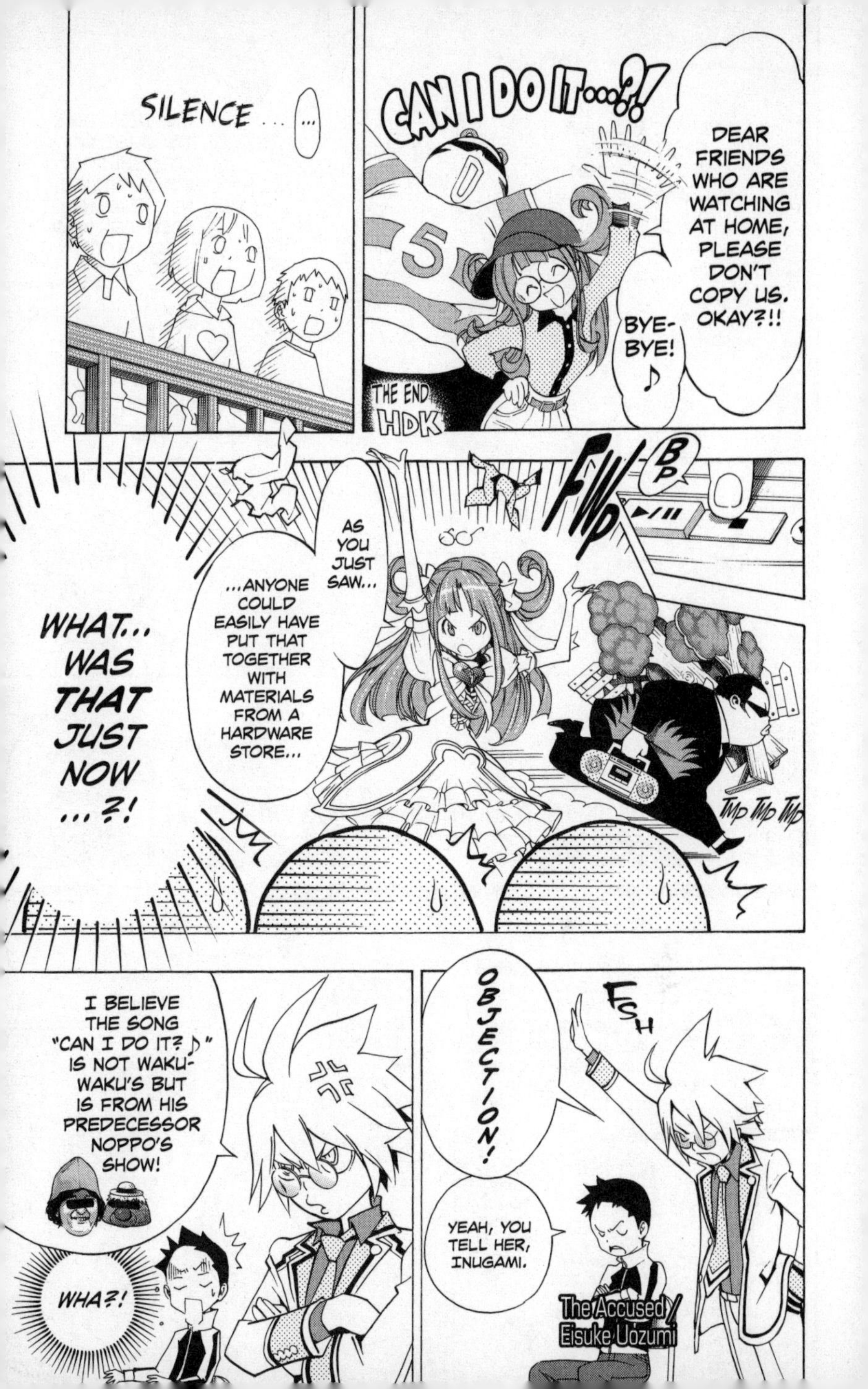
CAN I DO IT...?!
DEAR FRIENDS WHO ARE WATCHING AT HOME, PLEASE DON'T COPY US. OKAY?!!
BYE-BYE! ♪
THE END
HDK
SILENCE...
...
BP
FWP
AS YOU JUST SAW...
...ANYONE COULD EASILY HAVE PUT THAT TOGETHER WITH MATERIALS FROM A HARDWARE STORE...
TMP TMP TMP
WHAT... WAS THAT JUST NOW...?!
FSH
OBJECTION!
YEAH, YOU TELL HER, INUGAMI.
The Accused / Eisuke Uozumi
I BELIEVE THE SONG "CAN I DO IT?♪" IS NOT WAKU-WAKU'S BUT IS FROM HIS PREDECESSOR NOPPO'S SHOW!
WHA?!

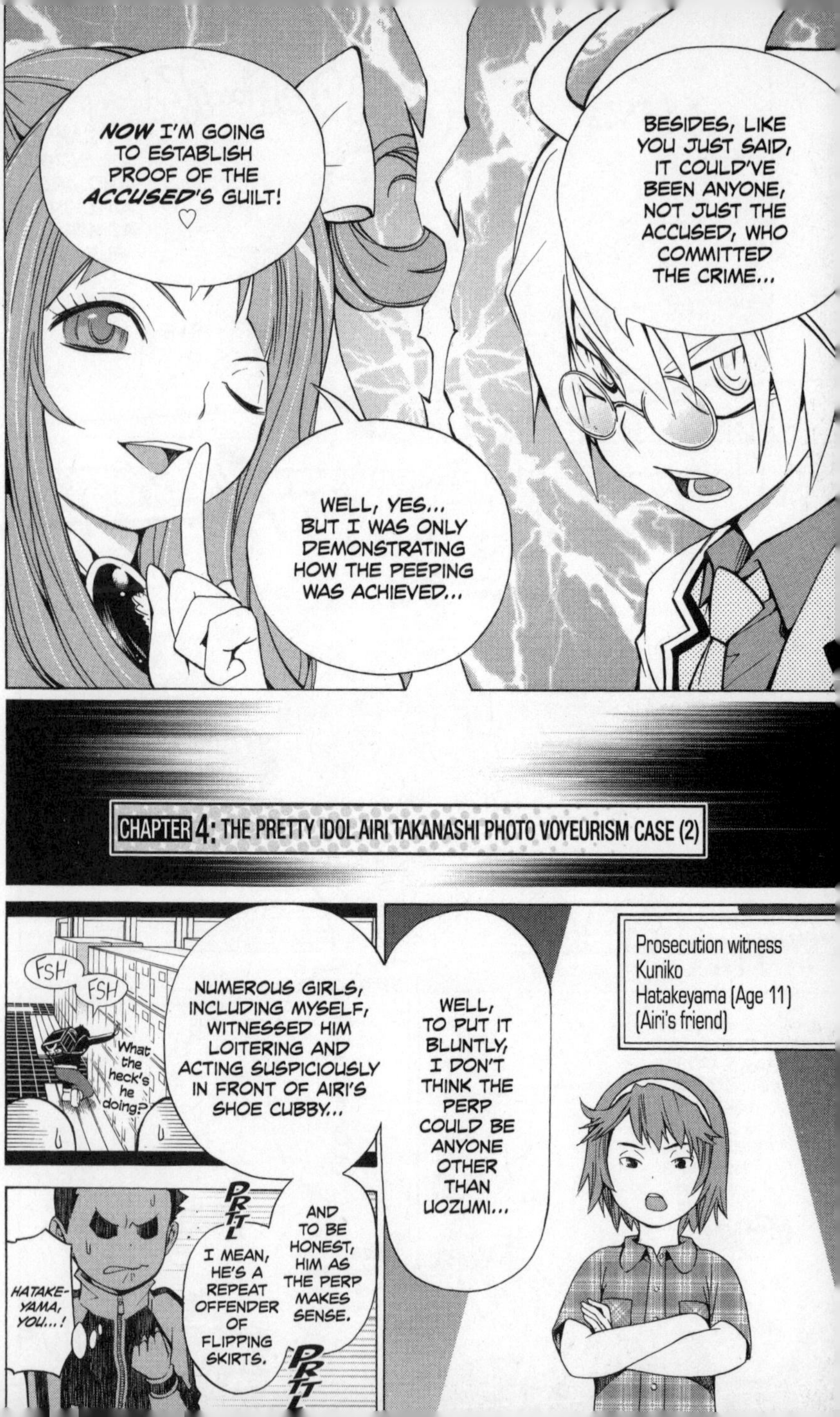
BESIDES, LIKE YOU JUST SAID, IT COULD'VE BEEN ANYONE, NOT JUST THE ACCUSED, WHO COMMITTED THE CRIME...
NOW I'M GOING TO ESTABLISH PROOF OF THE *ACCUSED*'S GUILT! ♡
WELL, YES... BUT I WAS ONLY DEMONSTRATING HOW THE PEEPING WAS ACHIEVED...
CHAPTER 4: THE PRETTY IDOL AIRI TAKANASHI PHOTO VOYEURISM CASE (2)
Prosecution witness Kuniko Hatakeyama (Age 11) (Airi's friend)
WELL, TO PUT IT BLUNTLY, I DON'T THINK THE PERP COULD BE ANYONE OTHER THAN UOZUMI...
NUMEROUS GIRLS, INCLUDING MYSELF, WITNESSED HIM LOITERING AND ACTING SUSPICIOUSLY IN FRONT OF AIRI'S SHOE CUBBY...
FSH
FSH
What the heck's he doing?
AND TO BE HONEST, HIM AS THE PERP MAKES SENSE.
I MEAN, HE'S A REPEAT OFFENDER OF FLIPPING SKIRTS.
PRTTL
PRTTL
HATAKE-YAMA, YOU...!

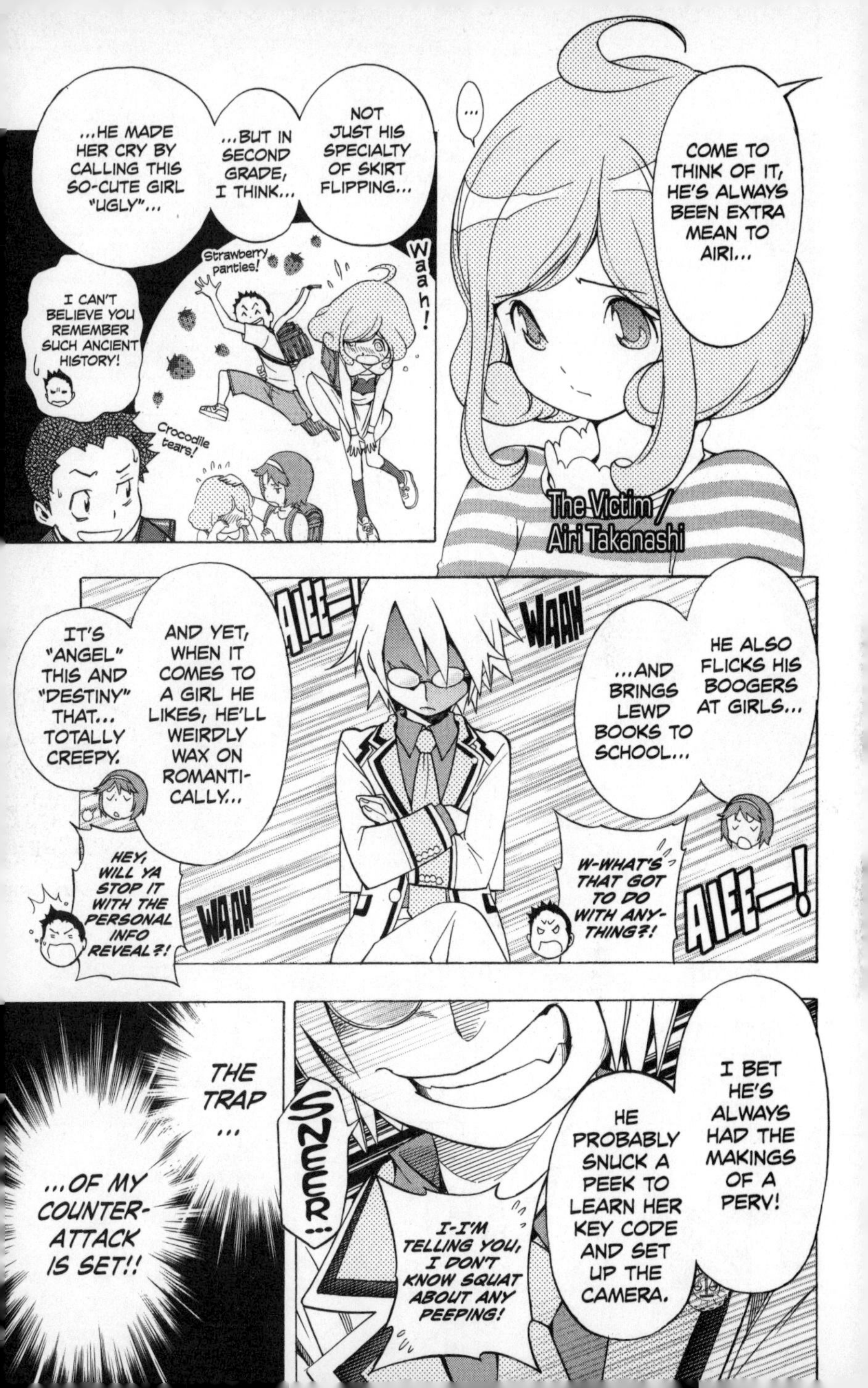
...
COME TO THINK OF IT, HE'S ALWAYS BEEN EXTRA MEAN TO AIRI...
The Victim / Airi Takanashi
NOT JUST HIS SPECIALTY OF SKIRT FLIPPING...
...BUT IN SECOND GRADE, I THINK...
...HE MADE HER CRY BY CALLING THIS SO-CUTE GIRL "UGLY"...
Waah!
Strawberry panties!
Crocodile tears!
I CAN'T BELIEVE YOU REMEMBER SUCH ANCIENT HISTORY!
HE ALSO FLICKS HIS BOOGERS AT GIRLS...
...AND BRINGS LEWD BOOKS TO SCHOOL...
AIEE—!
WAAH
W-WHAT'S THAT GOT TO DO WITH ANYTHING?!
AIEE—!
AND YET, WHEN IT COMES TO A GIRL HE LIKES, HE'LL WEIRDLY WAX ON ROMANTICALLY...
IT'S "ANGEL" THIS AND "DESTINY" THAT... TOTALLY CREEPY.
WAAH
HEY, WILL YA STOP IT WITH THE PERSONAL INFO REVEAL?!
I BET HE'S ALWAYS HAD THE MAKINGS OF A PERV!
HE PROBABLY SNUCK A PEEK TO LEARN HER KEY CODE AND SET UP THE CAMERA.
I-I'M TELLING YOU, I DON'T KNOW SQUAT ABOUT ANY PEEPING!
SNEER!!
THE TRAP...
...OF MY COUNTER-ATTACK IS SET!!

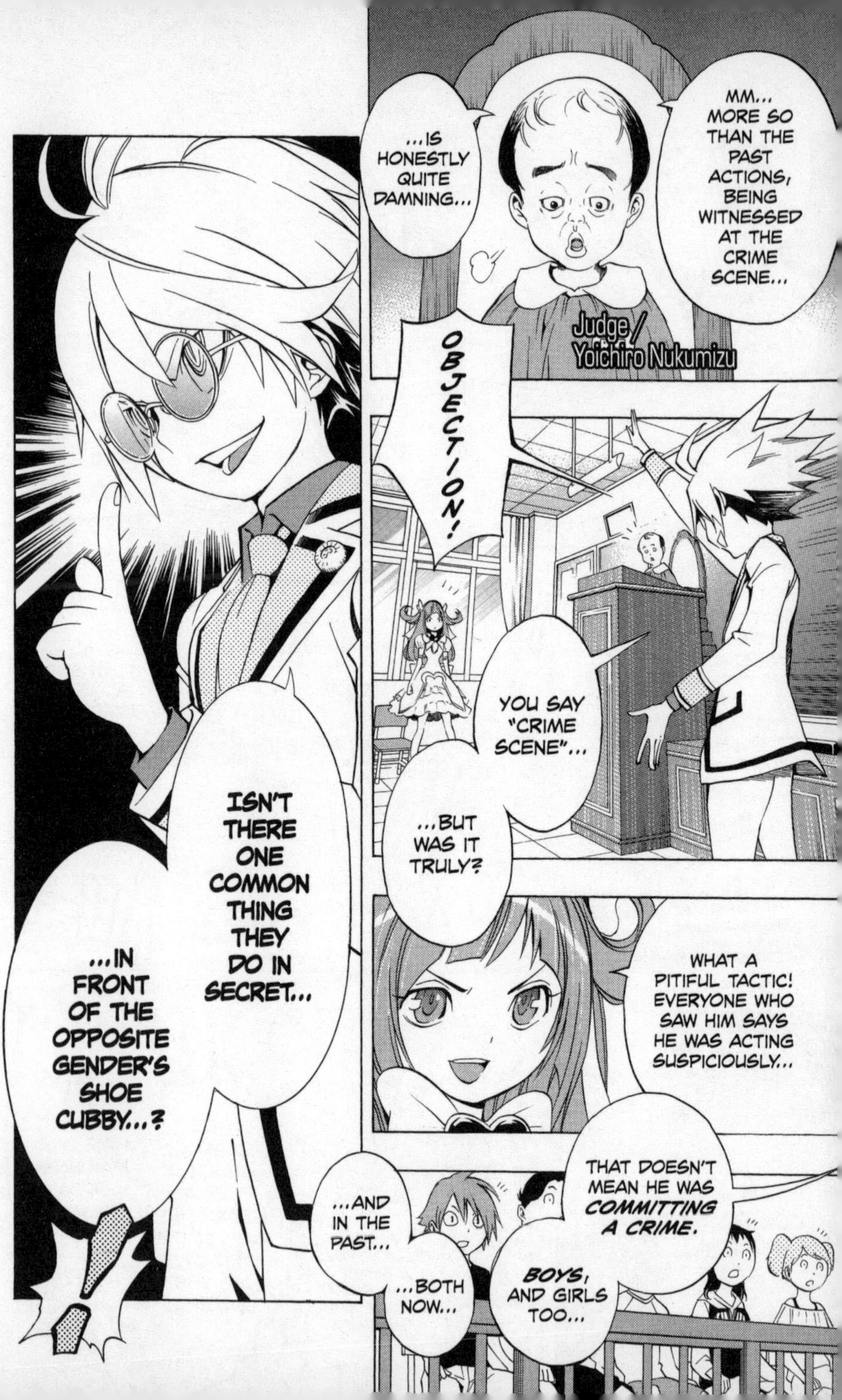
MM... MORE SO THAN THE PAST ACTIONS, BEING WITNESSED AT THE CRIME SCENE...
...IS HONESTLY QUITE DAMNING...
Judge / Yoichiro Nukumizu
OBJECTION!
YOU SAY "CRIME SCENE"...
...BUT WAS IT TRULY?
WHAT A PITIFUL TACTIC! EVERYONE WHO SAW HIM SAYS HE WAS ACTING SUSPICIOUSLY...
THAT DOESN'T MEAN HE WAS *COMMITTING A CRIME.*
BOYS, AND GIRLS TOO...
...BOTH NOW...
...AND IN THE PAST...
ISN'T THERE ONE COMMON THING THEY DO IN SECRET...
...IN FRONT OF THE OPPOSITE GENDER'S SHOE CUBBY...?
!

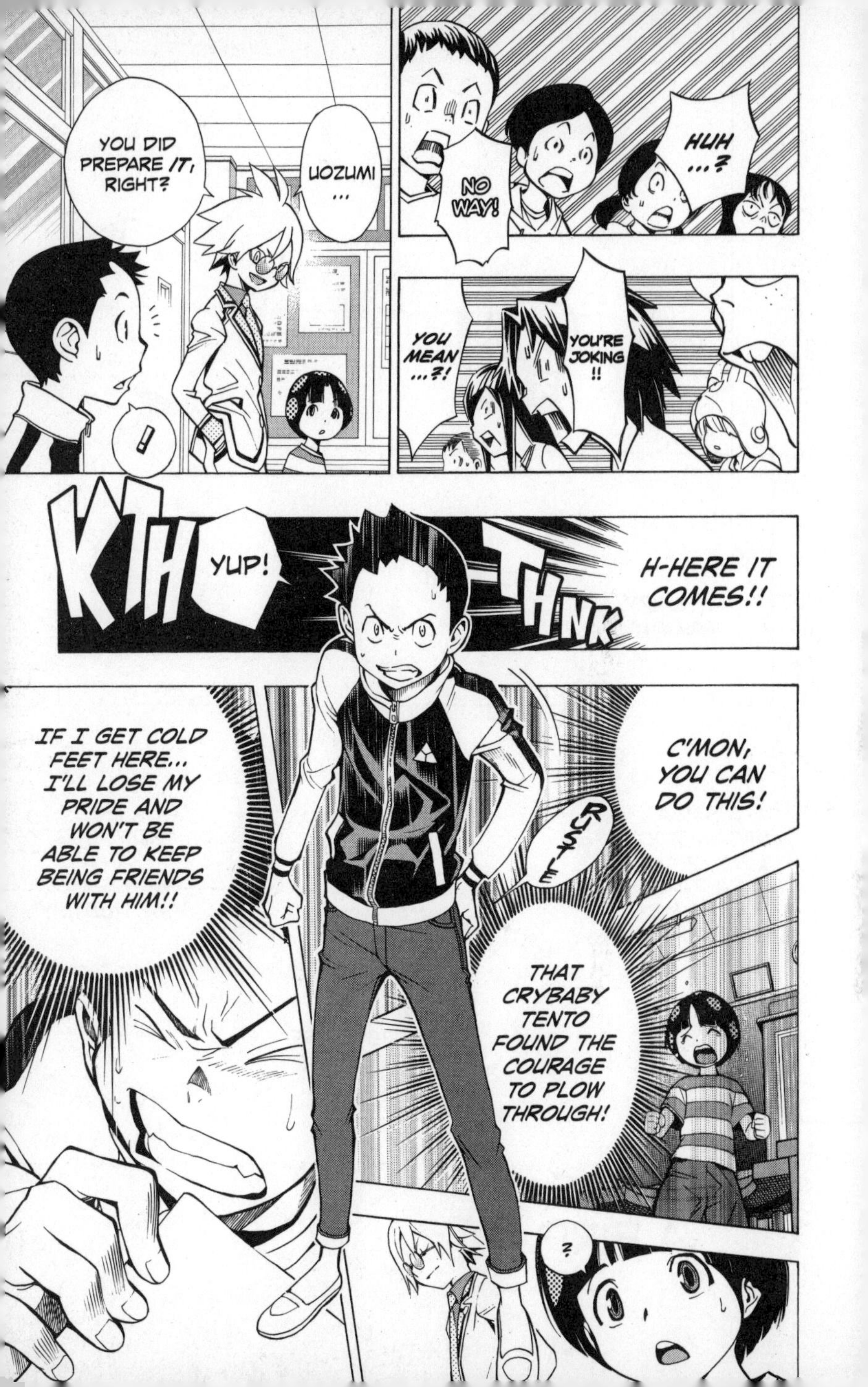
HUH ...?
NO WAY!
YOU'RE JOKING!!
YOU MEAN ...?!
UOZUMI ...
YOU DID PREPARE *IT*, RIGHT?
!
H-HERE IT COMES!!
THNK
YUP!
KTH
C'MON, YOU CAN DO THIS!
RUSTLE
IF I GET COLD FEET HERE... I'LL LOSE MY PRIDE AND WON'T BE ABLE TO KEEP BEING FRIENDS WITH HIM!!
THAT CRYBABY TENTO FOUND THE COURAGE TO PLOW THROUGH!
?

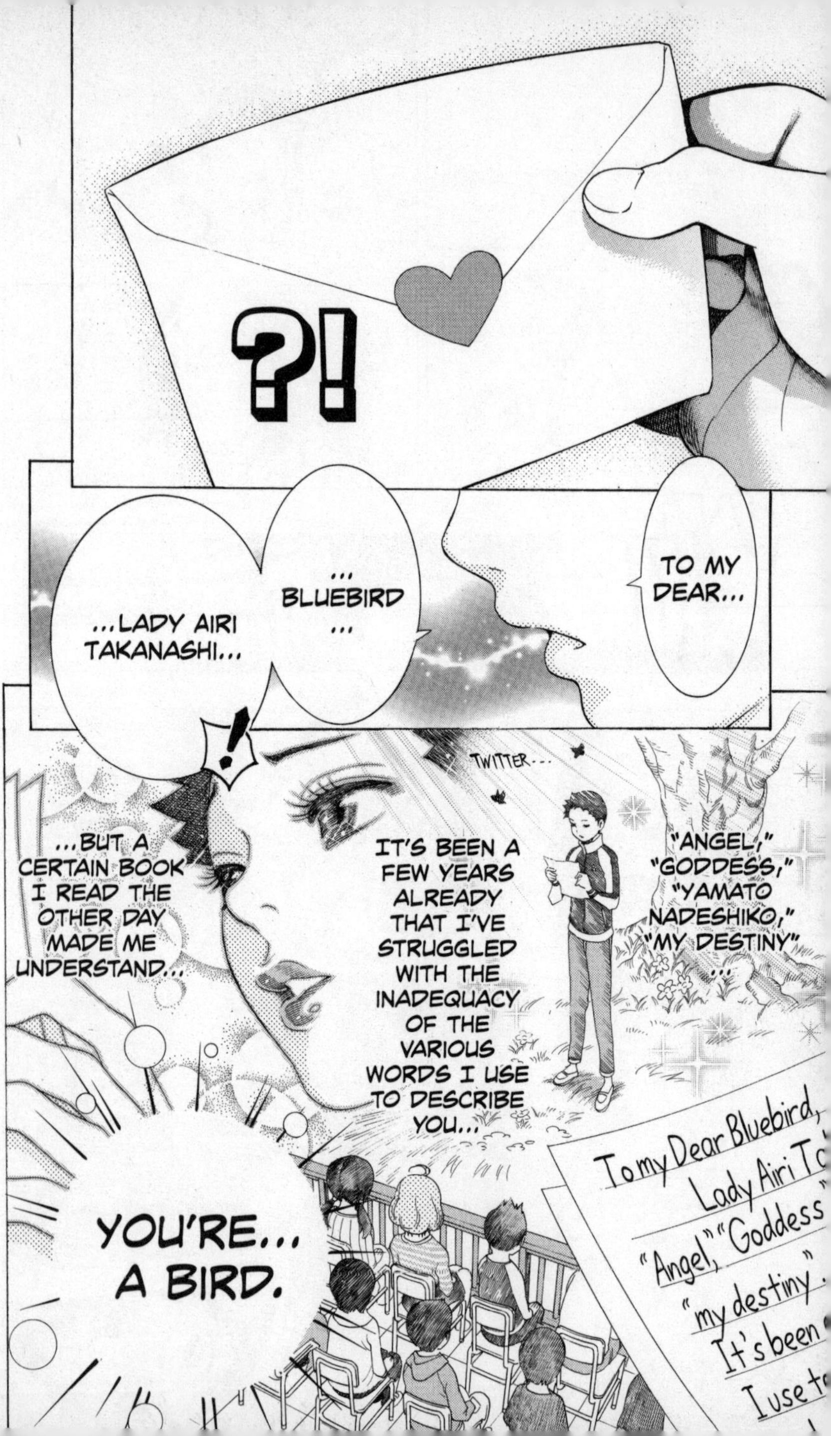
?!
TO MY DEAR...
... BLUEBIRD ...
...LADY AIRI TAKANASHI...
!
TWITTER...
"ANGEL," "GODDESS," "YAMATO NADESHIKO," "MY DESTINY"...
IT'S BEEN A FEW YEARS ALREADY THAT I'VE STRUGGLED WITH THE INADEQUACY OF THE VARIOUS WORDS I USE TO DESCRIBE YOU...
...BUT A CERTAIN BOOK I READ THE OTHER DAY MADE ME UNDERSTAND...
To my Dear Bluebird,
"Angel," "Goddess"
"my destiny."
It's been
YOU'RE... A BIRD.

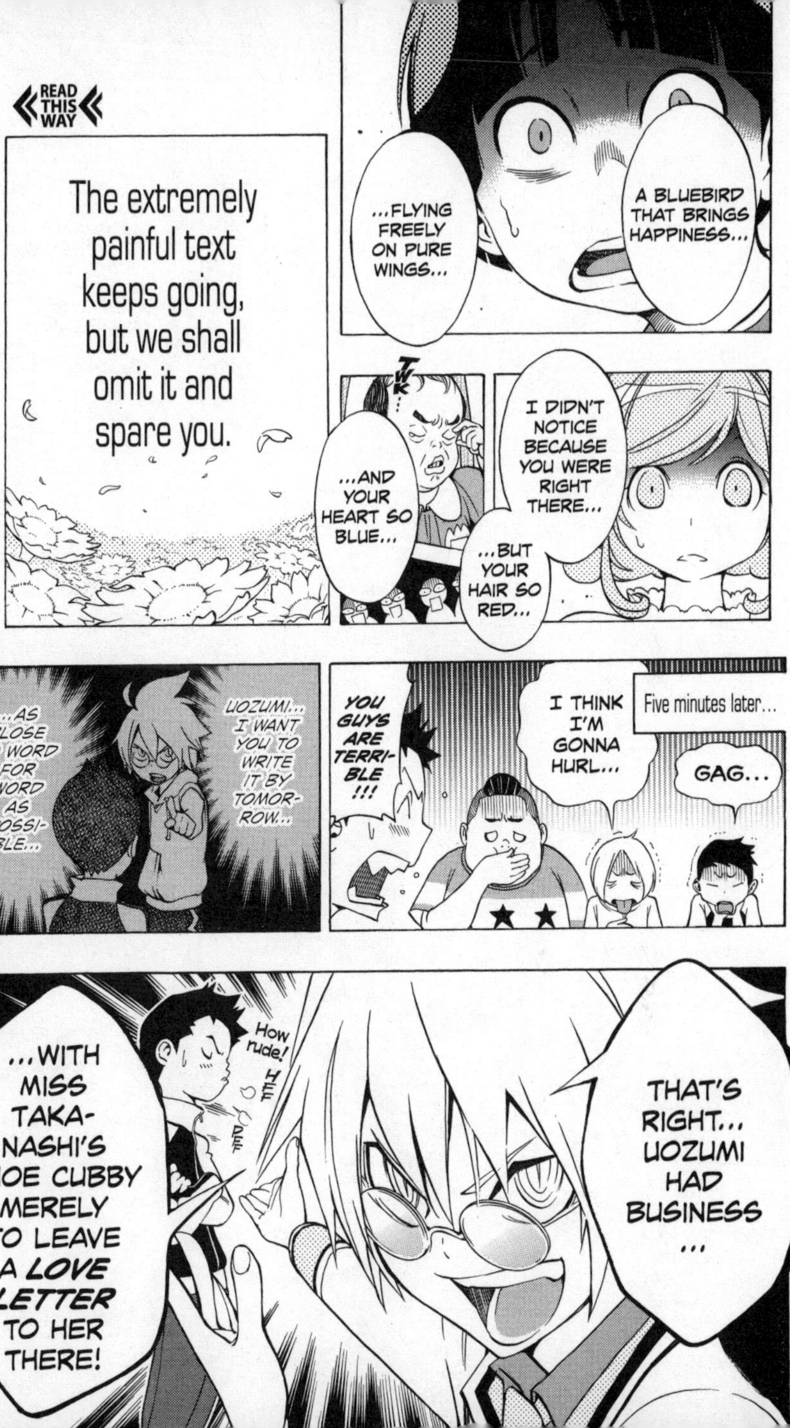
READ THIS WAY
A BLUEBIRD THAT BRINGS HAPPINESS...
...FLYING FREELY ON PURE WINGS...
I DIDN'T NOTICE BECAUSE YOU WERE RIGHT THERE...
...BUT YOUR HAIR SO RED...
TWK
...AND YOUR HEART SO BLUE...
The extremely painful text keeps going, but we shall omit it and spare you.
Five minutes later...
GAG...
I THINK I'M GONNA HURL...
YOU GUYS ARE TERRIBLE!!!
UOZUMI... I WANT YOU TO WRITE IT BY TOMORROW...
...AS CLOSE TO WORD FOR WORD AS POSSIBLE...
THAT'S RIGHT... UOZUMI HAD BUSINESS...
How rude!
...WITH MISS TAKANASHI'S SHOE CUBBY MERELY TO LEAVE A *LOVE LETTER* TO HER THERE!

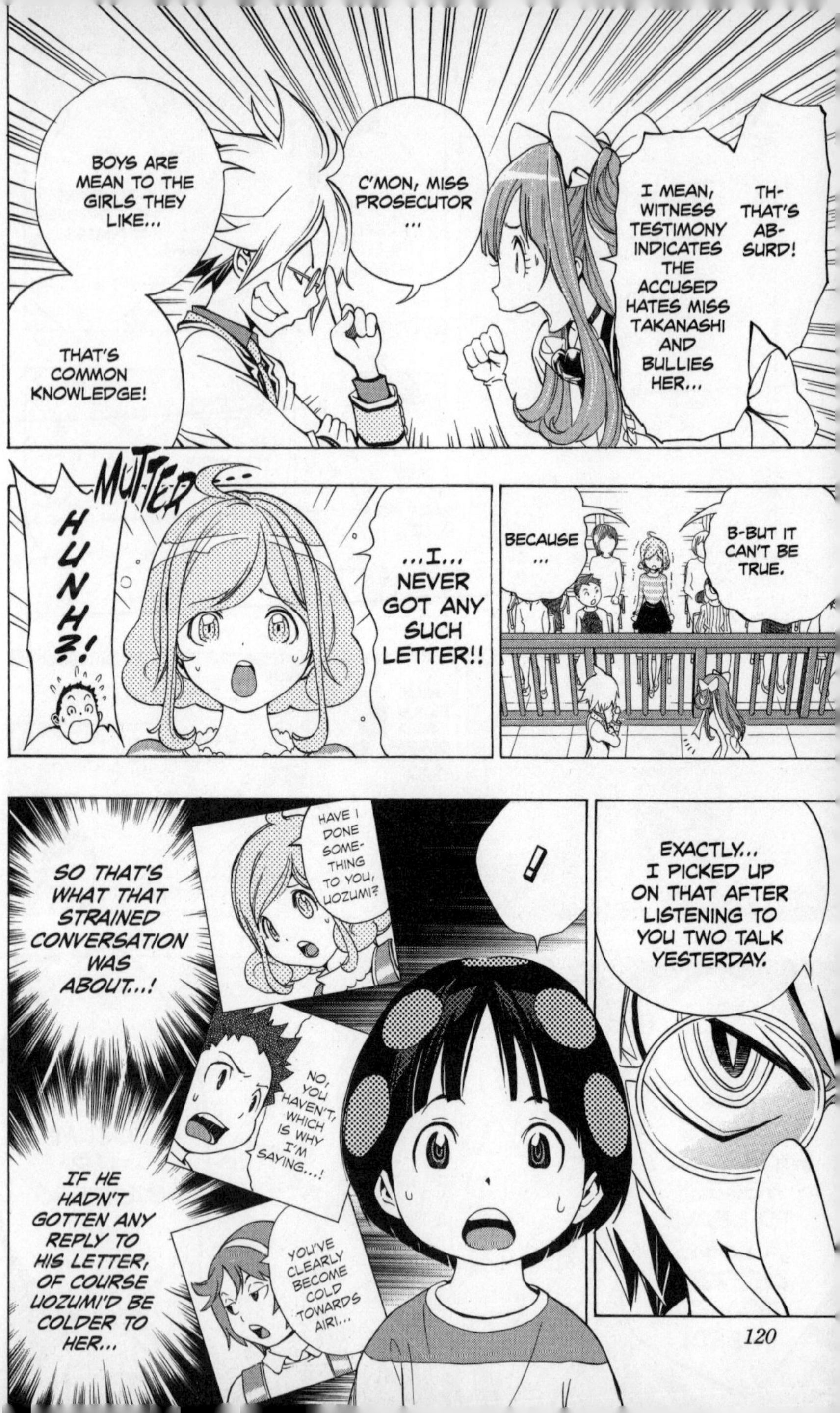
TH-THAT'S AB-SURD!
I MEAN, WITNESS TESTIMONY INDICATES THE ACCUSED HATES MISS TAKANASHI AND BULLIES HER...
C'MON, MISS PROSECUTOR...
BOYS ARE MEAN TO THE GIRLS THEY LIKE...
THAT'S COMMON KNOWLEDGE!
B-BUT IT CAN'T BE TRUE.
BECAUSE...
...I... NEVER GOT ANY SUCH LETTER!!
MUTTER
HUNH?!
EXACTLY... I PICKED UP ON THAT AFTER LISTENING TO YOU TWO TALK YESTERDAY.
!
HAVE I DONE SOMETHING TO YOU, UOZUMI?
SO THAT'S WHAT THAT STRAINED CONVERSATION WAS ABOUT...!
NO, YOU HAVEN'T, WHICH IS WHY I'M SAYING...!
YOU'VE CLEARLY BECOME COLD TOWARDS AIRI...
IF HE HADN'T GOTTEN ANY REPLY TO HIS LETTER, OF COURSE UOZUMI'D BE COLDER TO HER...

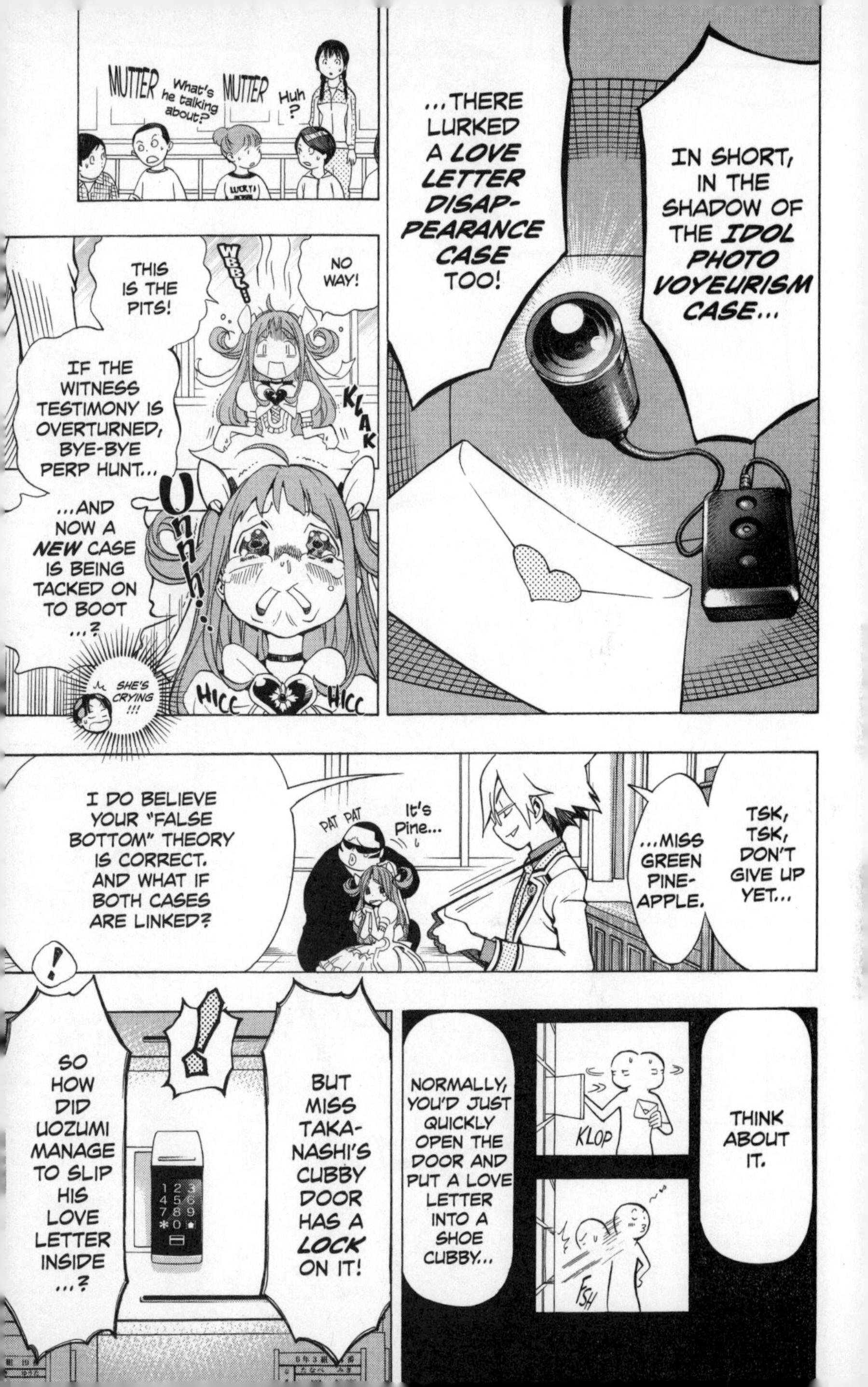
IN SHORT, IN THE SHADOW OF THE *IDOL PHOTO VOYEURISM CASE*...
...THERE LURKED A *LOVE LETTER DISAPPEARANCE CASE* TOO!
Huh?
MUTTER
What's he talking about?
MUTTER
NO WAY!
WBBL
THIS IS THE PITS!
IF THE WITNESS TESTIMONY IS OVERTURNED, BYE-BYE PERP HUNT...
KLAK
...AND NOW A *NEW* CASE IS BEING TACKED ON TO BOOT...?
Unnh!
HICC HICC
SHE'S CRYING!!!
TSK, TSK, DON'T GIVE UP YET...
...MISS GREEN PINE-APPLE.
It's fine...
PAT PAT
I DO BELIEVE YOUR "FALSE BOTTOM" THEORY IS CORRECT. AND WHAT IF BOTH CASES ARE LINKED?
!
THINK ABOUT IT.
NORMALLY, YOU'D JUST QUICKLY OPEN THE DOOR AND PUT A LOVE LETTER INTO A SHOE CUBBY...
KLOP
FSH
BUT MISS TAKA-NASHI'S CUBBY DOOR HAS A *LOCK* ON IT!
!
SO HOW DID UOZUMI MANAGE TO SLIP HIS LOVE LETTER INSIDE...?

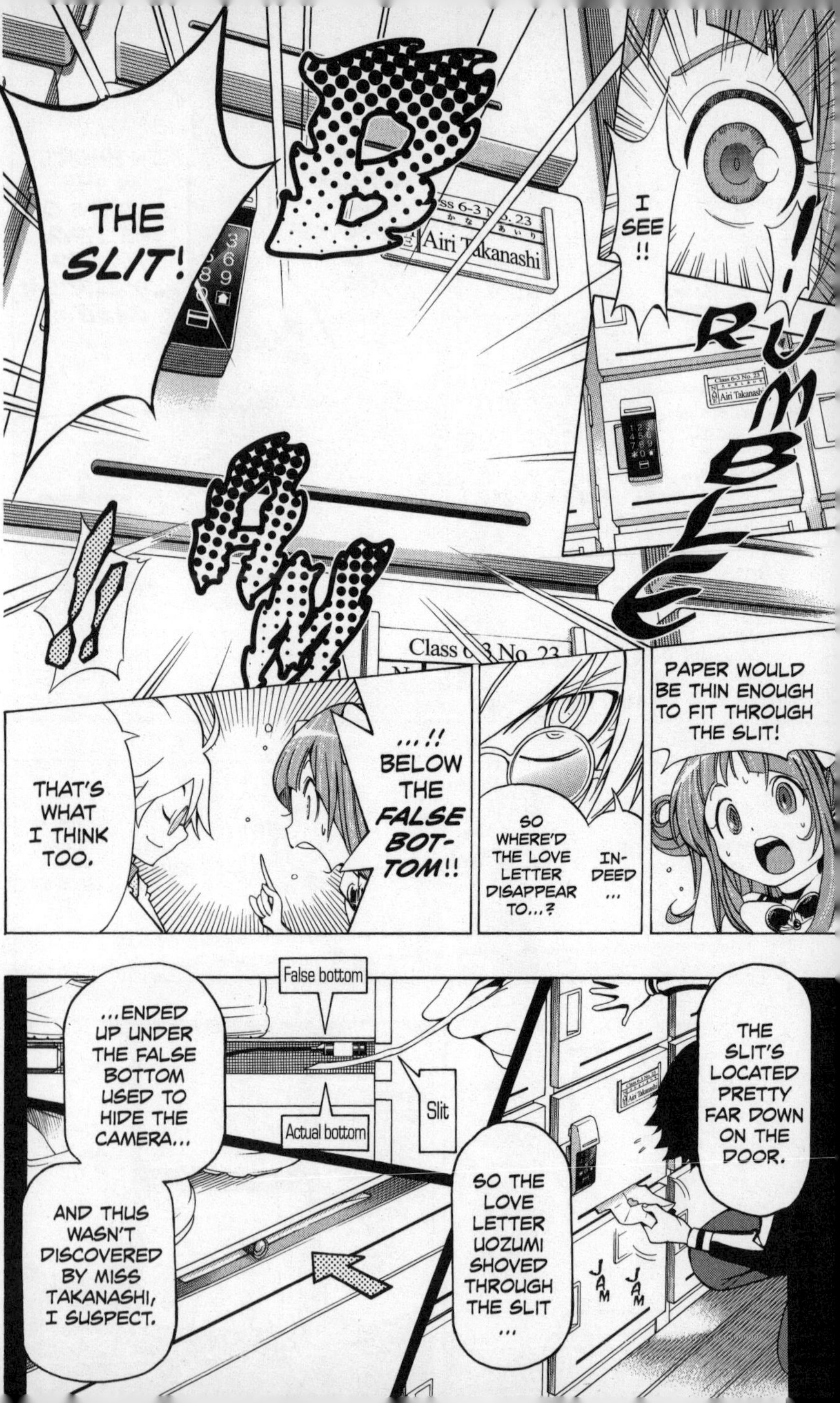
I SEE !!
RUMBLE
Class 6-3 No. 23
Airi Takanashi
THE SLIT!
PAPER WOULD BE THIN ENOUGH TO FIT THROUGH THE SLIT!
INDEED...
SO WHERE'D THE LOVE LETTER DISAPPEAR TO...?
...!! BELOW THE FALSE BOTTOM!!
THAT'S WHAT I THINK TOO.
THE SLIT'S LOCATED PRETTY FAR DOWN ON THE DOOR.
JAM JAM
SO THE LOVE LETTER UOZUMI SHOVED THROUGH THE SLIT...
...ENDED UP UNDER THE FALSE BOTTOM USED TO HIDE THE CAMERA...
False bottom
Slit
Actual bottom
AND THUS WASN'T DISCOVERED BY MISS TAKANASHI, I SUSPECT.

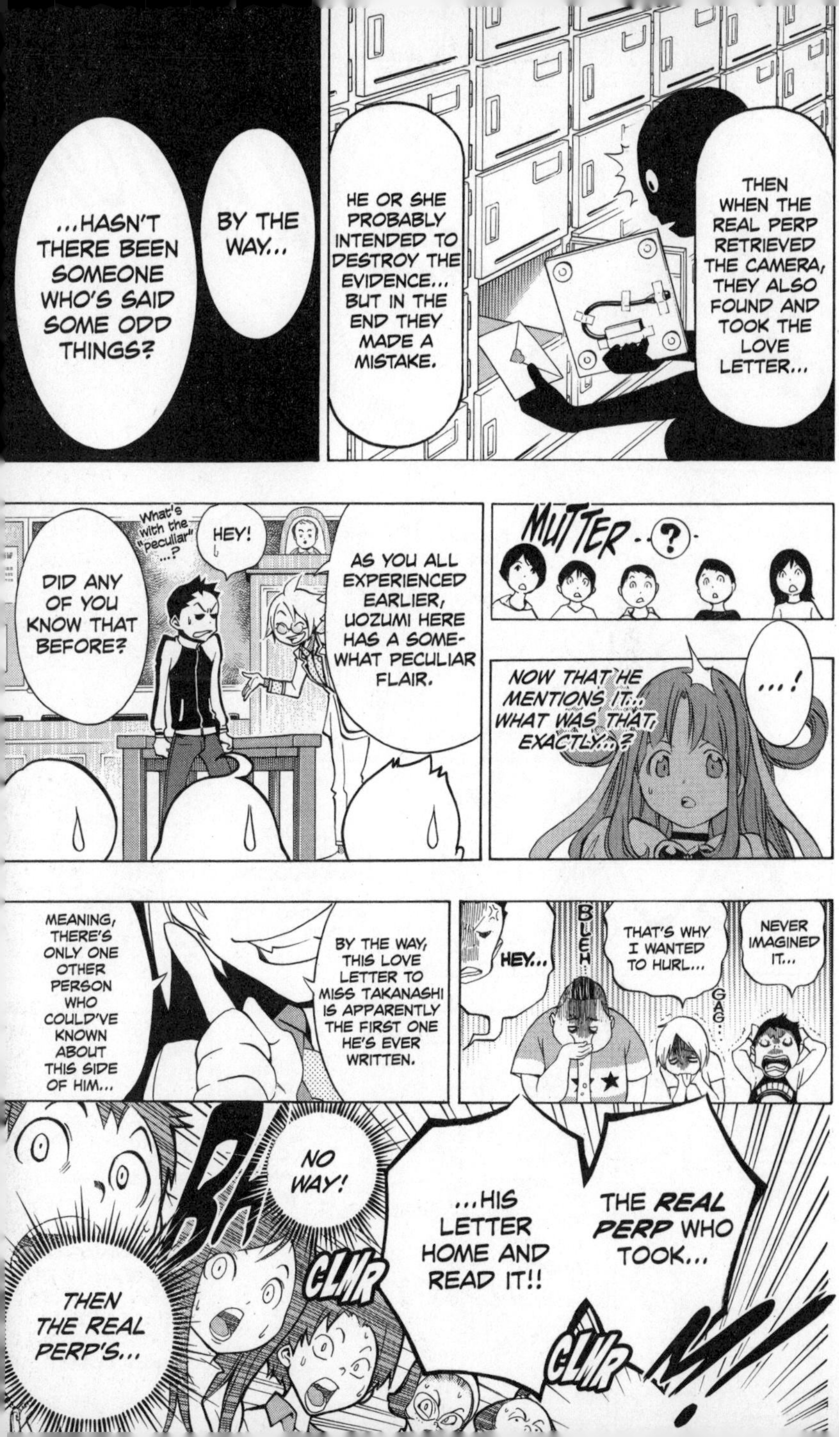
THEN WHEN THE REAL PERP RETRIEVED THE CAMERA, THEY ALSO FOUND AND TOOK THE LOVE LETTER...
HE OR SHE PROBABLY INTENDED TO DESTROY THE EVIDENCE... BUT IN THE END THEY MADE A MISTAKE.
BY THE WAY...
...HASN'T THERE BEEN SOMEONE WHO'S SAID SOME ODD THINGS?
MUTTER
?
...!
NOW THAT HE MENTIONS IT... WHAT WAS THAT, EXACTLY...?
AS YOU ALL EXPERIENCED EARLIER, UOZUMI HERE HAS A SOME-WHAT PECULIAR FLAIR.
HEY!
What's with the "peculiar"...?
DID ANY OF YOU KNOW THAT BEFORE?
NEVER IMAGINED IT...
THAT'S WHY I WANTED TO HURL...
BLEH
GAG...
HEY...
BY THE WAY, THIS LOVE LETTER TO MISS TAKANASHI IS APPARENTLY THE FIRST ONE HE'S EVER WRITTEN.
MEANING, THERE'S ONLY ONE OTHER PERSON WHO COULD'VE KNOWN ABOUT THIS SIDE OF HIM...
THE *REAL PERP* WHO TOOK...
...HIS LETTER HOME AND READ IT!!
NO WAY!
CLMR
THEN THE REAL PERP'S...
CLMR

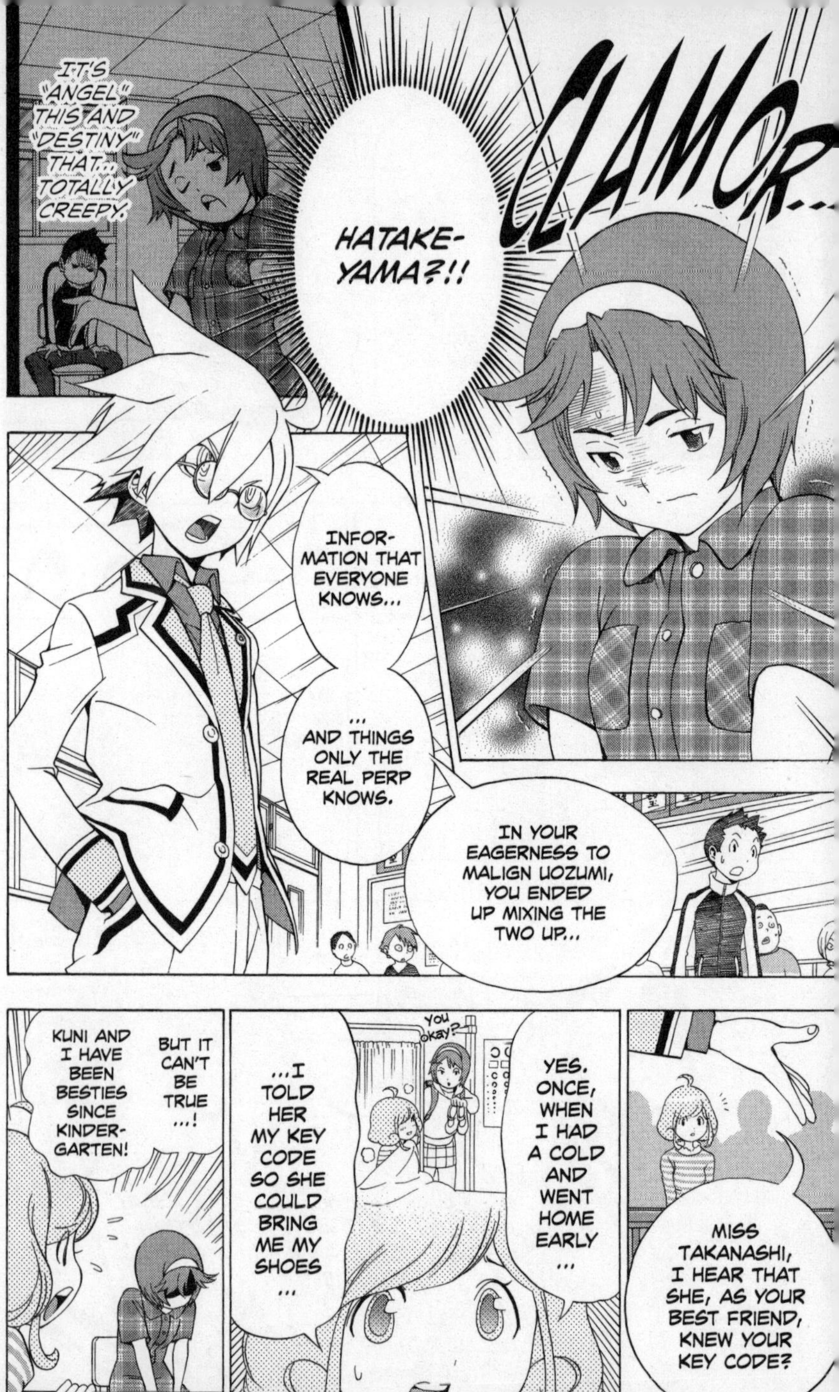
CLAMOR...
HATAKE-YAMA?!!
IT'S "ANGEL" THIS AND "DESTINY" THAT... TOTALLY CREEPY.
INFOR-MATION THAT EVERYONE KNOWS...
... AND THINGS ONLY THE REAL PERP KNOWS.
IN YOUR EAGERNESS TO MALIGN UOZUMI, YOU ENDED UP MIXING THE TWO UP...
MISS TAKANASHI, I HEAR THAT SHE, AS YOUR BEST FRIEND, KNEW YOUR KEY CODE?
YES. ONCE, WHEN I HAD A COLD AND WENT HOME EARLY ...
You okay?
...I TOLD HER MY KEY CODE SO SHE COULD BRING ME MY SHOES ...
BUT IT CAN'T BE TRUE ...!
KUNI AND I HAVE BEEN BESTIES SINCE KINDER-GARTEN!

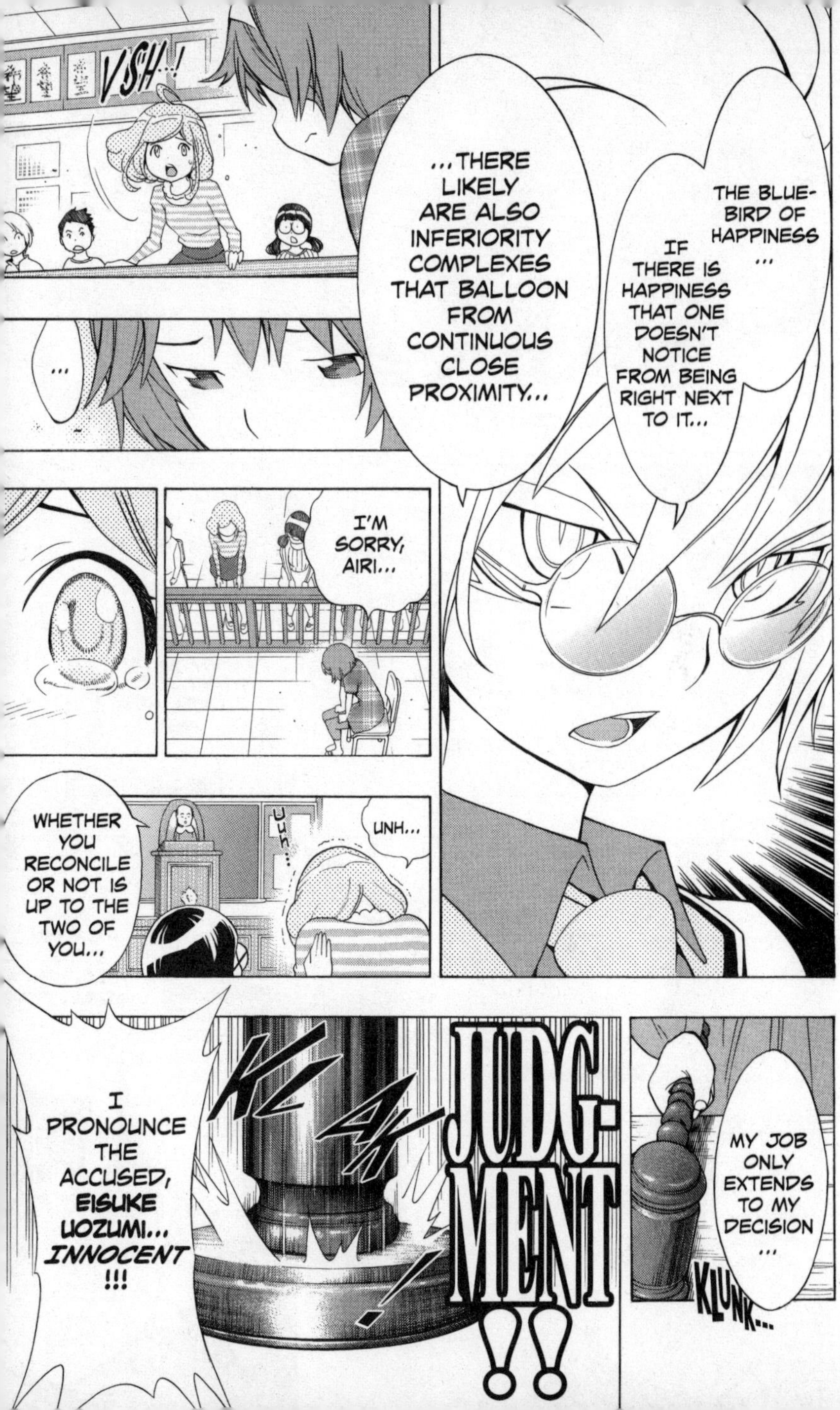
THE BLUE-BIRD OF HAPPINESS...
IF THERE IS HAPPINESS THAT ONE DOESN'T NOTICE FROM BEING RIGHT NEXT TO IT...
...THERE LIKELY ARE ALSO INFERIORITY COMPLEXES THAT BALLOON FROM CONTINUOUS CLOSE PROXIMITY...
VSH..!
...
I'M SORRY, AIRI...
UNH...
Uuh...
WHETHER YOU RECONCILE OR NOT IS UP TO THE TWO OF YOU...
MY JOB ONLY EXTENDS TO MY DECISION...
KLUNK...
JUDG-MENT!!
KLAK
I PRONOUNCE THE ACCUSED, EISUKE UOZUMI... INNOCENT!!!

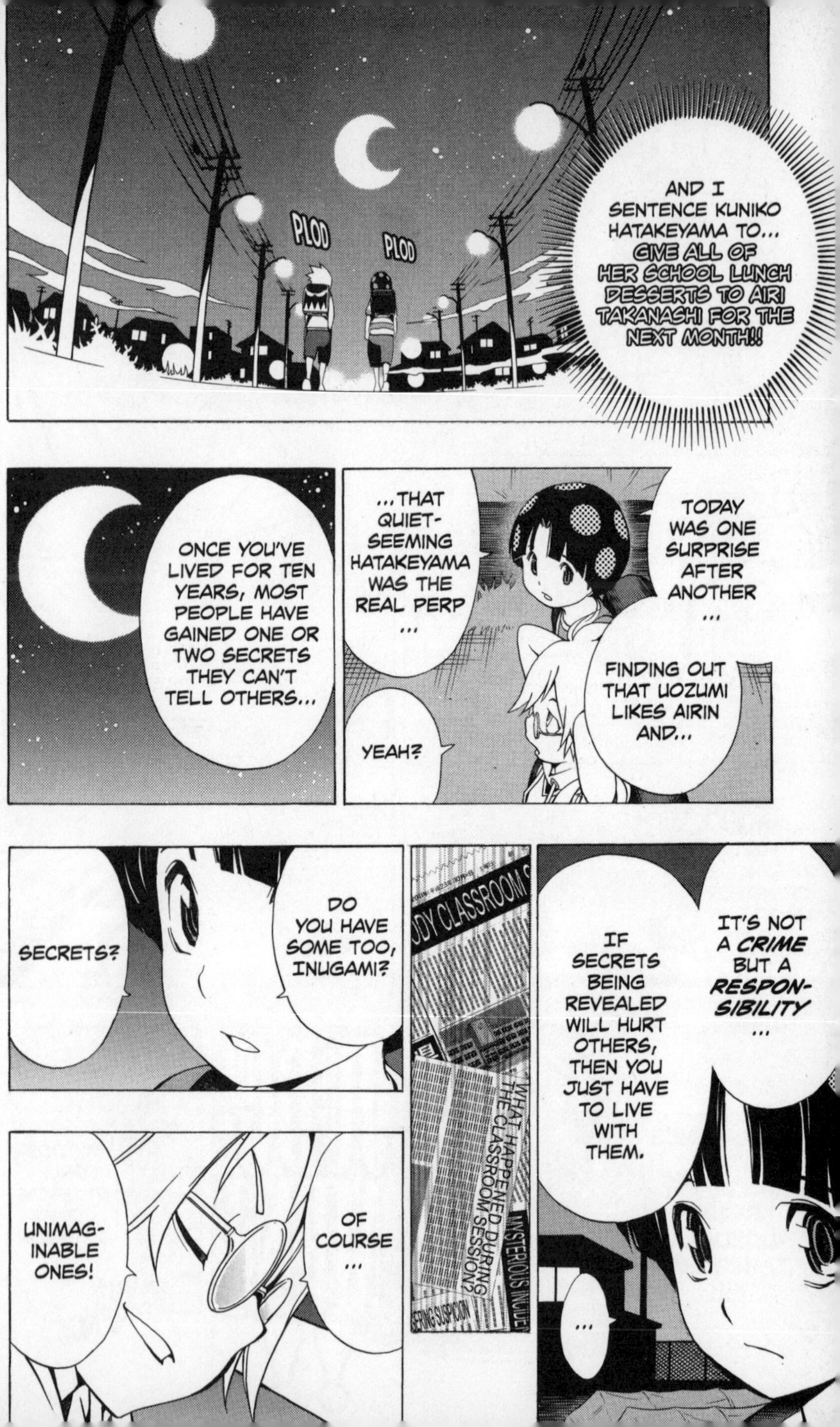
AND I SENTENCE KUNIKO HATAKEYAMA TO... GIVE ALL OF HER SCHOOL LUNCH DESSERTS TO AIRI TAKANASHI FOR THE NEXT MONTH!!
PLOD
PLOD
TODAY WAS ONE SURPRISE AFTER ANOTHER...
FINDING OUT THAT UOZUMI LIKES AIRIN AND...
...THAT QUIET-SEEMING HATAKEYAMA WAS THE REAL PERP...
YEAH?
ONCE YOU'VE LIVED FOR TEN YEARS, MOST PEOPLE HAVE GAINED ONE OR TWO SECRETS THEY CAN'T TELL OTHERS...
IT'S NOT A *CRIME* BUT A *RESPONSIBILITY*...
IF SECRETS BEING REVEALED WILL HURT OTHERS, THEN YOU JUST HAVE TO LIVE WITH THEM.
...
WHAT HAPPENED DURING THE CLASSROOM SESSION?
DO YOU HAVE SOME TOO, INUGAMI?
SECRETS?
OF COURSE...
UNIMAGINABLE ONES!

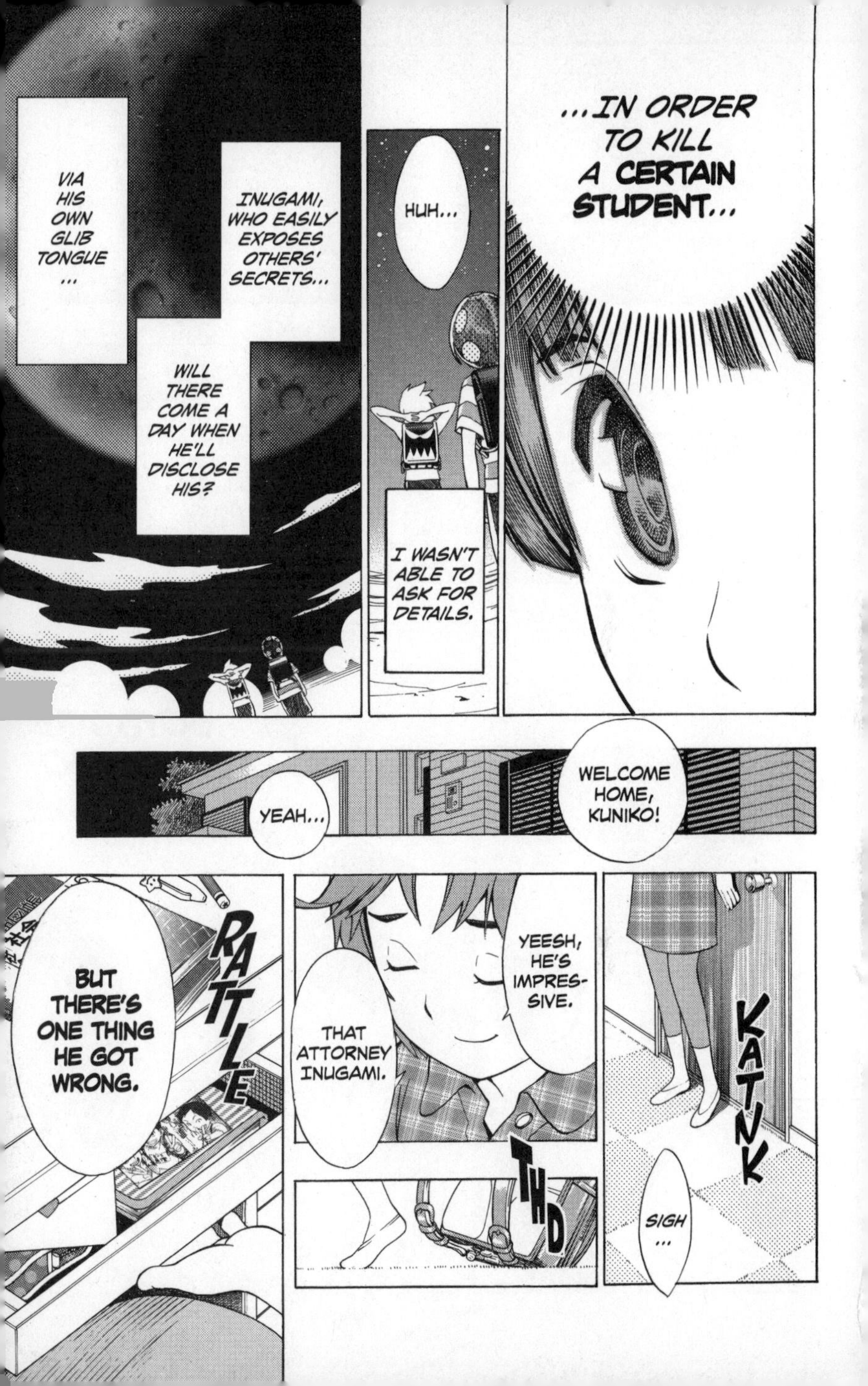
...IN ORDER TO KILL A CERTAIN STUDENT...
HUH...
I WASN'T ABLE TO ASK FOR DETAILS.
INUGAMI, WHO EASILY EXPOSES OTHERS' SECRETS...
VIA HIS OWN GLIB TONGUE...
WILL THERE COME A DAY WHEN HE'LL DISCLOSE HIS?
WELCOME HOME, KUNIKO!
YEAH...
KATNK
SIGH...
YEESH, HE'S IMPRES-SIVE.
THAT ATTORNEY INUGAMI.
THD
RATTLE
BUT THERE'S ONE THING HE GOT WRONG.

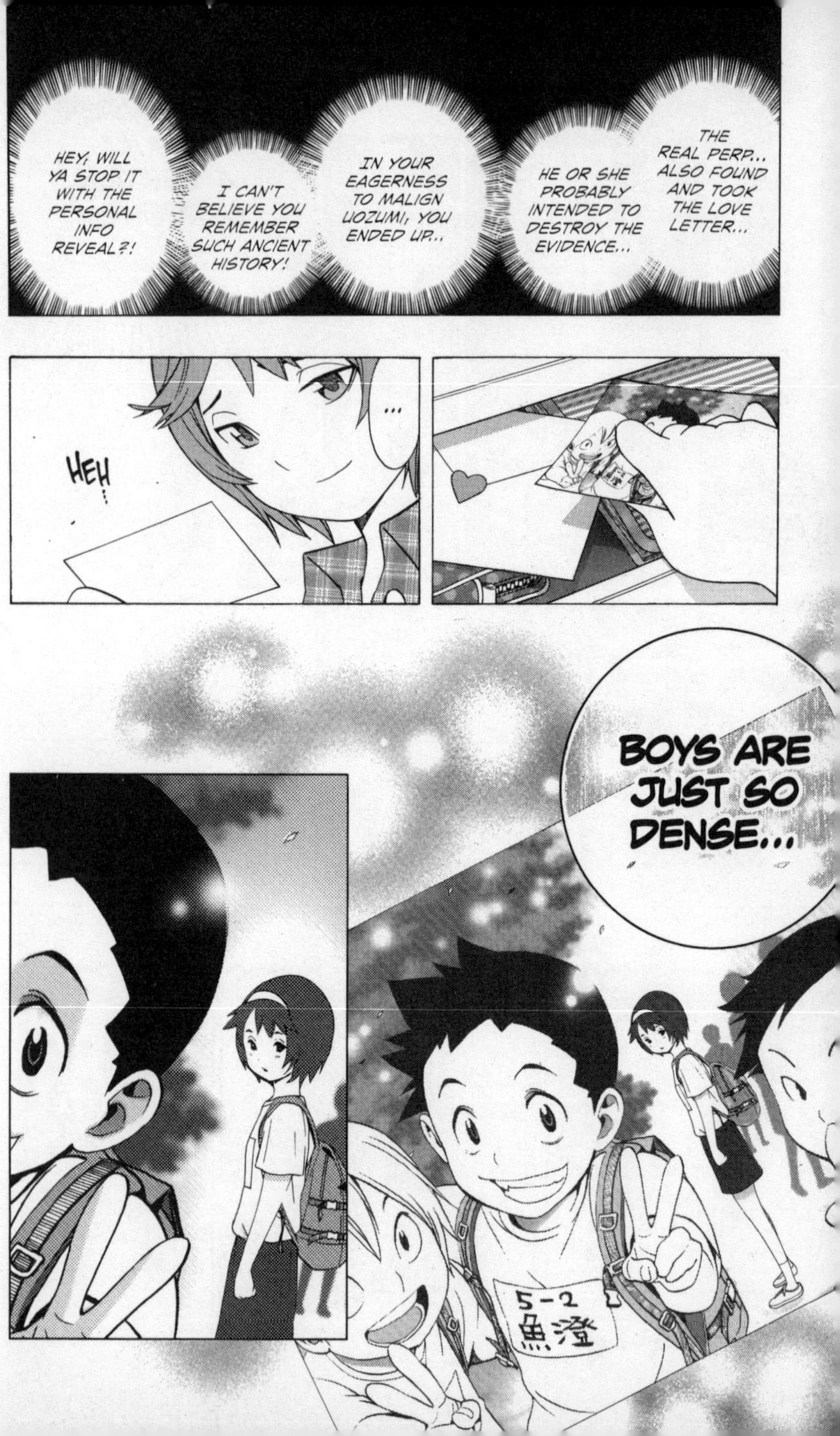
THE REAL PERP... ALSO FOUND AND TOOK THE LOVE LETTER...
HE OR SHE PROBABLY INTENDED TO DESTROY THE EVIDENCE...
IN YOUR EAGERNESS TO MALIGN UOZUMI, YOU ENDED UP...
I CAN'T BELIEVE YOU REMEMBER SUCH ANCIENT HISTORY!
HEY, WILL YA STOP IT WITH THE PERSONAL INFO REVEAL?!
...
HEH
BOYS ARE JUST SO DENSE...
5-2
魚澄

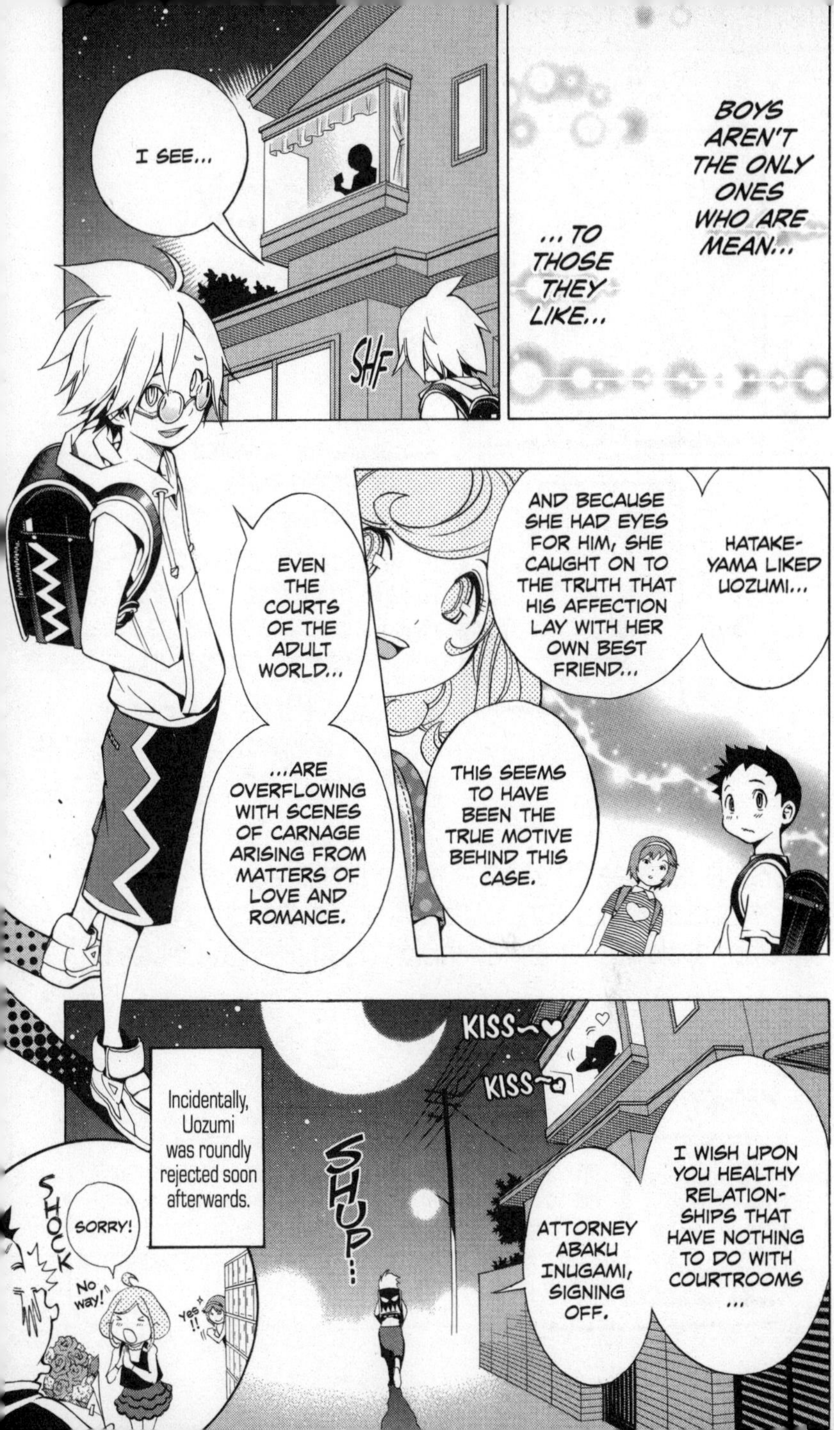
BOYS AREN'T THE ONLY ONES WHO ARE MEAN...
...TO THOSE THEY LIKE...
I SEE...
SHF
HATAKE-YAMA LIKED UOZUMI...
AND BECAUSE SHE HAD EYES FOR HIM, SHE CAUGHT ON TO THE TRUTH THAT HIS AFFECTION LAY WITH HER OWN BEST FRIEND...
THIS SEEMS TO HAVE BEEN THE TRUE MOTIVE BEHIND THIS CASE.
EVEN THE COURTS OF THE ADULT WORLD...
...ARE OVERFLOWING WITH SCENES OF CARNAGE ARISING FROM MATTERS OF LOVE AND ROMANCE.
KISS~♥
KISS~
I WISH UPON YOU HEALTHY RELATION-SHIPS THAT HAVE NOTHING TO DO WITH COURTROOMS...
ATTORNEY ABAKU INUGAMI, SIGNING OFF.
SHUP...
Incidentally, Uozumi was roundly rejected soon afterwards.
SORRY!
SHOCK
No way!
Yes!!

(Obata's final version)

Pine Hanzuki

Height: 4 ft. 10 in.
Dislikes: Abaku Inugami

(Enoki's draft version)

A dual-line thoroughbred elite. Her father is a prosecutor and her mother is a financial magnate.

As the heiress to the distinguished Hanzuki family known throughout the legal world, she is training as a grade school Prosecutor at her father's behest.

By the way, she states in chapter 1, "My favorite *Pretty Cure* character is Cure Peace," but...

...that is because Cure Peace was practically the only Cure girl I was familiar with. I later found out that there was a Cure Pine. I hereby apologize for any confusion that I may have caused.

☆ School Judgment Backstory ② ☆

Hatakeyama

In the original ending, she was a crazy girl who had photos of Uozumi plastered all over her room and face-planted and breathed heavily all over the love letter that he gave her to take home. My editor, Mr. Saito, stated coolly, "Isn't that a bit much?" Her image was later altered to that of an innocent young girl in love and made it through without further problems.

ABAKU INUGAMI...

Abaku Inug[a]

Date of Bir[th]
Blood Typ[e]
Address

Phone Nu[mber]

STARTED BEING ACTIVE AS AN *ATTORNEY* IN FOURTH GRADE.

BEFORE THAT, HE SPENT THREE YEARS INCARCERATED IN *ONIGASHIMA* ELEMENTARY.

AFTER THAT HE WON INNOCENT VERDICTS DURING NUMEROUS CLASS ARBITRATIONS...

HIS SUCCESS HAS EARNED HIM THE MONIKER OF ONE OF THE *THREE TONGUES*, THREE GRADE-SCHOOLERS SAID TO POSSESS A DIVINE TONGUE.

CHAPTER 5:
THE SHUICHI HIGASHIDE CHEATING CASE

IT'S BEEN *FIVE YEARS* SINCE THAT DAY...

WHAT THE HECK ARE YOU THINKING...

...YOU *BLOODY CLASSROOM* GHOST?!

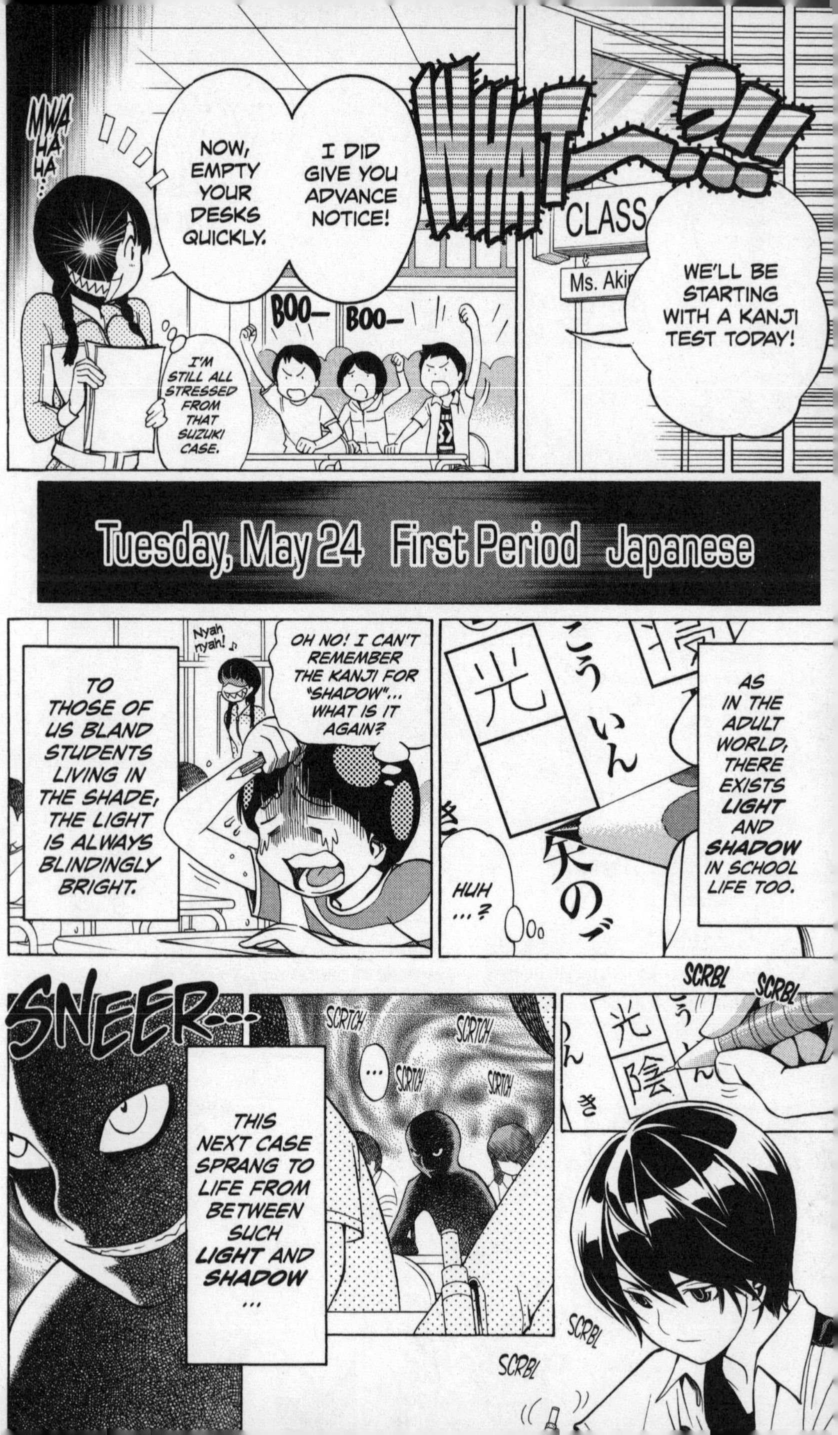
CLASS
Ms. Aki
WE'LL BE STARTING WITH A KANJI TEST TODAY!
WHAT—?!!
I DID GIVE YOU ADVANCE NOTICE!
NOW, EMPTY YOUR DESKS QUICKLY.
MWA HA HA...
BOO— BOO—
I'M STILL ALL STRESSED FROM THAT SUZUKI CASE.
Tuesday, May 24 First Period Japanese
AS IN THE ADULT WORLD, THERE EXISTS LIGHT AND SHADOW IN SCHOOL LIFE TOO.
こういん
光
矢の
HUH ...?
OH NO! I CAN'T REMEMBER THE KANJI FOR "SHADOW"... WHAT IS IT AGAIN?
Nyah nyah! ♪
TO THOSE OF US BLAND STUDENTS LIVING IN THE SHADE, THE LIGHT IS ALWAYS BLINDINGLY BRIGHT.
SCRBL SCRBL
光
陰
SCRBL
SCRBL
SNEER...
SCRTCH SCRTCH
...
SCRTCH SCRTCH
THIS NEXT CASE SPRANG TO LIFE FROM BETWEEN SUCH LIGHT AND SHADOW...

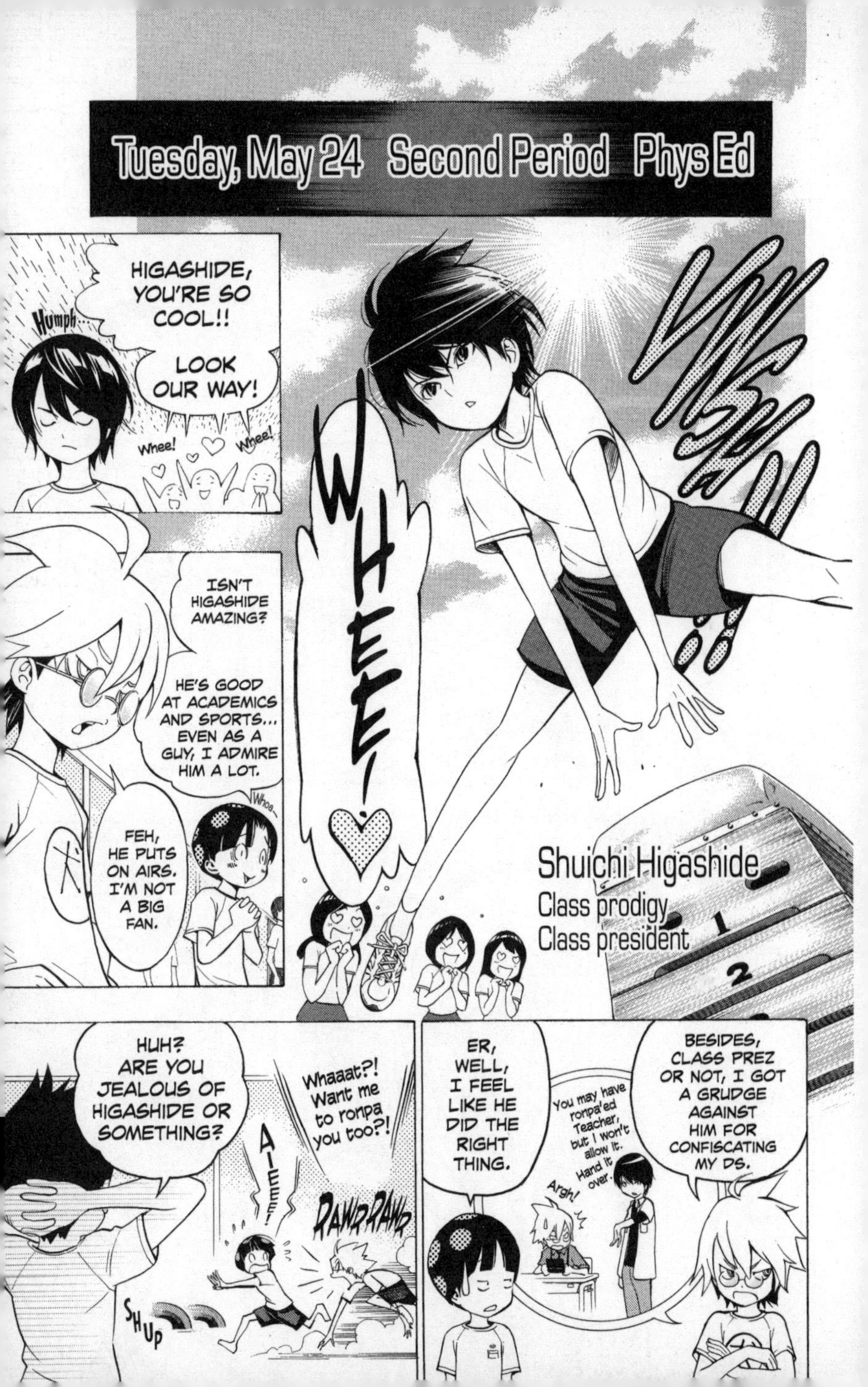
Tuesday, May 24 Second Period Phys Ed
WHISH!!
WHEEE!♥
Shuichi Higashide
Class prodigy
Class president
HIGASHIDE, YOU'RE SO COOL!!
LOOK OUR WAY!
Humph...
Whee!
Whee!
ISN'T HIGASHIDE AMAZING?
HE'S GOOD AT ACADEMICS AND SPORTS... EVEN AS A GUY, I ADMIRE HIM A LOT.
Whoa~
FEH, HE PUTS ON AIRS. I'M NOT A BIG FAN.
BESIDES, CLASS PREZ OR NOT, I GOT A GRUDGE AGAINST HIM FOR CONFISCATING MY DS.
ER, WELL, I FEEL LIKE HE DID THE RIGHT THING.
You may have ronpa'ed Teacher, but I won't allow it. Hand it over.
Argh!
HUH? ARE YOU JEALOUS OF HIGASHIDE OR SOMETHING?
Whaaat?! Want me to ronpa you too?!
AIEEE!
RAWR RAWR
SHUP

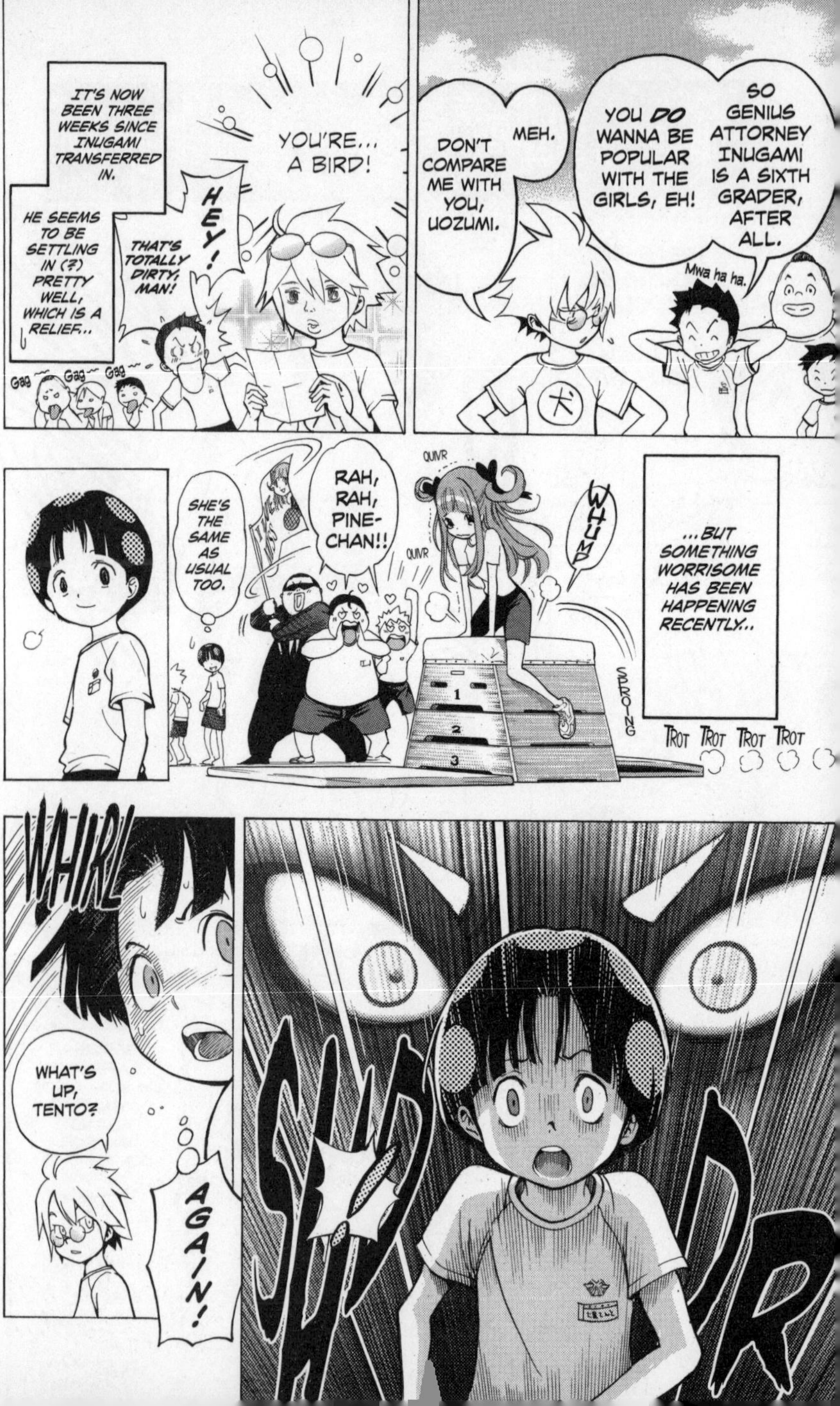
SO GENIUS ATTORNEY INUGAMI IS A SIXTH GRADER, AFTER ALL.
YOU DO WANNA BE POPULAR WITH THE GIRLS, EH!
Mwa ha ha.
MEH.
DON'T COMPARE ME WITH YOU, UOZUMI.
YOU'RE... A BIRD!
HEY!
THAT'S TOTALLY DIRTY, MAN!
IT'S NOW BEEN THREE WEEKS SINCE INUGAMI TRANSFERRED IN.
HE SEEMS TO BE SETTLING IN (?) PRETTY WELL, WHICH IS A RELIEF...
Gag~ Gag~ Gag~
...BUT SOMETHING WORRISOME HAS BEEN HAPPENING RECENTLY...
TROT TROT TROT TROT
WHUMP
SPROING
QUIVR
QUIVR
RAH, RAH, PINE-CHAN!!
SHE'S THE SAME AS USUAL TOO.
WHIRL
WHAT'S UP, TENTO?
AGAIN!

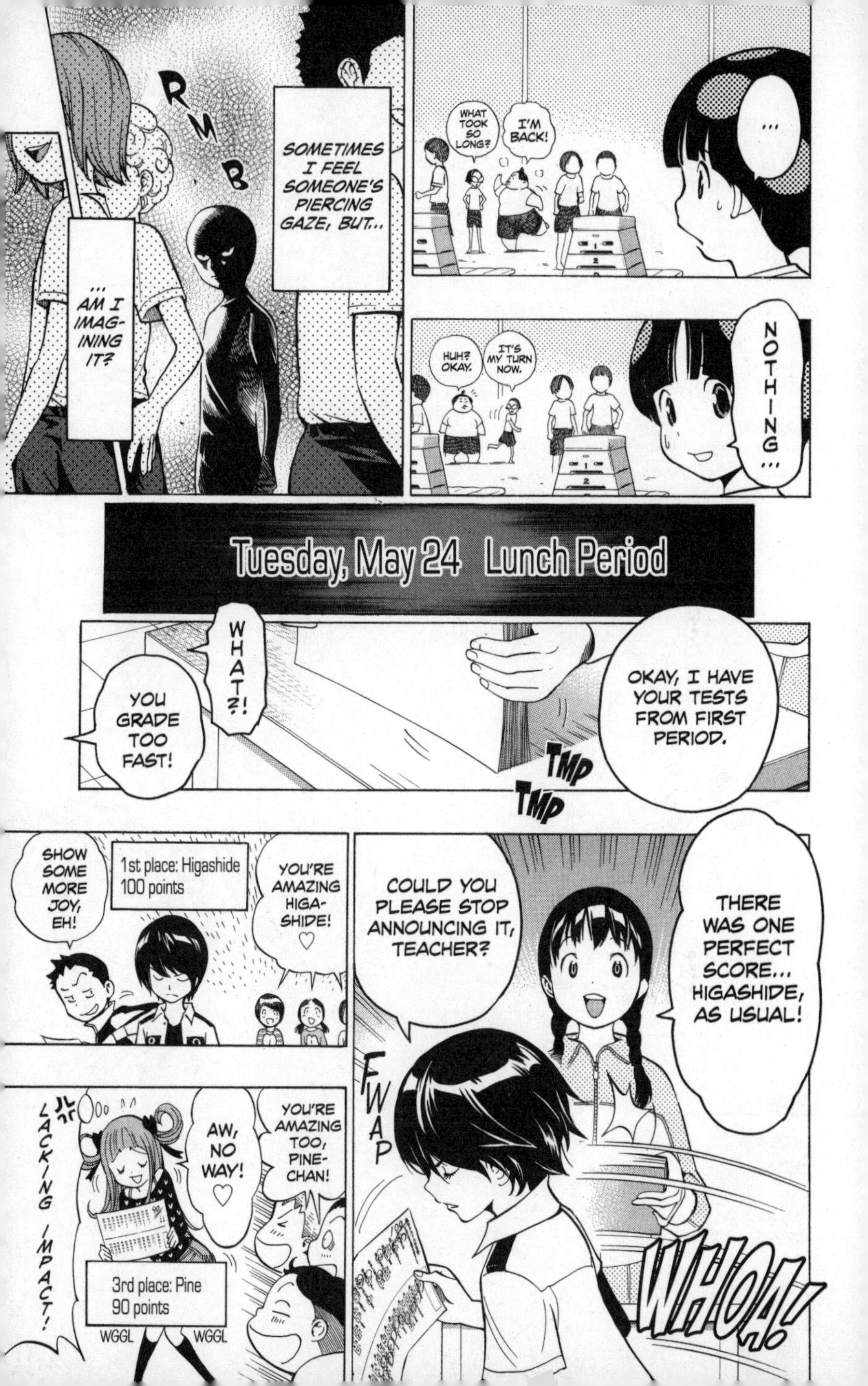

...
I'M BACK!
WHAT TOOK SO LONG?
NOTHING...
IT'S MY TURN NOW.
HUH? OKAY.
RMB
SOMETIMES I FEEL SOMEONE'S PIERCING GAZE, BUT...
...AM I IMAGINING IT?
Tuesday, May 24 Lunch Period
OKAY, I HAVE YOUR TESTS FROM FIRST PERIOD.
TMP TMP
WHAT?!
YOU GRADE TOO FAST!
THERE WAS ONE PERFECT SCORE... HIGASHIDE, AS USUAL!
COULD YOU PLEASE STOP ANNOUNCING IT, TEACHER?
FWAP
WHOA!!
YOU'RE AMAZING HIGASHIDE! ♡
1st place: Higashide 100 points
SHOW SOME MORE JOY, EH!
YOU'RE AMAZING TOO, PINE-CHAN!
AW, NO WAY! ♡
LACKING IMPACT!
3rd place: Pine 90 points
WGGL
WGGL

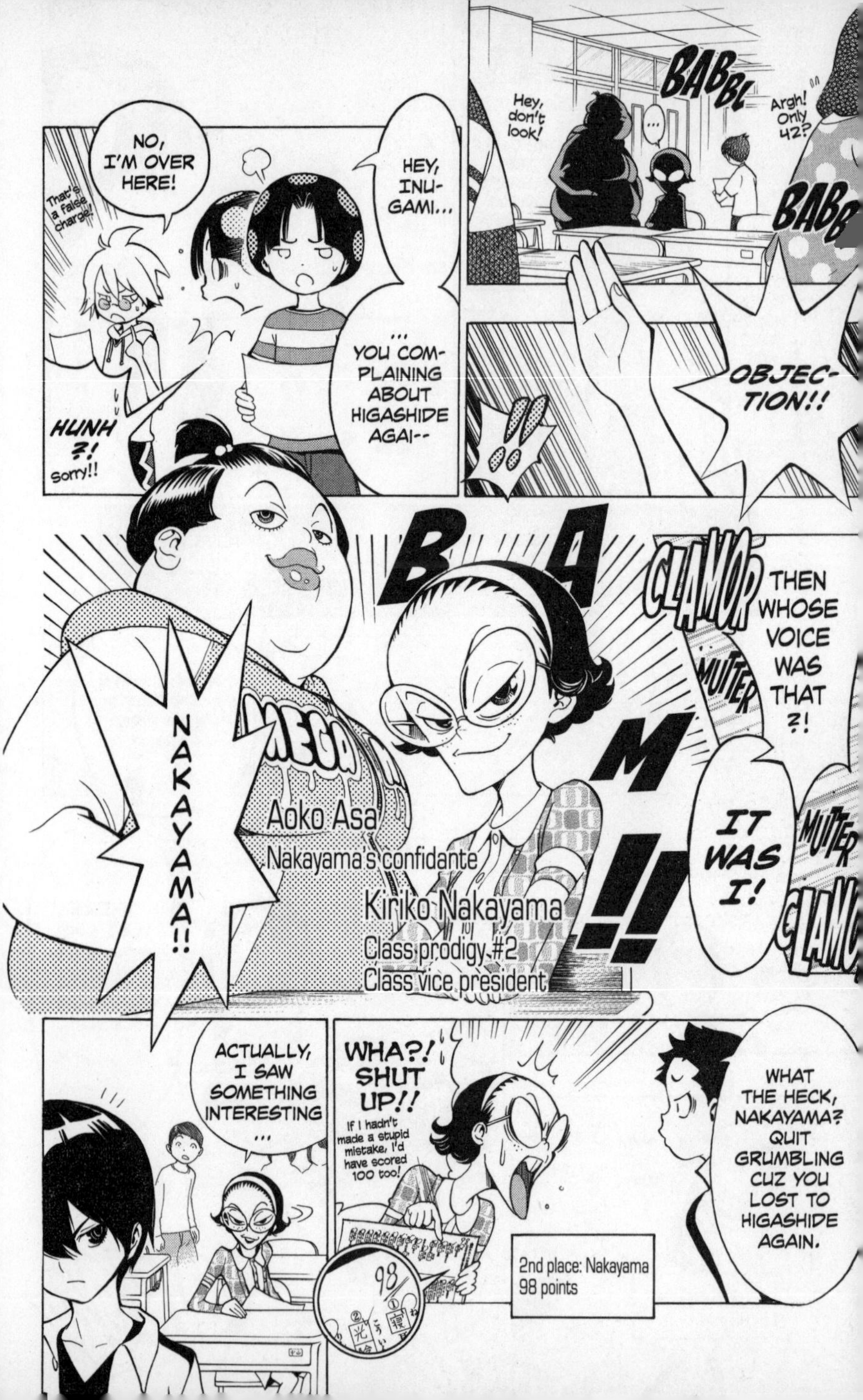
BABBL
Hey, don't look!
...
Argh! Only 42?
BABB
OBJECTION!!
HEY, INUGAMI...
... YOU COMPLAINING ABOUT HIGASHIDE AGAI--
NO, I'M OVER HERE!
That's a false charge!
HUNH?!
Sorry!!
BAM!!
CLAMOR
THEN WHOSE VOICE WAS THAT?!
MUTTER
IT WAS I!
MUTTER
CLAMO
NAKAYAMA!!
Aoko Asa
Nakayama's confidante
Kiriko Nakayama
Class prodigy #2
Class vice president
WHAT THE HECK, NAKAYAMA? QUIT GRUMBLING CUZ YOU LOST TO HIGASHIDE AGAIN.
2nd place: Nakayama
98 points
WHA?! SHUT UP!!
If I hadn't made a stupid mistake, I'd have scored 100 too!
98
ACTUALLY, I SAW SOMETHING INTERESTING ...

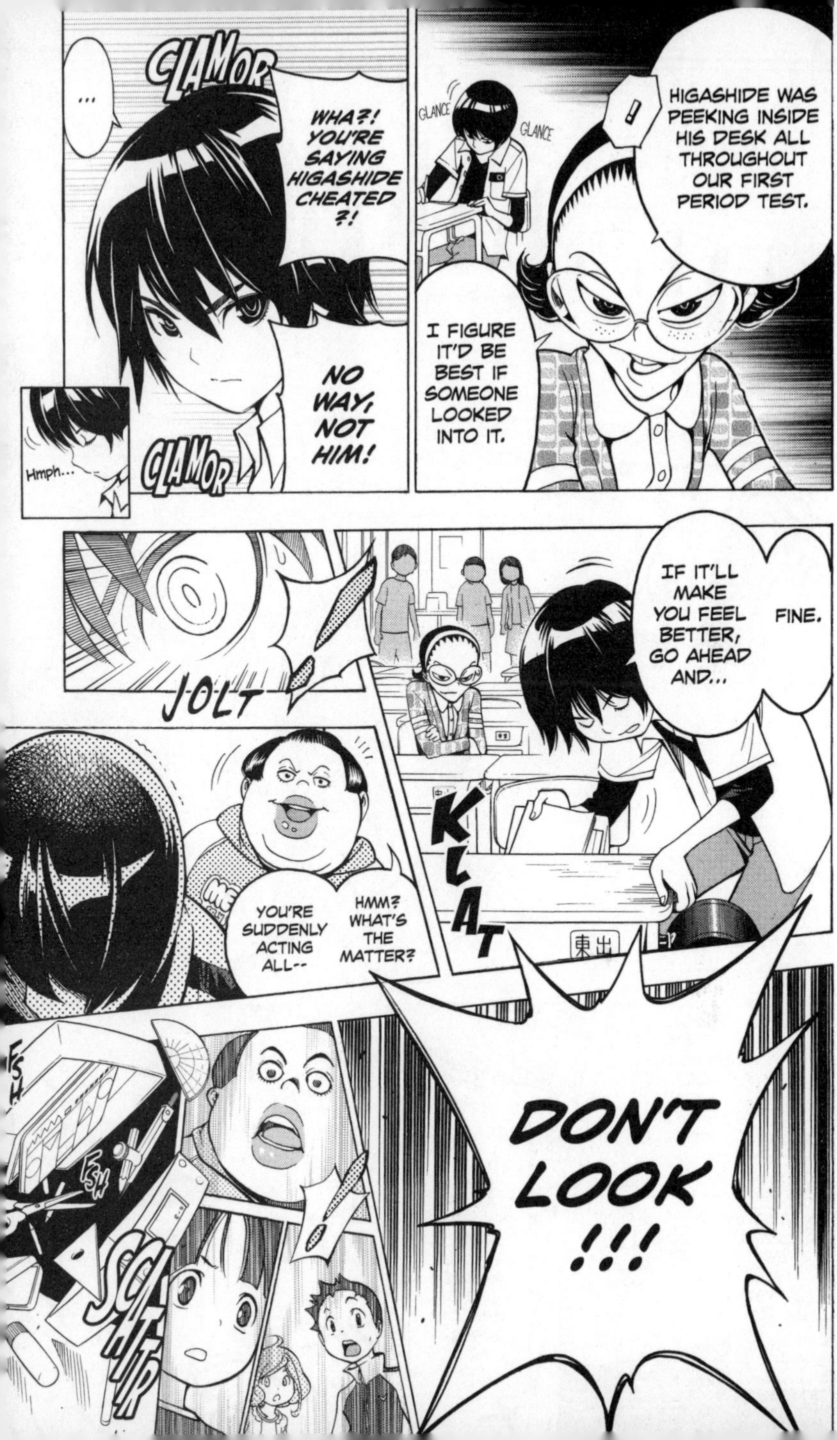
!
HIGASHIDE WAS PEEKING INSIDE HIS DESK ALL THROUGHOUT OUR FIRST PERIOD TEST.
GLANCE
GLANCE
I FIGURE IT'D BE BEST IF SOMEONE LOOKED INTO IT.
CLAMOR
WHA?! YOU'RE SAYING HIGASHIDE CHEATED?!
...
NO WAY, NOT HIM!
CLAMOR
Hmph...
FINE.
IF IT'LL MAKE YOU FEEL BETTER, GO AHEAD AND...
KLAT
JOLT
HMM? WHAT'S THE MATTER?
YOU'RE SUDDENLY ACTING ALL--
DON'T LOOK!!!
FSH
FSH
SCHTR

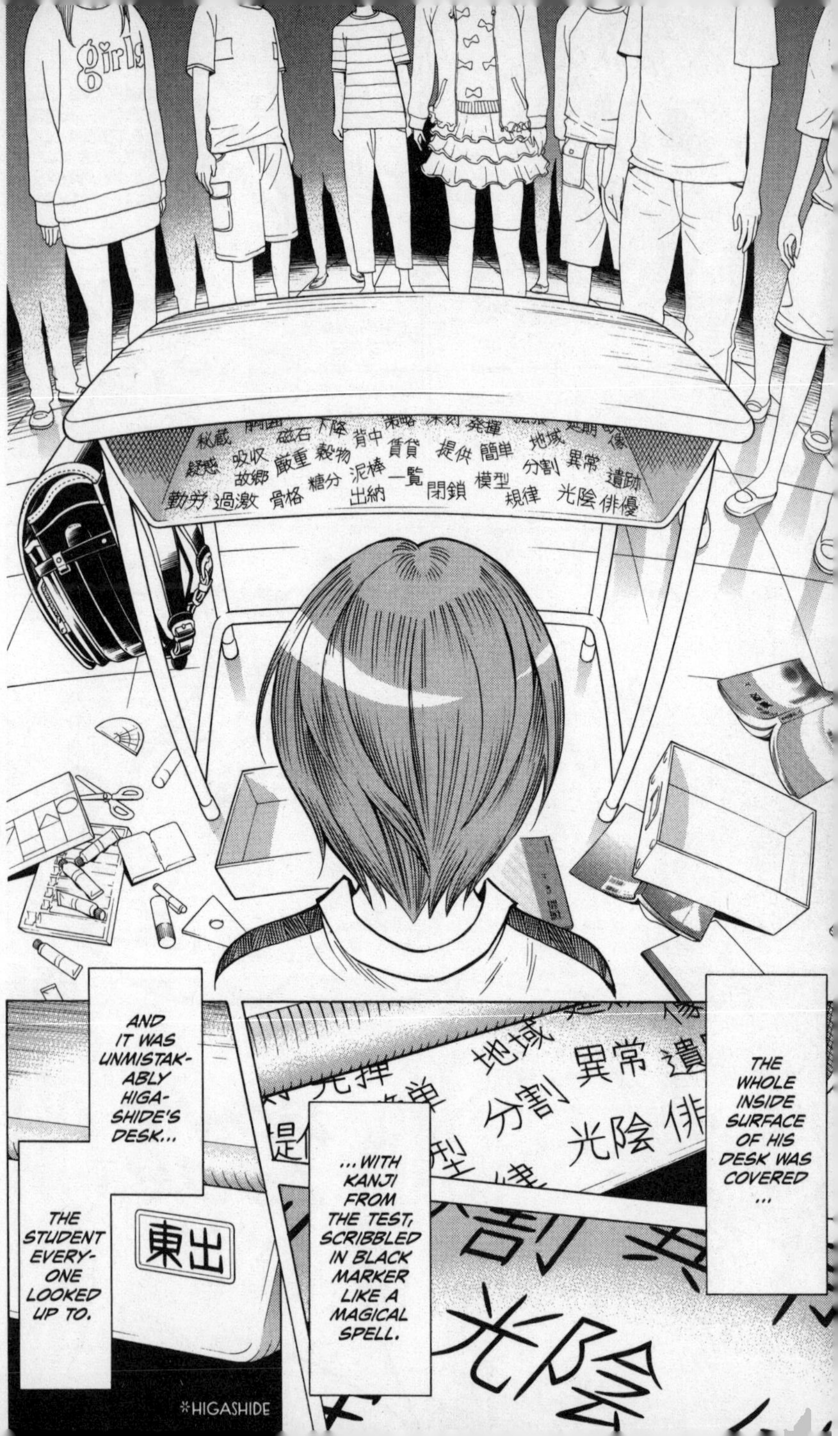
girls
THE WHOLE INSIDE SURFACE OF HIS DESK WAS COVERED...
...WITH KANJI FROM THE TEST, SCRIBBLED IN BLACK MARKER LIKE A MAGICAL SPELL.
AND IT WAS UNMISTAKABLY HIGASHIDE'S DESK...
THE STUDENT EVERYONE LOOKED UP TO.
東出
*HIGASHIDE

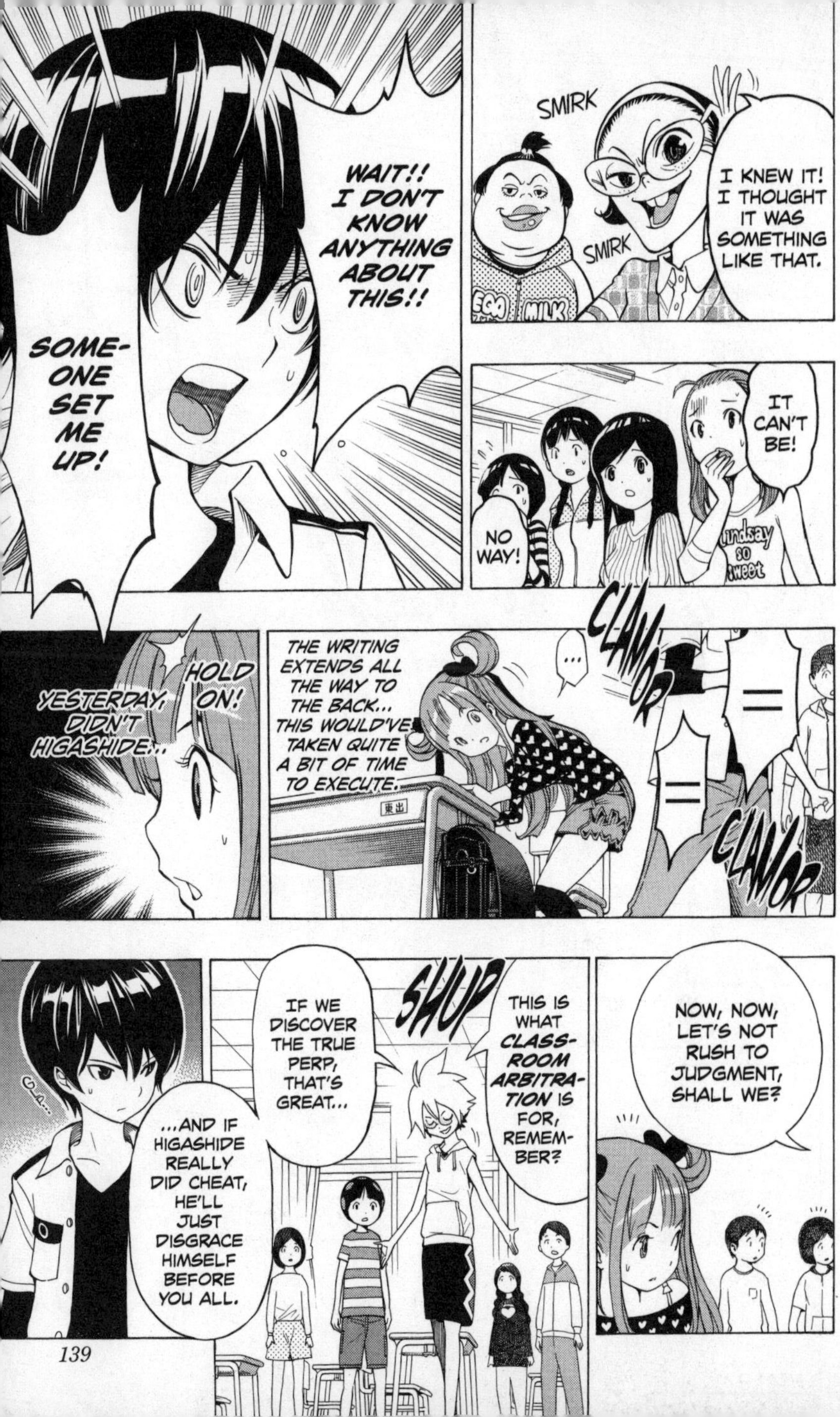
SMIRK
SMIRK
I KNEW IT! I THOUGHT IT WAS SOMETHING LIKE THAT.
IT CAN'T BE!
NO WAY!
WAIT!! I DON'T KNOW ANYTHING ABOUT THIS!!
SOME-ONE SET ME UP!
CLAMOR
...
CLAMOR
THE WRITING EXTENDS ALL THE WAY TO THE BACK... THIS WOULD'VE TAKEN QUITE A BIT OF TIME TO EXECUTE.
HOLD ON!
YESTERDAY, DIDN'T HIGASHIDE...
NOW, NOW, LET'S NOT RUSH TO JUDGMENT, SHALL WE?
SHUP
THIS IS WHAT CLASS-ROOM ARBITRA-TION IS FOR, REMEM-BER?
IF WE DISCOVER THE TRUE PERP, THAT'S GREAT...
...AND IF HIGASHIDE REALLY DID CHEAT, HE'LL JUST DISGRACE HIMSELF BEFORE YOU ALL.

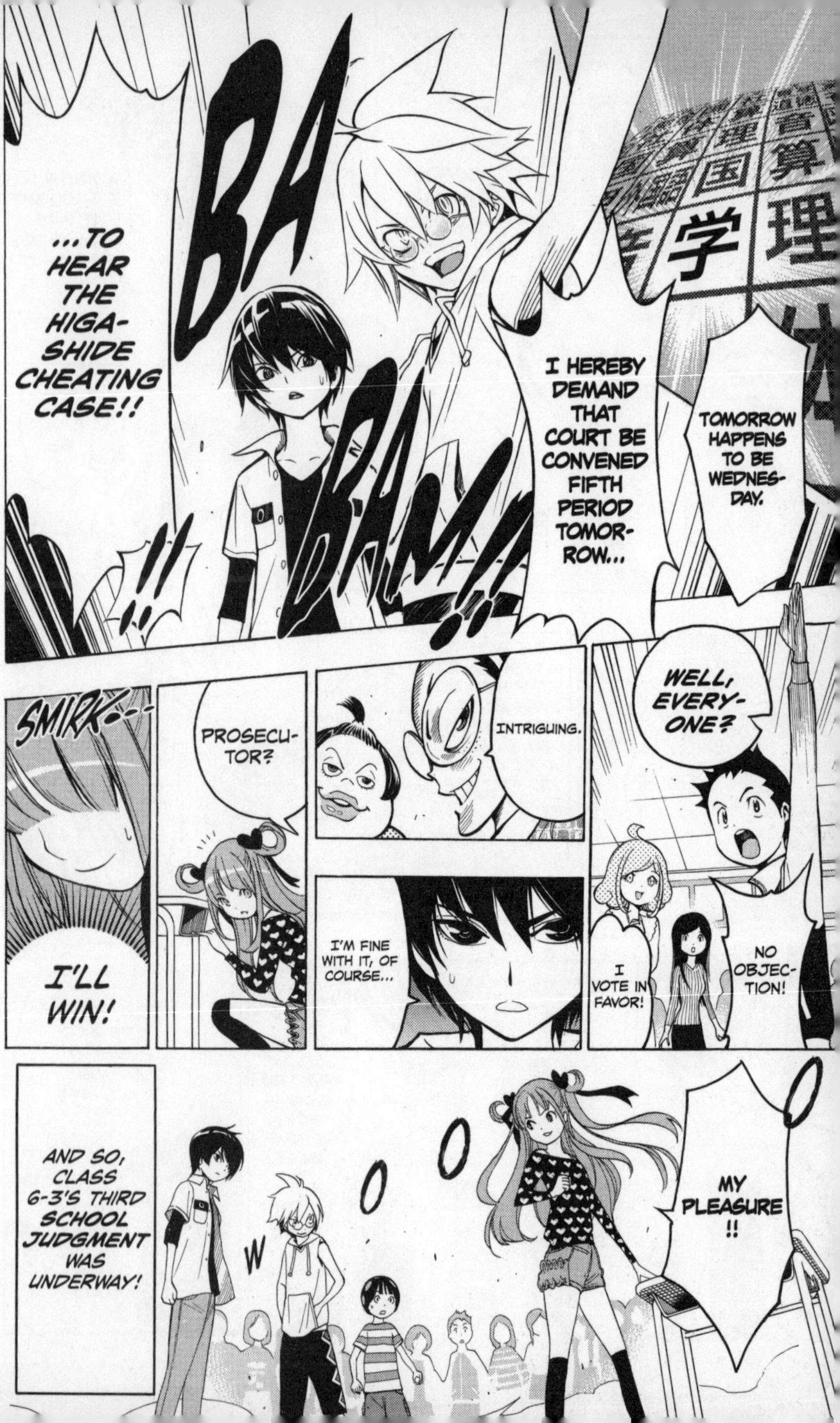
TOMORROW HAPPENS TO BE WEDNES-DAY.
I HEREBY DEMAND THAT COURT BE CONVENED FIFTH PERIOD TOMOR-ROW...
BA BAM!!
!!
...TO HEAR THE HIGA-SHIDE CHEATING CASE!!
WELL, EVERY-ONE?
NO OBJEC-TION!
I VOTE IN FAVOR!
INTRIGUING.
I'M FINE WITH IT, OF COURSE...
PROSECU-TOR?
SMIRK...
I'LL WIN!
MY PLEASURE!!
AND SO, CLASS 6-3'S THIRD SCHOOL JUDGMENT WAS UNDERWAY!

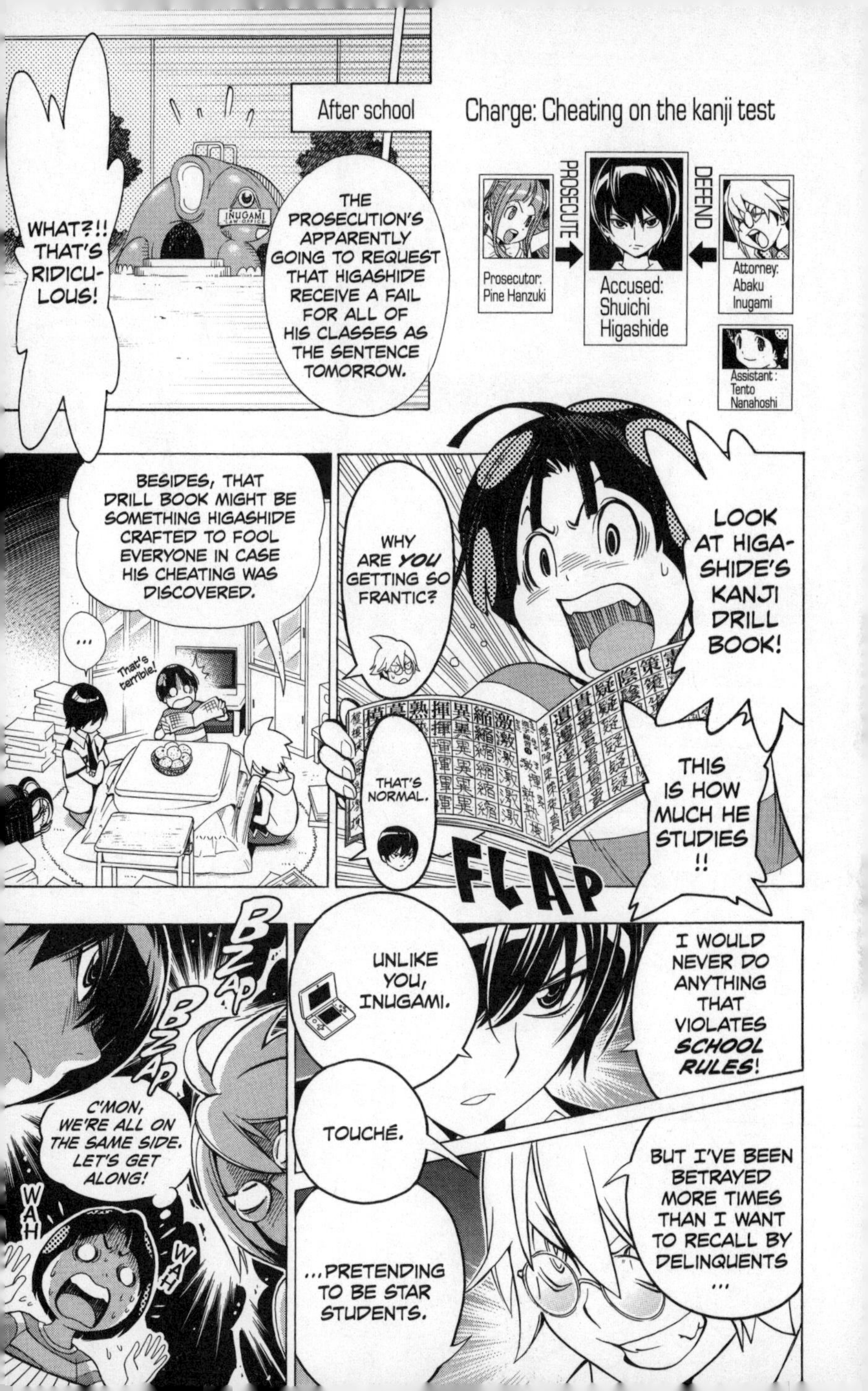

Charge: Cheating on the kanji test
PROSECUTE
DEFEND
Prosecutor: Pine Hanzuki
Accused: Shuichi Higashide
Attorney: Abaku Inugami
Assistant : Tento Nanahoshi
After school
INUGAMI LAW OFFICE
THE PROSECUTION'S APPARENTLY GOING TO REQUEST THAT HIGASHIDE RECEIVE A FAIL FOR ALL OF HIS CLASSES AS THE SENTENCE TOMORROW.
WHAT?!! THAT'S RIDICULOUS!
LOOK AT HIGASHIDE'S KANJI DRILL BOOK!
WHY ARE *YOU* GETTING SO FRANTIC?
THIS IS HOW MUCH HE STUDIES!!
THAT'S NORMAL.
FLAP
BESIDES, THAT DRILL BOOK MIGHT BE SOMETHING HIGASHIDE CRAFTED TO FOOL EVERYONE IN CASE HIS CHEATING WAS DISCOVERED.
...
That's terrible!
I WOULD NEVER DO ANYTHING THAT VIOLATES ***SCHOOL RULES***!
UNLIKE YOU, INUGAMI.
TOUCHÉ.
BUT I'VE BEEN BETRAYED MORE TIMES THAN I WANT TO RECALL BY DELINQUENTS ...
...PRETENDING TO BE STAR STUDENTS.
BZZAP
BZZAP
C'MON, WE'RE ALL ON THE SAME SIDE. LET'S GET ALONG!
WAH
WAH

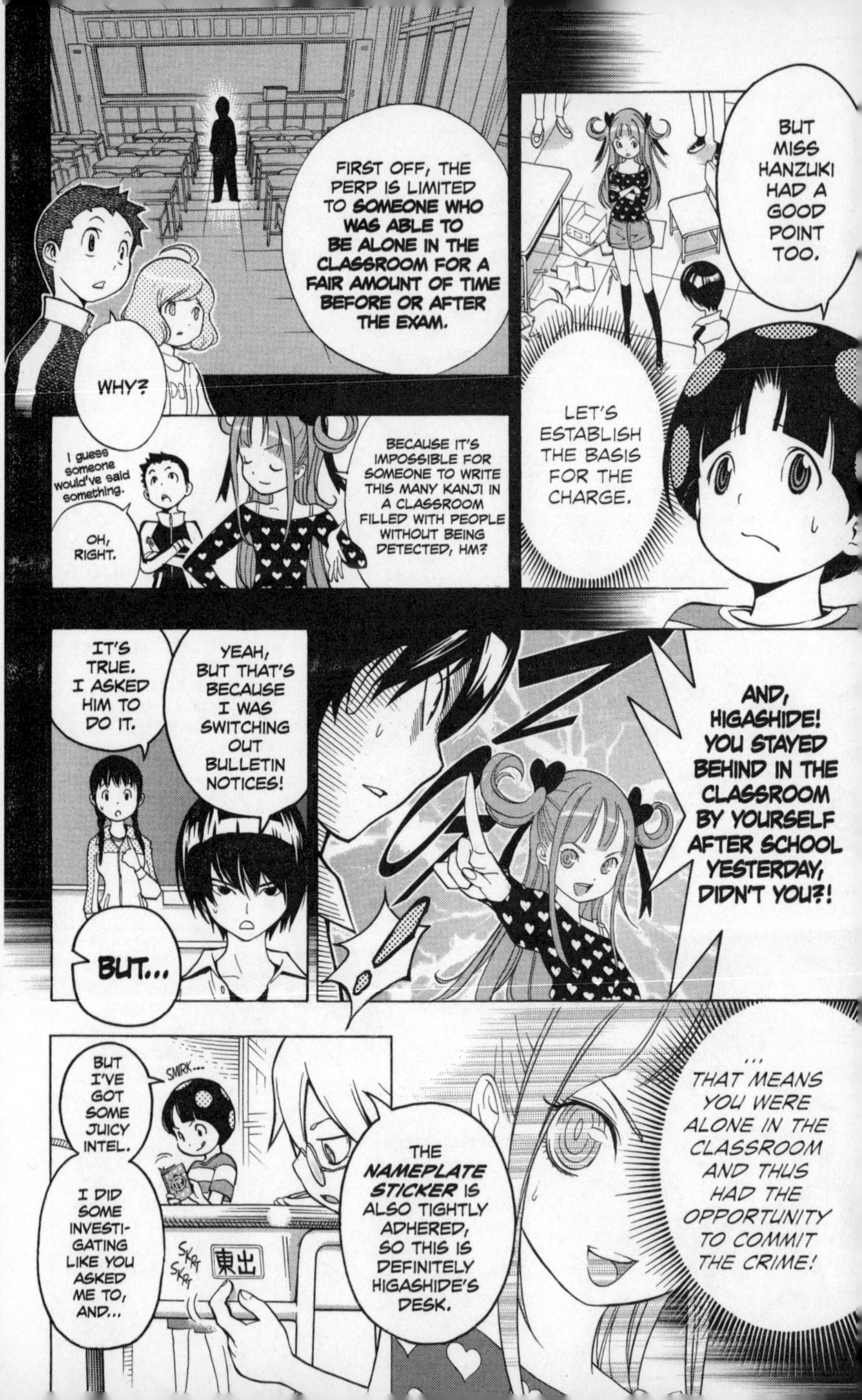
BUT MISS HANZUKI HAD A GOOD POINT TOO.
LET'S ESTABLISH THE BASIS FOR THE CHARGE.
FIRST OFF, THE PERP IS LIMITED TO **SOMEONE WHO WAS ABLE TO BE ALONE IN THE CLASSROOM FOR A FAIR AMOUNT OF TIME BEFORE OR AFTER THE EXAM.**
WHY?
BECAUSE IT'S IMPOSSIBLE FOR SOMEONE TO WRITE THIS MANY KANJI IN A CLASSROOM FILLED WITH PEOPLE WITHOUT BEING DETECTED, HM?
OH, RIGHT.
I guess someone would've said something.
AND, HIGASHIDE! YOU STAYED BEHIND IN THE CLASSROOM BY YOURSELF AFTER SCHOOL YESTERDAY, DIDN'T YOU?!
YEAH, BUT THAT'S BECAUSE I WAS SWITCHING OUT BULLETIN NOTICES!
IT'S TRUE. I ASKED HIM TO DO IT.
BUT...
...THAT MEANS YOU WERE ALONE IN THE CLASSROOM AND THUS HAD THE OPPORTUNITY TO COMMIT THE CRIME!
THE *NAMEPLATE STICKER* IS ALSO TIGHTLY ADHERED, SO THIS IS DEFINITELY HIGASHIDE'S DESK.
東出
SKRT SKRT
SMIRK...
BUT I'VE GOT SOME JUICY INTEL.
I DID SOME INVESTI-GATING LIKE YOU ASKED ME TO, AND...

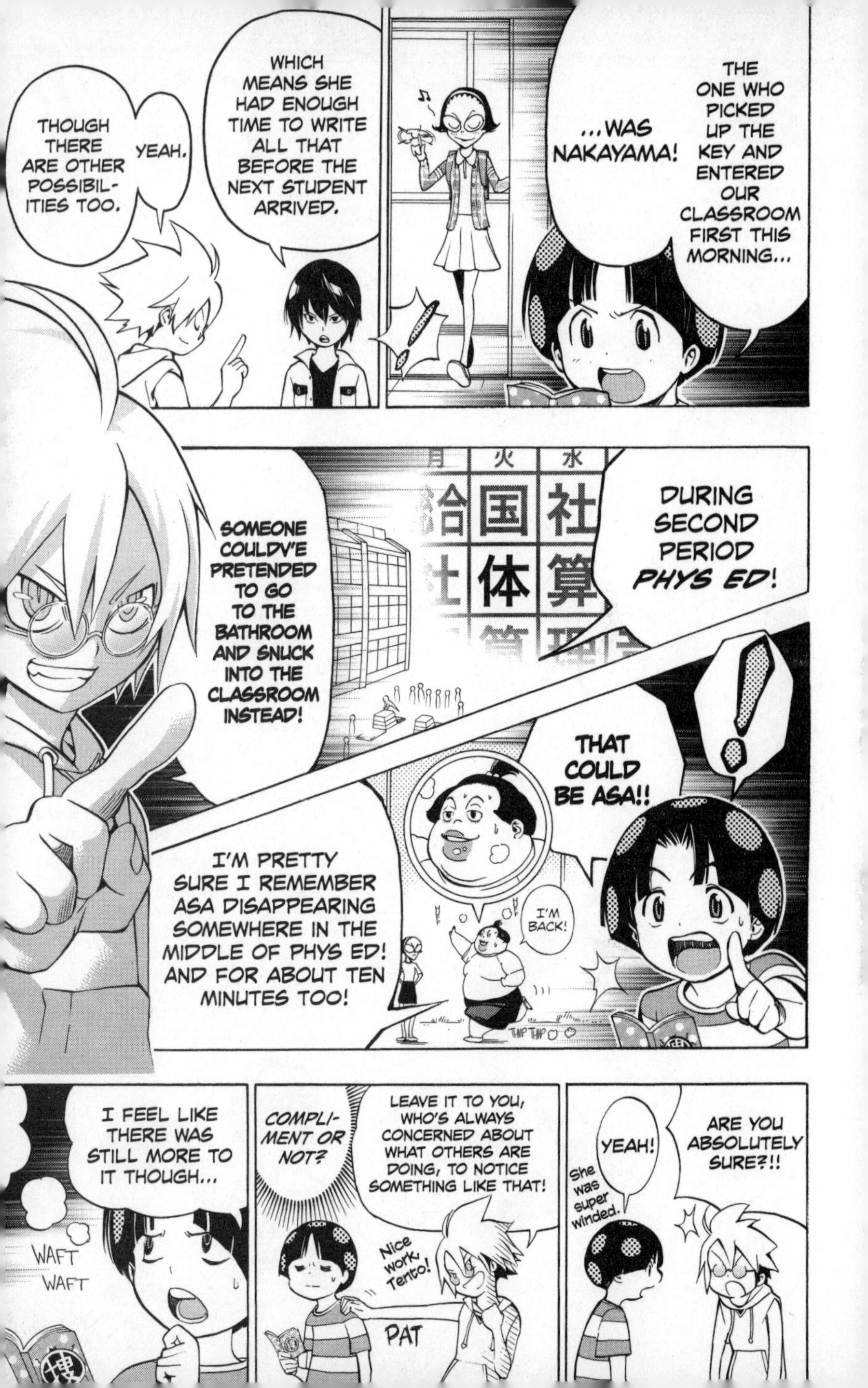
THE ONE WHO PICKED UP THE KEY AND ENTERED OUR CLASSROOM FIRST THIS MORNING...
...WAS NAKAYAMA!
WHICH MEANS SHE HAD ENOUGH TIME TO WRITE ALL THAT BEFORE THE NEXT STUDENT ARRIVED.
YEAH.
THOUGH THERE ARE OTHER POSSIBIL-ITIES TOO.
DURING SECOND PERIOD PHYS ED!
THAT COULD BE ASA!!
I'M PRETTY SURE I REMEMBER ASA DISAPPEARING SOMEWHERE IN THE MIDDLE OF PHYS ED! AND FOR ABOUT TEN MINUTES TOO!
I'M BACK!
SOMEONE COULDV'E PRETENDED TO GO TO THE BATHROOM AND SNUCK INTO THE CLASSROOM INSTEAD!
ARE YOU ABSOLUTELY SURE?!!
YEAH!
She was super winded.
LEAVE IT TO YOU, WHO'S ALWAYS CONCERNED ABOUT WHAT OTHERS ARE DOING, TO NOTICE SOMETHING LIKE THAT!
COMPLI-MENT OR NOT?
Nice work, Tento!
PAT
I FEEL LIKE THERE WAS STILL MORE TO IT THOUGH...
WAFT WAFT

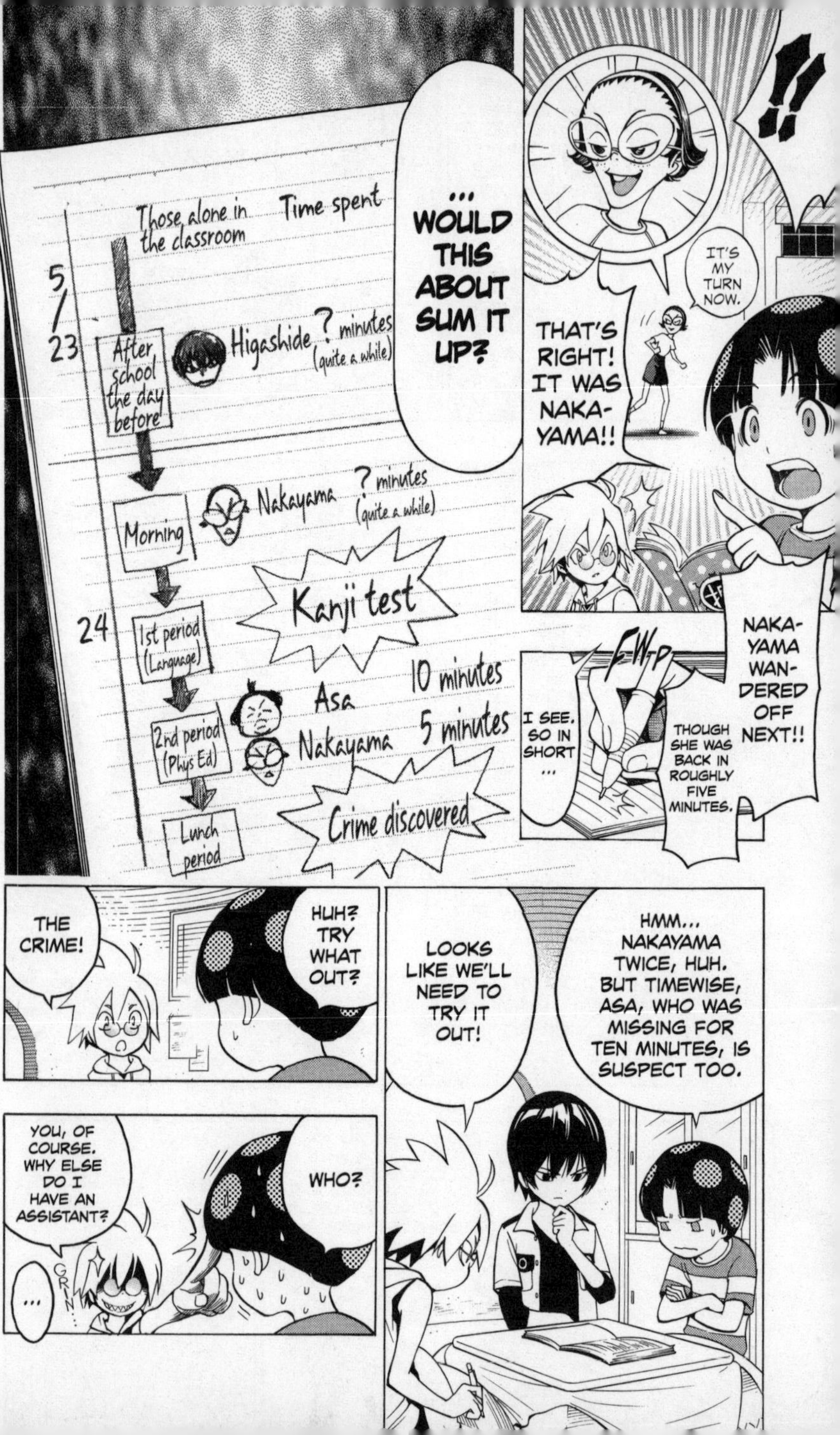
!!
IT'S MY TURN NOW.
THAT'S RIGHT! IT WAS NAKA-YAMA!!
NAKA-YAMA WAN-DERED OFF NEXT!!
THOUGH SHE WAS BACK IN ROUGHLY FIVE MINUTES.
FWIP
I SEE. SO IN SHORT ...
...WOULD THIS ABOUT SUM IT UP?
Those alone in the classroom
Time spent
5/23
After school the day before
Higashide
? minutes (quite a while)
Morning
Nakayama
? minutes (quite a while)
24
1st period (Language)
Kanji test
2nd period (Phys Ed)
Asa
10 minutes
Nakayama
5 minutes
Lunch period
Crime discovered
HMM... NAKAYAMA TWICE, HUH. BUT TIMEWISE, ASA, WHO WAS MISSING FOR TEN MINUTES, IS SUSPECT TOO.
LOOKS LIKE WE'LL NEED TO TRY IT OUT!
HUH? TRY WHAT OUT?
THE CRIME!
WHO?
YOU, OF COURSE. WHY ELSE DO I HAVE AN ASSISTANT?
GRIN...
...

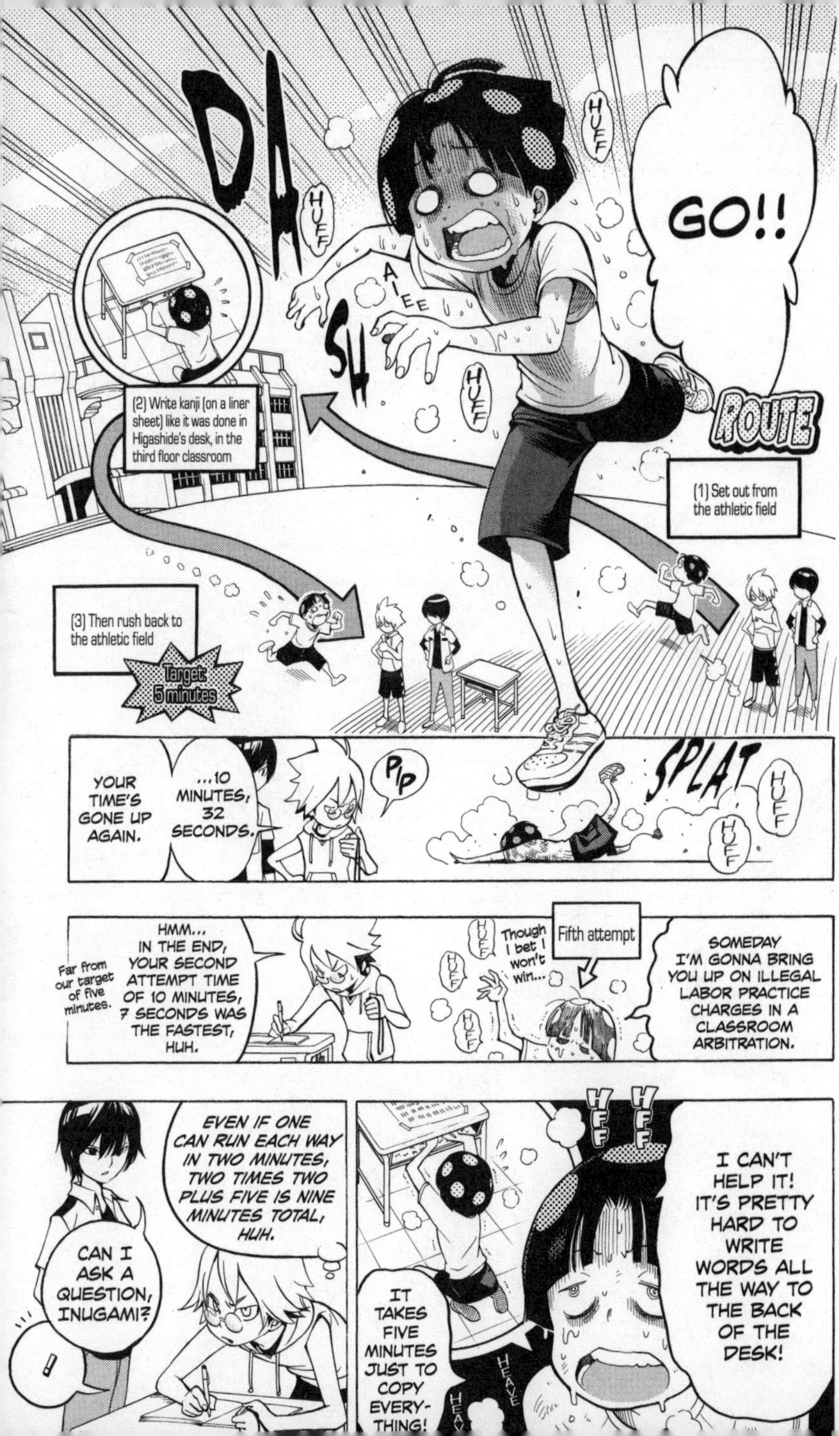
GO!!
HUFF
DA
HUFF
AIEEE
SH
HUFF
ROUTE
(1) Set out from the athletic field
(2) Write kanji (on a liner sheet) like it was done in Higashide's desk, in the third floor classroom
(3) Then rush back to the athletic field
Target: 5 minutes
SPLAT
HUFF
HUFF
PIP
...10 MINUTES, 32 SECONDS.
YOUR TIME'S GONE UP AGAIN.
SOMEDAY I'M GONNA BRING YOU UP ON ILLEGAL LABOR PRACTICE CHARGES IN A CLASSROOM ARBITRATION.
Fifth attempt
Though I bet I won't win...
HUFF
HUFF
HUFF
HMM... IN THE END, YOUR SECOND ATTEMPT TIME OF 10 MINUTES, 7 SECONDS WAS THE FASTEST, HUH.
Far from our target of five minutes.
HFF HFF
I CAN'T HELP IT! IT'S PRETTY HARD TO WRITE WORDS ALL THE WAY TO THE BACK OF THE DESK!
IT TAKES FIVE MINUTES JUST TO COPY EVERY-THING!
HEAVE
HEAVE
EVEN IF ONE CAN RUN EACH WAY IN TWO MINUTES, TWO TIMES TWO PLUS FIVE IS NINE MINUTES TOTAL, HUH.
CAN I ASK A QUESTION, INUGAMI?
!

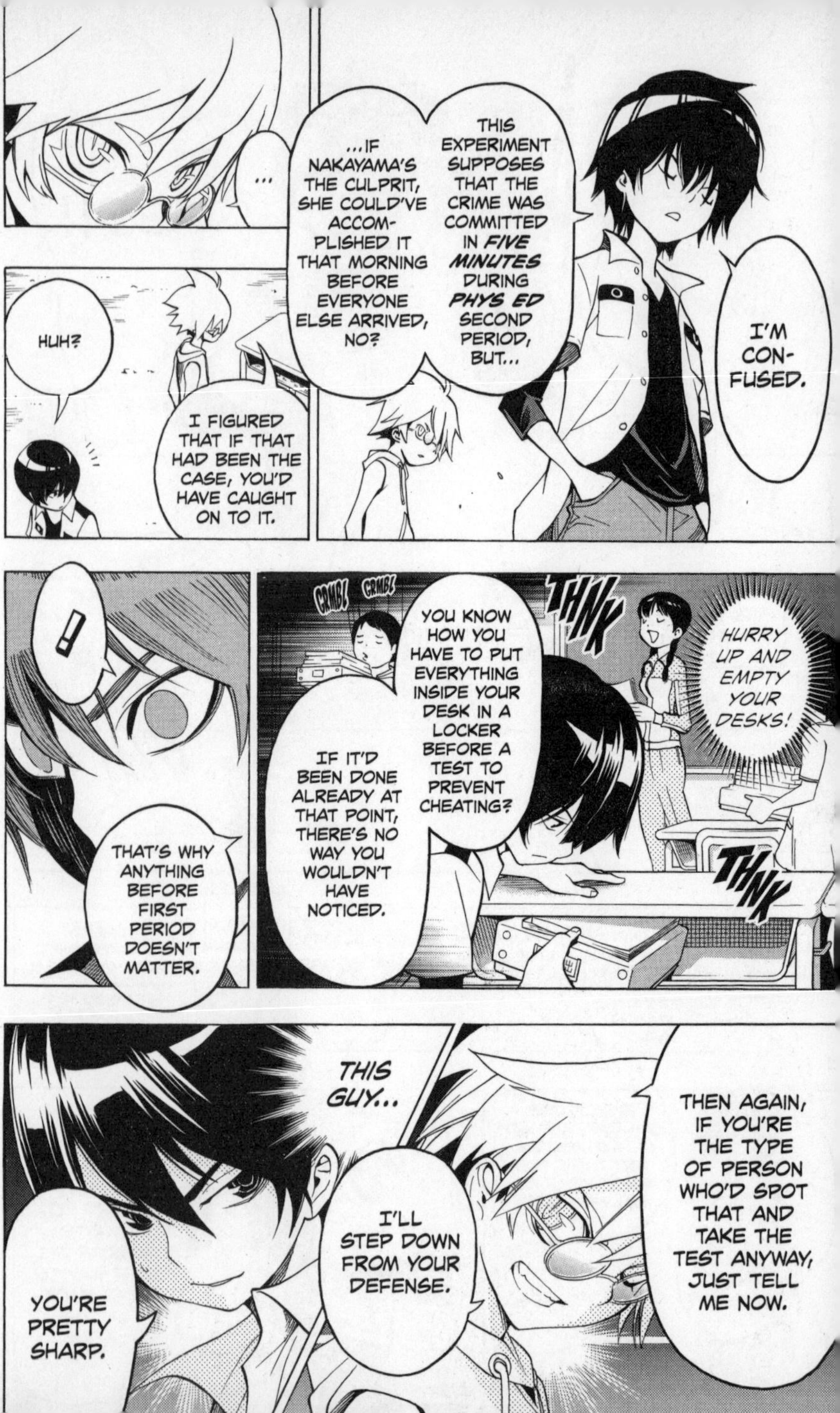
I'M CONFUSED.
THIS EXPERIMENT SUPPOSES THAT THE CRIME WAS COMMITTED IN *FIVE MINUTES* DURING *PHYS ED* SECOND PERIOD, BUT...
...IF NAKAYAMA'S THE CULPRIT, SHE COULD'VE ACCOMPLISHED IT THAT MORNING BEFORE EVERYONE ELSE ARRIVED, NO?
...
HUH?
I FIGURED THAT IF THAT HAD BEEN THE CASE, YOU'D HAVE CAUGHT ON TO IT.
HURRY UP AND EMPTY YOUR DESKS!
THNK
THNK
GRMBL
GRMBL
YOU KNOW HOW YOU HAVE TO PUT EVERYTHING INSIDE YOUR DESK IN A LOCKER BEFORE A TEST TO PREVENT CHEATING?
IF IT'D BEEN DONE ALREADY AT THAT POINT, THERE'S NO WAY YOU WOULDN'T HAVE NOTICED.
!
THAT'S WHY ANYTHING BEFORE FIRST PERIOD DOESN'T MATTER.
THEN AGAIN, IF YOU'RE THE TYPE OF PERSON WHO'D SPOT THAT AND TAKE THE TEST ANYWAY, JUST TELL ME NOW.
THIS GUY...
I'LL STEP DOWN FROM YOUR DEFENSE.
YOU'RE PRETTY SHARP.

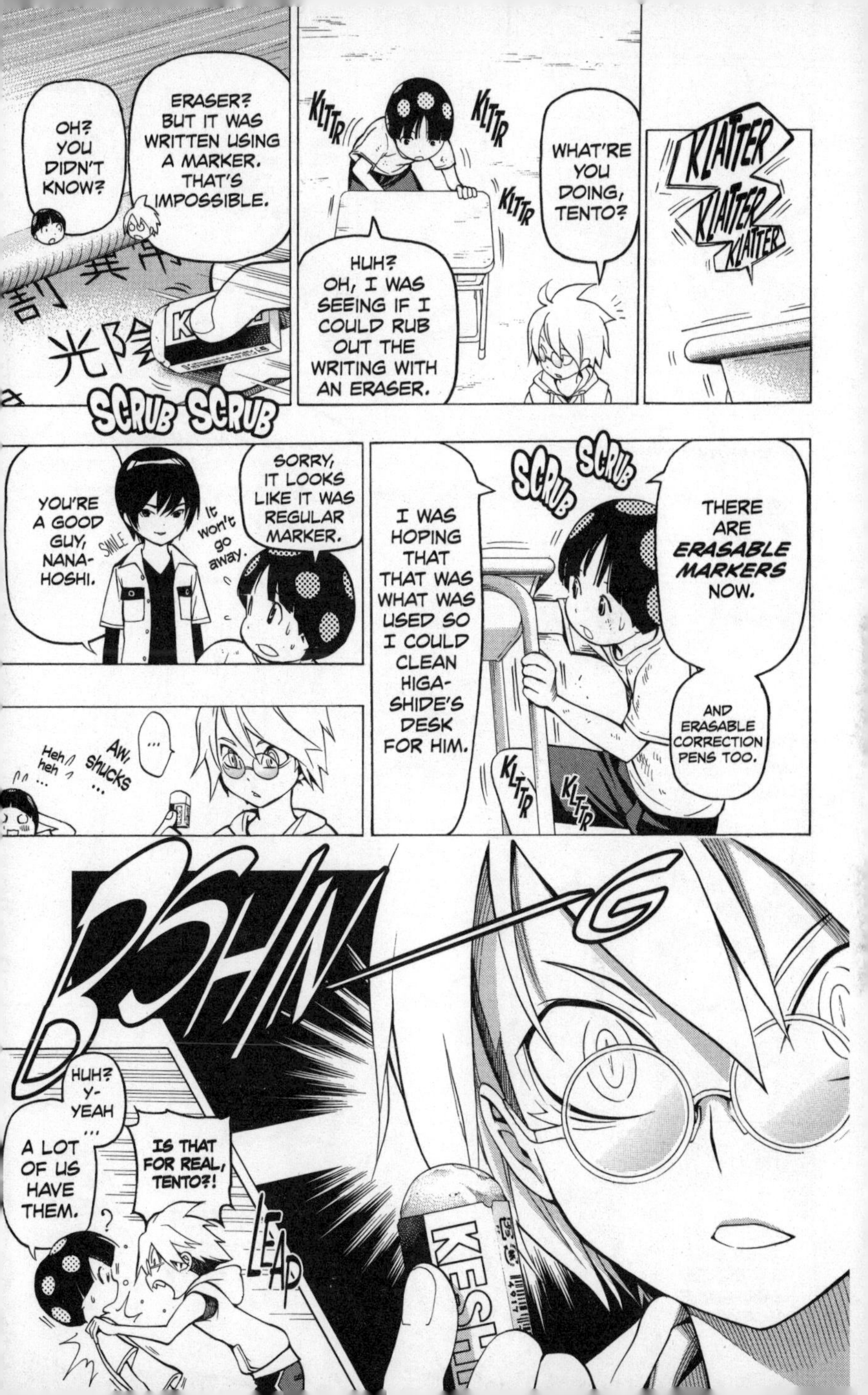
KLATTER
KLATTER
KLATTER
KLTTR
KLTTR
KLTTR
WHAT'RE YOU DOING, TENTO?
HUH? OH, I WAS SEEING IF I COULD RUB OUT THE WRITING WITH AN ERASER.
ERASER? BUT IT WAS WRITTEN USING A MARKER. THAT'S IMPOSSIBLE.
OH? YOU DIDN'T KNOW?
光陰
SCRUB SCRUB
SCRUB
SCRUB
THERE ARE ERASABLE MARKERS NOW.
AND ERASABLE CORRECTION PENS TOO.
I WAS HOPING THAT THAT WAS WHAT WAS USED SO I COULD CLEAN HIGA-SHIDE'S DESK FOR HIM.
KLTTR
KLTTR
SORRY, IT LOOKS LIKE IT WAS REGULAR MARKER.
It won't go away.
YOU'RE A GOOD GUY, NANA-HOSHI.
SMILE
...
Aw, shucks...
Heh heh...
BOSHING
IS THAT FOR REAL, TENTO?!
HUH? Y-YEAH...
A LOT OF US HAVE THEM.
?
LEAP
KESHI

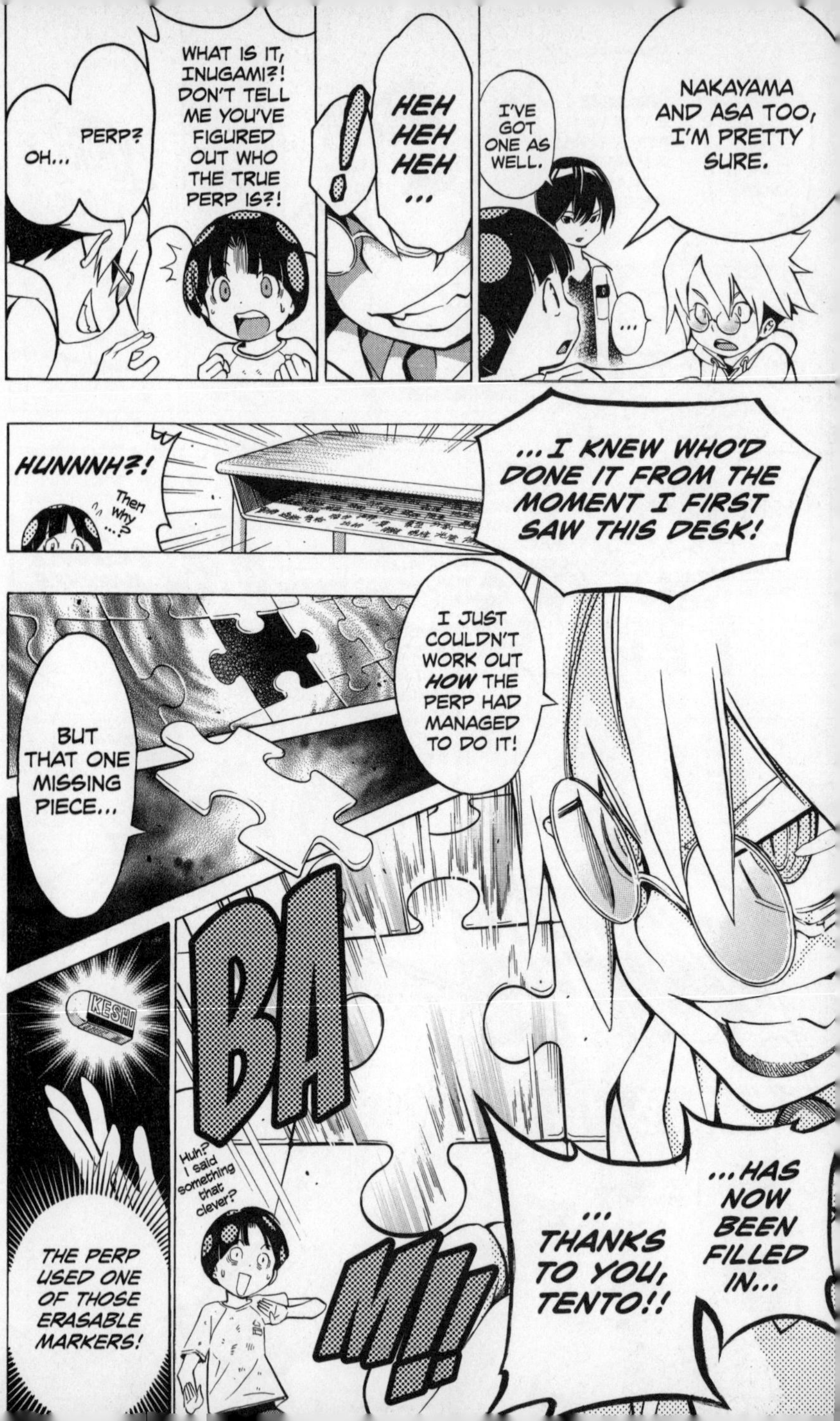
NAKAYAMA AND ASA TOO, I'M PRETTY SURE.
I'VE GOT ONE AS WELL.
...
HEH HEH HEH...
!
WHAT IS IT, INUGAMI?! DON'T TELL ME YOU'VE FIGURED OUT WHO THE TRUE PERP IS?!
PERP? OH...
...I KNEW WHO'D DONE IT FROM THE MOMENT I FIRST SAW THIS DESK!
HUNNNH?!
Then why...?
I JUST COULDN'T WORK OUT *HOW* THE PERP HAD MANAGED TO DO IT!
BUT THAT ONE MISSING PIECE...
...HAS NOW BEEN FILLED IN...
...THANKS TO YOU, TENTO!!
BAM!!
Huh? I said something that clever?
KESHI
THE PERP USED ONE OF THOSE ERASABLE MARKERS!

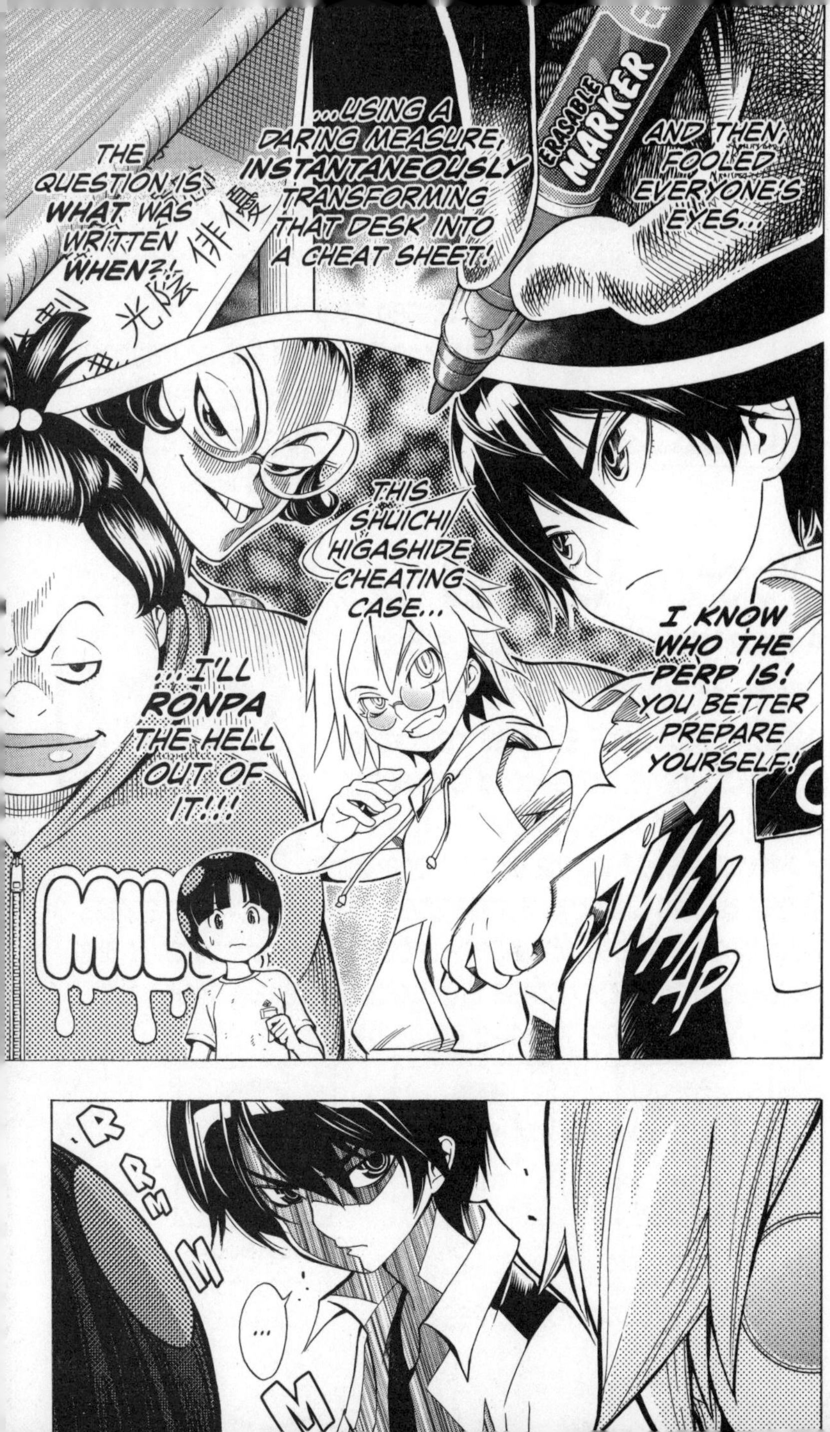
THE QUESTION IS WHAT WAS WRITTEN WHEN?!
...USING A DARING MEASURE, INSTANTANEOUSLY TRANSFORMING THAT DESK INTO A CHEAT SHEET!
ERASABLE MARKER
AND THEN, FOOLED EVERYONE'S EYES...
THIS SHUICHI HIGASHIDE CHEATING CASE...
...I'LL RONPA THE HELL OUT OF IT!!!
I KNOW WHO THE PERP IS! YOU BETTER PREPARE YOURSELF!
MIL
WHAP
RRMMM
...

Akane Akimoto

Class 6-3 homeroom teacher.

I wanted to pioneer a new loser-cute genre (of character), but unfortunately her loser side is too dominating, so she started to appear less and less.

Yoichiro Nukumizu (age 5)

A kindergartner judge, a.k.a. a Baby.

Due to an overwhelming number of negative reactions such as *revolting* and *sick*, he is the second character whose screen time got cut.

However, please let me explain one thing.

These Babies undergo accelerated aging due to the stress of judging others, but once they enter grade school, they are released from such stress and gradually regain their youth...!

In Lil' Nuku's case, it would go as below:

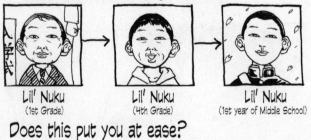

Lil' Nuku
(1st Grade)

Lil' Nuku
(4th Grade)

Lil' Nuku
(1st year of Middle School)

Does this put you at ease?

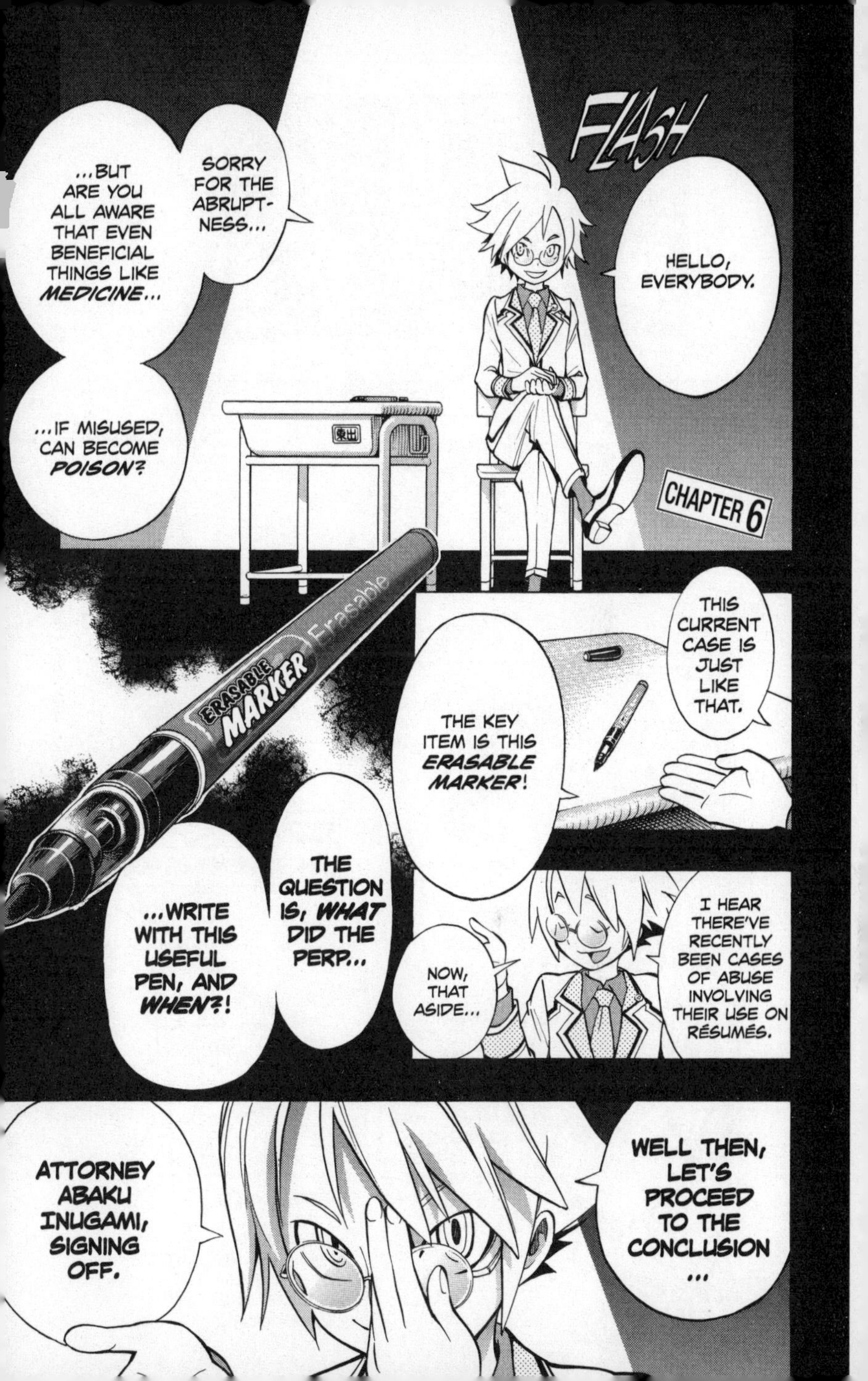
FLASH
HELLO, EVERYBODY.
SORRY FOR THE ABRUPTNESS...
...BUT ARE YOU ALL AWARE THAT EVEN BENEFICIAL THINGS LIKE *MEDICINE*...
...IF MISUSED, CAN BECOME *POISON*?
東出
CHAPTER 6
THIS CURRENT CASE IS JUST LIKE THAT.
THE KEY ITEM IS THIS *ERASABLE MARKER*!
ERASABLE MARKER
Erasable
I HEAR THERE'VE RECENTLY BEEN CASES OF ABUSE INVOLVING THEIR USE ON RÉSUMÉS.
NOW, THAT ASIDE...
THE QUESTION IS, *WHAT* DID THE PERP...
...WRITE WITH THIS USEFUL PEN, AND *WHEN*?!
WELL THEN, LET'S PROCEED TO THE CONCLUSION ...
ATTORNEY ABAKU INUGAMI, SIGNING OFF.

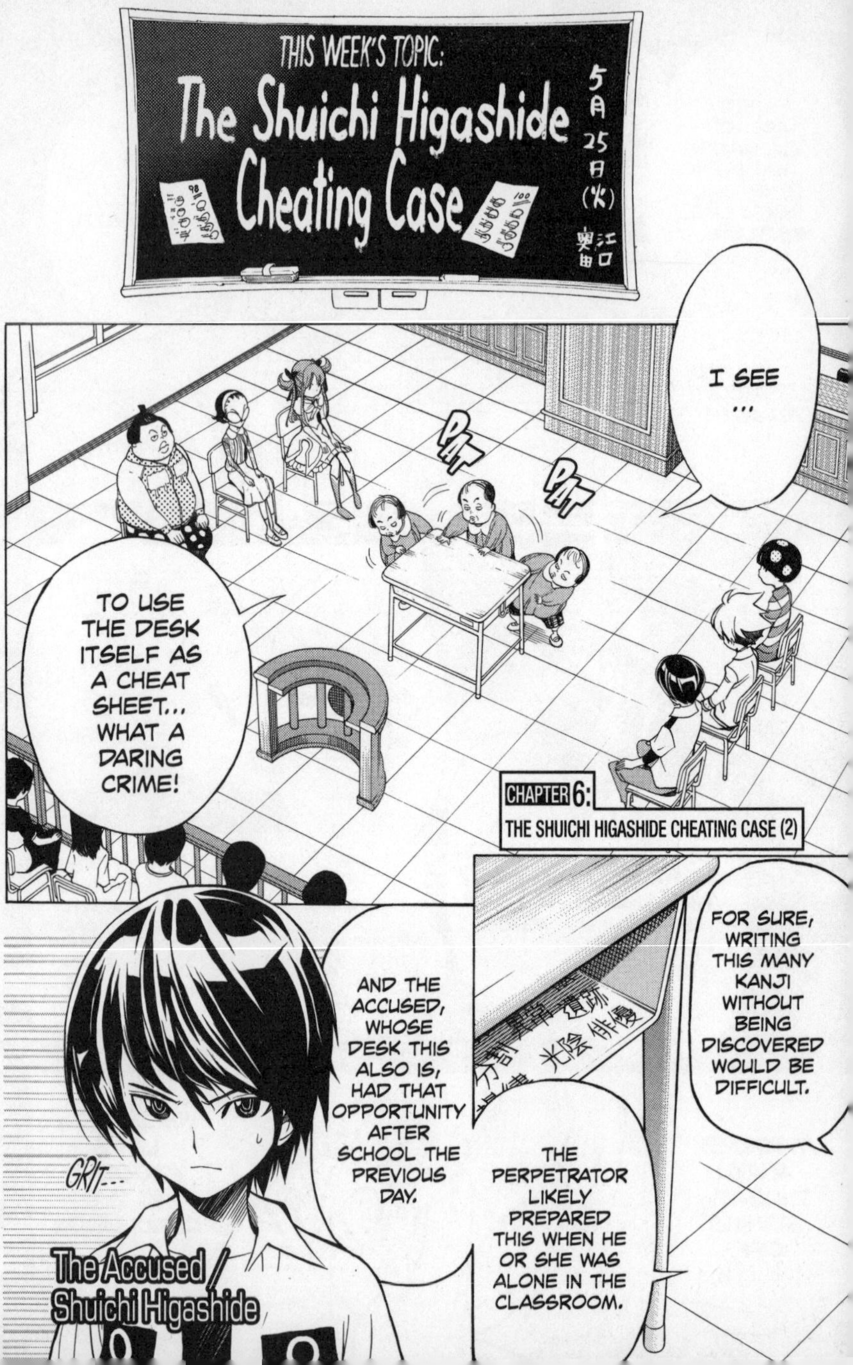
THIS WEEK'S TOPIC:
The Shuichi Higashide Cheating Case
5月25日(火)
江口
奥田
I SEE...
PAT
PAT
TO USE THE DESK ITSELF AS A CHEAT SHEET... WHAT A DARING CRIME!
CHAPTER 6:
THE SHUICHI HIGASHIDE CHEATING CASE (2)
FOR SURE, WRITING THIS MANY KANJI WITHOUT BEING DISCOVERED WOULD BE DIFFICULT.
THE PERPETRATOR LIKELY PREPARED THIS WHEN HE OR SHE WAS ALONE IN THE CLASSROOM.
AND THE ACCUSED, WHOSE DESK THIS ALSO IS, HAD THAT OPPORTUNITY AFTER SCHOOL THE PREVIOUS DAY.
GRIT...
The Accused / Shuichi Higashide

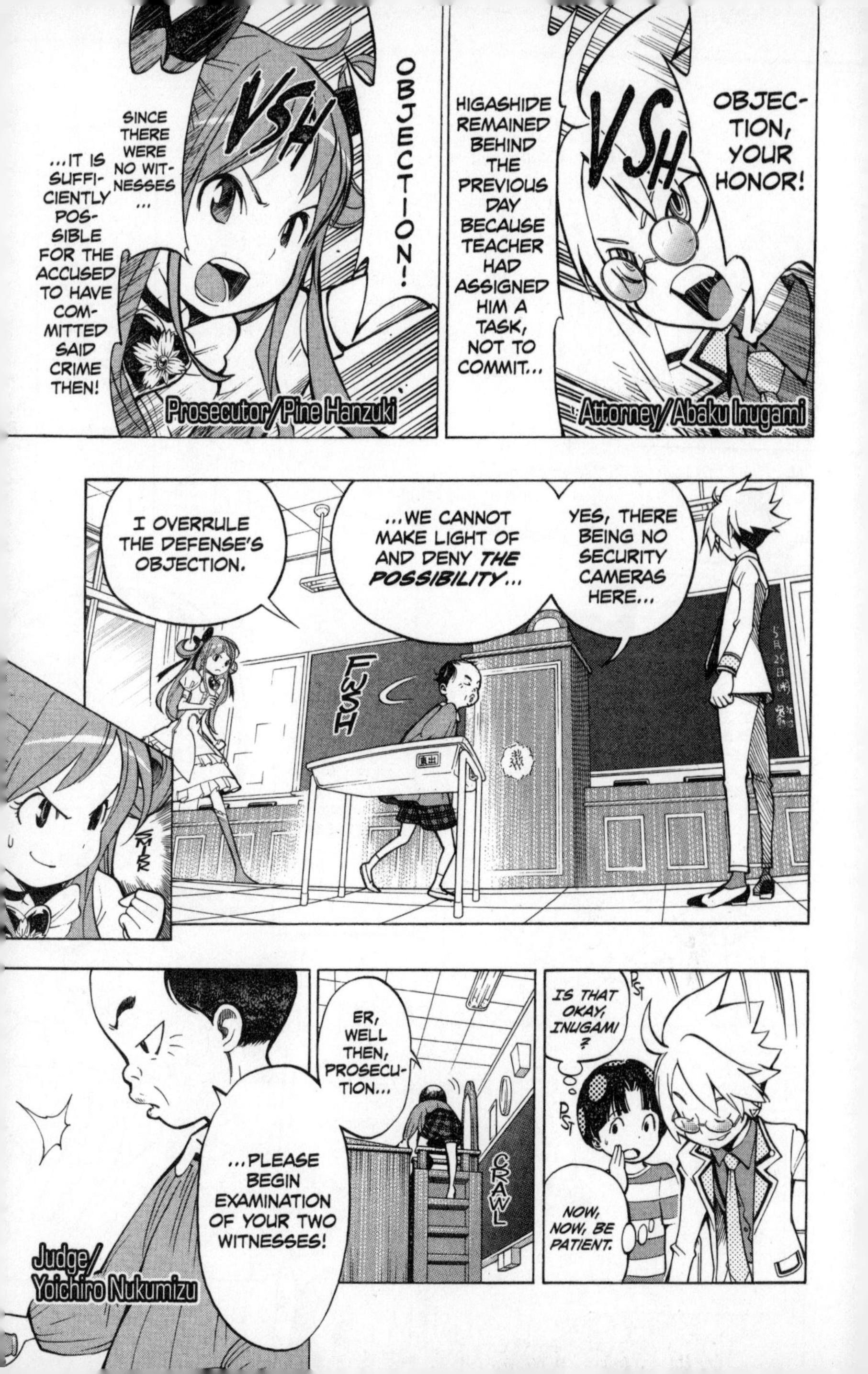
VSH
OBJECTION, YOUR HONOR!
HIGASHIDE REMAINED BEHIND THE PREVIOUS DAY BECAUSE TEACHER HAD ASSIGNED HIM A TASK, NOT TO COMMIT...
Attorney/Abaku Inugami
OBJECTION!
VSH
SINCE THERE WERE NO WITNESSES...
...IT IS SUFFICIENTLY POSSIBLE FOR THE ACCUSED TO HAVE COMMITTED SAID CRIME THEN!
Prosecutor/Pine Hanzuki
YES, THERE BEING NO SECURITY CAMERAS HERE...
...WE CANNOT MAKE LIGHT OF AND DENY *THE POSSIBILITY*...
I OVERRULE THE DEFENSE'S OBJECTION.
FWSH
SMIRK
PST
IS THAT OKAY, INUGAMI?
PST
NOW, NOW, BE PATIENT.
ER, WELL THEN, PROSECUTION...
CRAWL
...PLEASE BEGIN EXAMINATION OF YOUR TWO WITNESSES!
Judge/Yoichiro Nukumizu

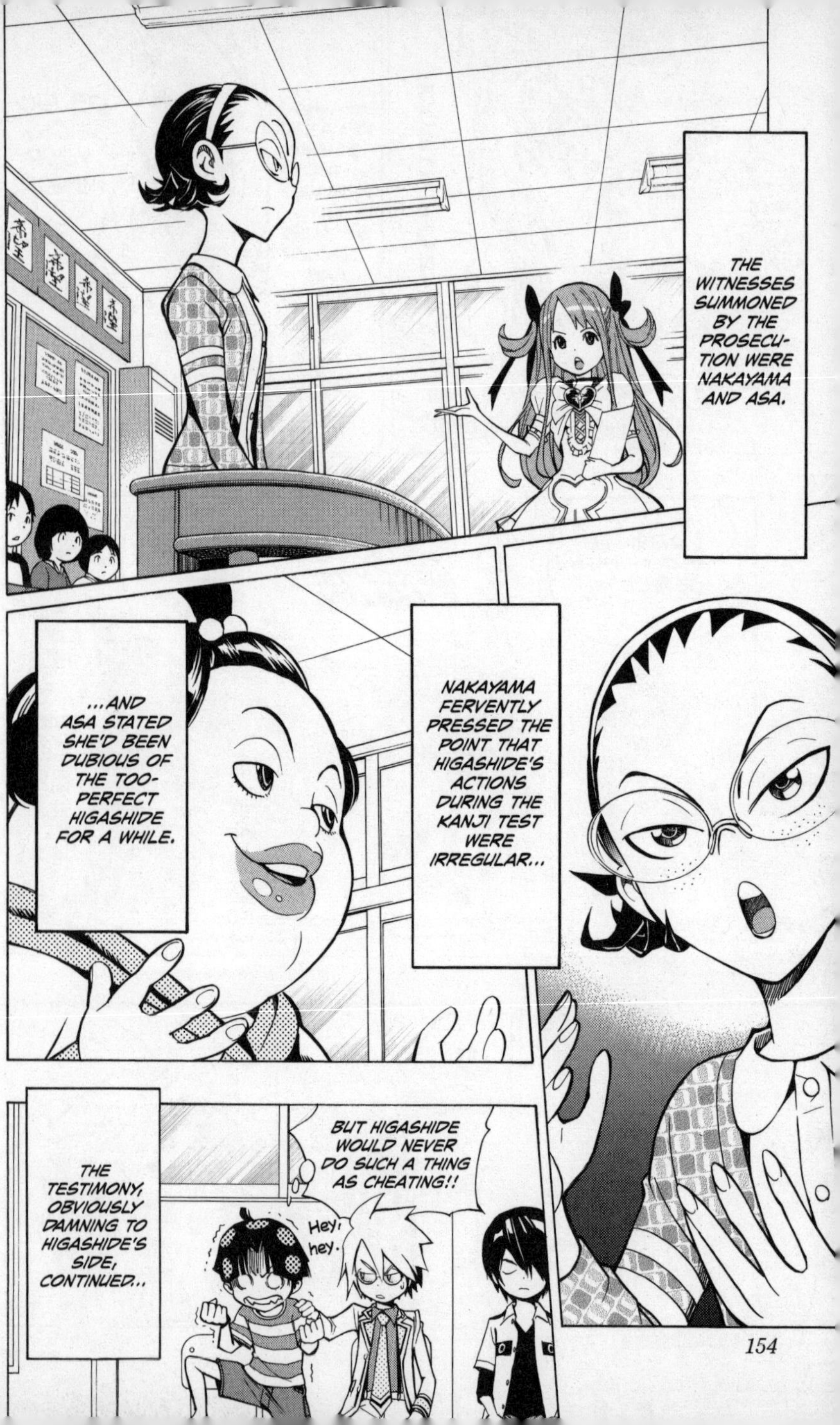
THE WITNESSES SUMMONED BY THE PROSECUTION WERE NAKAYAMA AND ASA.
NAKAYAMA FERVENTLY PRESSED THE POINT THAT HIGASHIDE'S ACTIONS DURING THE KANJI TEST WERE IRREGULAR...
...AND ASA STATED SHE'D BEEN DUBIOUS OF THE TOO-PERFECT HIGASHIDE FOR A WHILE.
BUT HIGASHIDE WOULD NEVER DO SUCH A THING AS CHEATING!!
Hey, hey.
THE TESTIMONY, OBVIOUSLY DAMNING TO HIGASHIDE'S SIDE, CONTINUED...

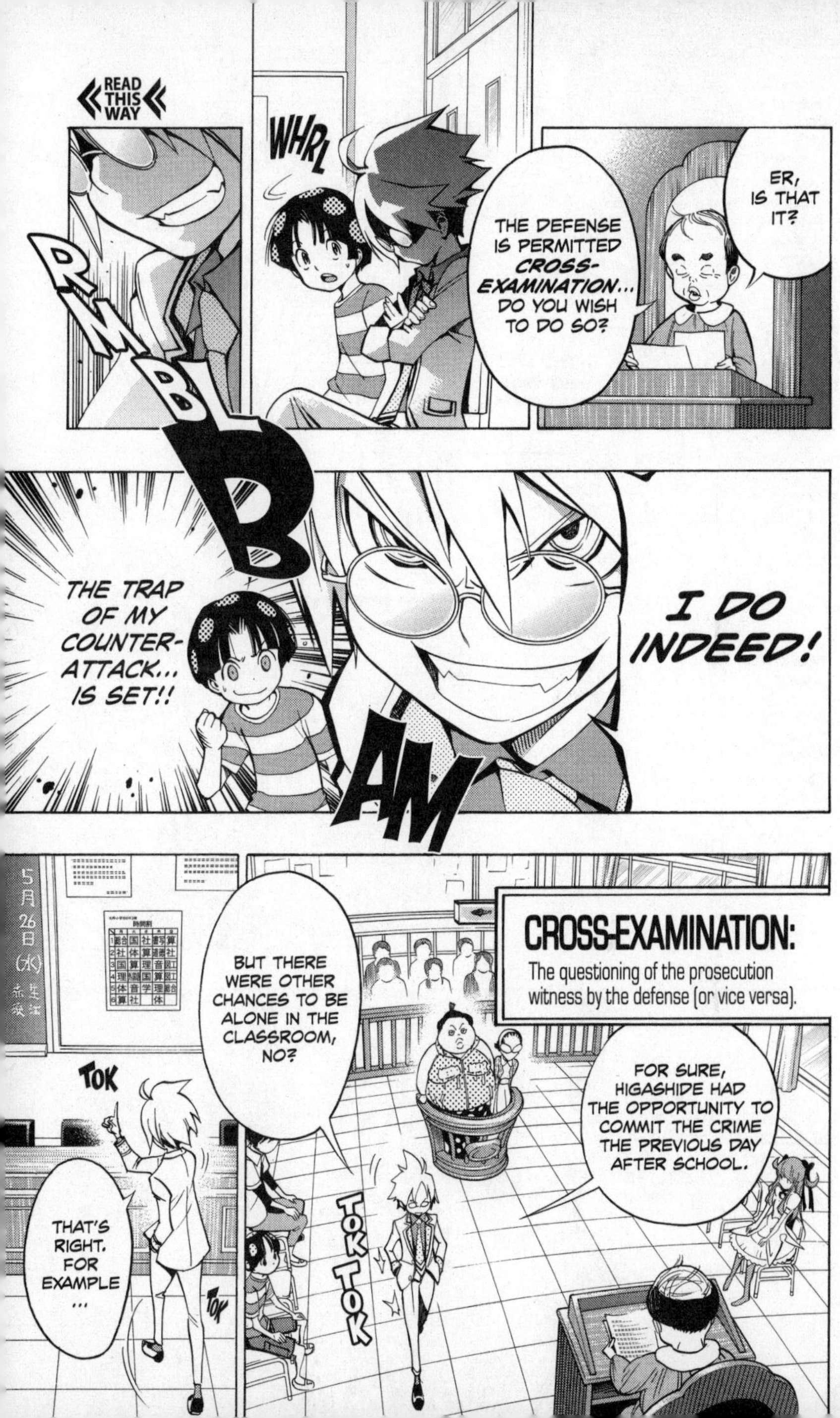

READ THIS WAY
ER, IS THAT IT?
THE DEFENSE IS PERMITTED CROSS-EXAMINATION... DO YOU WISH TO DO SO?
WHRL
RMBL
I DO INDEED!
BAM
THE TRAP OF MY COUNTER-ATTACK... IS SET!!
CROSS-EXAMINATION:
The questioning of the prosecution witness by the defense (or vice versa).
FOR SURE, HIGASHIDE HAD THE OPPORTUNITY TO COMMIT THE CRIME THE PREVIOUS DAY AFTER SCHOOL.
BUT THERE WERE OTHER CHANCES TO BE ALONE IN THE CLASSROOM, NO?
TOK TOK
TOK
TOK
THAT'S RIGHT. FOR EXAMPLE ...

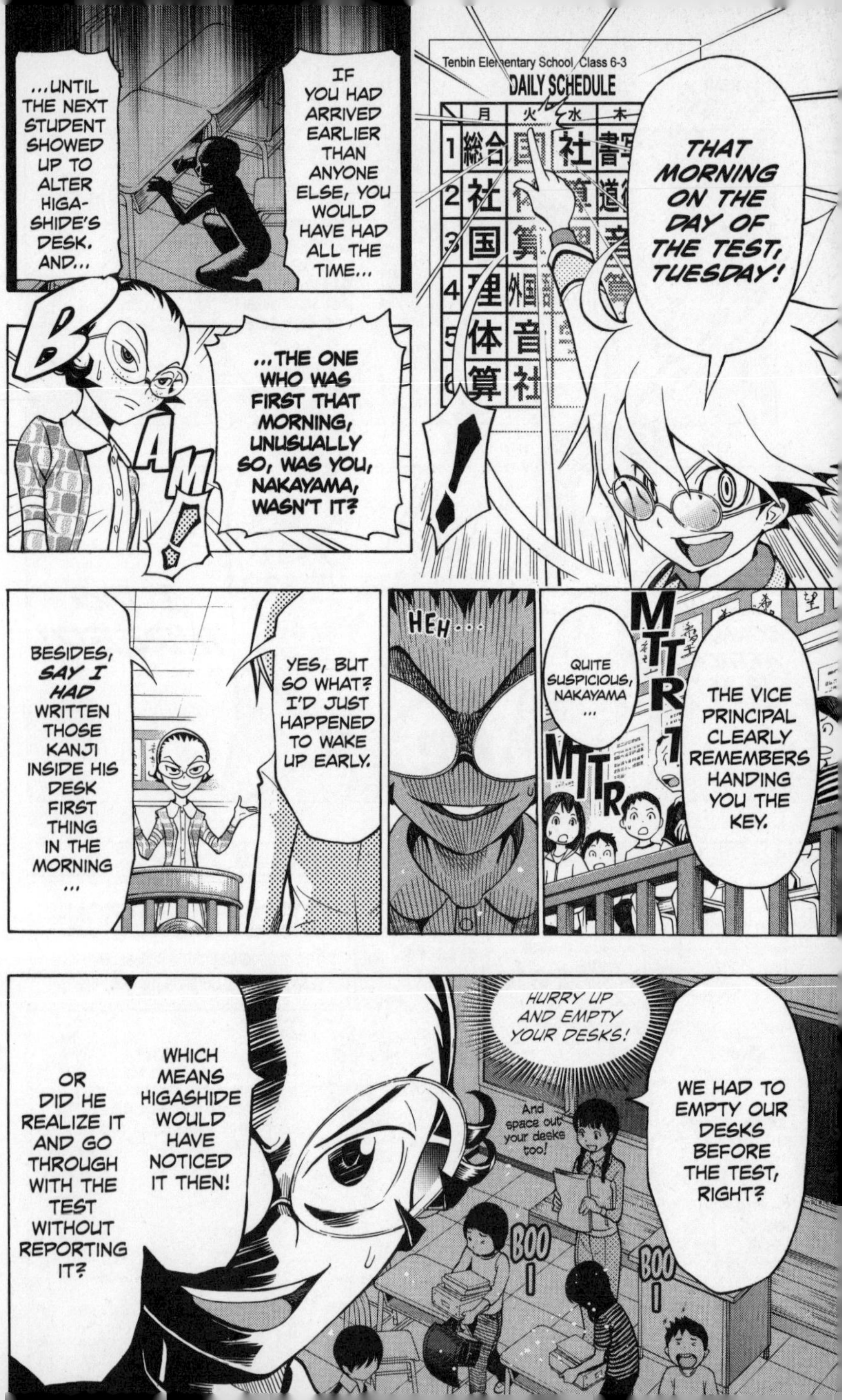

Tenbin Elementary School Class 6-3
DAILY SCHEDULE
THAT MORNING ON THE DAY OF THE TEST, TUESDAY!
!
IF YOU HAD ARRIVED EARLIER THAN ANYONE ELSE, YOU WOULD HAVE HAD ALL THE TIME...
...UNTIL THE NEXT STUDENT SHOWED UP TO ALTER HIGA-SHIDE'S DESK. AND...
...THE ONE WHO WAS FIRST THAT MORNING, UNUSUALLY SO, WAS YOU, NAKAYAMA, WASN'T IT?
BAM!
THE VICE PRINCIPAL CLEARLY REMEMBERS HANDING YOU THE KEY.
QUITE SUSPICIOUS, NAKAYAMA...
MTTR
MTTR
HEH...
YES, BUT SO WHAT? I'D JUST HAPPENED TO WAKE UP EARLY.
BESIDES, *SAY I HAD* WRITTEN THOSE KANJI INSIDE HIS DESK FIRST THING IN THE MORNING...
WE HAD TO EMPTY OUR DESKS BEFORE THE TEST, RIGHT?
HURRY UP AND EMPTY YOUR DESKS!
And space out your desks too!
BOOI
BOOI
WHICH MEANS HIGASHIDE WOULD HAVE NOTICED IT THEN!
OR DID HE REALIZE IT AND GO THROUGH WITH THE TEST WITHOUT REPORTING IT?

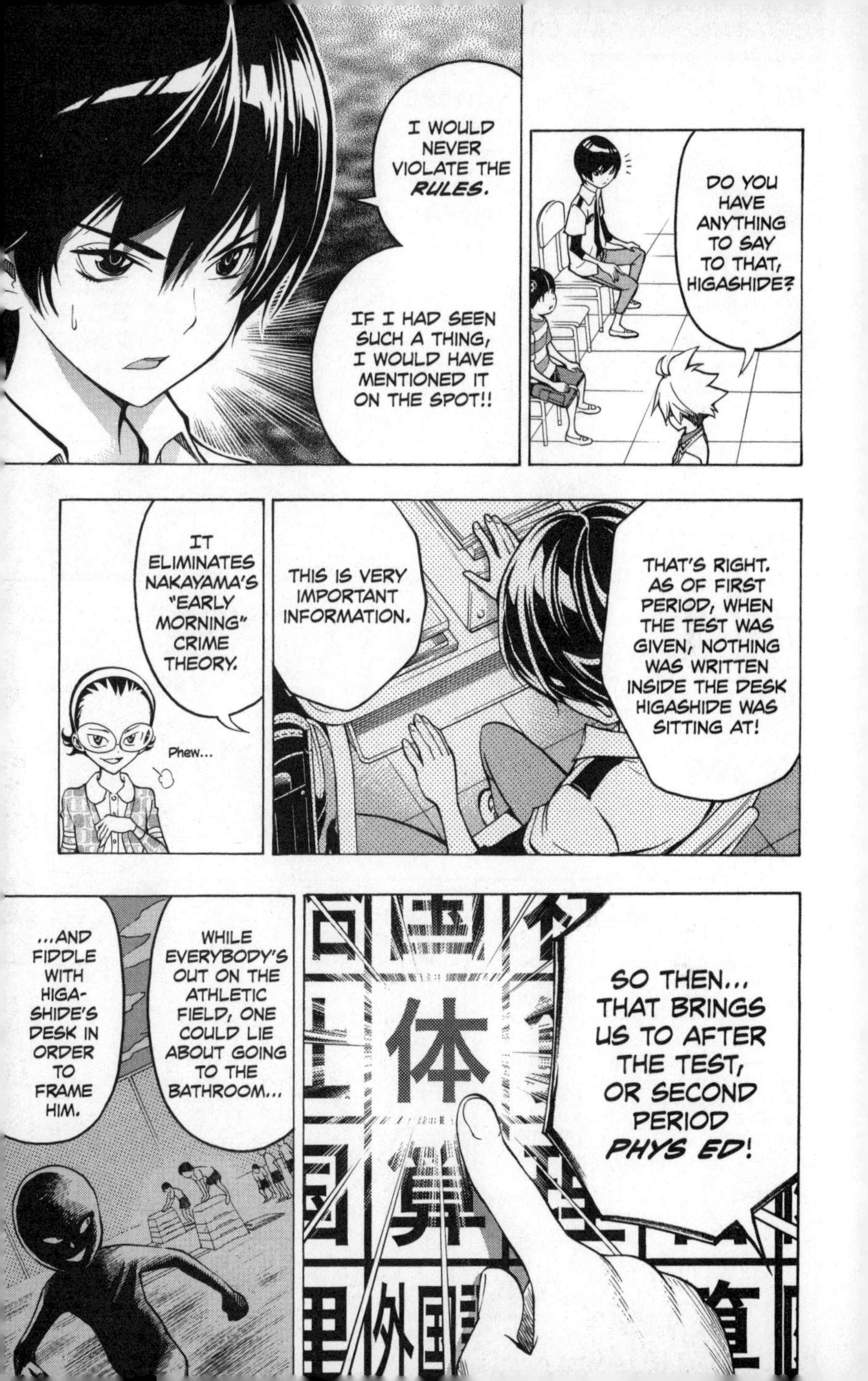
DO YOU HAVE ANYTHING TO SAY TO THAT, HIGASHIDE?
I WOULD NEVER VIOLATE THE *RULES.*
IF I HAD SEEN SUCH A THING, I WOULD HAVE MENTIONED IT ON THE SPOT!!
THAT'S RIGHT. AS OF FIRST PERIOD, WHEN THE TEST WAS GIVEN, NOTHING WAS WRITTEN INSIDE THE DESK HIGASHIDE WAS SITTING AT!
THIS IS VERY IMPORTANT INFORMATION.
IT ELIMINATES NAKAYAMA'S "EARLY MORNING" CRIME THEORY.
Phew...
体
SO THEN... THAT BRINGS US TO AFTER THE TEST, OR SECOND PERIOD *PHYS ED*!
WHILE EVERYBODY'S OUT ON THE ATHLETIC FIELD, ONE COULD LIE ABOUT GOING TO THE BATHROOM...
...AND FIDDLE WITH HIGA-SHIDE'S DESK IN ORDER TO FRAME HIM.

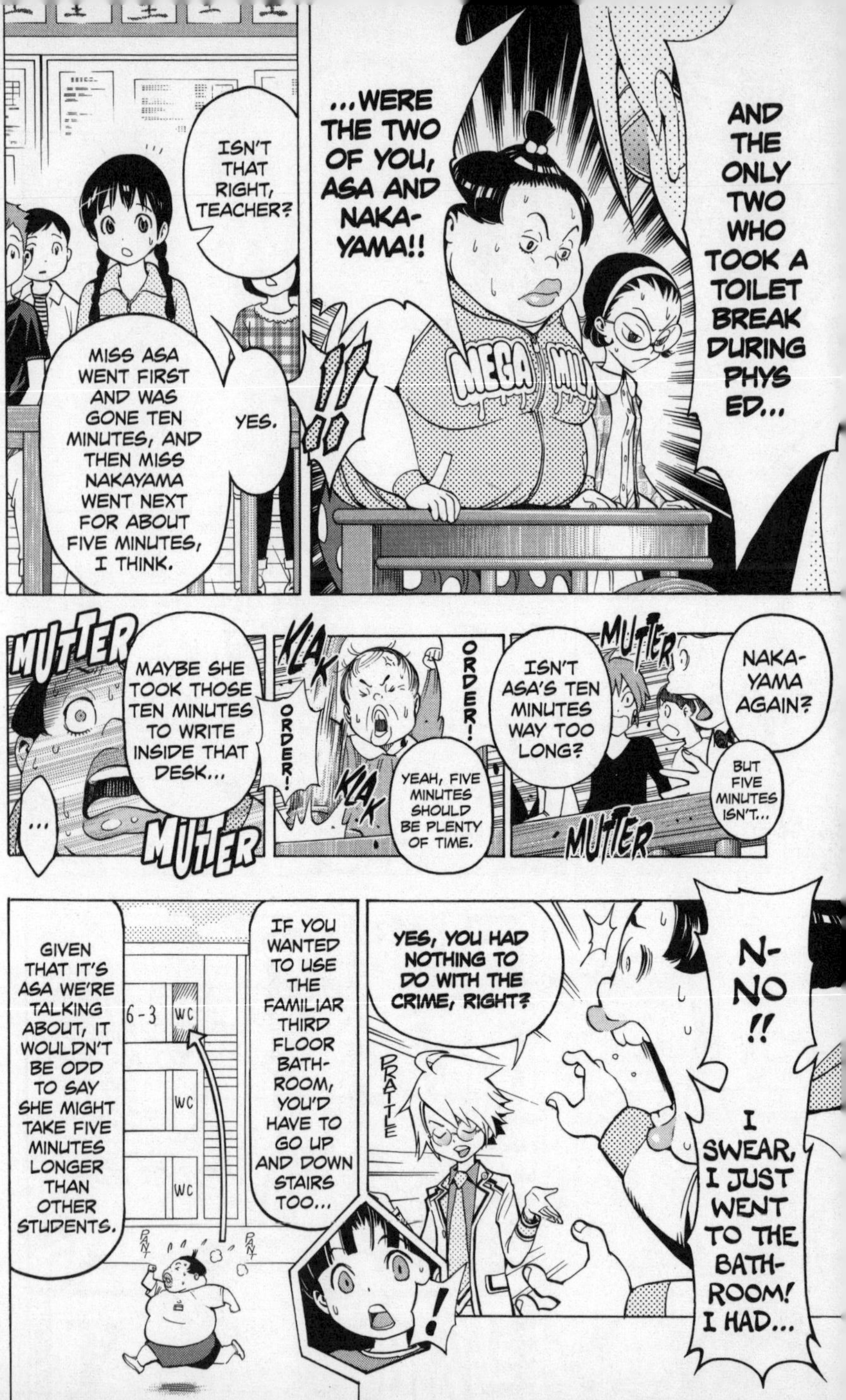
AND THE ONLY TWO WHO TOOK A TOILET BREAK DURING PHYS ED...
...WERE THE TWO OF YOU, ASA AND NAKAYAMA!!
!!
ISN'T THAT RIGHT, TEACHER?
YES.
MISS ASA WENT FIRST AND WAS GONE TEN MINUTES, AND THEN MISS NAKAYAMA WENT NEXT FOR ABOUT FIVE MINUTES, I THINK.
MUTTER
NAKAYAMA AGAIN?
BUT FIVE MINUTES ISN'T...
ISN'T ASA'S TEN MINUTES WAY TOO LONG?
MUTTER
ORDER!
KLAK
ORDER!
YEAH, FIVE MINUTES SHOULD BE PLENTY OF TIME.
KLAK
MUTTER
MAYBE SHE TOOK THOSE TEN MINUTES TO WRITE INSIDE THAT DESK...
...
MUTTER
N-NO!!
I SWEAR, I JUST WENT TO THE BATHROOM! I HAD...
YES, YOU HAD NOTHING TO DO WITH THE CRIME, RIGHT?
PRATTLE
!
IF YOU WANTED TO USE THE FAMILIAR THIRD FLOOR BATHROOM, YOU'D HAVE TO GO UP AND DOWN STAIRS TOO...
GIVEN THAT IT'S ASA WE'RE TALKING ABOUT, IT WOULDN'T BE ODD TO SAY SHE MIGHT TAKE FIVE MINUTES LONGER THAN OTHER STUDENTS.
6-3
WC
WC
WC
PANT
PANT

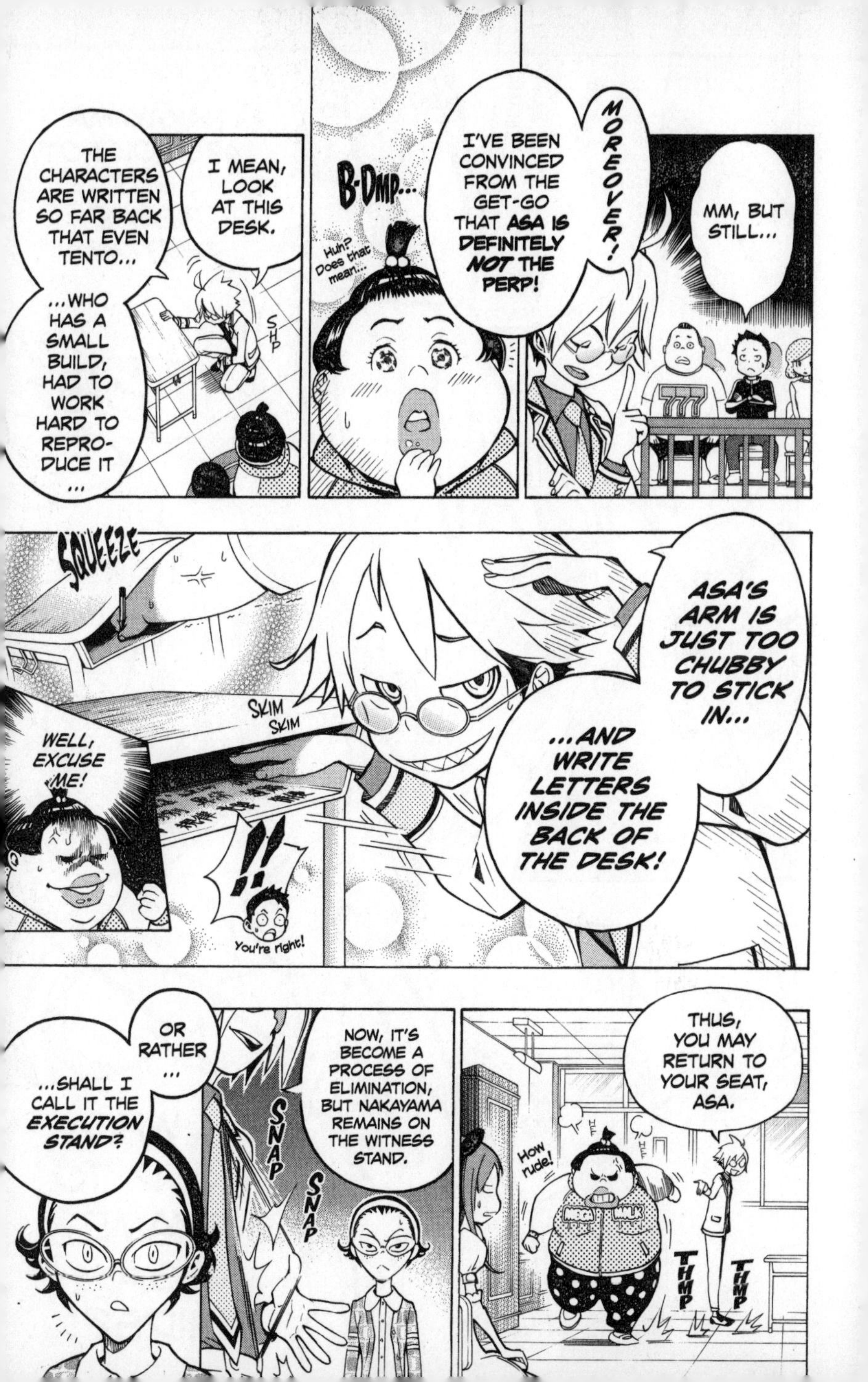
MM, BUT STILL...
MOREOVER!
I'VE BEEN CONVINCED FROM THE GET-GO THAT ASA IS DEFINITELY NOT THE PERP!
B-DMP...
Huh? Does that mean...
I MEAN, LOOK AT THIS DESK.
THE CHARACTERS ARE WRITTEN SO FAR BACK THAT EVEN TENTO...
...WHO HAS A SMALL BUILD, HAD TO WORK HARD TO REPRODUCE IT...
SHP
ASA'S ARM IS JUST TOO CHUBBY TO STICK IN...
...AND WRITE LETTERS INSIDE THE BACK OF THE DESK!
SQUEEZE
SKIM SKIM
!!
You're right!
WELL, EXCUSE ME!
THUS, YOU MAY RETURN TO YOUR SEAT, ASA.
HF HF
How rude!
THMP THMP
NOW, IT'S BECOME A PROCESS OF ELIMINATION, BUT NAKAYAMA REMAINS ON THE WITNESS STAND.
OR RATHER...
...SHALL I CALL IT THE EXECUTION STAND?
SNAP SNAP

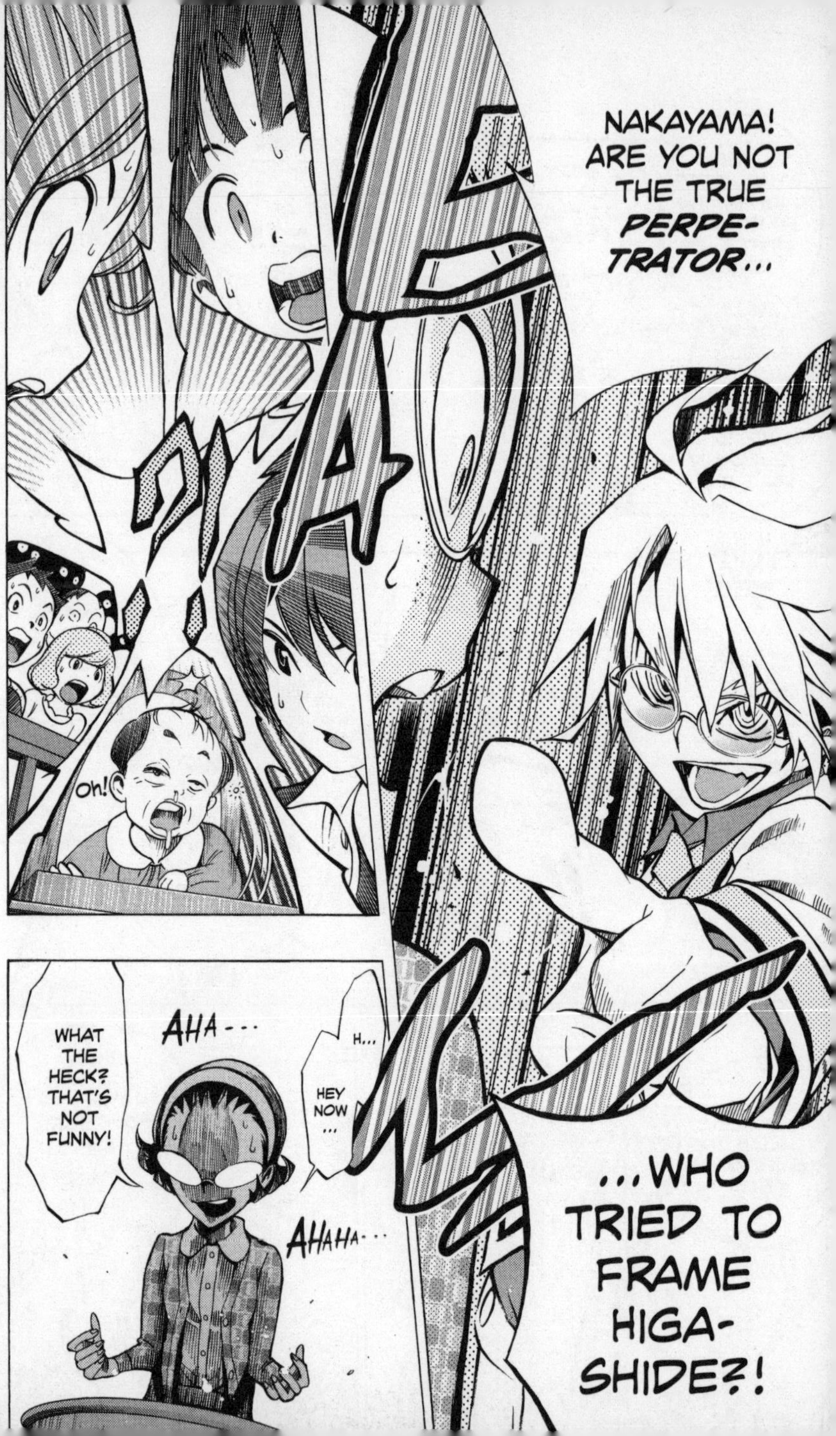
NAKAYAMA! ARE YOU NOT THE TRUE PERPE-TRATOR...
...WHO TRIED TO FRAME HIGA-SHIDE?!
?!
Oh!
H... HEY NOW...
AHA...
WHAT THE HECK? THAT'S NOT FUNNY!
AHAHA...

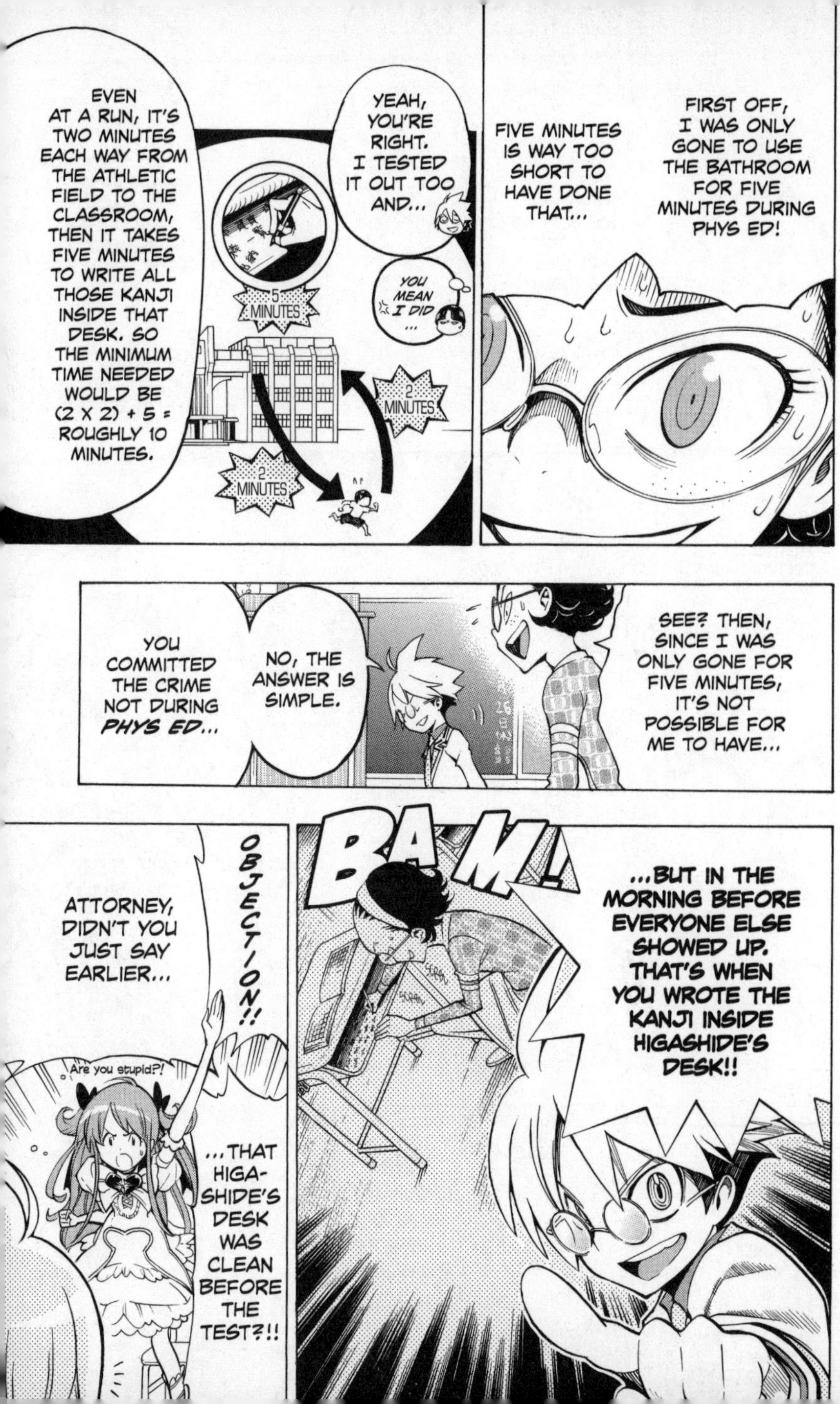
FIRST OFF, I WAS ONLY GONE TO USE THE BATHROOM FOR FIVE MINUTES DURING PHYS ED!
FIVE MINUTES IS WAY TOO SHORT TO HAVE DONE THAT...
YEAH, YOU'RE RIGHT. I TESTED IT OUT TOO AND...
EVEN AT A RUN, IT'S TWO MINUTES EACH WAY FROM THE ATHLETIC FIELD TO THE CLASSROOM, THEN IT TAKES FIVE MINUTES TO WRITE ALL THOSE KANJI INSIDE THAT DESK. SO THE MINIMUM TIME NEEDED WOULD BE (2 X 2) + 5 = ROUGHLY 10 MINUTES.
YOU MEAN I DID...
5 MINUTES
2 MINUTES
2 MINUTES
SEE? THEN, SINCE I WAS ONLY GONE FOR FIVE MINUTES, IT'S NOT POSSIBLE FOR ME TO HAVE...
NO, THE ANSWER IS SIMPLE.
YOU COMMITTED THE CRIME NOT DURING *PHYS ED*...
BAM!
...BUT IN THE MORNING BEFORE EVERYONE ELSE SHOWED UP. THAT'S WHEN YOU WROTE THE KANJI INSIDE HIGASHIDE'S DESK!!
OBJECTION!!
ATTORNEY, DIDN'T YOU JUST SAY EARLIER...
Are you stupid?!
...THAT HIGASHIDE'S DESK WAS CLEAN BEFORE THE TEST?!!

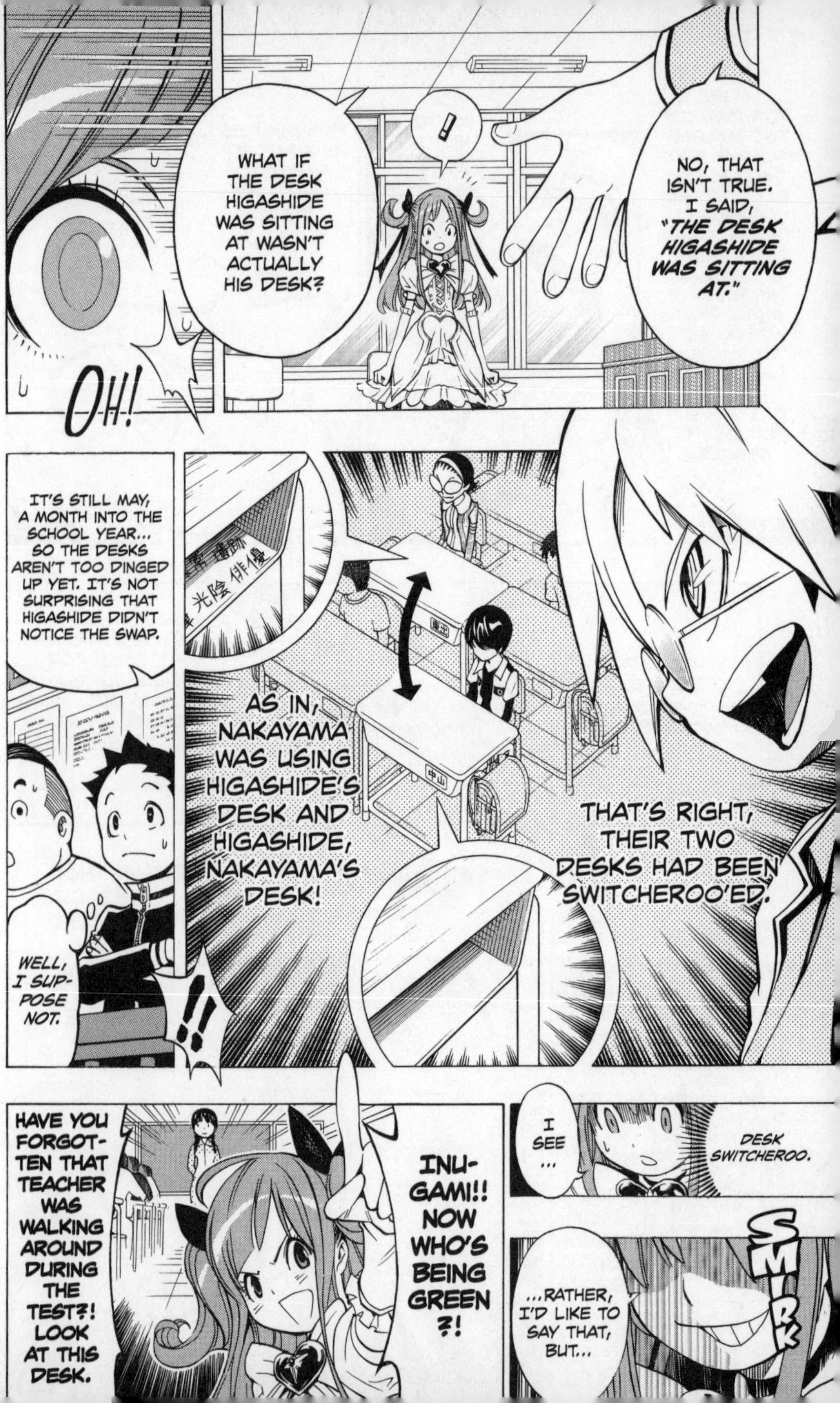

NO, THAT ISN'T TRUE. I SAID, *"THE DESK HIGASHIDE WAS SITTING AT."*
!
WHAT IF THE DESK HIGASHIDE WAS SITTING AT WASN'T ACTUALLY HIS DESK?
OH!
THAT'S RIGHT, THEIR TWO DESKS HAD BEEN SWITCHEROO'ED.
東出
中山
AS IN, NAKAYAMA WAS USING HIGASHIDE'S DESK AND HIGASHIDE, NAKAYAMA'S DESK!
!!
IT'S STILL MAY, A MONTH INTO THE SCHOOL YEAR... SO THE DESKS AREN'T TOO DINGED UP YET. IT'S NOT SURPRISING THAT HIGASHIDE DIDN'T NOTICE THE SWAP.
WELL, I SUPPOSE NOT.
DESK SWITCHEROO.
I SEE...
SMIRK
...RATHER, I'D LIKE TO SAY THAT, BUT...
INUGAMI!! NOW WHO'S BEING GREEN?!
HAVE YOU FORGOTTEN THAT TEACHER WAS WALKING AROUND DURING THE TEST?! LOOK AT THIS DESK.

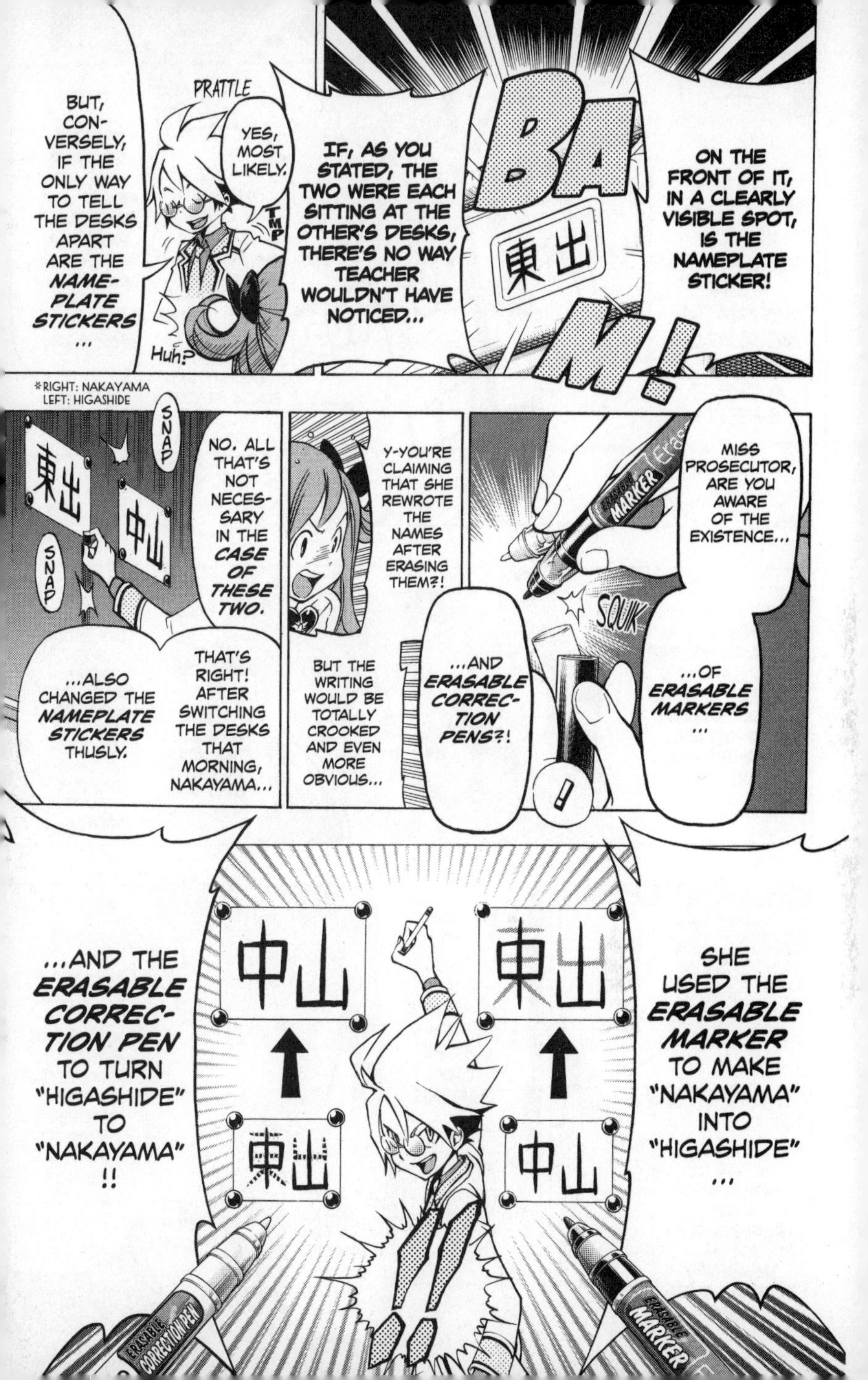

ON THE FRONT OF IT, IN A CLEARLY VISIBLE SPOT, IS THE NAMEPLATE STICKER!
BAM!
東出
IF, AS YOU STATED, THE TWO WERE EACH SITTING AT THE OTHER'S DESKS, THERE'S NO WAY TEACHER WOULDN'T HAVE NOTICED...
YES, MOST LIKELY.
PRATTLE
TMP
BUT, CONVERSELY, IF THE ONLY WAY TO TELL THE DESKS APART ARE THE *NAME-PLATE STICKERS*...
Huh?
*RIGHT: NAKAYAMA
LEFT: HIGASHIDE
MISS PROSECUTOR, ARE YOU AWARE OF THE EXISTENCE...
ERASABLE MARKER
...OF *ERASABLE MARKERS*...
SQUIK
...AND *ERASABLE CORRECTION PENS*?!
!
Y-YOU'RE CLAIMING THAT SHE REWROTE THE NAMES AFTER ERASING THEM?!
BUT THE WRITING WOULD BE TOTALLY CROOKED AND EVEN MORE OBVIOUS...
NO. ALL THAT'S NOT NECESSARY IN THE *CASE OF THESE TWO.*
SNAP
東出
中山
SNAP
THAT'S RIGHT! AFTER SWITCHING THE DESKS THAT MORNING, NAKAYAMA...
...ALSO CHANGED THE *NAMEPLATE STICKERS* THUSLY.
SHE USED THE *ERASABLE MARKER* TO MAKE "NAKAYAMA" INTO "HIGASHIDE"...
...AND THE *ERASABLE CORRECTION PEN* TO TURN "HIGASHIDE" TO "NAKAYAMA"!!
中山
東出
東出
中山
ERASABLE MARKER
ERASABLE CORRECTION PEN

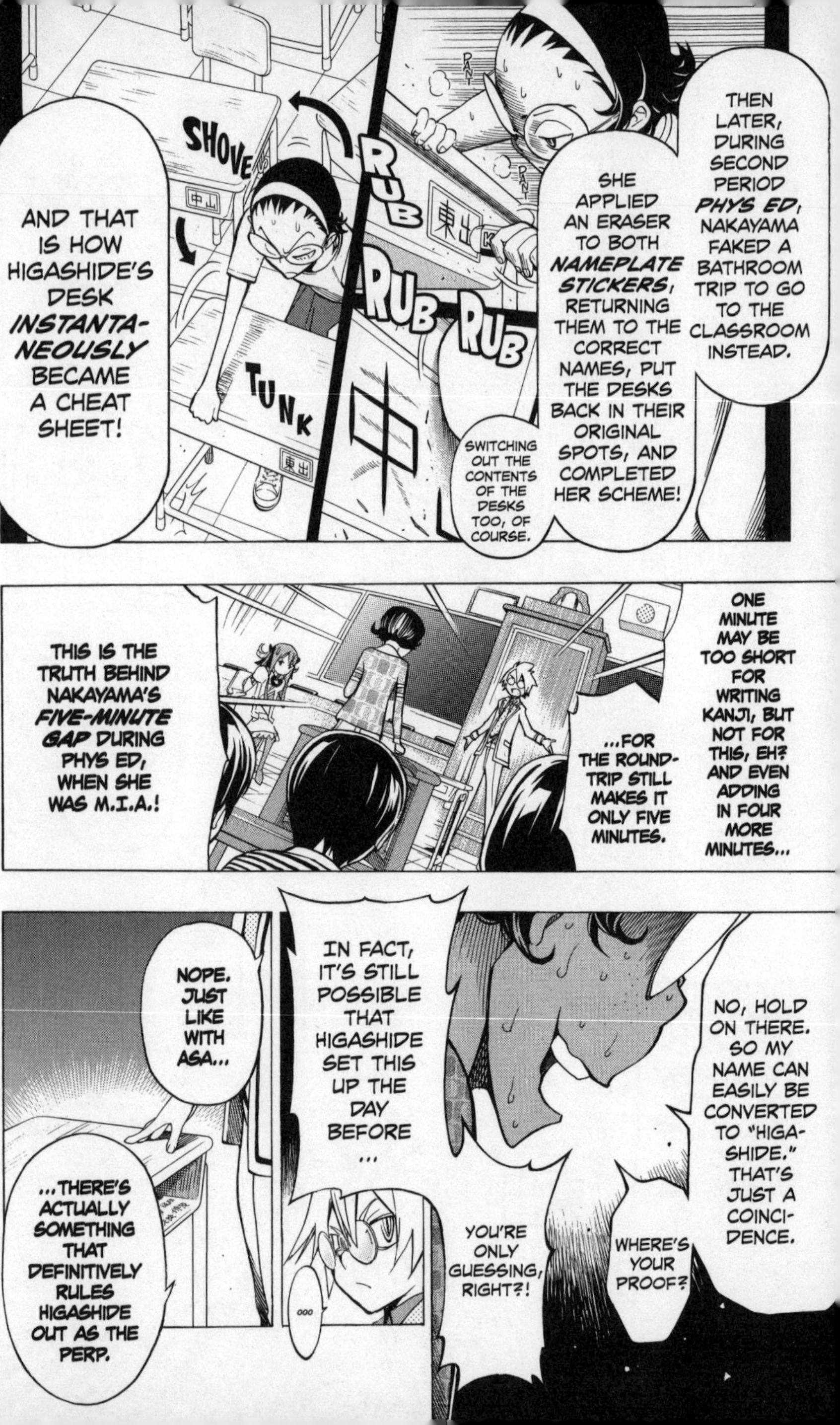
THEN LATER, DURING SECOND PERIOD *PHYS ED*, NAKAYAMA FAKED A BATHROOM TRIP TO GO TO THE CLASSROOM INSTEAD.
PANT
PANT
SHE APPLIED AN ERASER TO BOTH *NAMEPLATE STICKERS*, RETURNING THEM TO THE CORRECT NAMES, PUT THE DESKS BACK IN THEIR ORIGINAL SPOTS, AND COMPLETED HER SCHEME!
SWITCHING OUT THE CONTENTS OF THE DESKS TOO, OF COURSE.
RUB
RUB
RUB
SHOVE
TUNK
AND THAT IS HOW HIGASHIDE'S DESK *INSTANTANEOUSLY* BECAME A CHEAT SHEET!
ONE MINUTE MAY BE TOO SHORT FOR WRITING KANJI, BUT NOT FOR THIS, EH? AND EVEN ADDING IN FOUR MORE MINUTES...
...FOR THE ROUND-TRIP STILL MAKES IT ONLY FIVE MINUTES.
THIS IS THE TRUTH BEHIND NAKAYAMA'S *FIVE-MINUTE GAP* DURING PHYS ED, WHEN SHE WAS M.I.A.!
NO, HOLD ON THERE. SO MY NAME CAN EASILY BE CONVERTED TO "HIGASHIDE." THAT'S JUST A COINCIDENCE.
WHERE'S YOUR PROOF?
YOU'RE ONLY GUESSING, RIGHT?!
IN FACT, IT'S STILL POSSIBLE THAT HIGASHIDE SET THIS UP THE DAY BEFORE...
ooo
NOPE. JUST LIKE WITH ASA...
...THERE'S ACTUALLY SOMETHING THAT DEFINITIVELY RULES HIGASHIDE OUT AS THE PERP.

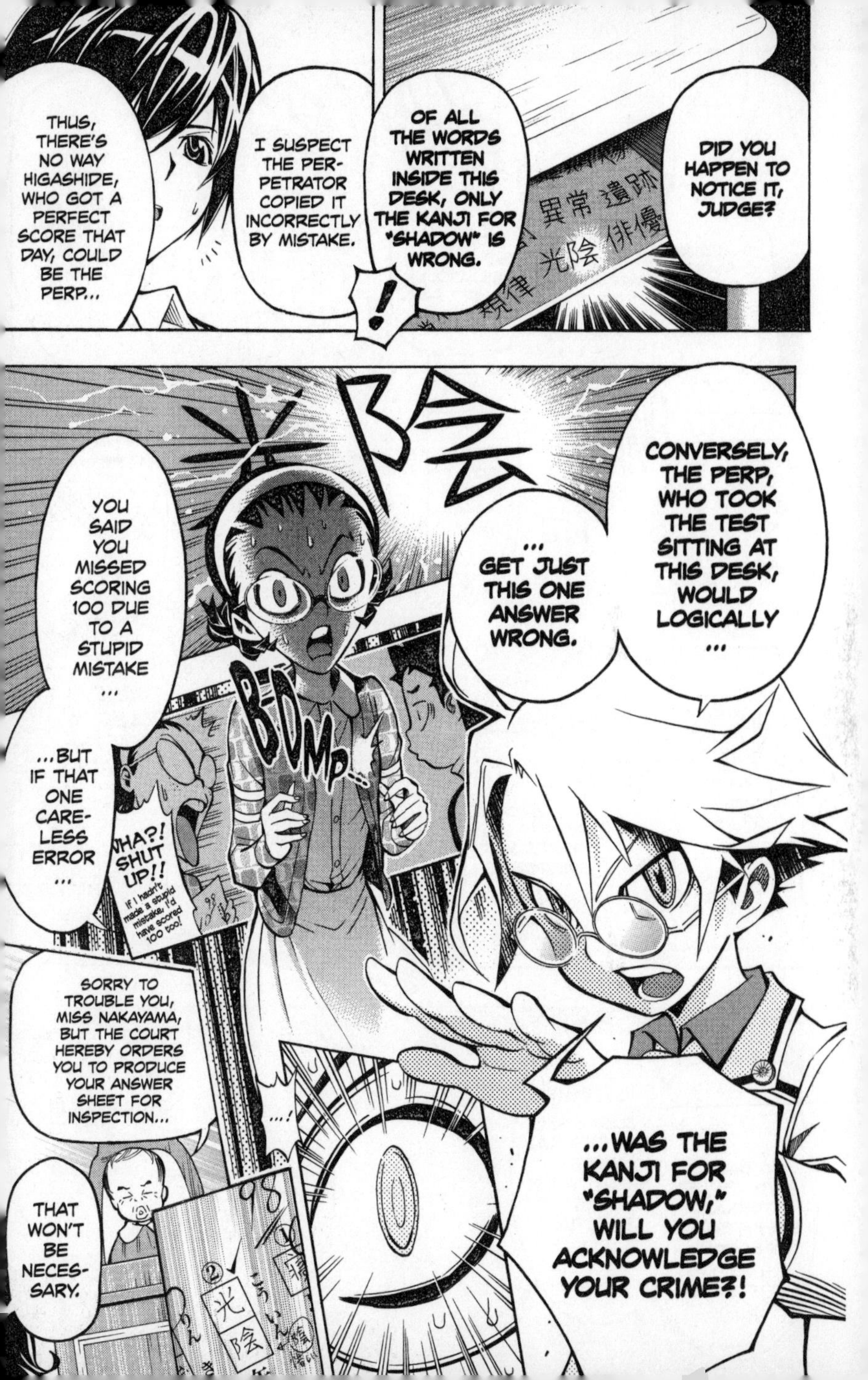
DID YOU HAPPEN TO NOTICE IT, JUDGE?
OF ALL THE WORDS WRITTEN INSIDE THIS DESK, ONLY THE KANJI FOR "SHADOW" IS WRONG.
I SUSPECT THE PER-PETRATOR COPIED IT INCORRECTLY BY MISTAKE.
!
THUS, THERE'S NO WAY HIGASHIDE, WHO GOT A PERFECT SCORE THAT DAY, COULD BE THE PERP...
CONVERSELY, THE PERP, WHO TOOK THE TEST SITTING AT THIS DESK, WOULD LOGICALLY ...
... GET JUST THIS ONE ANSWER WRONG.
YOU SAID YOU MISSED SCORING 100 DUE TO A STUPID MISTAKE ...
BDMP
WHA?! SHUT UP!!
If I hadn't made a stupid mistake, I'd have scored 100 too!
...BUT IF THAT ONE CARE-LESS ERROR ...
...WAS THE KANJI FOR "SHADOW," WILL YOU ACKNOWLEDGE YOUR CRIME?!
...!
SORRY TO TROUBLE YOU, MISS NAKAYAMA, BUT THE COURT HEREBY ORDERS YOU TO PRODUCE YOUR ANSWER SHEET FOR INSPECTION...
THAT WON'T BE NECES-SARY.

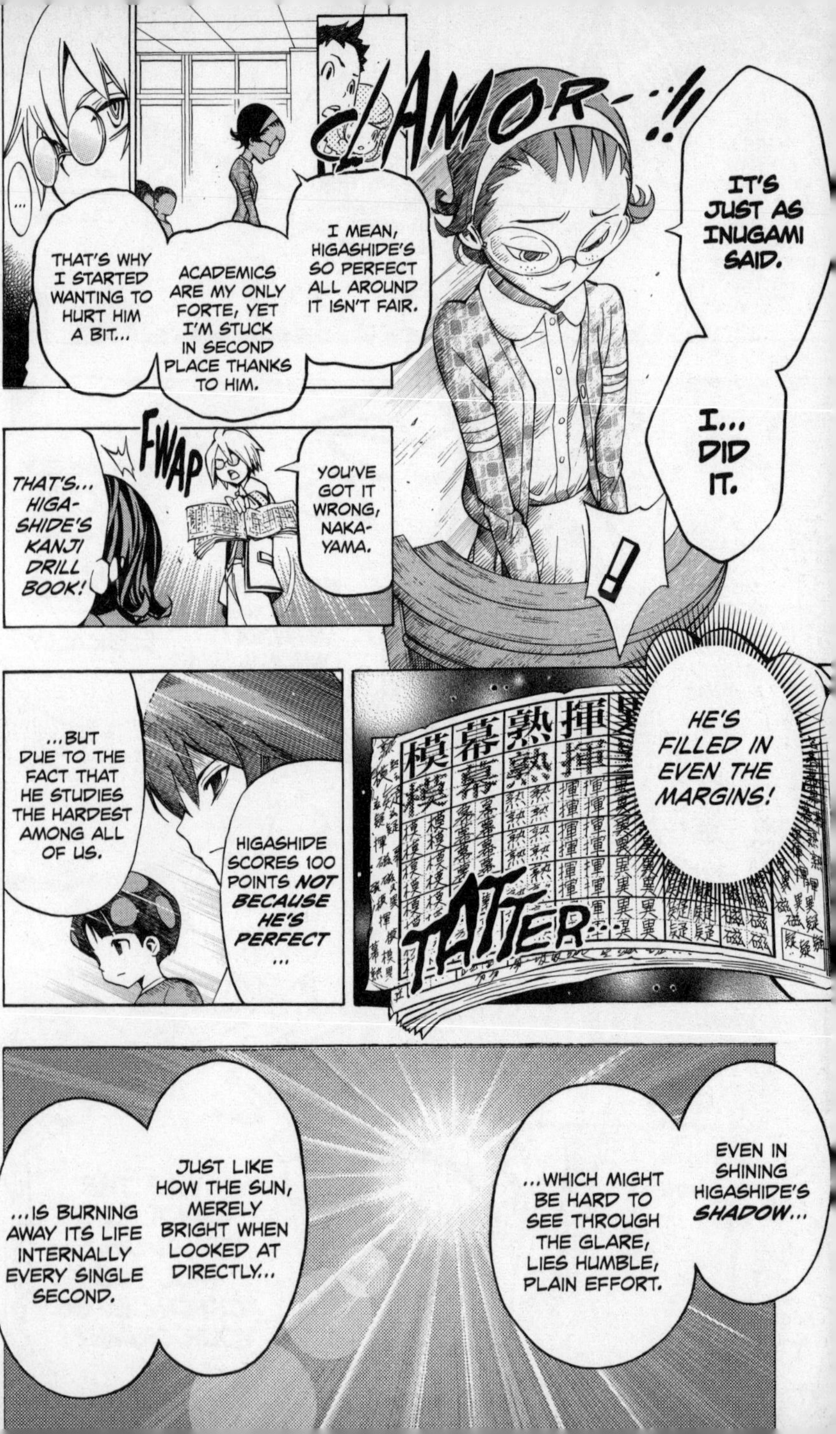
CLAMOR--..!!
IT'S JUST AS INUGAMI SAID.
I... DID IT.
!
I MEAN, HIGASHIDE'S SO PERFECT ALL AROUND IT ISN'T FAIR.
ACADEMICS ARE MY ONLY FORTE, YET I'M STUCK IN SECOND PLACE THANKS TO HIM.
THAT'S WHY I STARTED WANTING TO HURT HIM A BIT...
...
YOU'VE GOT IT WRONG, NAKAYAMA.
FWAP
THAT'S... HIGASHIDE'S KANJI DRILL BOOK!
HE'S FILLED IN EVEN THE MARGINS!
TATTER...
HIGASHIDE SCORES 100 POINTS *NOT BECAUSE HE'S PERFECT*...
...BUT DUE TO THE FACT THAT HE STUDIES THE HARDEST AMONG ALL OF US.
EVEN IN SHINING HIGASHIDE'S *SHADOW*...
...WHICH MIGHT BE HARD TO SEE THROUGH THE GLARE, LIES HUMBLE, PLAIN EFFORT.
JUST LIKE HOW THE SUN, MERELY BRIGHT WHEN LOOKED AT DIRECTLY...
...IS BURNING AWAY ITS LIFE INTERNALLY EVERY SINGLE SECOND.

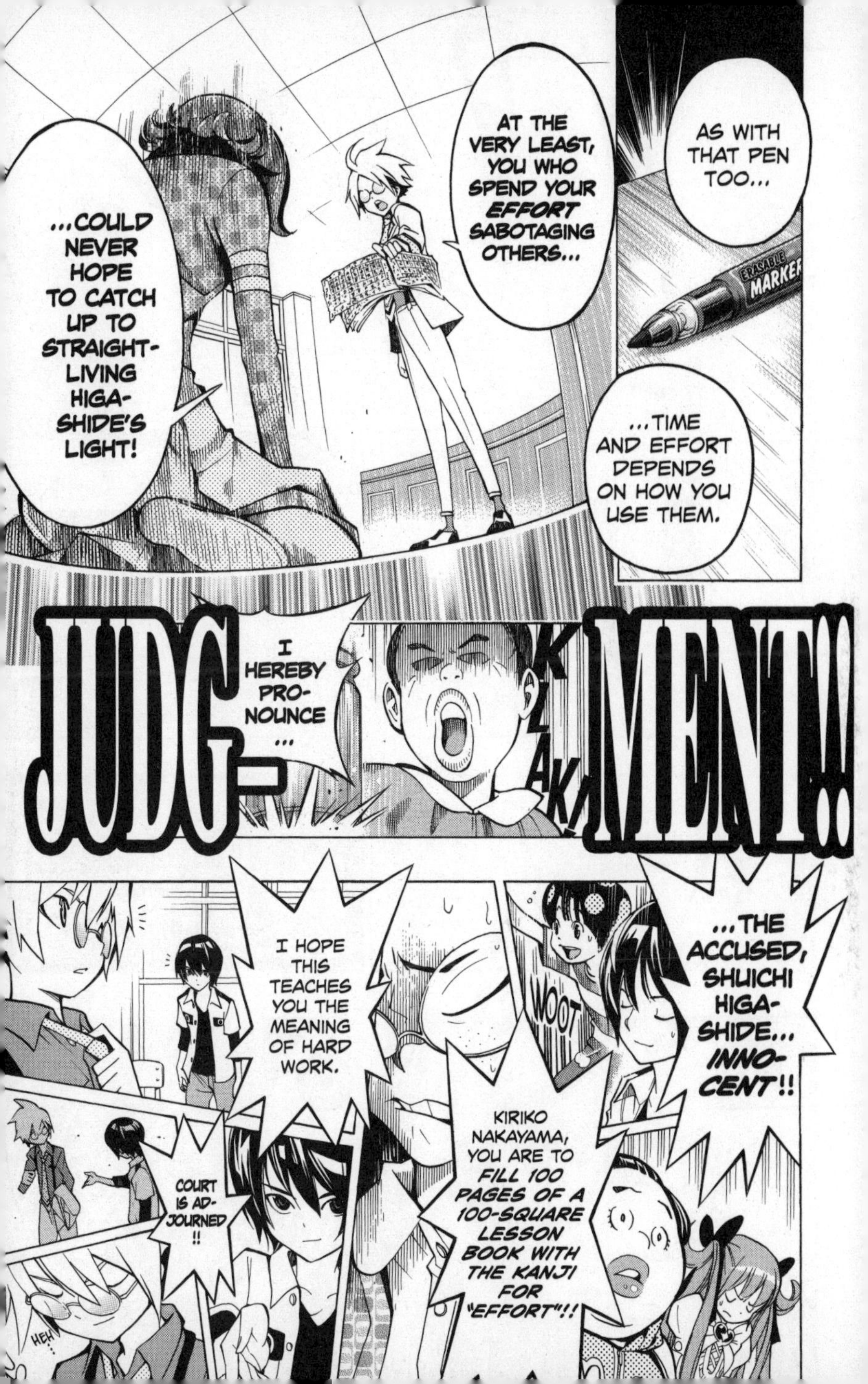
AS WITH THAT PEN TOO...
ERASABLE MARKER
...TIME AND EFFORT DEPENDS ON HOW YOU USE THEM.
AT THE VERY LEAST, YOU WHO SPEND YOUR *EFFORT* SABOTAGING OTHERS...
...COULD NEVER HOPE TO CATCH UP TO STRAIGHT-LIVING HIGA-SHIDE'S LIGHT!
I HEREBY PRO-NOUNCE...
JUDG-
KZAAK!
MENT!!
...THE ACCUSED, SHUICHI HIGA-SHIDE... *INNO-CENT*!!
WOOT
KIRIKO NAKAYAMA, YOU ARE TO *FILL 100 PAGES OF A 100-SQUARE LESSON BOOK WITH THE KANJI FOR "EFFORT"*!!
I HOPE THIS TEACHES YOU THE MEANING OF HARD WORK.
COURT IS AD-JOURNED!!
HEH...

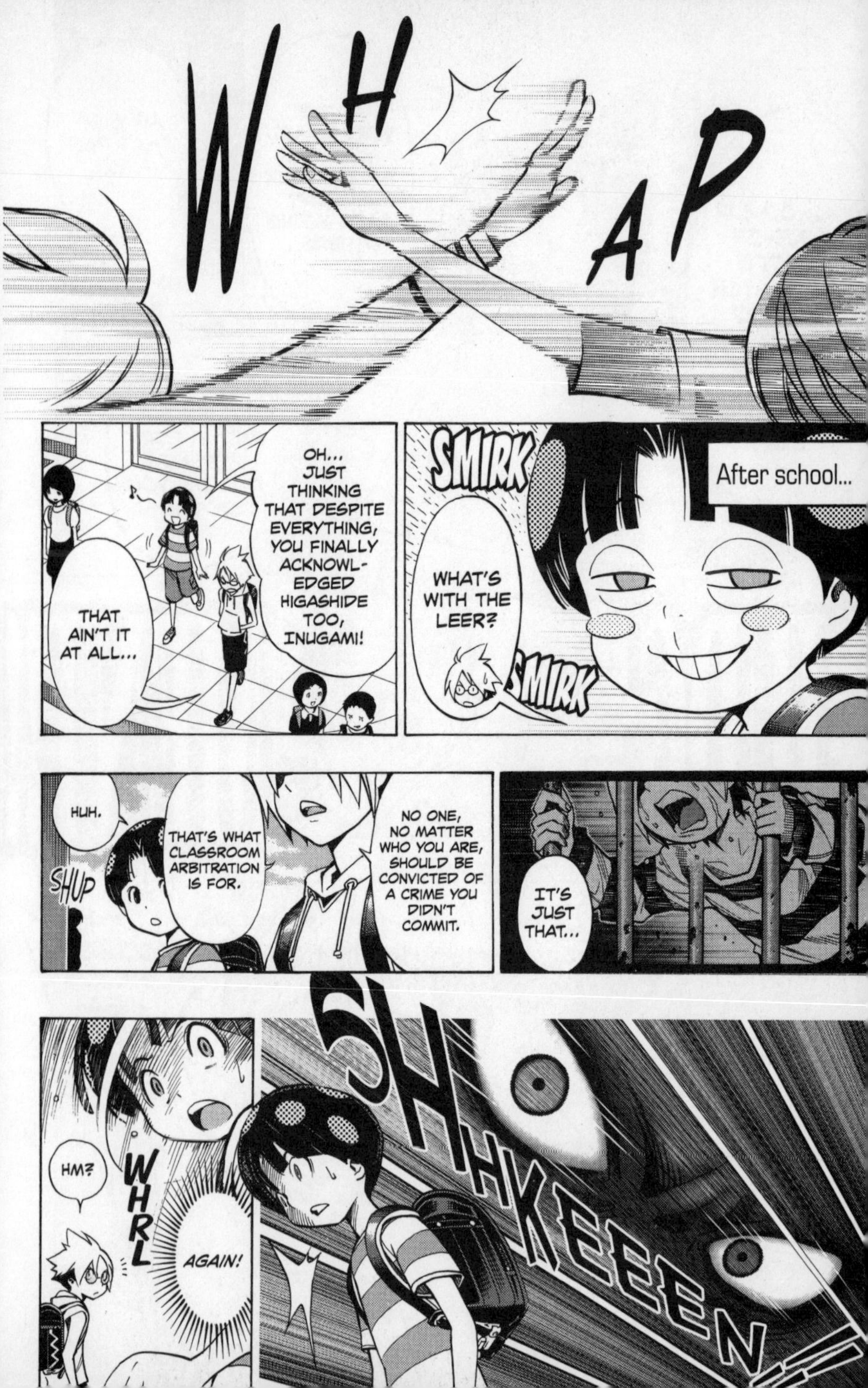
WHAP
After school...
SMIRK
WHAT'S WITH THE LEER?
SMIRK
OH... JUST THINKING THAT DESPITE EVERYTHING, YOU FINALLY ACKNOWL-EDGED HIGASHIDE TOO, INUGAMI!
THAT AIN'T IT AT ALL...
IT'S JUST THAT...
NO ONE, NO MATTER WHO YOU ARE, SHOULD BE CONVICTED OF A CRIME YOU DIDN'T COMMIT.
THAT'S WHAT CLASSROOM ARBITRATION IS FOR.
HUH.
SHUP
SHHKEEEN
AGAIN!
WHRL
HM?

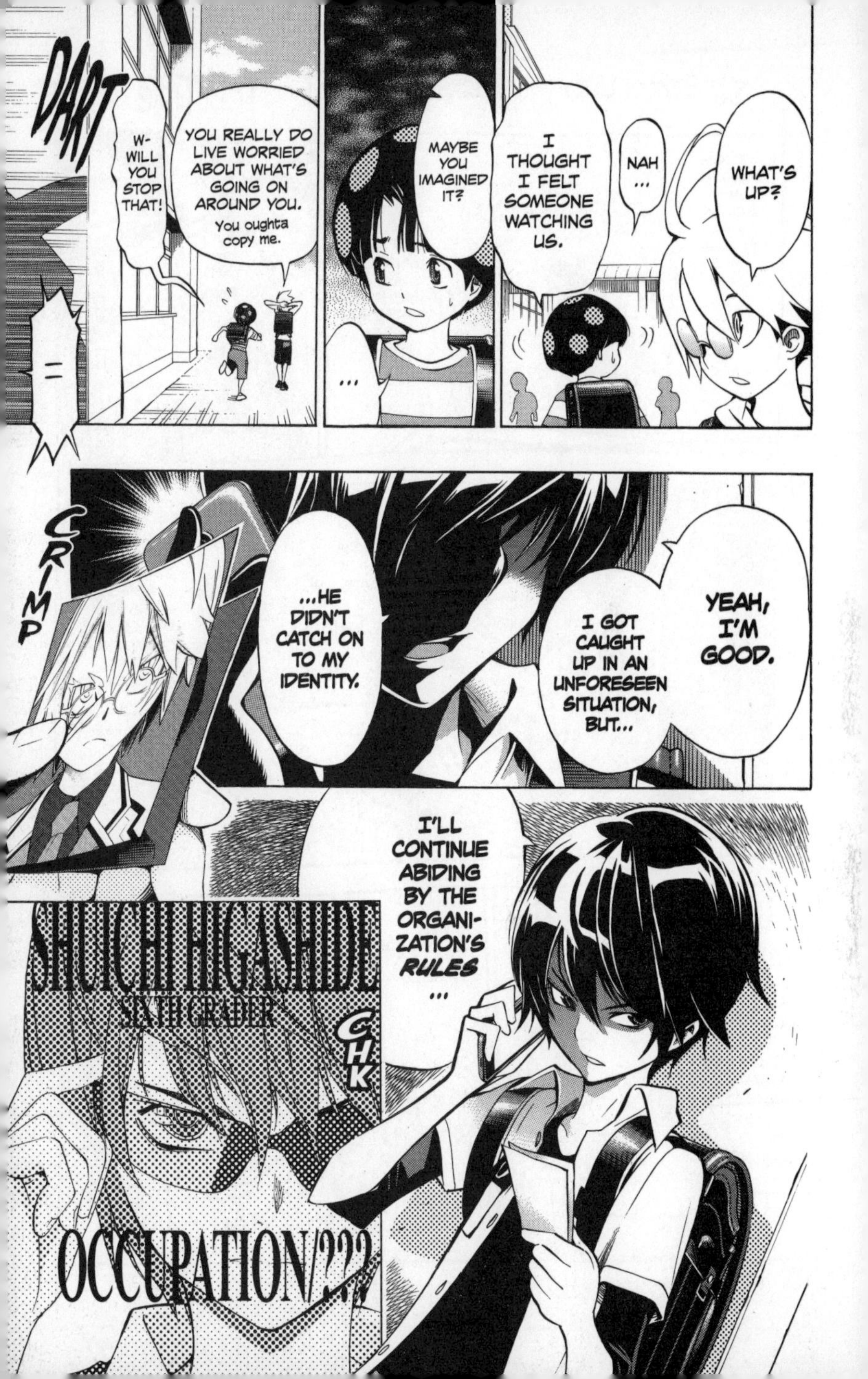
WHAT'S UP?
NAH...
I THOUGHT I FELT SOMEONE WATCHING US.
MAYBE YOU IMAGINED IT?
...
YOU REALLY DO LIVE WORRIED ABOUT WHAT'S GOING ON AROUND YOU. You oughta copy me.
W-WILL YOU STOP THAT!
DART
YEAH, I'M GOOD.
I GOT CAUGHT UP IN AN UNFORESEEN SITUATION, BUT...
...HE DIDN'T CATCH ON TO MY IDENTITY.
CRIMP
I'LL CONTINUE ABIDING BY THE ORGANI-ZATION'S RULES...
CHK
SHUICHI HIGASHIDE
SIXTH GRADER
OCCUPATION/???

☆ School Judgment Backstory ③ ☆ The Title

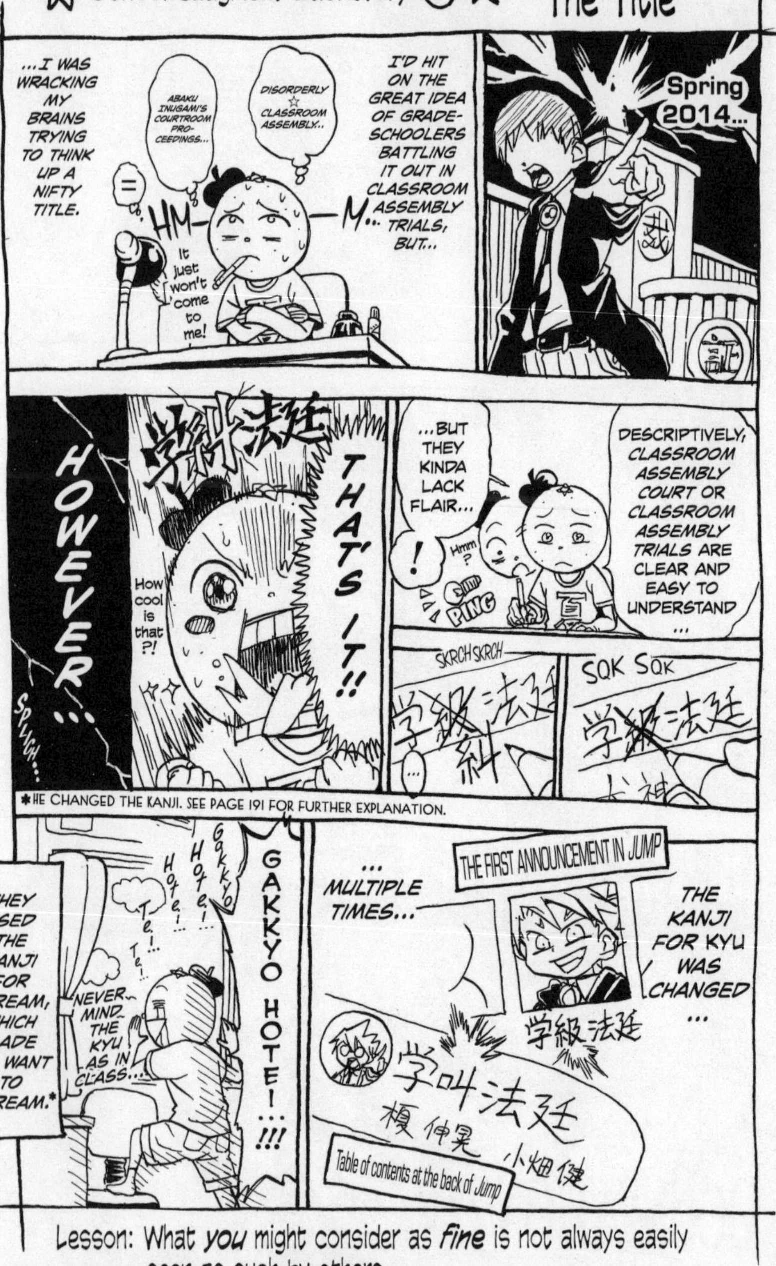
Spring 2014...
I'D HIT ON THE GREAT IDEA OF GRADE-SCHOOLERS BATTLING IT OUT IN CLASSROOM ASSEMBLY TRIALS, BUT...
DISORDERLY ☆ CLASSROOM ASSEMBLY...
ABAKU INUGAMI'S COURTROOM PROCEEDINGS...
...I WAS WRACKING MY BRAINS TRYING TO THINK UP A NIFTY TITLE.
HM—M...
It just won't come to me!
DESCRIPTIVELY, CLASSROOM ASSEMBLY COURT OR CLASSROOM ASSEMBLY TRIALS ARE CLEAR AND EASY TO UNDERSTAND...
...BUT THEY KINDA LACK FLAIR...
Hmm?
!
PING
SQK SQK
学級法廷
SKRCH SKRCH
学級法廷
糾
...
学叫法廷
THAT'S IT!!
How cool is that?!
HOWEVER...
SPLUGH...
*HE CHANGED THE KANJI. SEE PAGE 191 FOR FURTHER EXPLANATION.
THE KANJI FOR KYU WAS CHANGED...
THE FIRST ANNOUNCEMENT IN JUMP
...MULTIPLE TIMES...
学級法廷
学叫法廷
榎伸晃 小畑健
Table of contents at the back of Jump
GAKKYO HOTE!...!!!
Gakkyo Hote!
Hote!...
Te!...
Te!...
NEVERMIND THE KYU AS IN CLASS...
THEY USED THE KANJI FOR SCREAM, WHICH MADE ME WANT TO SCREAM.*

Lesson: What *you* might consider as *fine* is not always easily seen as such by others.

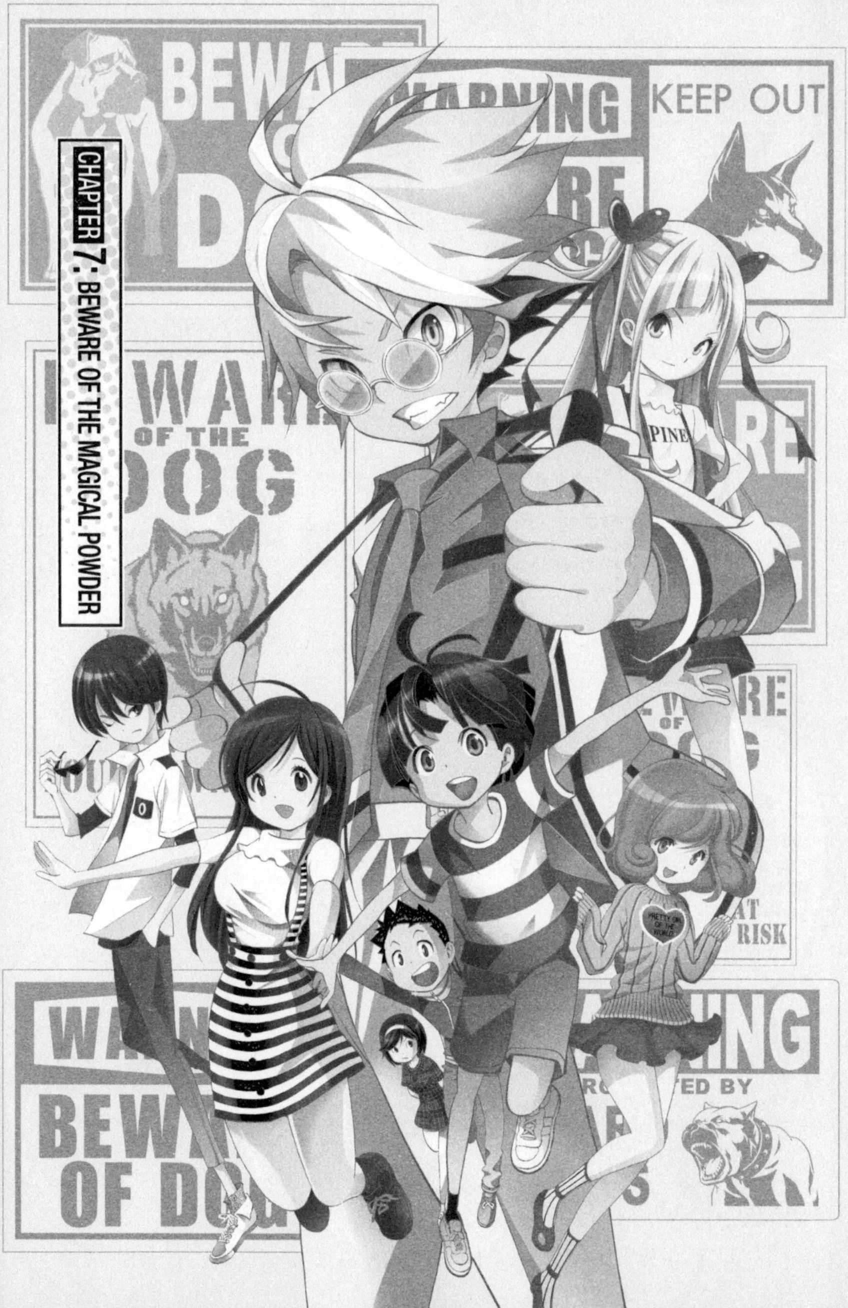
CHAPTER 7: BEWARE OF THE MAGICAL POWDER
KEEP OUT
WARNING
OF THE
DOG
PINE
RISK
BEWA
OF DO

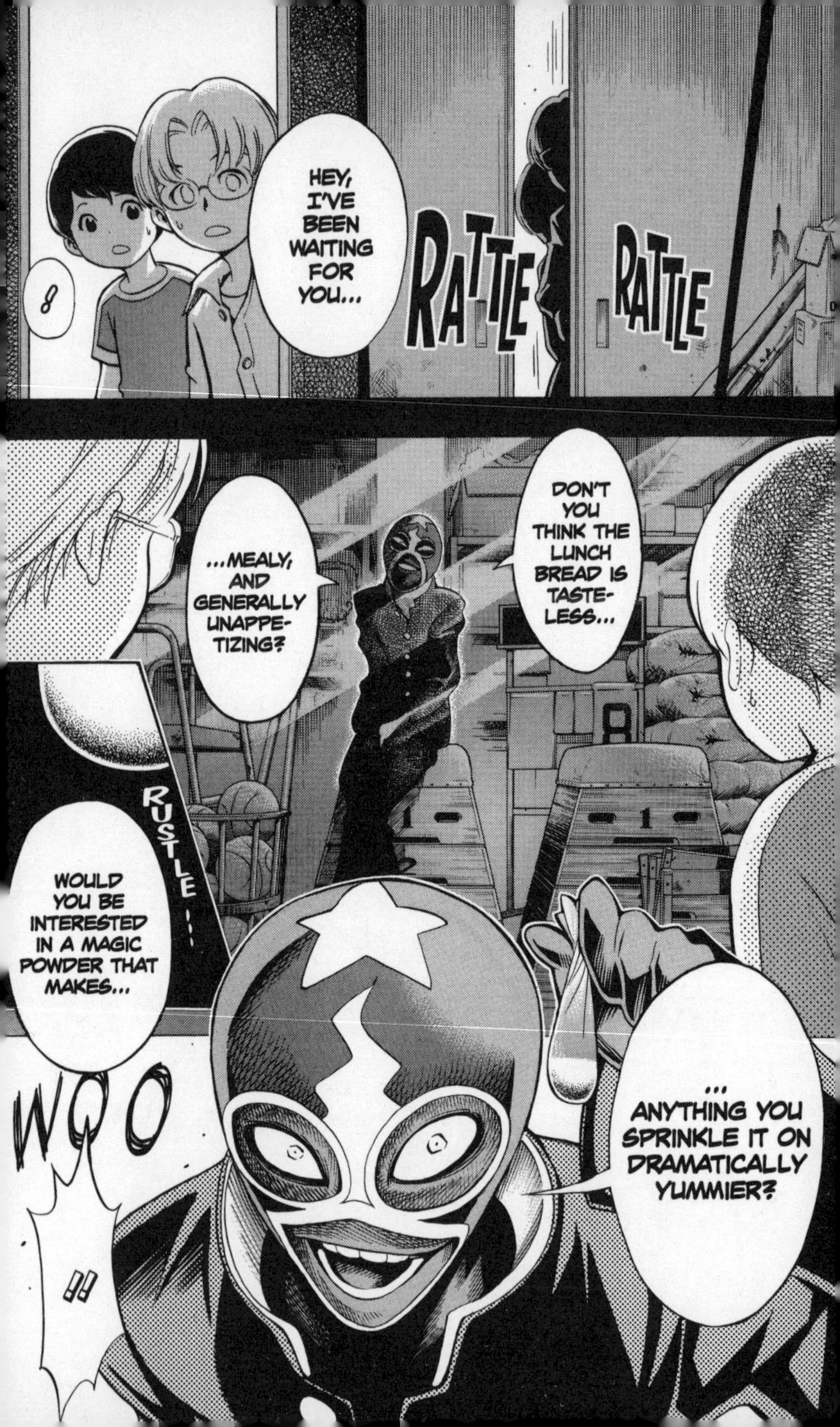
RATTLE
RATTLE
HEY, I'VE BEEN WAITING FOR YOU...
DON'T YOU THINK THE LUNCH BREAD IS TASTE-LESS...
...MEALY, AND GENERALLY UNAPPE-TIZING?
RUSTLE...
WOULD YOU BE INTERESTED IN A MAGIC POWDER THAT MAKES...
...ANYTHING YOU SPRINKLE IT ON DRAMATICALLY YUMMIER?
WOO
!!

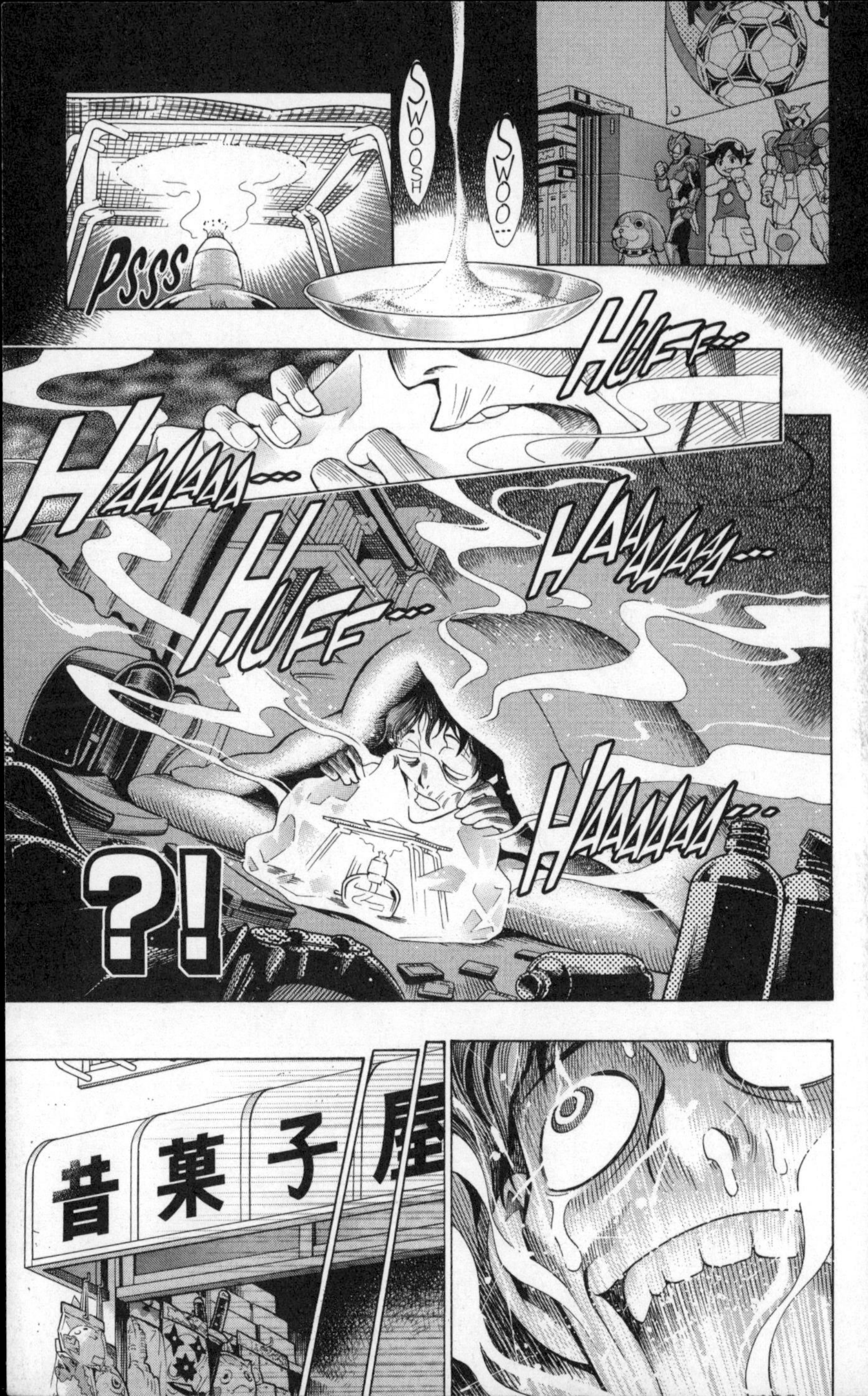
SWOOSH
SWOOO...
PSSS
HUFF...
HAAAAAA...
HAAAAA...
HUFF...
HAAAAAA...
?!
昔菓子屋

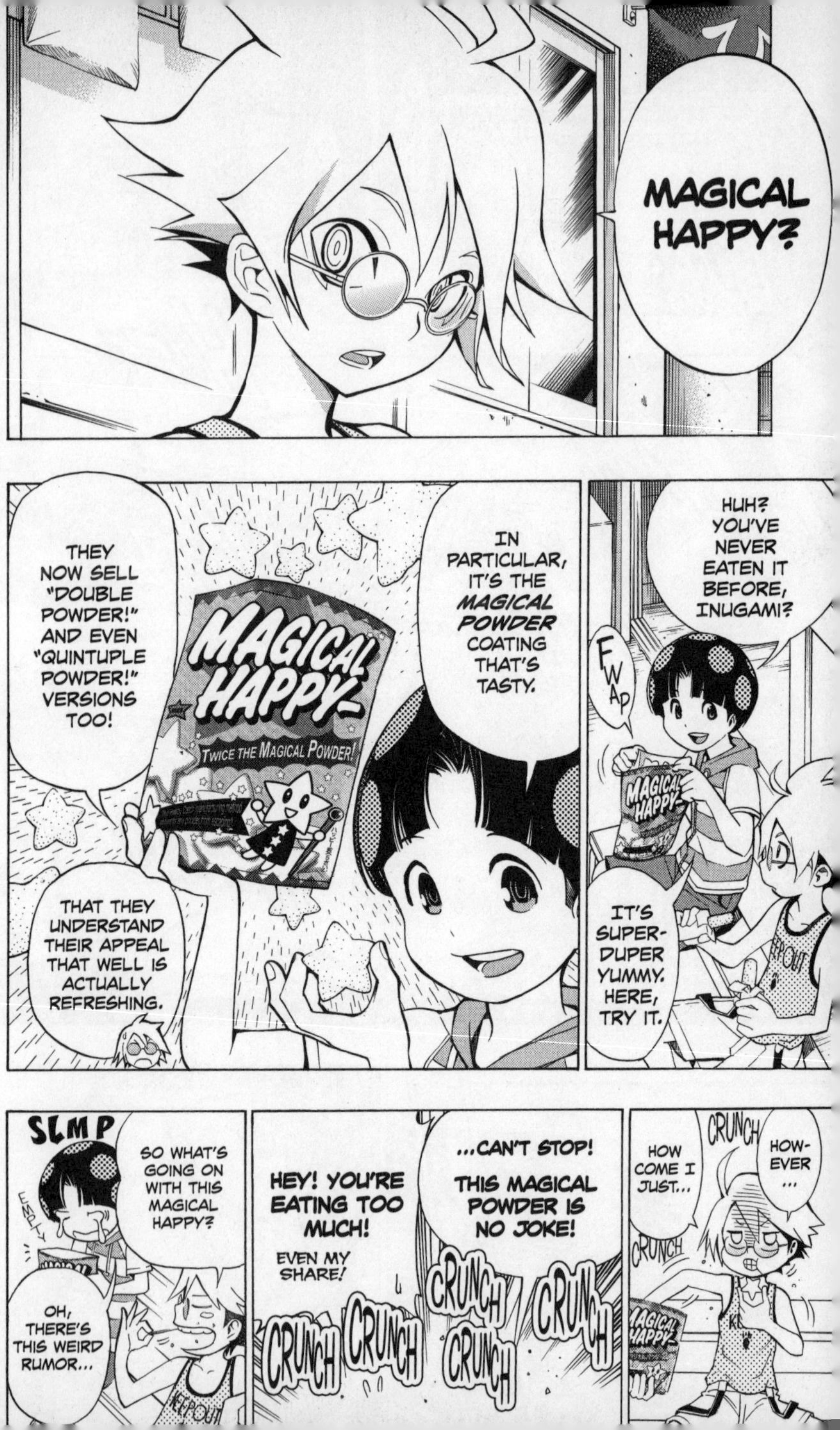
MAGICAL HAPPY?
HUH? YOU'VE NEVER EATEN IT BEFORE, INUGAMI?
FWAP
MAGICAL HAPPY
IT'S SUPER-DUPER YUMMY. HERE, TRY IT.
IN PARTICULAR, IT'S THE MAGICAL POWDER COATING THAT'S TASTY.
MAGICAL HAPPY
TWICE THE MAGICAL POWDER!
THEY NOW SELL "DOUBLE POWDER!" AND EVEN "QUINTUPLE POWDER!" VERSIONS TOO!
THAT THEY UNDERSTAND THEIR APPEAL THAT WELL IS ACTUALLY REFRESHING.
HOW-EVER...
CRUNCH
HOW COME I JUST...
CRUNCH
MAGICAL HAPPY
...CAN'T STOP!
THIS MAGICAL POWDER IS NO JOKE!
HEY! YOU'RE EATING TOO MUCH!
EVEN MY SHARE!
CRUNCH CRUNCH CRUNCH CRUNCH CRUNCH CRUNCH
SLMP
SO WHAT'S GOING ON WITH THIS MAGICAL HAPPY?
EMPTY
OH, THERE'S THIS WEIRD RUMOR...

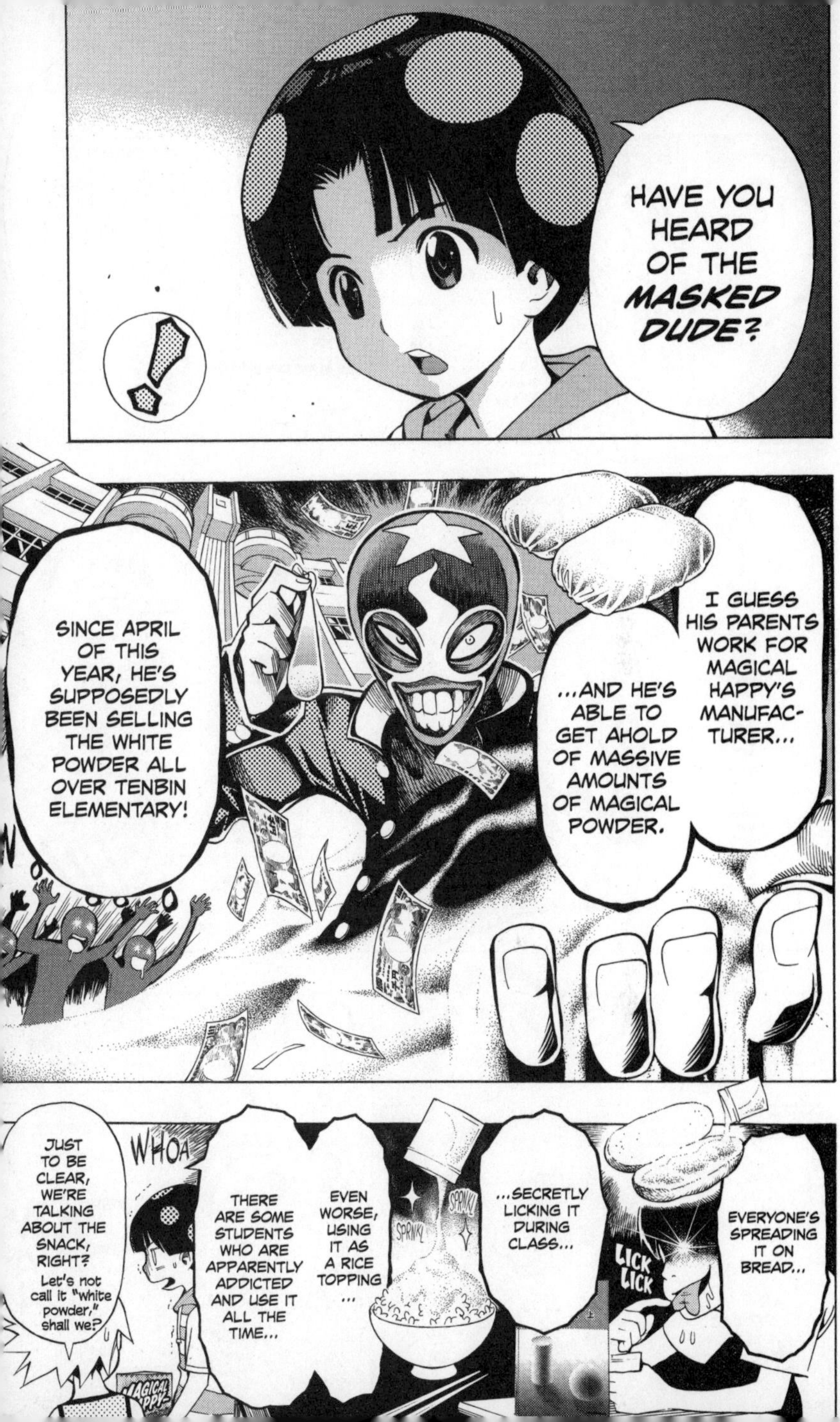

HAVE YOU HEARD OF THE *MASKED DUDE?*
I GUESS HIS PARENTS WORK FOR MAGICAL HAPPY'S MANUFAC-TURER...
...AND HE'S ABLE TO GET AHOLD OF MASSIVE AMOUNTS OF MAGICAL POWDER.
SINCE APRIL OF THIS YEAR, HE'S SUPPOSEDLY BEEN SELLING THE WHITE POWDER ALL OVER TENBIN ELEMENTARY!
EVERYONE'S SPREADING IT ON BREAD...
LICK LICK
...SECRETLY LICKING IT DURING CLASS...
SPRNKL
SPRNKL
EVEN WORSE, USING IT AS A RICE TOPPING ...
THERE ARE SOME STUDENTS WHO ARE APPARENTLY ADDICTED AND USE IT ALL THE TIME...
WHOA
JUST TO BE CLEAR, WE'RE TALKING ABOUT THE SNACK, RIGHT?
Let's not call it "white powder," shall we?

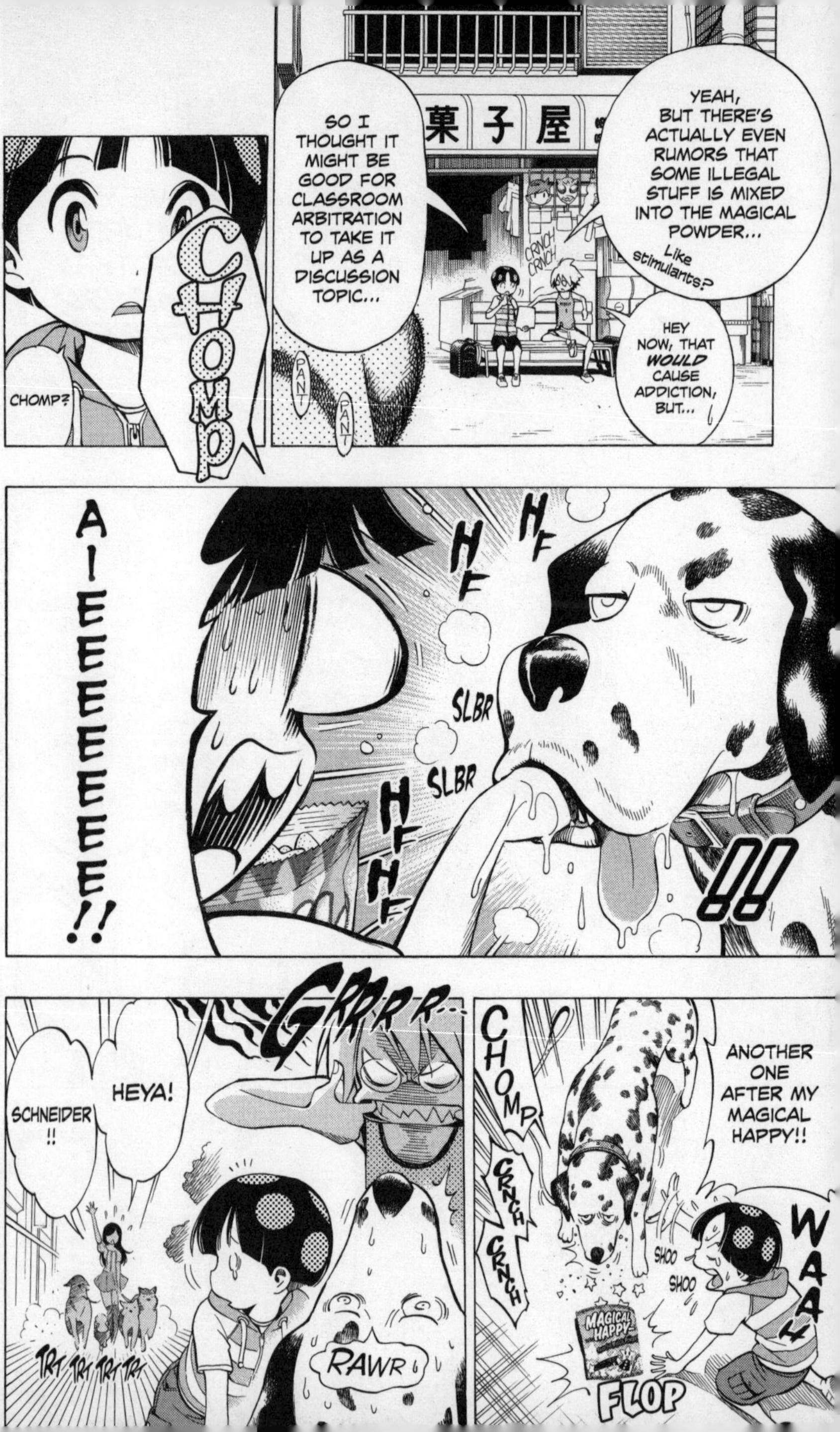

YEAH, BUT THERE'S ACTUALLY EVEN RUMORS THAT SOME ILLEGAL STUFF IS MIXED INTO THE MAGICAL POWDER...
Like stimulants?
HEY NOW, THAT WOULD CAUSE ADDICTION, BUT...
SO I THOUGHT IT MIGHT BE GOOD FOR CLASSROOM ARBITRATION TO TAKE IT UP AS A DISCUSSION TOPIC...
CRNCH CRNCH
PANT
PANT
CHOMP
CHOMP?
HF
HF
!!
SLBR
SLBR
HFHFHF
AIEEEEEEEEEE!!
ANOTHER ONE AFTER MY MAGICAL HAPPY!!
WAAAH
SHOO
SHOO
CHOMP
CRNCH
CRNCH
MAGICAL HAPPY
FLOP
GRRRR...
HEYA!
SCHNEIDER!!
RAWR
TRT TRT TRT TRT

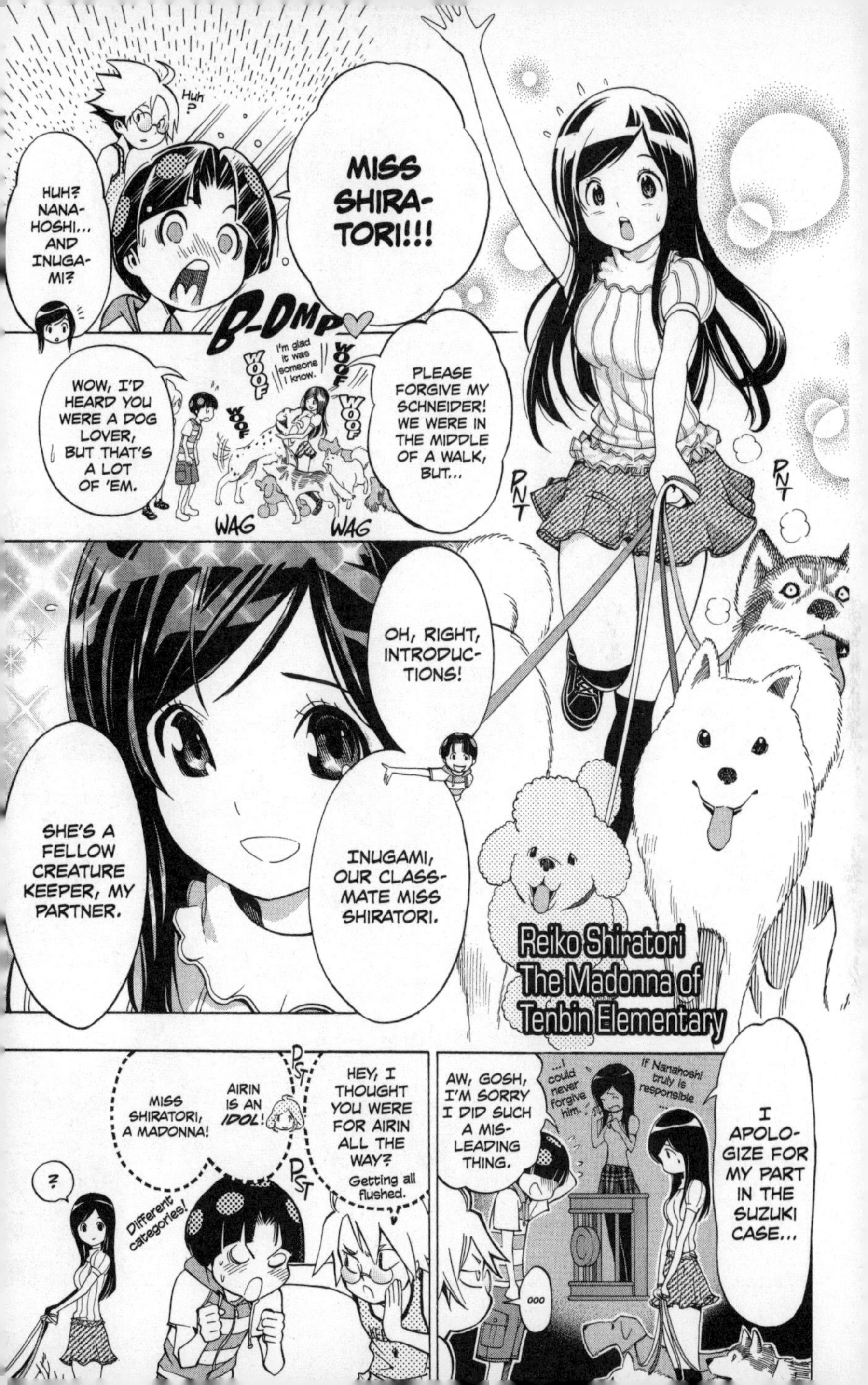
PNT
PNT
Reiko Shiratori The Madonna of Tenbin Elementary
MISS SHIRA-TORI!!!
Huh?
HUH? NANA-HOSHI... AND INUGA-MI?
B-DMP
PLEASE FORGIVE MY SCHNEIDER! WE WERE IN THE MIDDLE OF A WALK, BUT...
WOOF
I'm glad it was someone I know.
WOOF
WOOF
WOOF
WOW, I'D HEARD YOU WERE A DOG LOVER, BUT THAT'S A LOT OF 'EM.
WAG
WAG
OH, RIGHT, INTRODUC-TIONS!
INUGAMI, OUR CLASS-MATE MISS SHIRATORI.
SHE'S A FELLOW CREATURE KEEPER, MY PARTNER.
I APOLO-GIZE FOR MY PART IN THE SUZUKI CASE...
If Nanahoshi truly is responsible...
...I could never forgive him.
AW, GOSH, I'M SORRY I DID SUCH A MIS-LEADING THING.
ooo
HEY, I THOUGHT YOU WERE FOR AIRIN ALL THE WAY?
Getting all flushed.
PST
PST
AIRIN IS AN IDOL!
MISS SHIRATORI, A MADONNA!
Different categories!
?

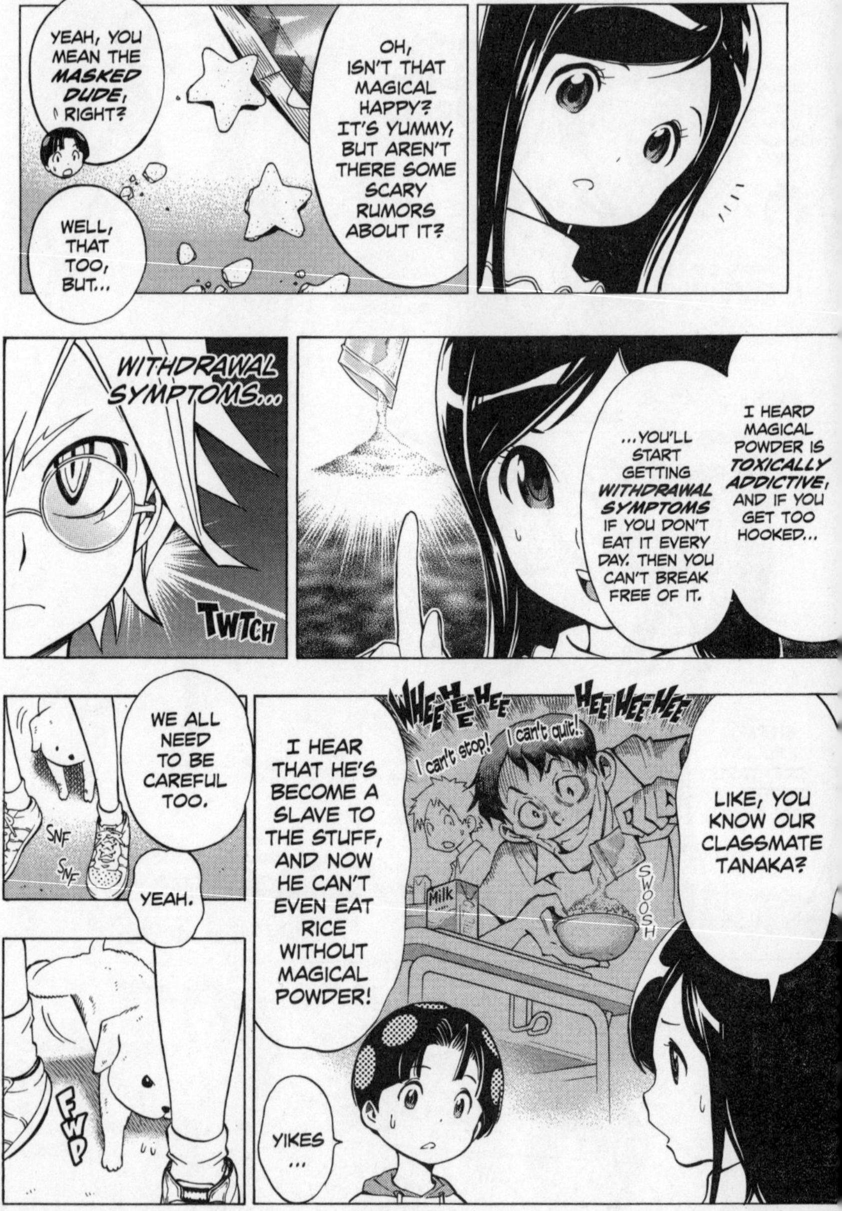
OH, ISN'T THAT MAGICAL HAPPY? IT'S YUMMY, BUT AREN'T THERE SOME SCARY RUMORS ABOUT IT?
YEAH, YOU MEAN THE MASKED DUDE, RIGHT?
WELL, THAT TOO, BUT...
I HEARD MAGICAL POWDER IS TOXICALLY ADDICTIVE, AND IF YOU GET TOO HOOKED...
...YOU'LL START GETTING WITHDRAWAL SYMPTOMS IF YOU DON'T EAT IT EVERY DAY. THEN YOU CAN'T BREAK FREE OF IT.
WITHDRAWAL SYMPTOMS...
TWTCH
LIKE, YOU KNOW OUR CLASSMATE TANAKA?
HEE HEE HEE
WHEE HEE HEE
I can't quit!
I can't stop!
SWOOSH
Milk
I HEAR THAT HE'S BECOME A SLAVE TO THE STUFF, AND NOW HE CAN'T EVEN EAT RICE WITHOUT MAGICAL POWDER!
YIKES...
WE ALL NEED TO BE CAREFUL TOO.
SNF
SNF
YEAH.
FWP

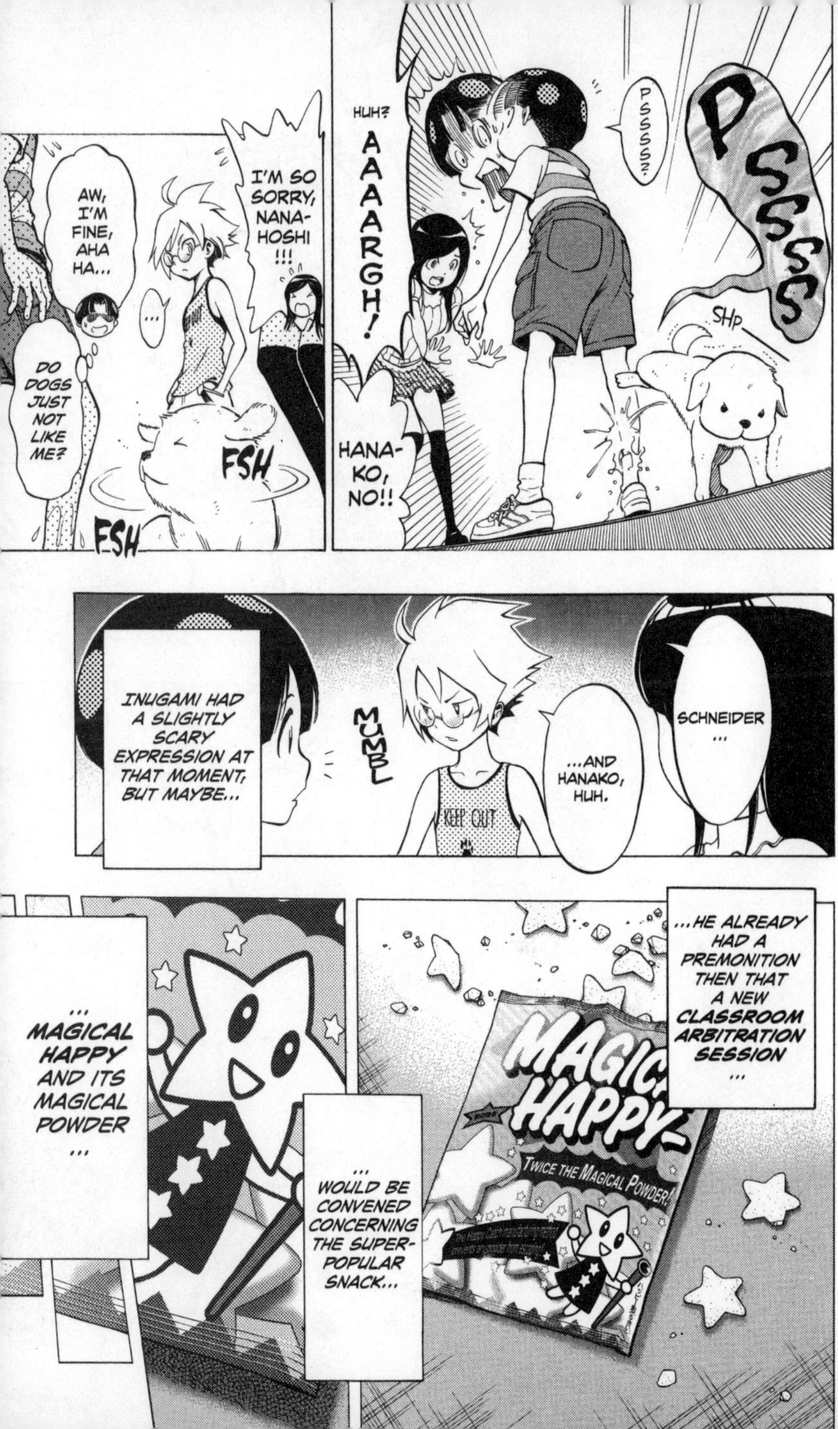
PSSSS
PSSSS?
HUH?
AAAARGH!
HANAKO, NO!!
SHp
I'M SO SORRY, NANA-HOSHI!!!
AW, I'M FINE, AHA HA...
...
DO DOGS JUST NOT LIKE ME?
FSH
FSH
SCHNEIDER...
...AND HANAKO, HUH.
MUMBL
INUGAMI HAD A SLIGHTLY SCARY EXPRESSION AT THAT MOMENT, BUT MAYBE...
...HE ALREADY HAD A PREMONITION THEN THAT A NEW CLASSROOM ARBITRATION SESSION...
MAGICAL HAPPY
TWICE THE MAGICAL POWDER!
...WOULD BE CONVENED CONCERNING THE SUPER-POPULAR SNACK...
...MAGICAL HAPPY AND ITS MAGICAL POWDER...

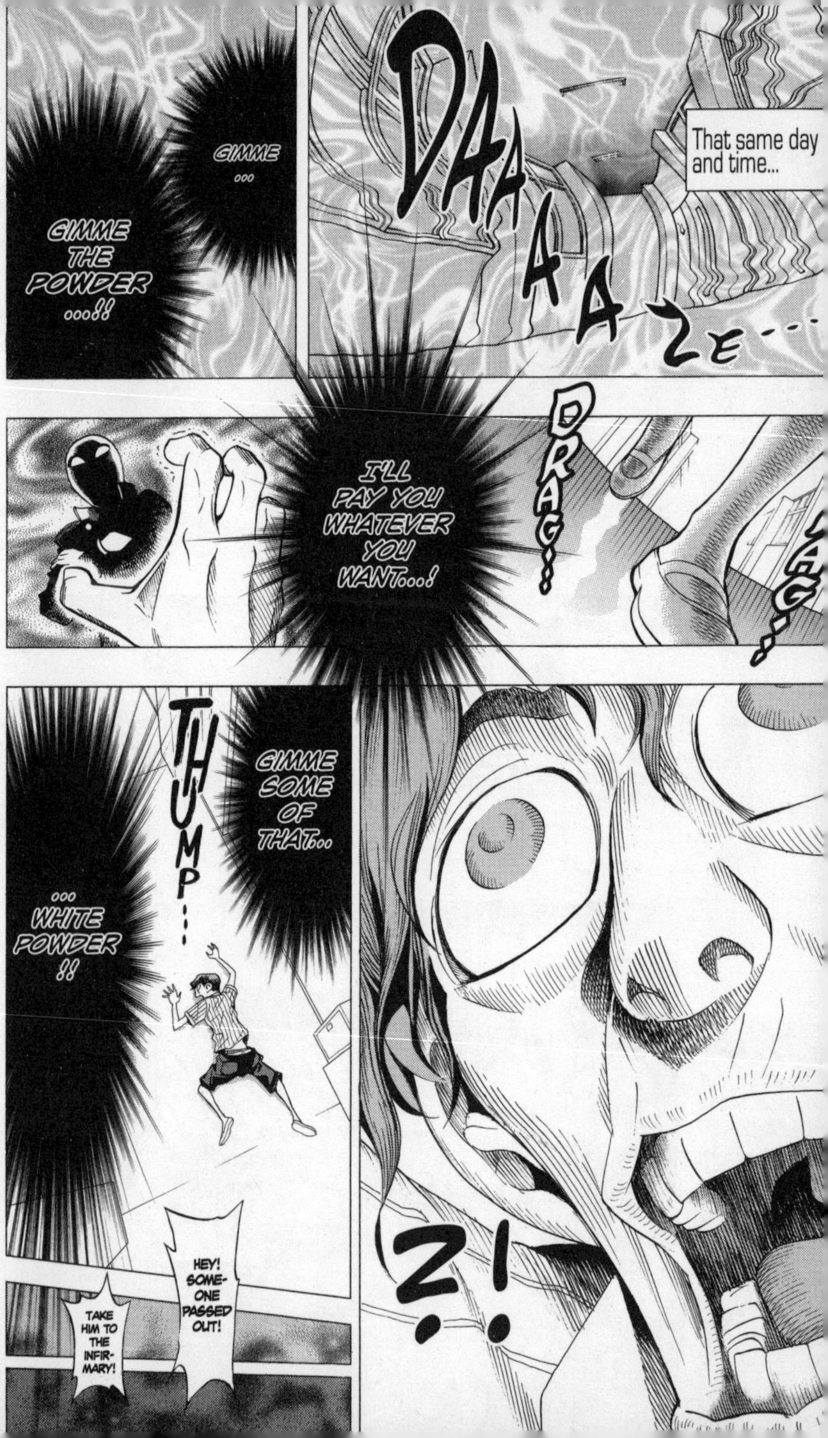
That same day and time...
DAAAAZE...
GIMME...
GIMME THE POWDER...!!
DRAG...
AG...
I'LL PAY YOU WHATEVER YOU WANT...!
Z!!
GIMME SOME OF THAT...
...WHITE POWDER!!
THUMP...
HEY! SOME-ONE PASSED OUT!
TAKE HIM TO THE INFIR-MARY!

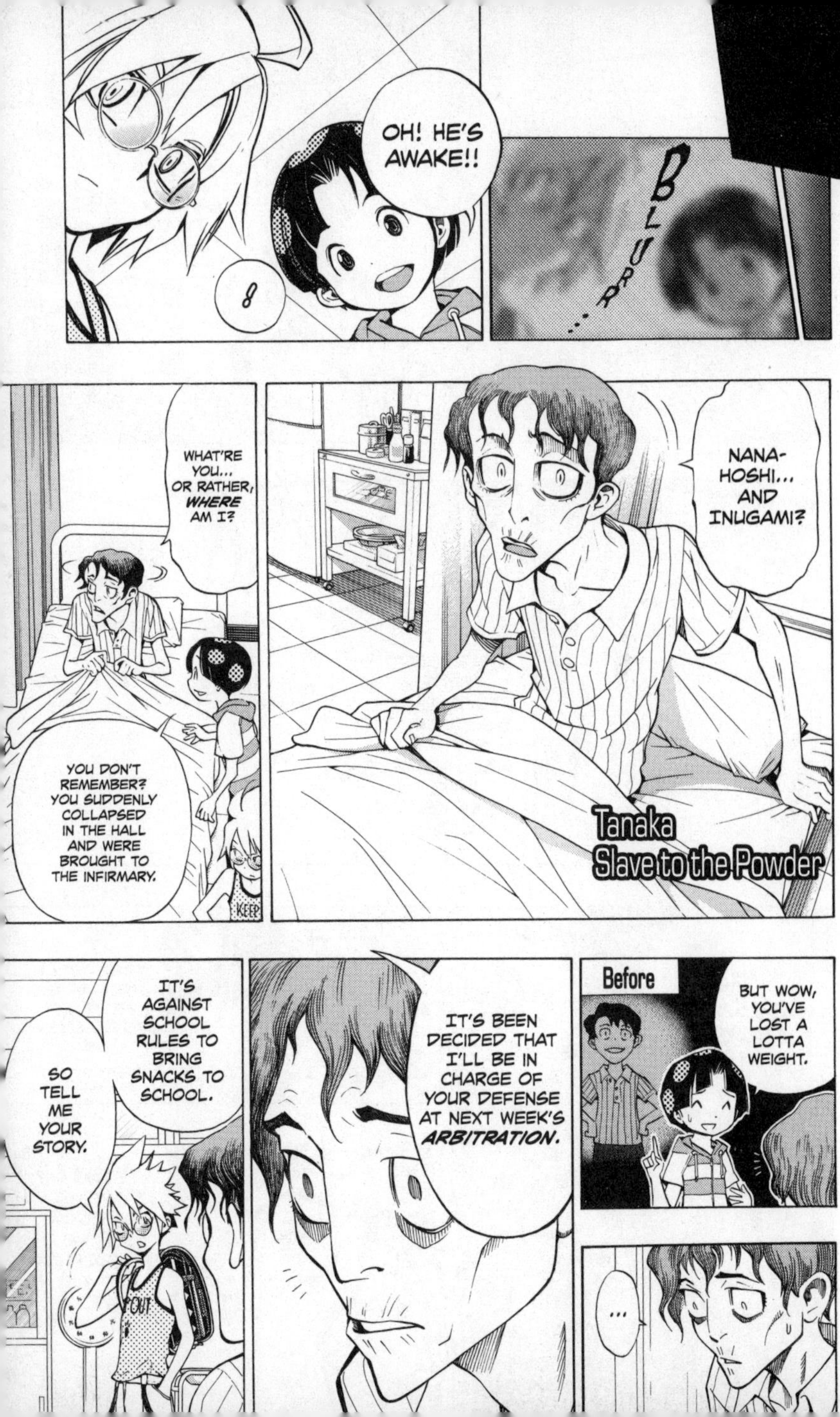
BLURR...
OH! HE'S AWAKE!!
!
NANA-HOSHI... AND INUGAMI?
Tanaka Slave to the Powder
WHAT'RE YOU... OR RATHER, *WHERE* AM I?
YOU DON'T REMEMBER? YOU SUDDENLY COLLAPSED IN THE HALL AND WERE BROUGHT TO THE INFIRMARY.
Before
BUT WOW, YOU'VE LOST A LOTTA WEIGHT.
...
IT'S BEEN DECIDED THAT I'LL BE IN CHARGE OF YOUR DEFENSE AT NEXT WEEK'S *ARBITRATION*.
IT'S AGAINST SCHOOL RULES TO BRING SNACKS TO SCHOOL.
SO TELL ME YOUR STORY.

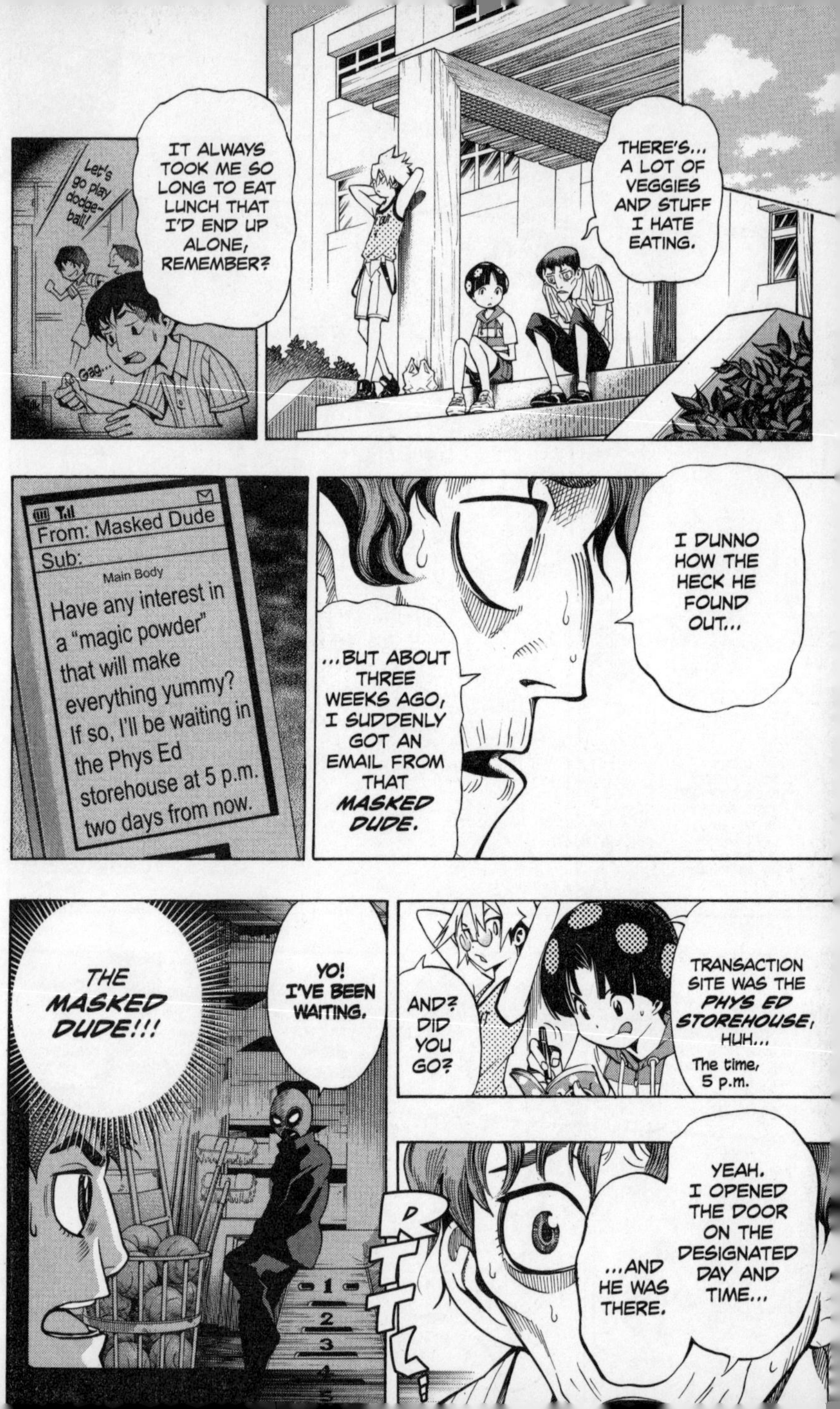
THERE'S... A LOT OF VEGGIES AND STUFF I HATE EATING.
IT ALWAYS TOOK ME SO LONG TO EAT LUNCH THAT I'D END UP ALONE, REMEMBER?
Let's go play dodge-ball!
Gag...
I DUNNO HOW THE HECK HE FOUND OUT...
...BUT ABOUT THREE WEEKS AGO, I SUDDENLY GOT AN EMAIL FROM THAT *MASKED DUDE*.
From: Masked Dude
Sub:
Main Body
Have any interest in a "magic powder" that will make everything yummy? If so, I'll be waiting in the Phys Ed storehouse at 5 p.m. two days from now.
TRANSACTION SITE WAS THE *PHYS ED STOREHOUSE*, HUH...
The time, 5 p.m.
AND? DID YOU GO?
YEAH. I OPENED THE DOOR ON THE DESIGNATED DAY AND TIME...
...AND HE WAS THERE.
RTTL
YO! I'VE BEEN WAITING.
THE *MASKED DUDE*!!!
1
2
3

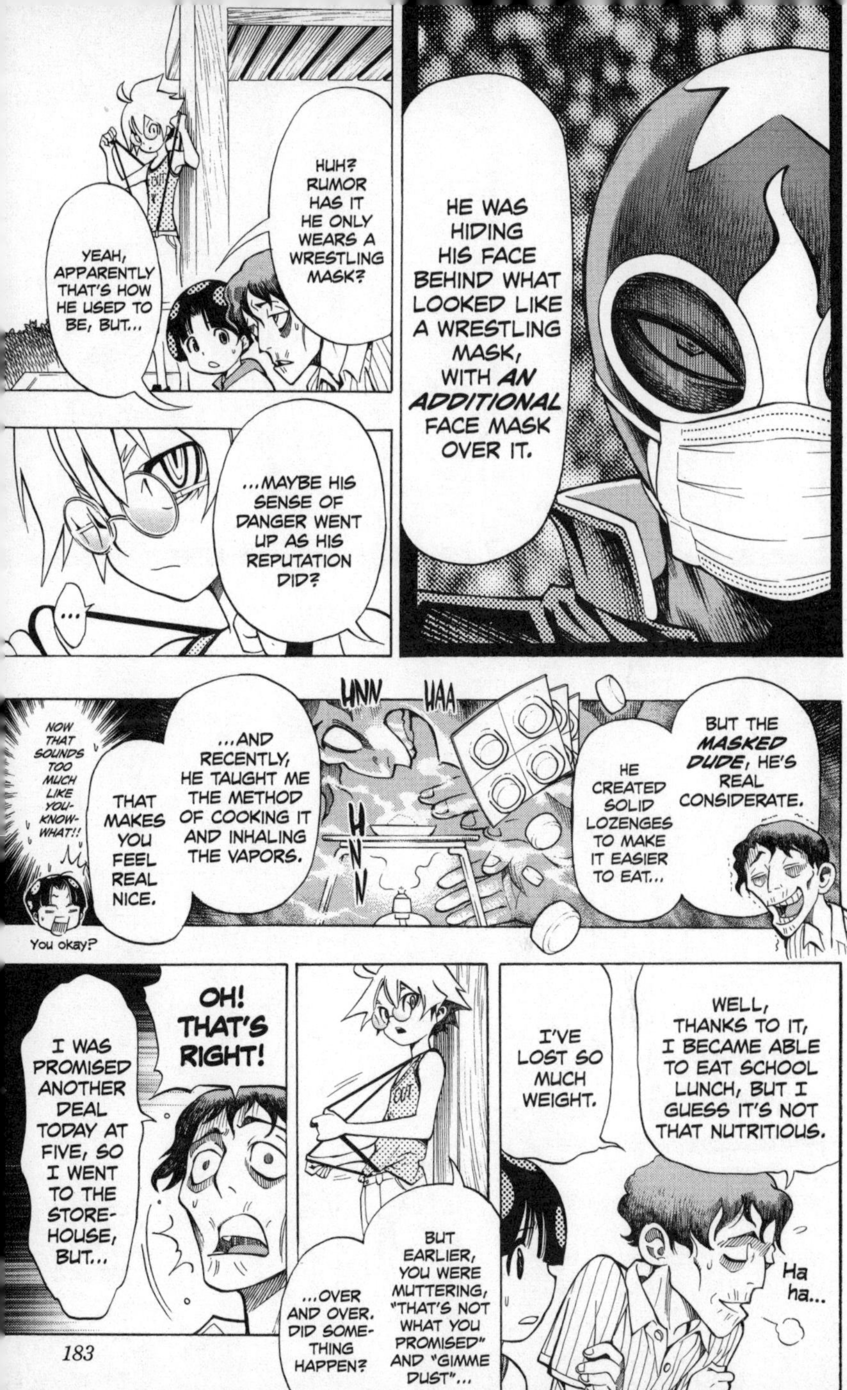
HE WAS HIDING HIS FACE BEHIND WHAT LOOKED LIKE A WRESTLING MASK, WITH ***AN ADDITIONAL*** FACE MASK OVER IT.
HUH? RUMOR HAS IT HE ONLY WEARS A WRESTLING MASK?
YEAH, APPARENTLY THAT'S HOW HE USED TO BE, BUT...
...MAYBE HIS SENSE OF DANGER WENT UP AS HIS REPUTATION DID?
...
BUT THE ***MASKED DUDE***, HE'S REAL CONSIDERATE.
HE CREATED SOLID LOZENGES TO MAKE IT EASIER TO EAT...
UAA
UNN
HNN
...AND RECENTLY, HE TAUGHT ME THE METHOD OF COOKING IT AND INHALING THE VAPORS.
THAT MAKES YOU FEEL REAL NICE.
NOW THAT SOUNDS TOO MUCH LIKE YOU-KNOW-WHAT!!
You okay?
WELL, THANKS TO IT, I BECAME ABLE TO EAT SCHOOL LUNCH, BUT I GUESS IT'S NOT THAT NUTRITIOUS.
I'VE LOST SO MUCH WEIGHT.
Ha ha...
BUT EARLIER, YOU WERE MUTTERING, "THAT'S NOT WHAT YOU PROMISED" AND "GIMME DUST"...
...OVER AND OVER. DID SOMETHING HAPPEN?
OH! THAT'S RIGHT!
I WAS PROMISED ANOTHER DEAL TODAY AT FIVE, SO I WENT TO THE STOREHOUSE, BUT...

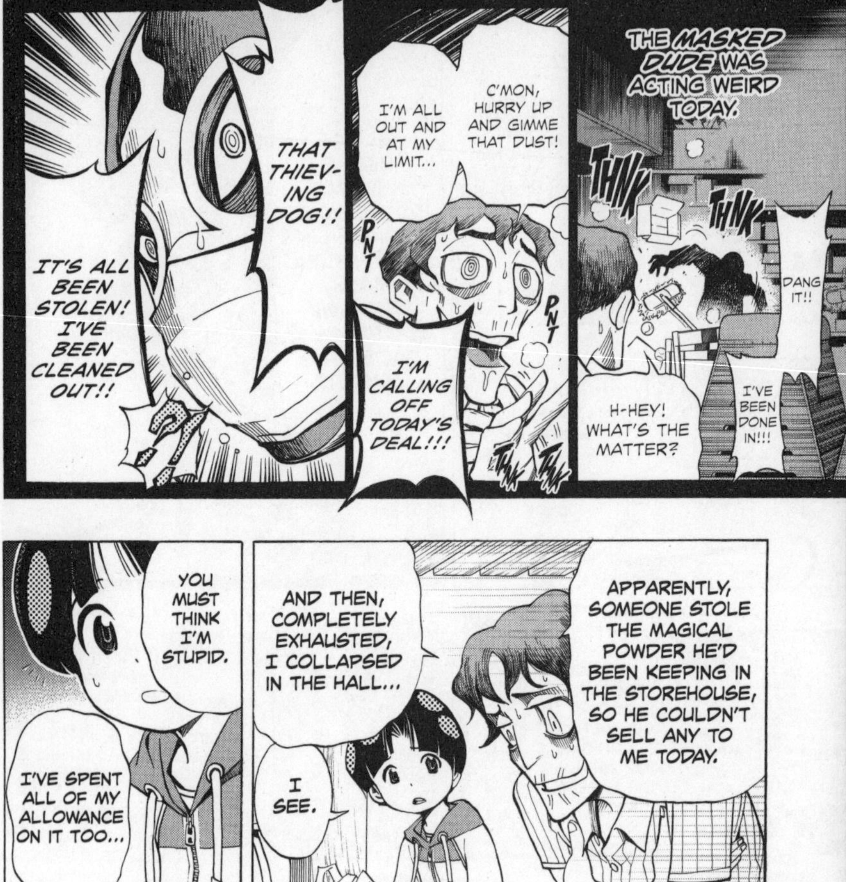
THE MASKED DUDE WAS ACTING WEIRD TODAY.
THNK
THNK
DANG IT!!
I'VE BEEN DONE IN!!!
H-HEY! WHAT'S THE MATTER?
C'MON, HURRY UP AND GIMME THAT DUST!
I'M ALL OUT AND AT MY LIMIT...
PNT
PNT
I'M CALLING OFF TODAY'S DEAL!!!
THNK
THNK
THAT THIEVING DOG!!
IT'S ALL BEEN STOLEN! I'VE BEEN CLEANED OUT!!
APPARENTLY, SOMEONE STOLE THE MAGICAL POWDER HE'D BEEN KEEPING IN THE STOREHOUSE, SO HE COULDN'T SELL ANY TO ME TODAY.
AND THEN, COMPLETELY EXHAUSTED, I COLLAPSED IN THE HALL...
I SEE.
YOU MUST THINK I'M STUPID.
I'VE SPENT ALL OF MY ALLOWANCE ON IT TOO...

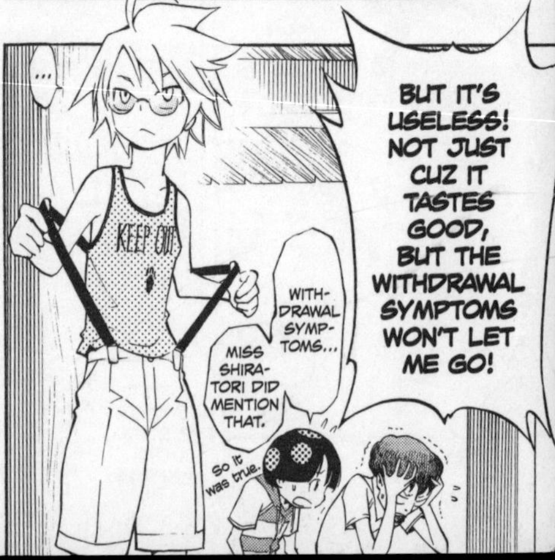
BUT IT'S USELESS! NOT JUST CUZ IT TASTES GOOD, BUT THE WITHDRAWAL SYMPTOMS WON'T LET ME GO!
...
KEEP OUT
WITHDRAWAL SYMPTOMS...
MISS SHIRATORI DID MENTION THAT.
So it was true.

WITHDRAWAL SYMPTOMS:

Symptoms such as headaches and hallucinations that torment those who use narcotics or stimulants and then quit taking them. Because they desire the drugs again in order to escape said symptoms, a vicious cycle is created.

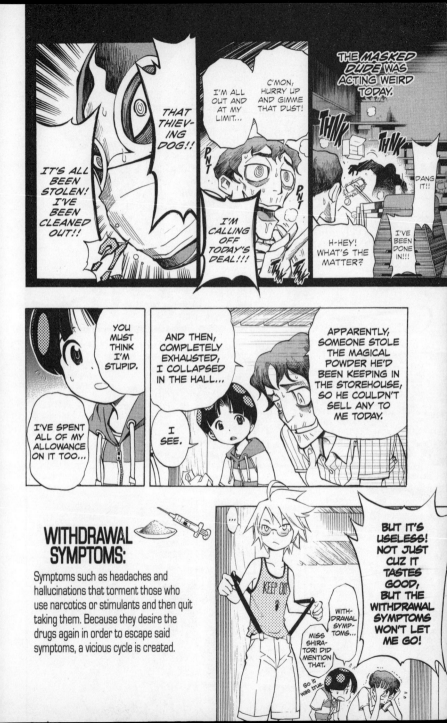

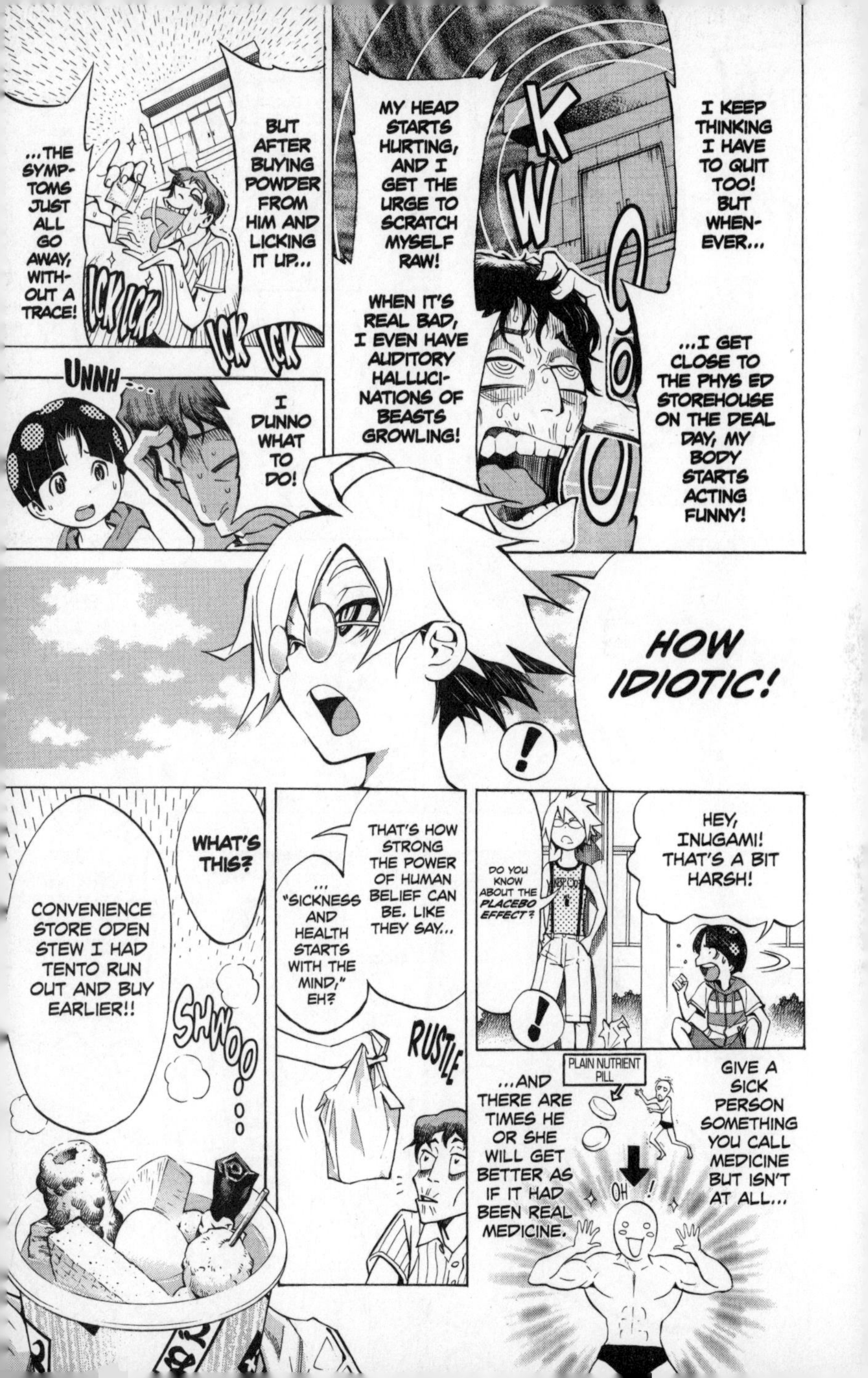
I KEEP THINKING I HAVE TO QUIT TOO! BUT WHENEVER...
...I GET CLOSE TO THE PHYS ED STOREHOUSE ON THE DEAL DAY, MY BODY STARTS ACTING FUNNY!
MY HEAD STARTS HURTING, AND I GET THE URGE TO SCRATCH MYSELF RAW!
WHEN IT'S REAL BAD, I EVEN HAVE AUDITORY HALLUCINATIONS OF BEASTS GROWLING!
KWOOOO
BUT AFTER BUYING POWDER FROM HIM AND LICKING IT UP...
...THE SYMPTOMS JUST ALL GO AWAY, WITHOUT A TRACE!
ICK ICK ICK ICK
UNNH...
I DUNNO WHAT TO DO!
HOW IDIOTIC!
!
HEY, INUGAMI! THAT'S A BIT HARSH!
DO YOU KNOW ABOUT THE PLACEBO EFFECT?
!
GIVE A SICK PERSON SOMETHING YOU CALL MEDICINE BUT ISN'T AT ALL...
...AND THERE ARE TIMES HE OR SHE WILL GET BETTER AS IF IT HAD BEEN REAL MEDICINE.
PLAIN NUTRIENT PILL
OH!
THAT'S HOW STRONG THE POWER OF HUMAN BELIEF CAN BE. LIKE THEY SAY...
..."SICKNESS AND HEALTH STARTS WITH THE MIND," EH?
RUSTLE
WHAT'S THIS?
CONVENIENCE STORE ODEN STEW I HAD TENTO RUN OUT AND BUY EARLIER!!
SHWOOO

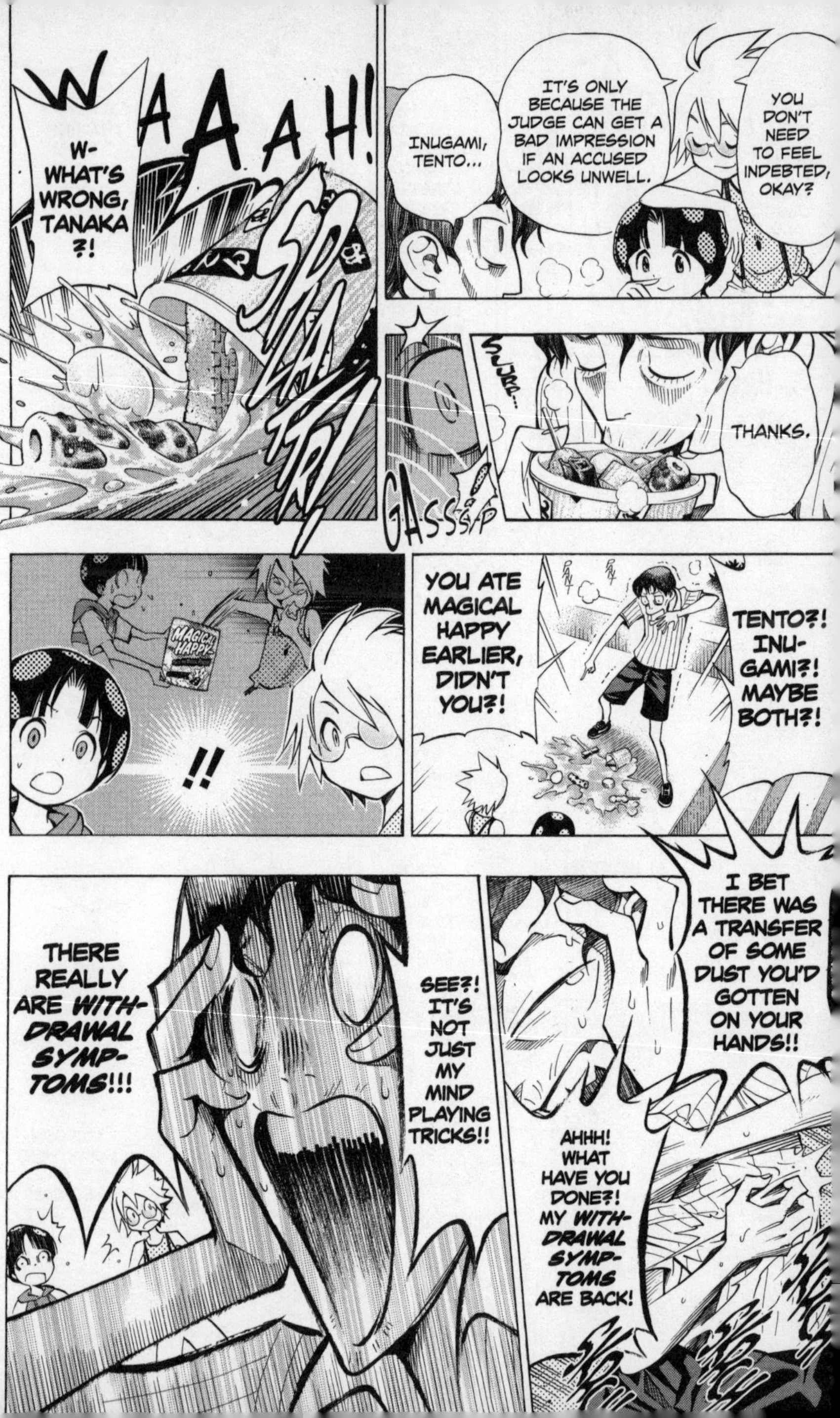

YOU DON'T NEED TO FEEL INDEBTED, OKAY?
IT'S ONLY BECAUSE THE JUDGE CAN GET A BAD IMPRESSION IF AN ACCUSED LOOKS UNWELL.
INUGAMI, TENTO...
THANKS.
WAAAH!
W-WHAT'S WRONG, TANAKA?!
TENTO?! INU-GAMI?! MAYBE BOTH?!
YOU ATE MAGICAL HAPPY EARLIER, DIDN'T YOU?!
MAGICAL HAPPY
!!
I BET THERE WAS A TRANSFER OF SOME DUST YOU'D GOTTEN ON YOUR HANDS!!
AHHH! WHAT HAVE YOU DONE?! MY *WITH-DRAWAL SYMP-TOMS* ARE BACK!
SEE?! IT'S NOT JUST MY MIND PLAYING TRICKS!!
THERE REALLY ARE *WITH-DRAWAL SYMP-TOMS*!!!

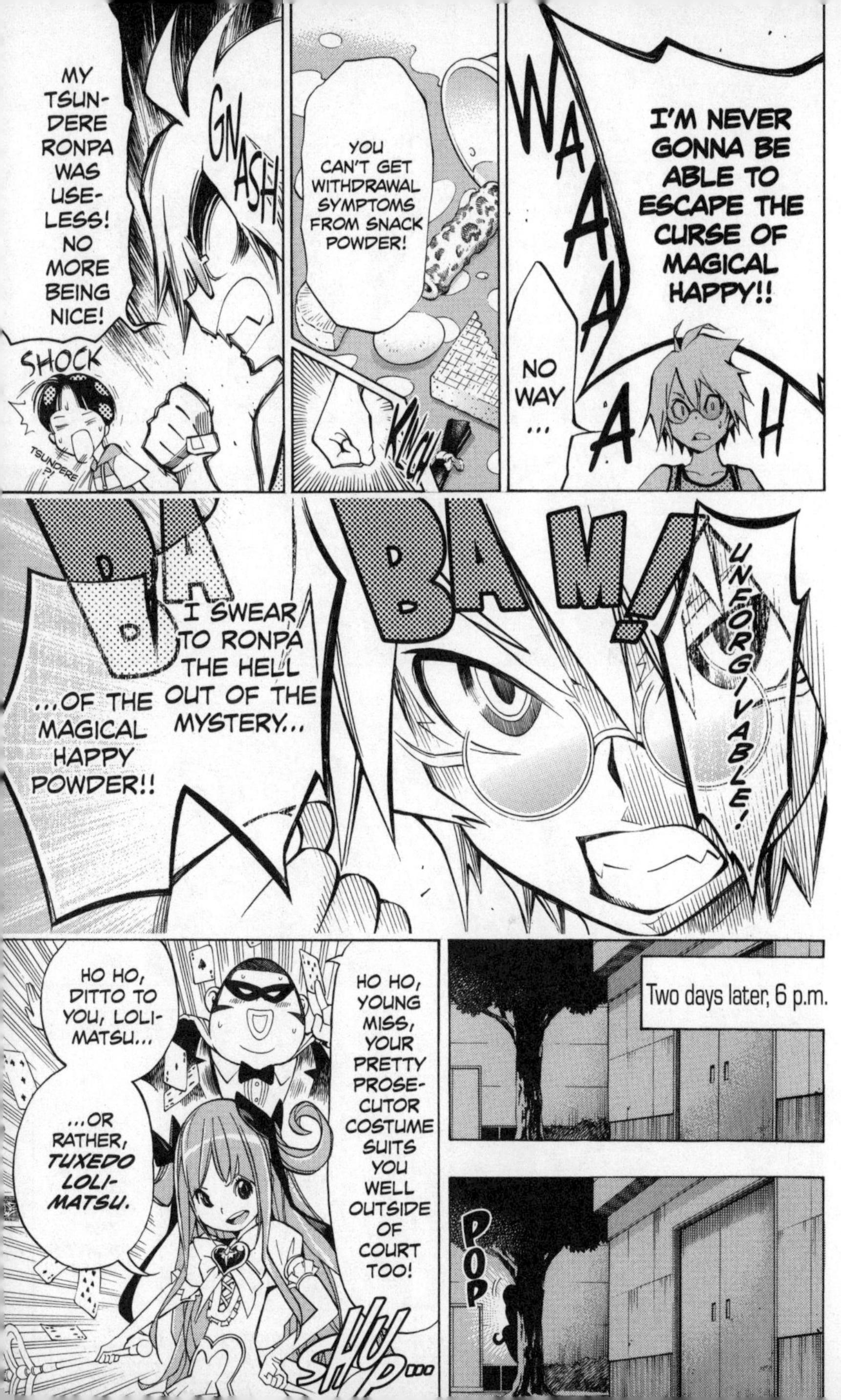
WAAAAAH
I'M NEVER GONNA BE ABLE TO ESCAPE THE CURSE OF MAGICAL HAPPY!!
NO WAY ...
YOU CAN'T GET WITHDRAWAL SYMPTOMS FROM SNACK POWDER!
KLINCH
GNASH
MY TSUN-DERE RONPA WAS USE-LESS! NO MORE BEING NICE!
SHOCK
TSUNDERE ?!
BAM!
UNFORGIVABLE!
DA
I SWEAR TO RONPA THE HELL OUT OF THE MYSTERY...
...OF THE MAGICAL HAPPY POWDER!!
Two days later, 6 p.m.
POP
HO HO, YOUNG MISS, YOUR PRETTY PROSE-CUTOR COSTUME SUITS YOU WELL OUTSIDE OF COURT TOO!
HO HO, DITTO TO YOU, LOLI-MATSU...
...OR RATHER, *TUXEDO LOLI-MATSU.*
SHUP...

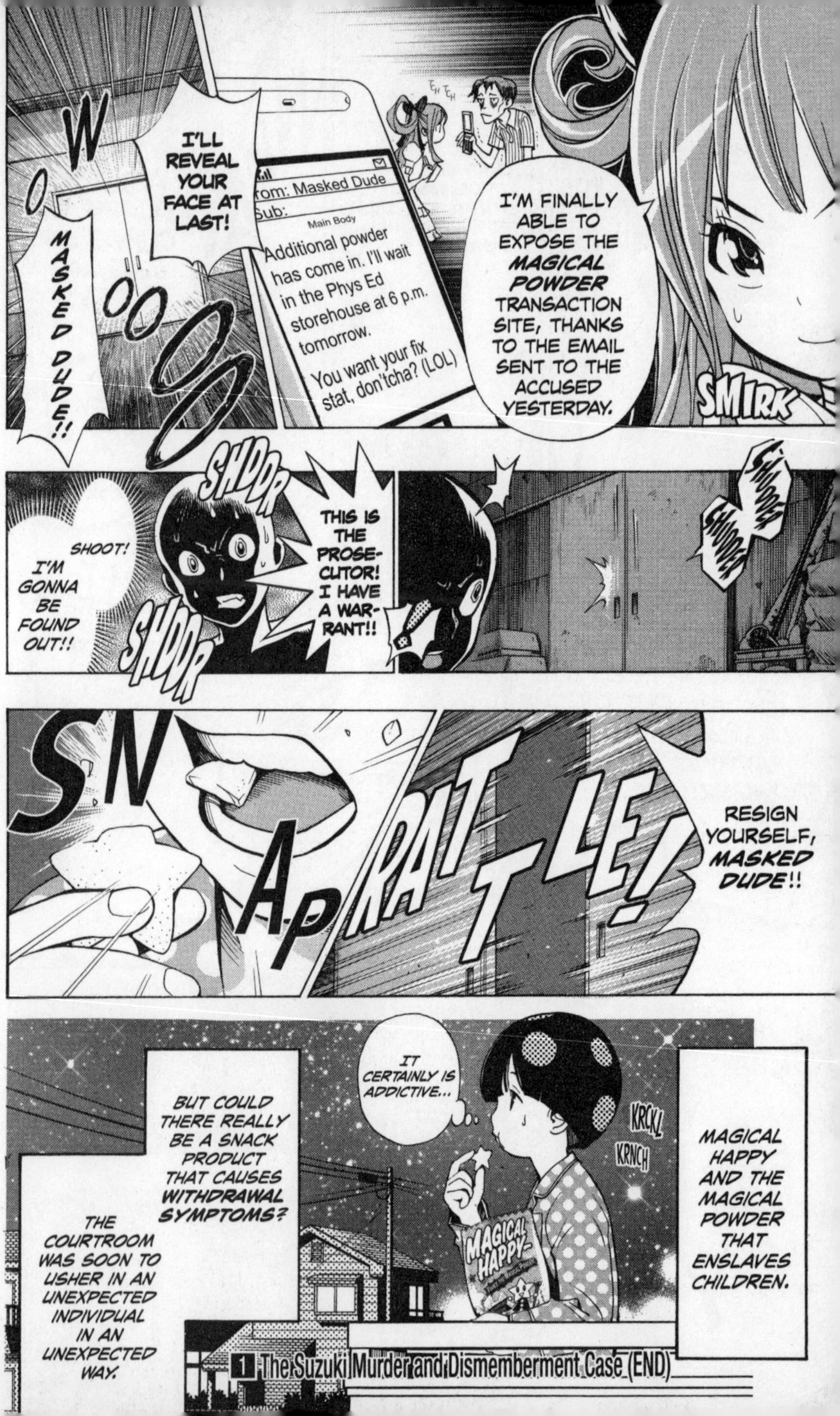
I'M FINALLY ABLE TO EXPOSE THE MAGICAL POWDER TRANSACTION SITE, THANKS TO THE EMAIL SENT TO THE ACCUSED YESTERDAY.
SMIRK
TCH TCH
From: Masked Dude
Sub:
Main Body
Additional powder has come in. I'll wait in the Phys Ed storehouse at 6 p.m. tomorrow.
You want your fix stat, don'tcha? (LOL)
I'LL REVEAL YOUR FACE AT LAST!
WOOOOO
MASKED DUDE!!
THIS IS THE PROSECUTOR! I HAVE A WARRANT!!
SHDDR SHDDR
SHOOT! I'M GONNA BE FOUND OUT!!
RESIGN YOURSELF, MASKED DUDE!!
RATTLE!
SNAP
MAGICAL HAPPY AND THE MAGICAL POWDER THAT ENSLAVES CHILDREN.
KRCKL
KRNCH
IT CERTAINLY IS ADDICTIVE...
BUT COULD THERE REALLY BE A SNACK PRODUCT THAT CAUSES WITHDRAWAL SYMPTOMS?
MAGICAL HAPPY
THE COURTROOM WAS SOON TO USHER IN AN UNEXPECTED INDIVIDUAL IN AN UNEXPECTED WAY.
1 The Suzuki Murder and Dismemberment Case (END)

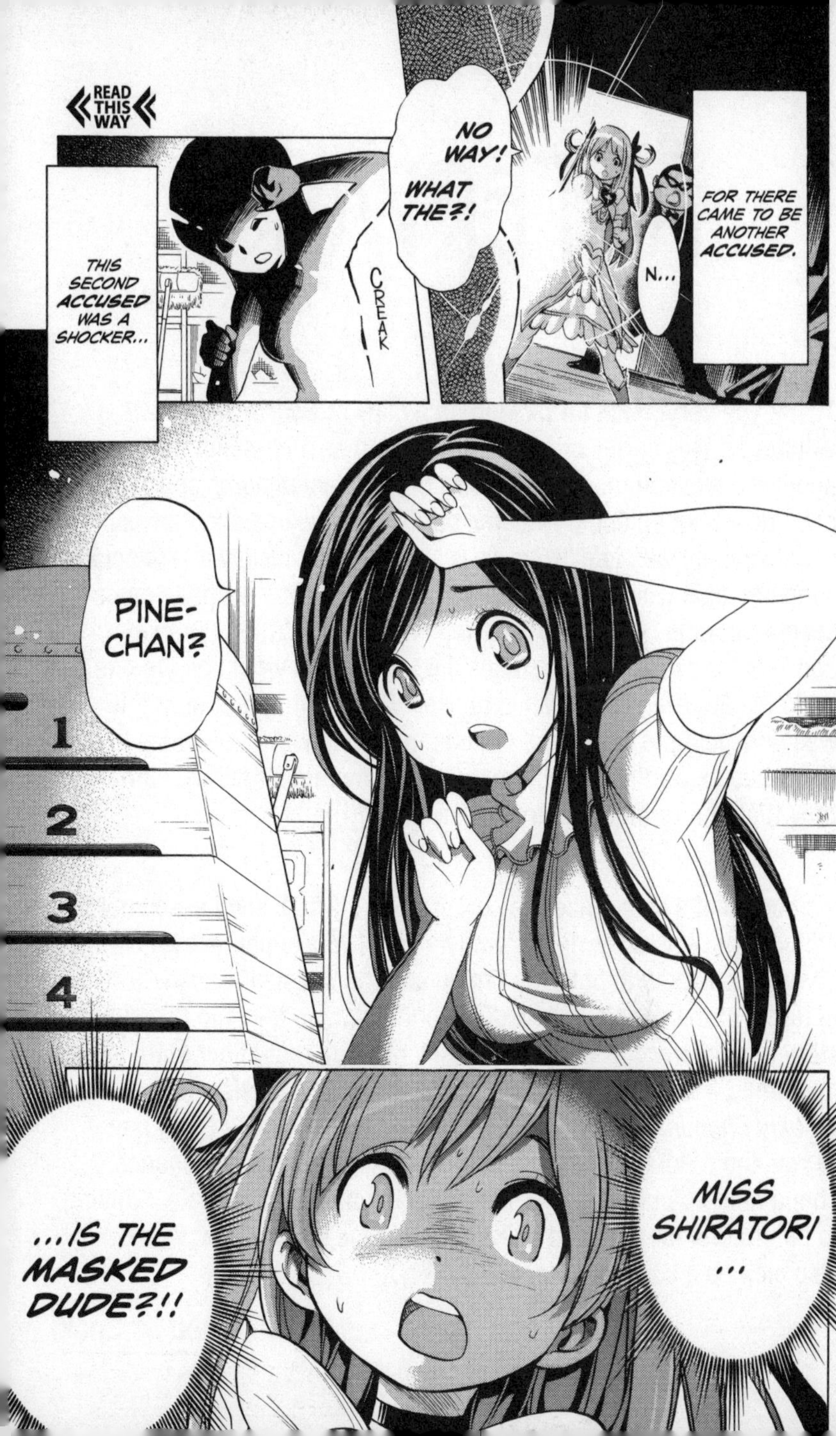
READ THIS WAY
FOR THERE CAME TO BE ANOTHER ACCUSED.
N...
NO WAY!
WHAT THE?!
THIS SECOND ACCUSED WAS A SHOCKER...
CREAK
PINE-CHAN?
MISS SHIRATORI ...
...IS THE MASKED DUDE?!!

AFTERWORD

Thank you very much for picking up a copy of *School Judgment* volume 1!! This series originally started out as a one-shot that appeared two summers ago as part of the *Shonen Jump* app Jump LIVE (now Shonen Jump+). Later, during discussions about possible serialization, I was told "Your art is lacking," and luckily it was decided someone else would do the art. But an even greater surprise came several months later when it turned out that the "God of Drawing" and "Walking Artistic Skill" Takeshi Obata Sensei would be the one to do the art. I felt like I was in heaven. Considering that at first it was only going to be around ten chapters long and is now able to be published in graphic novel form just like any regular series, I am truly thankful from the bottom of my heart.

It's been half a year since the serialization started, and I asked my editor, "I'm very lucky, right?" And he said I was super lucky as in I had good luck with both the timing and the people involved. In terms of the people involved, of course I mean the help this simple story has received from Obata Sensei, plus the rest of our staff, my family, friends, my editor Mr. Saito and everyone else on the *Weekly Shonen Jump* editorial team. This also includes every one of you, the readers, who have decided to give this story a chance. I hope to keep pursuing this quest for enlightenment while continuing to be grateful for my good luck. It'd make me happy if you would also pick up a copy of volume 2!

Nobuaki Enoki

COURT IS NOW IN SESSION

Hi! Thank you for reading *School Judgment: Gakkyu Hotei!* There are quite a few instances in this series where knowledge of the Japanese language is a key part of understanding the cases and extra pages, so I would like to take the time to explain some of this to you!

学 *(gaku)*
(kanji on wall, p. 5)

This kanji appears in multiple places throughout *School Judgment*, including in the Japanese title. The kanji can mean "education," "study," "learn" or "school," depending on the context.

Chalkboard
(pgs. 5, 25)

The writing on the chalkboard says, "Friday, May 6th. Classroom helpers: Sasaki and Nakamura."

Inugami
(p. 11)

Pine refers to Inugami as a dog or puppy on multiple occasions. While it sounds like she is doing it just to be mean, Inugami's name is written with the kanji 犬神, which mean "dog" and "god," respectively. So when she is calling him a dog, she is actually making a joke about his name. This is why on page 133, Inugami has 犬 *(inu)* written on his shirt.

Sweetshop
(pgs. 18, 173)

Abaku and Tento are sitting in front of a sweetshop. The snack Abaku is eating is called an *Umai Dog* or "Yummy Dog."

Pine Half-Baked
(p. 21)

Pine's last name, Hanzuki, is written with the kanji for "discriminate" and "moon." The way that Abaku says it here, however, implies that she is half-baked or physically underdeveloped.

Chalkboard
(p. 27)

The date reads April 25. The children are tallying the votes for "eat" and "don't eat." In Japanese, the strokes in the kanji 正 *(sei)*, meaning "correct" or "justice," are used the same way we use tally marks in English.

裁 *(sai)*
(kanji on judge's stand, p. 46)

This kanji comes from the word, 裁判所 *(saibasho)*, which means "courthouse."

証 *(sho)*
(kanji on witness stand, p. 46)

This kanji means "evidence." It is also used in the word 証人 *(shonin)*, which means "witness." This sign refers to the witness stand.

○ vs. ✓
(pgs. 71, 136)

Tento marked his answer with a circle rather than a check mark, and Kiriko's wrong answer was marked with a check mark. In Japan the circle means something is correct or okay, while the check mark is like an X through a wrong answer. So when Tento circled his ballot instead of writing a check mark, that meant he was affirming his answer, "yes."

Chalkboard
(p. 97)

The writing on the chalkboard says, "Tuesday, May 17th. Classroom helpers: Yashima and Akagi."

The Bluebird of Happiness
(p. 125)

This refers to the play *The Blue Bird* by Maurice Maeterlinck, in which two children seek the bluebird of happiness.

The Kanji Test
(pgs. 132, 136, 138)

The kanji featured in this chapter, 光 (*hikari*) and 陰 (*kage*), mean "light" and "shadow." The kanji in this lesson are a reference to how Kiriko lives in Higashide's shadow as the second best. When writing kanji, stroke order and placement are really important. If you look closely at Kiriko's answer, the seventh stroke in her answer for "shadow" is different from Higashide's. She also wrote the same kanji wrong in the desk she switched with Higashide's. Since he is so diligent, that desk could not have been his.

体 (*karada*)
(kanji on schedule, p. 143)

This kanji means "body." It refers to physical education or gym class on the class schedule.

Chalkboard
(p. 152)

The writing on the chalkboard says, "Wednesday, May 25th. Classroom helpers: Eguchi and Okuda."

Gakkyu Hotei Title
(p. 170)

This author comment page explains the history of the original Japanese title, *Gakkyu Hotei*. In Japanese, a lot of words are pronounced the same. While explaining how the title got switched, you can see that the second kanji changes multiple times on the page to read either 糾 (accusation), 級 (class) or 叫 (screaming). The first two are read as *kyu* while the last one is read as *kyo*. *Gakkyu* consists of two kanji (学級), but the author intentionally changed 級 to 糾. While they all sound similar, the meanings are quite different. At the end, the author is screaming because of the mistakes, which is a pun on how the second kanji was changed to mean "scream."

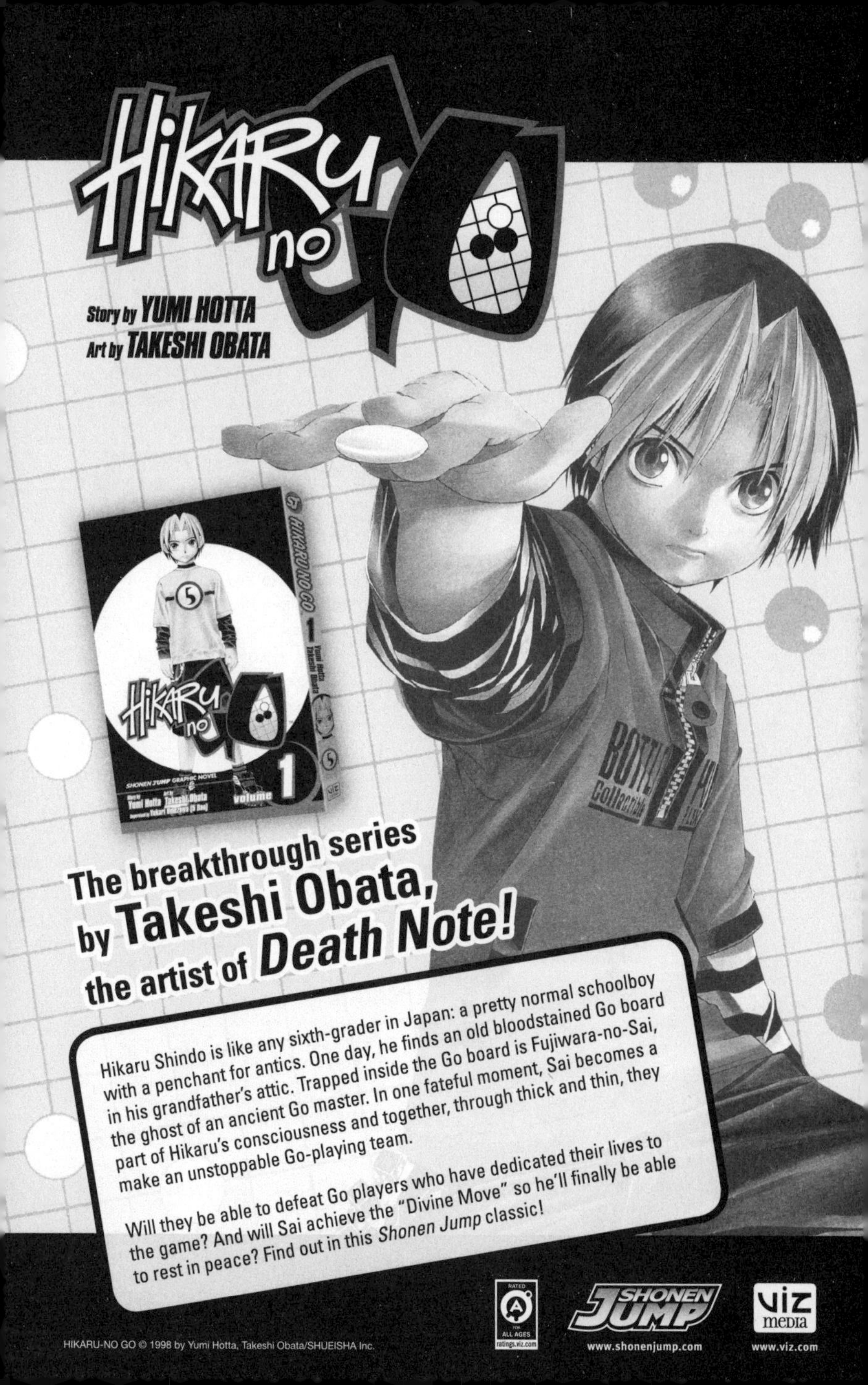
HIKARU no GO
Story by YUMI HOTTA
Art by TAKESHI OBATA
HIKARU NO GO
1
Yumi Hotta
Takeshi Obata
SHONEN JUMP GRAPHIC NOVEL
volume 1
The breakthrough series
by Takeshi Obata,
the artist of Death Note!
Hikaru Shindo is like any sixth-grader in Japan: a pretty normal schoolboy with a penchant for antics. One day, he finds an old bloodstained Go board in his grandfather's attic. Trapped inside the Go board is Fujiwara-no-Sai, the ghost of an ancient Go master. In one fateful moment, Sai becomes a part of Hikaru's consciousness and together, through thick and thin, they make an unstoppable Go-playing team.
Will they be able to defeat Go players who have dedicated their lives to the game? And will Sai achieve the "Divine Move" so he'll finally be able to rest in peace? Find out in this Shonen Jump classic!
RATED A FOR ALL AGES
ratings.viz.com
SHONEN JUMP
VIZ media
HIKARU-NO GO © 1998 by Yumi Hotta, Takeshi Obata/SHUEISHA Inc.
www.shonenjump.com
www.viz.com

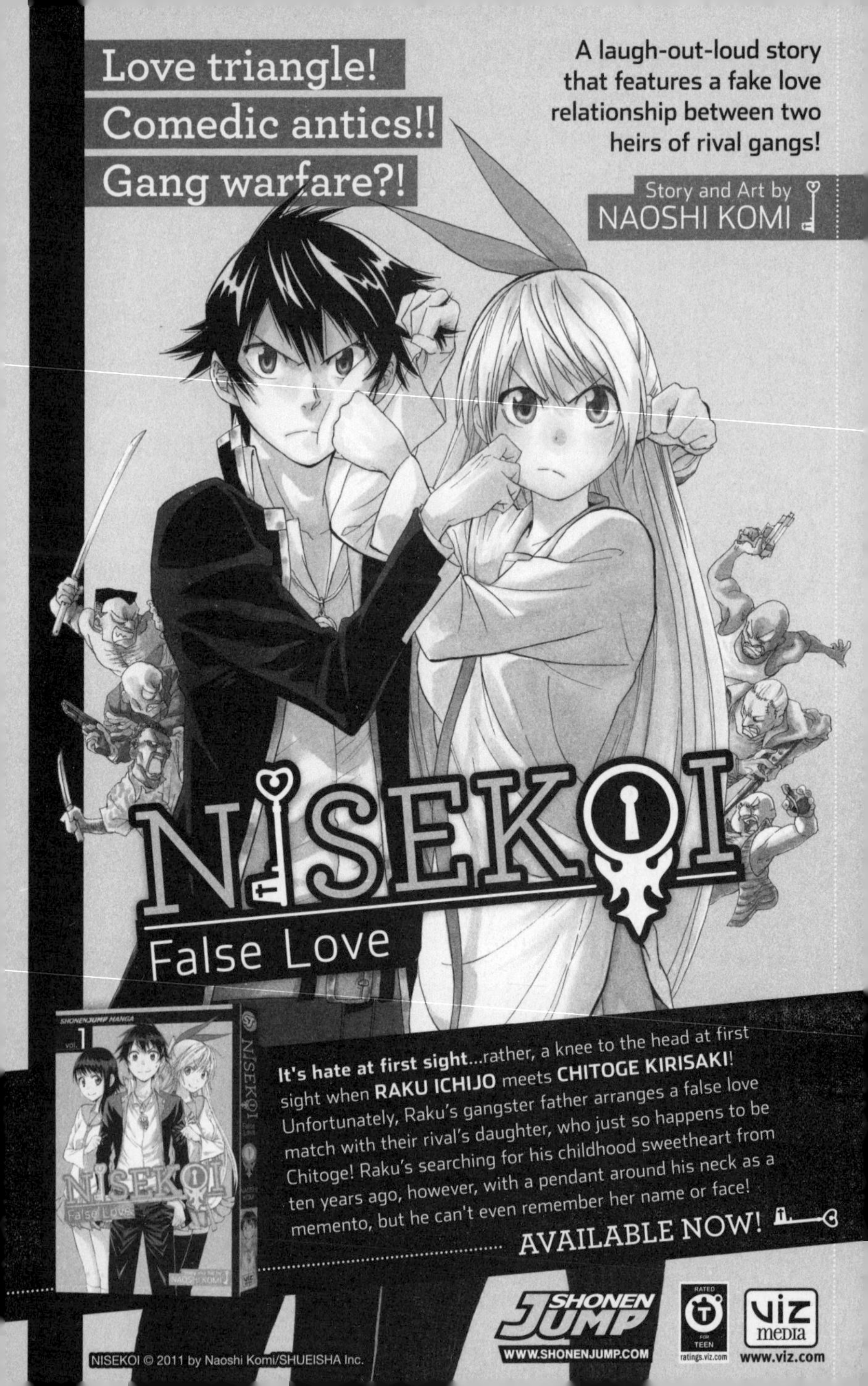
Love triangle!
Comedic antics!!
Gang warfare?!
A laugh-out-loud story that features a fake love relationship between two heirs of rival gangs!
Story and Art by
NAOSHI KOMI
NISEKOI
False Love
SHONENJUMP MANGA
vol. 1
It's hate at first sight...rather, a knee to the head at first sight when RAKU ICHIJO meets CHITOGE KIRISAKI! Unfortunately, Raku's gangster father arranges a false love match with their rival's daughter, who just so happens to be Chitoge! Raku's searching for his childhood sweetheart from ten years ago, however, with a pendant around his neck as a memento, but he can't even remember her name or face!
AVAILABLE NOW!
SHONEN JUMP
WWW.SHONENJUMP.COM
RATED T FOR TEEN
ratings.viz.com
VIZ media
www.viz.com
NISEKOI © 2011 by Naoshi Komi/SHUEISHA Inc.

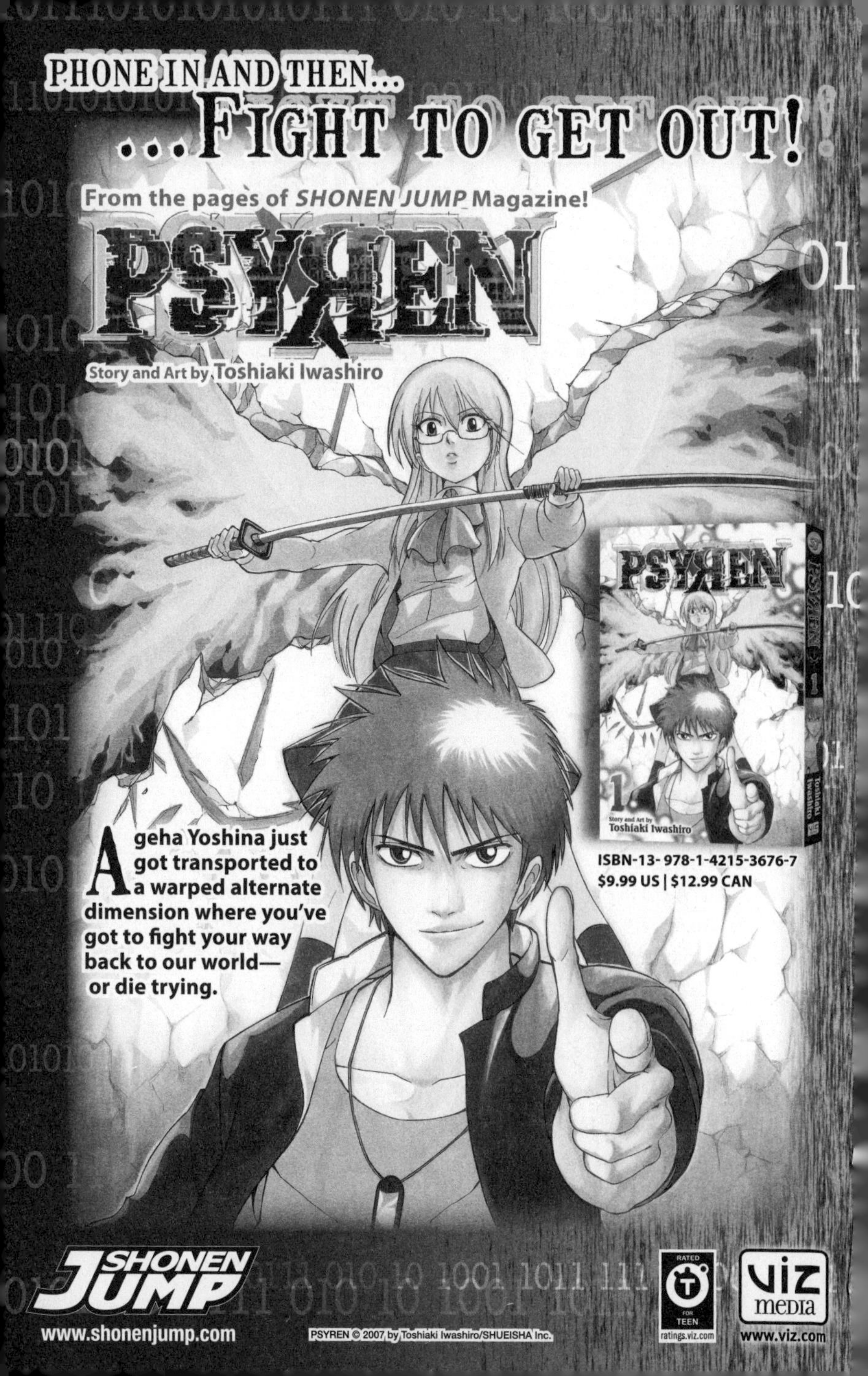
PHONE IN AND THEN...
...FIGHT TO GET OUT!
From the pages of SHONEN JUMP Magazine!
PSYREN
Story and Art by Toshiaki Iwashiro
Ageha Yoshina just got transported to a warped alternate dimension where you've got to fight your way back to our world—or die trying.
PSYREN
1
Story and Art by Toshiaki Iwashiro
ISBN-13- 978-1-4215-3676-7
$9.99 US | $12.99 CAN
SHONEN JUMP
www.shonenjump.com
PSYREN © 2007 by Toshiaki Iwashiro/SHUEISHA Inc.
RATED T FOR TEEN
ratings.viz.com
VIZ media
www.viz.com

YOU'RE READING THE WRONG WAY!

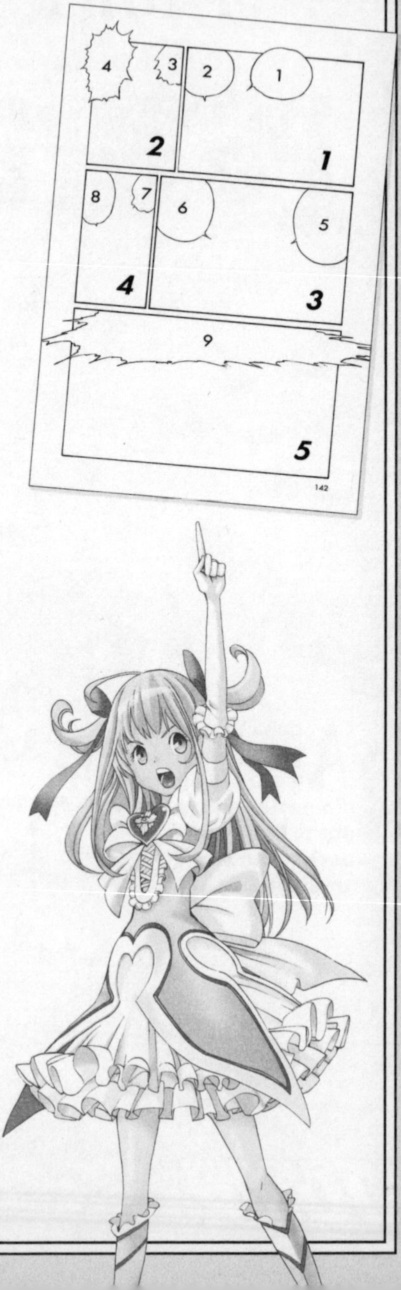
1
2
3
4
1
2
5
6
7
8
3
4
9
5
142

School Judgment: Gakkyu Hotei

reads from right to left, starting in the upper-right corner. Japanese is read from right to left, meaning that action, sound effects and word-balloon order are completely reversed from English order.